Praise for *Number Talks: Fractions, Decimals, and Percentages*

Number Talks: Fractions, Decimals, and Percentages is a welcomed resource for upper elementary and middle school teachers. The research data is convincing and the examples shed light on a topic that has challenged every teacher I know, including myself. The many figures give clear, conceptual information about the various strategies used for computing fractions and how they relate to whole number operations. We finally have a resource that helps educators and students remember not only how to divide fractions but also what it actually means to divide fractions and why we get a bigger answer than we started with.

—Lucy West, educator; author; and founder and CEO, Metamorphosis Teaching Learning Communities

Like its predecessor, this one's a winner. *Number Talks: Fractions, Decimals, and Percentages* builds on and extends the well-respected success of *Number Talks: Whole Number Computation*. It fully addresses fractions, decimals, and percentages with a particular focus on addressing challenges related to reasoning, multiple interpretations, and multiple representations. It engages teachers; the videos and talks become a personal professional development opportunity.

—Francis (Skip) Fennell, L. Stanley Bowlsbey Professor of Education and Graduate and Professional Studies Emeritus; Project Director, Elementary Mathematics Specialists and Teacher Leaders Project, McDaniel College; Past President, NCTM; and Past President, AMTE

Number Talks has created a positive, exciting, and refreshing culture around mathematics at our school. Through the talks, students challenge themselves in a nurturing and supportive environment; the strategies they discover give them confidence to tackle more complex problems.

—Michele Lenertz, Principal, Washington Elementary, Riverside, California

In *Number Talks,* the messages being communicated to students are that flexibility is valued, *every* person can contribute, and we learn from each other by communicating clearly. Because these messages are embedded in rich conversations about computation and properties of numbers—in short sessions of time, no less—the talks become the perfect venues for coaching and learning together with colleagues.

—Justin Johns, mathematics coach, American Embassy School, New Delhi, India

Number Talks is a great resource to help students think, reason, and build confidence in their mathematical thinking. The best part is that students want to share their ideas during a number talk. Every morning in my class, I have one or two students enthusiastically ask, "When are we doing number talks?" That's how I know this resource is so powerful.

—Nanette Shonwise, Numeracy Facilitator, Sudbury Catholic District School Boa

In this essential resource, Sherry and Ann tackle one of the most important content areas in all of school mathematics—fractions. Building on the proven effectiveness of number talks, they show teachers a clear picture of what classrooms can look like and offer concrete steps to stimulate the kind of rich discourse that helps students make sense of numbers, gain confidence, and develop the critical skills they need for the future.

—Cathy L. Seeley, NCTM, Past President; author of *Faster Isn't Smarter* and *Smarter Than We Think*; and educational speaker

Number Talks: Fractions, Decimals, and Percentages provides our teachers with in-depth knowledge and learning as they collaborate and plan for increasingly high and rigorous standards for our students. The Number Talks series has been an essential part of our math program for more than five years. Ten minutes a day has had a powerful impact on learning—students and staff love number talks!

—Denise Meister, Principal, Worsham Elementary, Aldine, Texas

In our classes where number talks have been happening regularly, we have seen shifts in student voice and communication in math. Teachers are empowered and more confident with their mathematical modeling; as a school, our mistakes are valued and our collective strategies are growing.

—Kim Bentley and Sarah Fleming, teachers, International School of Bangkok, Thailand

Since implementing number talks at our school, there has been a tangible "buzz." Our teachers have fully supported this initiative and have reported that student understanding and enthusiasm have grown exponentially. Number talks are a favorite part of math workshop—students will even remind teachers when it's time for them!

—Allison Ziemer, Junior School Vice Principal, United World College of South East Asia, Dover Campus, Singapore

Parrish's first book, *Number Talks: Whole Number Computation*, popularized the very concept and approach of number talks with a primary focus on whole numbers in grades K–5. This second resource in the series tackles the much more intricate realm of fractions, decimals, and percentages. It extends what students have hopefully experienced previously to these far more complex and often seriously confusing topics that build on whole number fluency and understanding to rational numbers.

—Steve Leinwand, *American Institutes for Research*

Number Talks is a rich professional learning resource that stands out because it is also a practical manual for day-to-day lessons. When we began implementing number talks using this resource, there was an immediate and visible impact on student engagement and learning. The energy and excitement in the classrooms are palpable for students and teachers alike!

—Carol Little, math coordinator, The American School of Doha, Qatar

NUMBER TALKS

FRACTIONS, DECIMALS, AND PERCENTAGES

A Multimedia Professional Learning Resource

SHERRY PARRISH AND ANN DOMINICK
Foreword by Steve Leinwand

Math Solutions
Sausalito, California, USA

Math Solutions
One Harbor Drive, Suite 101
Sausalito, California, USA 94965
www.mathsolutions.com

Copyright © 2016 by Sherry Parrish and Ann Dominick

The publisher grants permission to individual teachers who have purchased this book to copy the reproducible material as needed for use with their own students. Reproduction for an entire school district, or commercial or any other use, in any form or by any means, is prohibited without written permission from the publisher, except for the inclusion of brief quotations in a review. Notice of copyright must appear on all copies of copyrighted materials.

Library of Congress Cataloging-in-Publication Data
Names: Parrish, Sherry. | Dominick, Ann (Ann McNamee)
Title: Number talks. Fractions, decimals, and percentages : a multimedia professional learning resource / Sherry Parrish, Ann Dominick ; foreword by Steve Leinwand.
Other titles: Fractions, decimals, and percentages
Description: Sausalito, California : Math Solutions, [2016] | Includes bibliographical references.
Identifiers: LCCN 2016037553 | ISBN 9781935099758
Subjects: LCSH: Fractions—Study and teaching. | Decimal fractions—Study and teaching. | Percentage—Study and teaching. | Ratio and proportion—Study and teaching.
Classification: LCC QA137 .P37 2016 | DDC 513.2/6—dc23
LC record available at https://lccn.loc.gov/2016037553

ISBN-13: 978-1-935099-75-8
ISBN-10: 1-935099-75-2

Math Solutions is a division of Houghton Mifflin Harcourt.

MATH SOLUTIONS® and associated logos are trademarks or registered trademarks of Houghton Mifflin Harcourt Publishing Company. Other company names, brand names, and product names are the property and/or trademarks of their respective owners.

Executive Editor: Jamie A. Cross
Production Manager: Denise A. Botelho
Cover design: Wanda Espana/Wee Design Group
Interior design: MPS Limited
Composition: MPS Limited
Cover and interior images: Friday's Films
Videographer: Friday's Films, www.fridaysfilms.com

Printed in the United States of America.
1 2 3 4 5 6 7 8 9 10 0014 25 24 23 22 21 20 19 18 17 16
4510002177 ABCDE

A Message from Math Solutions

We at Math Solutions believe that teaching math well calls for increasing our understanding of the math we teach, seeking deeper insights into how students learn mathematics, and refining our lessons to best promote students' learning.

Math Solutions shares classroom-tested lessons and teaching expertise from our faculty of professional development consultants as well as from other respected math educators. Our publications are part of the nationwide effort we've made since 1984 that now includes

- more than five hundred face-to-face professional development programs each year for teachers and administrators in districts across the country;
- professional development books that span all math topics taught in kindergarten through high school;
- videos for teachers and for parents that show math lessons taught in actual classrooms;
- on-site visits to schools to help refine teaching strategies and assess student learning; and
- free online support, including grade-level lessons, book reviews, inservice information, and district feedback, all in our Math Solutions Online Newsletter.

For information about all of the products and services we have available, please visit our website at *www.mathsolutions.com.* You can also contact us to discuss math professional development needs by calling (800) 868-9092 or by sending an email to *info@mathsolutions.com.*

We're always eager for your feedback and interested in learning about your particular needs. We look forward to hearing from you.

To my grandchildren . . . Maggie, Charlie, Abby, Jack, Blakely, Brooke, and Jake . . . may you always look for the beauty and elegance of mathematics and experience the joy of finding understanding from within.

~Sherry Parrish

To John, Theresa, Michael, Will, and Suzanne—my balcony people who keep the learning fun.

~Ann Dominick

Brief Contents

To purchase the reproducible versions of the area, set, and linear models in this resource, visit www.mathsolutions.com/numbertalksfdp_reproducibles.

Contents

To purchase the reproducible versions of the area, set, and linear models in this resource, visit www.mathsolutions.com/numbertalksfdp_reproducibles.

Foreword

Number Talks is a powerful, accessible, and informative journey through mathematical understanding and the pedagogical strategies that support its development. Broadly and consistently implementing the ideas and techniques presented by the authors can change lives—ours as teachers of mathematics and those of our students—as we work to build a deep and lasting sense of fractions, decimals, and percentages in our students.

Done right, there is something so engaging, so mathematically rich and yes, even so magical, about a number talk. Pose a straightforward exercise or simple word problem, give students time to solve it mentally, and then open the floodgates of thinking and reasoning with little more than asking, "How did you get your answer?" "Who did it differently?" and "How are our approaches similar and different?"

As authors Sherry Parrish and Ann Dominick remind us in Chapter 1, we all share a common goal when it comes to mathematics: We want our students to "become mathematically proficient, reason mathematically, and compute with accuracy, flexibility, and efficiency." It's one thing to state such a mom-and-apple-pie goal. It's quite another to propose and describe practical and powerful strategies for meeting this goal. However, that is exactly why this resource is so helpful. *Number Talks* models how the techniques of conducting mathematical number talks and number strings enable students to grapple with number relationships, analyze their justifications and explanations, and communicate and solidify these critical understandings.

Parrish's first book, *Number Talks: Whole Number Computation,* popularized the very concept and approach of number talks with a primary focus on whole numbers in grades K–5. This second resource in the series tackles the much more intricate realm of fractions, decimals, and percentages. It extends what students have hopefully experienced previously to these far more complex and often seriously confusing topics that build on whole number fluency and understanding to rational numbers.

Just consider how many fourth and fifth graders are taught, confused, and even mathematically damaged by the approach of remembering and regurgitating that the "one correct way" to add $\frac{1}{2}$ and $\frac{7}{8}$ is to mindlessly get a common denominator of 8, convert the $\frac{1}{2}$ to $\frac{4}{8}$, and then add the numerators and "keep the denominator"—because "that's the rule"—to get the correct answer of $\frac{11}{8}$. And based on years of test scores, this makes frighteningly little sense to hundreds of millions of students.

Now envision, as described on pages 23–24, this same class where, through the process of number talks, we see a decidedly different mindset about teaching mathematics in practice.

- One student argues that $\frac{7}{8}$ is the same as $\frac{1}{2}+\frac{3}{8}$ so $\frac{1}{2}+\frac{7}{8}$ is the same as $\frac{1}{2}+\frac{1}{2}+\frac{3}{8}$ or $1+\frac{3}{8}$ or $1\frac{3}{8}$.
- Another student proposes that you can rename $\frac{1}{2}$ as $\frac{4}{8}$ and that means that there is a total of $\frac{11}{8}$.
- A third student announces that, thinking of her ruler, she can decompose $\frac{1}{2}$ into $\frac{3}{8}$ and $\frac{1}{8}$, and since $\frac{1}{8}+\frac{7}{8}$ is 1, the sum must be $1\frac{3}{8}$.

When each of these approaches is recorded and discussed in the manner so clearly modeled throughout this resource, we move from the limits of "remember and regurgitate" to the impact of a classroom dominated by "pause, reason, explain, and connect."

What has always impressed me about both the simplicity and the power of number talks done well is how they help to shift our teaching mindsets from "our telling" to "their thinking." What has dazzled me in dozens of classrooms is how effortlessly a number talk surfaces alternative approaches and multiple representations that, although raised by only a few students, inform the learning of the entire class. What has amazed me is how seamlessly a number talk raises big ideas like equivalents, place value, representations, the meaning of operations and properties of numbers—all essential and unifying ideas for all mathematics learning. And what has astounded me is how frequently a number talk surfaces common misconceptions and common errors that can be resolved well before they grow into major impediments.

We often think that the mathematical practices of reasoning and problem solving require rich and complex problems. But then we discover that a sixth-grade classroom discussion launched by a number talk about $17\frac{1}{4} - 9\frac{5}{8}$ can thoroughly engage students in constructing viable arguments and critiquing the reasoning of others—thereby operationalizing one of the key Common Core Standards for Mathematical Practice in a much more efficient and accessible manner.

As the reader sees over and over again in the diverse examples that Parrish and Dominick present and describe in great detail, a number talk is the diametric opposite of teaching students the one right way to get the one right answer. Instead, an effective number talk celebrates different approaches and values different ways of thinking. As such, number talks place sense making exactly where it belongs—in the forefront of every mathematics lesson.

Helping students develop deep and lasting number sense around fractions, decimals, and percentages is *not* easy. Eliciting, justifying, and connecting alternative approaches—including some that are at first alien to us—is *not easy.* Initially implementing successful number talks with our students is *not* easy. But by taking some of the same small risks as teachers that we expect our students to take, together we can blend the critical goals of deeper number sense and computational fluency with the techniques of number talks to create far more effective learning experiences and much greater success for our students.

I sincerely hope that every reader of this book learns as much from it as I have and, starting today, is as motivated to transfer these ideas into daily classroom practice.

—Steve Leinwand, American Institutes for Research

Acknowledgments

This book would not have been possible without the influence of Dr. Constance Kamii on both of our lives. For more than 30 years, Connie has touched us through sharing Piaget's teachings and giving a consistent message that children can invent their own strategies. We are grateful for the countless times she planned lessons with us, visited our classrooms to offer meaningful feedback, and encouraged us to take steps to shift our teaching practice from "teaching by telling" to asking students to think, reason, and only do what makes sense. Connie, we are forever grateful to you for helping us learn to listen to children and for making a difference in who we are as teachers. Your dedication and unwavering passion has changed our lives for the better and continues to impact teachers and students.

We are grateful to Charlotte Brown for believing in us, supporting us, and encouraging us to step out a little farther than we thought we could. We are also grateful for Faye Clark and Bernie Mullins. This project would not have been possible without you. Many late nights were spent over cups of tea as you shared your expertise and belief in this book. Thank you for giving us your wisdom, knowledge, and insights, and for cheering us all along the way.

Many thanks to Jamie Cross, Patty Clark, and Denise Botelho for your passion, insight, and attention to detail throughout this project. Your unique gifts allowed you to thoughtfully listen to our ideas and make them into a cohesive reality. We are forever grateful to Perry Pickert and Friday's Films for capturing the essence of number talks through film and providing others with a vision of this elegant but simple routine. Most importantly, we are indebted to Lori St. Clair Rhodes,

Maria Barry, Katherine Alexander, Laura Kretschmar and all of the students who were willing to share their ideas, strategies, and expertise so others could follow in their footsteps.

Finally, we thank our families who provided the encouragement, patience and support we needed throughout this journey.

How to Use This Resource

Introduction

Watch the video clip "Introduction."

Talk with a friend or colleague; what do you see in the introduction that makes you most excited about *Number Talks: Fractions, Decimals, and Percentages?*

To view this video clip, scan the QR code or access via mathsolutions.com /NTFDPintro

Number Talks: Fractions, Decimals, and Percentages was created in response to the requests of teachers—teachers who want to implement number talks but are unsure of how to begin and teachers who are seasoned in this art of instruction but want support in crafting purposeful problems. The primary purpose of this resource is to help teachers begin

or refine their use of number talks with fractions, decimals, and percentages. The video clips give readers the opportunity to access authentic classroom number talks with third- through sixth-grade students. The video clips also provide a visual platform for teachers to reflect on their current practices and target essential understandings from their readings.

Regardless of where you are in your number talk journey, it is important to establish a common understanding of number talks before immersing yourself in this resource. Number talks can be best described as classroom conversations around purposefully crafted problems that are solved mentally. The problems in a number talk are designed to help students focus on number relationships and number theory. Students are given problems in either a whole- or small-group setting and are asked to mentally solve them one at a time. By sharing and defending their various solutions and strategies, students have the opportunity to collectively reason about numbers while building connections to key conceptual ideas in mathematics. A typical classroom number talk can be conducted in five to fifteen minutes.

Overview of *Number Talks: Fractions, Decimals, and Percentages*

Number Talks: Fractions, Decimals, and Percentages is part of the Number Talks series. In this resource, we focus only on positive rational numbers. The term *rational numbers* comes from the word *ratio*. It means any number that can be made by dividing an integer by a non-zero integer. For example:

- $\frac{3}{4}$ is a rational number (3 divided by 4, or the ratio of 3 to 4)
- 0.25 is a rational number $\left(\frac{1}{4}\right)$
- 1 is a rational number $\left(\frac{3}{3}\right)$
- 6 is a rational number $\left(\frac{6}{1}\right)$
- 3.45 is a rational number $\left(\frac{345}{100}\right)$
- -5.2 is a rational number $\left(-\frac{52}{10}\right)$

Negative integers and whole numbers are rational numbers, because they can be made by dividing an integer by a nonzero integer. For example, -2 and 3 can be expressed as fractions, $-\frac{2}{1}$ and $\frac{3}{1}$ respectively.

In this resource, we focus exclusively on positive rational numbers and on parts of a whole, or fractional reasoning.

While *Number Talks: Fractions, Decimals, and Percentages* is intended to be read from cover to cover, it is designed in such a way as to meet a range of needs. To accomplish this goal, the resource is organized into the following sections.

Reference Tables

Reference tables provide ease in locating featured number talks by chapter or grade level.

Introduction

The Introduction chapter looks at research on why students struggle with fractions, decimals, and percentages, building a context for why number talks address this area are critical.

Section I: Understanding Number Talks

Chapters 1 and 2 discuss the key elements of the practice of number talks and how to establish procedures and expectations for implementation.

Section II: Number Talks to Help Students Build Fractional Reasoning

Chapters 3, 4, and 5 concentrate on the essential understandings for reasoning with fractions, decimals, and percentages and incorporate number talks to strategically target these areas.

Section III: Number Talks to Help Students Operate with Fractions and Decimals

Chapters 6, 7, 8, and 9 focus on operations with fractions. The number talk goals for third- through seventh-grade students are addressed and accompanied by addition, subtraction, multiplication, and division number talks to help students develop strategies for these operations. Examples of classroom student-teacher dialogues are also included for each operation.

Chapter 10 addresses goals for reasoning and computing with decimals, and incorporates specific number talks to help students develop computation strategies for each operation.

The Video Clips

Many of the chapters feature video clips of actual classroom number talks in grades 3–6. Each clip is accompanied by a series of guided questions and reflections crafted to address specific ideas discussed in the corresponding chapter.

How to Access Online Video Clips

Readers have several options for accessing the video clips. Either scan the QR code (with a QR code reader app of your choice) that appears within the video clip section in the text or enter the corresponding URLs in your browser. If you would like to access all the clips at once, follow these instructions:

1. Go to mathsolutions.com/myvideos and click or tap the Create New Account button at the bottom of the Log In form.
2. Create an account, even if you have created one with Math Solutions bookstore. You will receive a confirmation email when your account has been created.
3. Once your account has been created, you will be taken to the Product Registration page. Click Register on the product you would like to access (in this case, *Number Talks: Fractions, Decimals, and Percentages*).
4. Enter key code **NTFDP** and click or tap the Submit Key Code button.
5. Click or tap the Complete Registration button.
6. To access videos at any time, visit your account page.

A Note About Captions (Subtitles) for Videos

To turn on captions, click on the "CC" watermark in the upper lefthand corner of the video. Select English and play the video. To turn off captions, click on the "CC" watermark and select Off.

Guidelines for Watching Videos of Teaching

The teachers who agreed to be recorded in these videos have complex and challenging classrooms, just like you. When we watch videos of others it is easy to see things that we might do differently. It is then all too easy to move to a critical stance, focusing on what the teacher "should" have done differently. But we have found that such a stance is not helpful for learning.

These videos are not scripted or rehearsed. They are real classroom sessions. Remember that teaching is a complicated activity, in which the teacher is required to do many things at once. As you watch these videos, alone or with others, we recommend following these rules:

1. Assume that there are many things you don't know about the students, the classroom, and the shared history of the teacher and students in the video.
2. Assume good intent and expertise on the part of the teacher. If you cannot understand his or her actions, try to hypothesize what might have motivated him or her.
3. Keep focused on your observations about what students are getting out of the talk and interaction.
4. Keep focused on how the classroom discourse is serving the mathematical goals of the lesson.

Source: From *Talk Moves: A Teacher's Guide for Using Talk Moves to Support the Common Core and More, Third Edition* by Suzanne H. Chapin, Catherine O'Connor, and Nancy Canavan Anderson (Math Solutions, 2013, xxi).

Reproducibles

The reproducibles listed below are enlarged versions of the area, set, and linear models that appear in Chapters 4, 6, 7, and 8 of this resource. These user-friendly, reproducible formats are not included with this resource; however, they can be purchased separately at mathsolutions.com/numbertalksfdp_reproducibles.

Area Models

Reproducible 1 Reasoning About Equal Parts of a Fraction: Which of these models represent $\left(\frac{1}{2}, \frac{1}{4}, \frac{1}{8}, \frac{1}{3}, \frac{1}{6}\right)$ of the whole?

Reproducible 2 Reasoning About Equivalence Among Fractions: Can you see $\left(\frac{1}{2}, \frac{1}{4}, \frac{1}{8}, \frac{1}{3}, \frac{1}{6}\right)$ of the whole? Can you see $\left(\frac{1}{2}, \frac{1}{4}, \frac{1}{8}, \frac{1}{3}, \frac{1}{6}\right)$ in a different way? How can you prove your thinking?

Reproducible 3 Using Area Models Partitioned into Common Denominators: How can you solve ___ + ___? How can you use what we already know to solve this next problem?

Reproducible 4 Using Area Models Requiring Partitioning: How can you solve ___+___? How can you use what we already know to solve this next problem?

Reproducible 5 Using Area Models Partitioned into Eighths and Twelfths: What is ___ − ___? How do you know? How can you use what we already know to solve the next problem?

Reproducible 6 Models to Focus on the Shifting Whole: What is ___ of ___? How do you know? How can you use what we already know to solve this next problem?

Set Models

Reproducible 7 Can you see $\left(\frac{1}{2}, \frac{1}{4}, \frac{1}{8}, \frac{1}{3}, \frac{1}{6}\right)$ of the whole? Can you see $\left(\frac{1}{2}, \frac{1}{4}, \frac{1}{8}, \frac{1}{3}, \frac{1}{6}\right)$ in a different way? How can you prove your thinking?

Linear Models

Reproducible 8 0 to 1 Number line

Reproducible 9 0 to 2 Number Line

Reproducible 10 0 to 4 Number Line

Reproducible 11 1 to 2 Number Line

Reproducible 12 −1 to 1 Number Line

Reproducible 13 −2 to 2 Number line

Reproducible 14 Various Number Lines: Where should ____ be placed? How do you know?

Reproducible 15 0 to 2 Number Line, Partitioned into $\frac{1}{4}$s

Reproducible 16 0 to 2 Number Line, Partitioned into $\frac{1}{2}$s and $\frac{1}{3}$s

Video Clips by Chapter

Chapter and Page Number	Video Clip	Title	Grade/Teacher
Chapter 1			
14	1.1	$16 \times \frac{2}{8}$: Why Number Talks?	Grade 5/Alexander
22	1.2	$4 \times \frac{1}{2}$: Establishing a Safe Learning Community	Grade 5/Alexander
36	1.3	Placing 0.89 on the Number Line: Number Talks and the Standards for Mathematical Practice	Grade 4/Dominick
Chapter 2			
42	2.1	Using Hand Signals and Wait Time	Grade 6/Kretschmar
45	2.2	$1\frac{1}{2} \times \frac{2}{5}$: Using Turn and Talk with a Number Talk	Grade 6/Kretschmar
56	2.3	$\frac{1}{2} + \frac{7}{8}$: Thinking About Efficient Strategies	Grade 4/Parrish

(continued)

Chapter and Page Number	Video Clip	Title	Grade/Teacher
Chapter 4			
74	4.1	What is $\frac{3}{4}$ of 12? Using a Story Context	Grade 3/St. Clair Rhodes
84	4.2	The Fraction Kit: A Conversation About Equivalence	Grade 3/St. Clair Rhodes
107	4.3	Comparing $\frac{24}{50}$ and $\frac{21}{40}$	Grade 4/Dominick
Chapter 5			
119	5.1	$\frac{1}{4} \times \frac{1}{3}$: Connecting Fractions to Percentages	Grade 5/Alexander
127	5.2	Placing 0.9, 0.13, 0.255 on the Number Line: Connecting Fractions to Decimals	Grade 6/Kretschmar
Chapter 6			
138	6.1	$\frac{1}{2} + \frac{5}{6}$: Developing Addition Strategies with Fractions	Grade 4/Parrish
149	6.2	Are the Addends Equal to 1? Using Area Models with Addition of Fractions	Grade 3/St. Clair Rhodes
169	6.3	$\frac{1}{2} + \frac{1}{2}, \frac{1}{2} + \frac{3}{4}$: Developing Addition Strategies with Fractions	Grade 4/Parrish
Chapter 7			
189	7.1	$\frac{3}{4} - \frac{3}{8}$: Developing Subtraction Strategies with Fractions	Grade 4/Parrish

Chapter and Page Number	Video Clip	Title	Grade/Teacher
Chapter 8			
227	8.1	$\frac{1}{4} \times \frac{1}{3}$: Developing Multiplication Strategies with Fractions	Grade 5/Alexander
231	8.2	$\frac{1}{2}$ of 12, $\frac{1}{4}$ of 12: Developing Multiplication Strategies with Fractions	Grade 3/St. Clair Rhodes
247	8.3	$1\frac{1}{3} \times \frac{3}{4}$: Developing Multiplication Strategies with Fractions	Grade 6/Kretschmar
265	8.4	Doubling and Halving to Solve $\frac{1}{4} \times \frac{2}{3}$	Grade 5/Alexander
Chapter 9			
281	9.1	$1 \div \frac{3}{8}$: Developing Division Strategies with Fractions	Grade 6/Kretschmar
299	9.2	$6 \div 3, 3 \div 1\frac{1}{2}, 1\frac{1}{2} \div \frac{3}{4}$: Proportional Reasoning String	Grade 6 /Kretschmar

Video Clips by Grade, Including Demographics

Lighthouse Community Charter School
The student body at Lighthouse Community Charter School, a K–12 school in Oakland, California, comprises 81 percent Hispanic, 9 percent African American, 5 percent Multiethnic, 3 percent Asian/Pacific Islander, 1 percent Middle Eastern, and 1 percent Caucasian. Eighty-one percent of students are English learners. Eighty-six percent of the students receive free or reduced price lunch.

South Shades Crest Elementary School
The student body at South Shades Crest Elementary School, a K–4 school in Hoover, Alabama, comprises 57 percent Caucasian, 28 percent African American, 8 percent Asian, 6 percent Hispanic, and less than 1 percent American Indian/Multiethnic/Pacific Islander/Other. Twenty-four percent of the students receive free or reduced price lunch.

Vincent Elementary School
The student body at Vincent Elementary School, a K–5 school in Vincent, Alabama, comprises 75 percent Caucasian, 23 percent African American, 2 percent Hispanic, and less than 1 percent Asian. Sixty percent of the students receive free or reduced price lunch.

Grade	Teacher	Video Clips
3	Ms. St. Clair Rhodes is a Nationally Board Certified Teacher and has been teaching elementary grade children for twenty-seven years. She is currently the mathematics coach at South Shades Crest Elementary. She believes that all children can learn, and she enjoys helping students develop a love of learning and a passion for mathematics.	4.1 What is $\frac{3}{4}$ of 12? Using a Story Context 4.2 The Fraction Kit: A Conversation About Equivalence 6.2 Are the Addends Equal to 1? Using Area Models with Addition of Fractions 8.2 $\frac{1}{2}$ of 12, $\frac{1}{4}$ of 12: Developing Multiplication Strategies with Fractions
4	Dr. Parrish is the author of *Number Talks: Whole Number Computation* and coauthor of *Number Talks: Fractions, Decimals, and Percentages.* She is thrilled to be a guest teacher in Ms. Barry's class and is always amazed at the mathematical thinking of students.	2.3 $\frac{1}{2}+\frac{7}{8}$: Thinking About Efficient Strategies 6.1 $\frac{1}{2}+\frac{5}{6}$: Developing Addition Strategies with Fractions 6.3 $\frac{1}{2}+\frac{1}{2}, \frac{1}{2}+\frac{3}{4}$: Developing Addition Strategies with Fractions 7.1 $\frac{3}{4}-\frac{3}{8}$: Developing Subtraction Strategies with Fractions

Grade	Teacher	Video Clips
4	 Dr. Dominick is coauthor of *Number Talks: Fractions, Decimals, and Percentages* and is excited to be a guest teacher in Ms. Barry's class. She loves being part of a classroom community where students are excited about learning mathematics.	1.3 Placing 0.89 on the Number Line: Number Talks and the Standards for Mathematical Practice 4.3 Comparing $\frac{24}{50}$ and $\frac{21}{40}$
5	 Ms. Alexander has been in education for ten years; she spent seven years teaching fifth grade and two years teaching fourth grade. She is currently a mathematics coach at Vincent Elementary School in Vincent, Alabama. She believes that all children deserve the opportunity to understand why math makes sense and to share their thinking.	1.1 $16 \times \frac{2}{8}$: Why Number Talks? 1.2 $4 \times \frac{1}{2}$: Establishing a Safe Learning Community 5.1 $\frac{1}{4} \times \frac{1}{3}$: Connecting Fractions to Percentages 8.1 $\frac{1}{4} \times \frac{1}{3}$: Developing Multiplication Strategies with Fractions 8.4 Doubling and Halving to Solve $\frac{1}{4} \times \frac{2}{3}$

(continued)

Grade	Teacher	Video Clips
6	 Ms. Kretschmar teaches fifth- and sixth-grade math and science at Lighthouse Community Charter School. She has been teaching and learning from her students for seventeen years. She puts a high priority on looking deeply at student work and listening to student thinking to inform instruction.	2.1 Using Hand Signals and Wait Time 2.2 $1\frac{1}{2} \times \frac{2}{5}$: Using Turn and Talk with a Number Talk 5.2 Placing 0.9, 0.13, 0.255 on the Number Line: Connecting Fractions to Decimals 8.3 $1\frac{1}{3} \times \frac{3}{4}$: Developing Multiplication Strategies with Fractions 9.1 $1 \div \frac{3}{8}$: Developing Division Strategies with Fractions 9.2 $6 \div 3, 3 \div 1\frac{1}{2}, 1\frac{1}{2} \div \frac{3}{4}$: Proportional Reasoning String

INTRODUCTION

Why Fractions, Decimals, and Percentages?

In this section we tackle the "why"—why fractions, decimals, and percentages?—sharing a broad spectrum of compelling research and data. We open with data that show a history of the ongoing struggle students have with fractions, and we discuss the reasons this needs to change. We then take a closer look at why the process of working with fractions, decimals, and percentages can be so challenging for students who often struggle with making connections to other areas of mathematics. Finally, we explore how this struggle can be related to the way students are frequently taught procedural methods versus conceptual processes.

OVERVIEW

Fractions Are a Critical Foundation in Mathematics

In 2008, the National Mathematics Advisory Panel stated that proficiency with fractions should be a major goal of K–8 education. The panel described this area of mathematics as a Critical Foundation for Algebra and made the following recommendation:

> *The most important foundational skill not presently developed appears to be proficiency with fractions (including decimals, percent, and negative fractions). The teaching of fractions must be acknowledged as critically important and improved before an increase in student achievement in algebra can be expected. (xvii, 17)*

Many teachers can identify with the panel's finding that proficiency with fractions is underdeveloped; our own memories of learning about fractions consist primarily of dividing pizzas, pies, and candy bars and memorizing procedures for computation. When we were students, our sole access to a solution was often limited to following the rule of invert and multiply to divide, multiplying across the "top" and the "bottom" to find a product, or using cross multiplication to compare two fractions. As we progressed from grade to grade, we continued to follow these procedures to reach a short-term goal of getting a correct answer; consequently, we did not readily acquire the lifelong goal of developing fractional reasoning.

Evidence of Our Struggles (the Data from Research)

So how did the National Mathematics Advisory Panel conclude that "the most important foundational skill not presently developed appears to be proficiency with fractions"? Let's look at the data. The panel's findings were corroborated with a survey of 1,000 U.S. algebra teachers, who indicated that a lack of fractional knowledge was the second biggest problem students faced in being prepared to learn algebra. The final report also shared the following data, which indicate that difficulties with fractions, decimals, and percentages extend beyond the K–12 populations and into the general adult population:

- 78 percent of adults cannot explain how to compute the interest paid on a loan;

- 71 percent cannot calculate miles per gallon on a trip; and
- 58 percent cannot calculate a 10 percent tip for a lunch bill.

Other studies support this perspective, reinforcing the idea that fluency with fractions, decimals, and percentages is a critical gatekeeper to higher mathematics (Booth and Newton 2012; Geary et al. 2012; Siegler et al. 2012).

Data from student performance on the *National Assessment of Educational Progress* (NAEP) provides an overarching perspective on American students' difficulties with fractional reasoning from the late 1970s to the present. Consider the following examples:

1978 NAEP

When eighth-grade students were asked to estimate the sum for $\frac{12}{13} + \frac{7}{8}$:

- only 24 percent questioned could correctly answer 2;
- 28 percent chose 19;
- 27 percent chose 21;
- 14 percent indicated that they did not know; and
- 7 percent selected 1. (Carpenter et al. 1981)

2004 NAEP

- When asked to shade $\frac{1}{3}$ of a rectangle, 27 percent of the eighth graders questioned could not do this;
- 45 percent of the eighth graders could not solve a word problem that required division with fractions; and
- only 50 percent of the eighth graders could successfully order $\frac{2}{7}$, $\frac{1}{12}$, and $\frac{5}{9}$.

2009 NAEP

- Almost 75 percent of the fourth graders questioned could not choose a fraction, from four common fractions, that was closest to $\frac{1}{2}$; and
- less than 30 percent of the eleventh graders could correctly change 0.029 into $\frac{29}{1000}$.

Concern about the lack of understanding around fractional reasoning is warranted, and if a shift is not made, the impact on adult mathematical literacy as well as secondary education and mathematics in general could be far reaching (Hecht and Vagi 2010; Mazzocco and Devlin 2008).

Why Do Students Struggle with Fractions, Decimals, and Percentages?

As shared thus far, the struggles that people of all ages frequently have with understanding and operating with fractions, decimals, and percentages are well-documented, but this overwhelming evidence begs the question, "Why are they difficult?" In the following pages, we attempt to answer this through two perspectives: a look at the unique mathematical challenges that surface, and a look at procedural versus conceptual knowledge.

Mathematical Areas Linked to Students' Difficulties with Fractions

Student difficulties with fractions can often be linked to three issues: whole number reasoning, multiple interpretations, and multiple representations.

Three Issues Linked to Student Difficulties with Fractions

1. Whole Number Reasoning
2. Multiple Interpretations
3. Multiple Representations

Learn More...

Chapter 3 further discusses the idea of inappropriate whole number reasoning and how to confront this misconception when comparing and ordering fractions on a number line.

Whole Number Reasoning

A typical sequence in mathematics curricula and instruction starts with whole number reasoning and operations on whole numbers. However, as students begin to understand and make generalizations in this area of mathematics, they often make assumptions that the characteristics of and operations on whole numbers also apply to rational numbers. It is common for students to inaccurately apply what they know and understand about whole numbers and whole number operations to rational numbers.

Learn More...

As a reminder, the term *rational numbers* comes from the word *ratio*. It means any number that can be made by dividing an integer by a nonzero integer. We first talk about this in the "How to Use This Resource" section.

While some characteristics of whole numbers and rational numbers are similar, there are also many characteristics that are not interchangeable (Siegler et al. 2013). For example, with whole numbers there is an exact counting sequence with an exact successor for each number counted. If a student is counting by ones and has already counted 1, 2, 3, 4, 5, the number "6" is the only correct option for the next number in the sequence. When counting by fractions, however, there are multiple equivalent representations for every possible fraction, so counting in a fraction sequence can yield multiple answers. For example, if students are counting by fourths and begin with $\frac{1}{4}$, the next numbers in the sequence could be $\frac{2}{4}$, $\frac{4}{8}$, $\frac{3}{6}$, 0.50, and so forth. If we think about counting sequences represented on a number line, only one whole number can be represented at one specific point, whereas multiple fractions with the same value can be represented at one specific point on a number line.

Also, learners often assume that operating with fractions will result in the same outcomes as operating with whole numbers. For example, when students operate with whole numbers, they often generalize that multiplication produces a larger quantity and division results in a smaller one. The same generalizations do not hold true when operating with fractions:

Learn More...

Chapter 8 and Chapter 9 offer number talks specifically for helping students move beyond assumptions that the characteristics of and operations on whole numbers also apply to rational numbers.

1. When we multiply a given number by a proper fraction, the result is a smaller amount (e.g., $6 \times \frac{1}{2} = 3$).
2. When we divide a given number by a nonzero proper fraction, the result is larger (e.g., $6 \div \frac{1}{2} = 12$).

From a procedural perspective, there are also differences between operating on whole numbers and fractions. Traditionally, for example, students must align whole numbers to the right when adding, but they must align the decimal points when adding decimals. In this way, the so-called rules change. Yet without conceptual understanding, students do not have a foundation for understanding these rules or a framework for remembering when to apply specific rules, such as when to cross multiply or find a common denominator. When teachers present the rules without ensuring that they are embedded in students' conceptual understanding, there are many places where confusion may arise.

An example of a situation in which students may inappropriately apply whole number reasoning to fractions is when ordering fractions from least to greatest. Consider the fractions $\frac{1}{3}$, $\frac{1}{2}$, and $\frac{1}{4}$. A common error students make when placing these fractions on a number line is to focus solely on the denominators as whole numbers and then order them by those denominators (in this case, 3, 2, 4). Students who use this inappropriate whole number reasoning—that is, 2 is followed by 3, which is followed by 4—typically order the fractions as $\frac{1}{2}$, $\frac{1}{3}$, and $\frac{1}{4}$ like this:

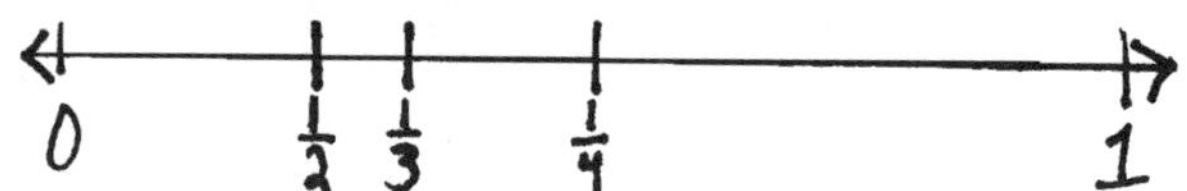

> **Learn More...**
>
> Each chapter in Section III, Number Talks to Help Students Operate with Fractions, offers specific suggestions for using contexts with fractions. See Chapters 4–9.

Multiple Interpretations

Another reason many students struggle as they work with fractions is that they can have different meanings or interpretations depending on the context or situation in which they are used (Brousseau, Brousseau, and Warfield 2004; Cramer, Post, and del Mas 2002; National Research Council [NRC] 2001). Without a context, it is difficult to determine if a fraction should be interpreted as a part–whole relationship, a measure, a ratio, a quotient, or an operator. To better understand this idea, see Figure I–1 on the next page, which looks at how context can influence the interpretation of the fraction $\frac{3}{4}$ (Wong and Evans 2007).

Multiple Representations

A third unique challenge that surfaces in understanding fractions is that there are multiple representations for the same quantity. A rational number can be represented as a common fraction, as a decimal fraction, or as a percent. To understand that $\frac{1}{2}$ can be represented and used three ways—as 50%, as an equivalent decimal fraction (0.5, 0.50, 0.500), and as an equivalent fraction $\left(\frac{2}{4}, \frac{3}{6}, \frac{4}{8}\right)$—requires reasoning about all representations simultaneously (NRC 2001). In order for students to understand and apply fractional reasoning, they must develop an understanding of equivalence as well as the ability to use all representations interchangeably while considering the unique applications of each representation.

Interpretation	Context
Part–Whole Relationship In this situation the fraction focuses on how many parts there are in relationship to parts in the whole.	$\frac{3}{4}$ of a dozen cookies have sprinkles. $\frac{3}{4}$ of a brownie was eaten. $\frac{3}{4}$ of the jewels are red.
Measure In this situation a fraction represents the measure of a distance, an amount, or a region and focuses on the relationship between the part and the whole. This interpretation requires students to focus on the individual unit and consider how many of those units are within the whole.	A recipe requires $\frac{3}{4}$ of a cup of sugar. Miguel ran $\frac{3}{4}$ of a mile.
Ratio A fraction as a ratio represents a comparison of either a part-to-part or part-to-whole relationship.	3 girls to 4 boys (part-to-part) 3 girls to 4 students (part-to-whole)
Quotient When interpreting a fraction as a quotient, the fraction represents the result when two integers are divided.	3 cookies are shared with 4 people; each person receives $\frac{3}{4}$ of a cookie.
An Operator When a fraction is used as an operator, it is used as a function or a rule to allow the fraction to become a number that acts on another number. The situation in which this occurs is always multiplicative.	Use $\frac{3}{4}$ of 12 feet of ribbon. Sonia ate $\frac{3}{4}$ of 2 pizzas.

Figure I–1. *How Context Influences the Interpretation of the Fraction* $\frac{3}{4}$

Procedural Knowledge Linked to Students' Difficulties with Fractions

Conventional instruction with rational numbers tends to be procedure- or rule-based (NRC 2001). A typical classroom lesson begins with the teacher showing a rule or procedure, asking students to repeatedly practice until they can perform it automatically, then assessing the speed and accuracy with which the procedure or rule is executed.

The statement "Yours is not to wonder why, just invert and multiply" is characteristic of most rational number instruction. The unfortunate message that students receive, whether unintended or not, is that reasoning and conceptual understanding are not important, but memorized algorithms and rules are. In interviews with community college students, Givvin, Stigler, and Thompson (2011) found that 77 percent of the students believed that math was only about memorizing rules and procedures without understanding or sense making.

There is much evidence that teaching by telling rules—particularly before students have developed a conceptual framework and explored opportunities to build their own knowledge of rational numbers—impedes understanding (Mack 1990; NRC 2001; Peck and Jencks 1981; Wearne and Kouba 2000). Even in classrooms with a direct teaching approach, students struggle to correctly execute the algorithms or rules, and few can explain why the procedures work (NRC 2001).

The work done by Van de Walle, Karp, and Bay-Williams (2010) further supports the mounting evidence that memorization of rules hinders sense making. They indicated that teaching rational number procedures before students construct understanding of this system of numbers results in two negative outcomes:

1. Students do not develop a sense of correctness or reasonableness of an answer when they blindly follow memorized rules.

2. Students become confused about which procedures to use for different applications and often forget the memorized algorithms.

Evidence that a conventional approach to teaching fractions has led to a widespread lack of understanding has resulted in gradual shifts in the mathematics content standards toward understanding and reasoning with rational numbers. Documents such as the National Council of Teachers of Mathematics (NCTM) *Principles and Standards for School Mathematics* (2000) provide an initial catalyst in this direction, and the

Common Core State Standards for Mathematics lay the groundwork for moving from innumeracy in this area to accuracy, fluency, and efficiency grounded in understanding.

Providing learners with a framework for understanding existing procedures and developing conceptual understanding is a needed shift. Educators and researchers alike express their concerns regarding the premature use of algorithms before students have an opportunity to construct meaning and reason about mathematical relationships (Kamii and Dominick 1997; Mueller, Yankelewitz, and Maher 2010). Too often we place procedures first and hope understanding will follow. Research continues to confirm that conceptual understanding directly impacts students' abilities to understand and correctly apply procedures (Hallett, Nunes, and Bryant 2010; Siegler, Thompson, and Schneider 2011). This same perspective is supported in the National Council of Teachers of Mathematics (NCTM) *Principles to Actions* (2014).

This resource continues to focus on the overwhelming research that points to the importance of building conceptual understanding of fractions, decimals, and percentages before procedural knowledge. The routine of number talks is used as a vehicle to focus on the essential understandings of rational numbers and develop a robust understanding of this realm of number.

Learn More...

The chapters in Section III, Number Talks to Help Students Operate with Fractions and Decimals, provide number talk strings designed to help students build strategies grounded in understanding when computing with fractions.

Looking Ahead

This introductory chapter addressed a couple of big "whys"—why fractions are critical in the study of mathematics and why fractions are so challenging for students. Chapter 1 continues to build on these ideas, addressing the important role that number talks have in teaching and learning fractions. It takes a focused look at four foundational principles of number talks, as well as how number talks elicit the Standards for Mathematical Practice.

Connecting the Chapter to Your Practice

1. How do the research results presented in this chapter mirror what you have seen or might expect to see with your students?
2. What evidence have you seen that indicates your students are using whole number reasoning inappropriately?
3. How would you describe the difference between procedural and conceptual knowledge?
4. What interpretations of fractions do we as teachers tend to expose students to more often than others?
5. What steps can we take as teachers to broaden students' thinking about the different ways fractions can be interpreted?
6. Fractions are a pivotal point at which students often decide they are not "good at math." What can we as teachers do to turn these students around with regard to understanding fractions?

Section I

Understanding Number Talks

CHAPTER 1

What Is a Number Talk?

Number Talks \'nəm-bər\ \'tōks\

1. A five- to fifteen-minute classroom conversation around purposefully crafted problems that are solved mentally.
2. The best part of a teacher's day.

This chapter builds an understanding of number talks by first addressing their importance (Why number talks?), then thoughtfully looking at four foundational principles and concluding with a look at how number talks elicit the Standards for Mathematical Practice. Through video clips, classroom dialogue, and numerous mathematical examples, the chapter emphasizes the importance of creating a learning community, selecting purposeful problems, and purposefully recording (writing) students' thinking during a number talk. All of this prepares readers for a focus on the last foundational principle—know when to ask and when to tell—and why it's crucial for educators to shift from the traditional role of "teacher as teller" to that of "teacher as facilitator, questioner, listener, and learner."

OVERVIEW

$16 \times \frac{2}{8}$: Why Number Talks?

Classroom Clip 1.1

To view this video clip, scan the QR code or access via mathsolutions .com/NTFDP1.1

Consider the following questions as you watch this number talk from a fifth-grade classroom:

1. What do you see happening in this number talk?
2. What do you notice about what the students are doing and saying?
3. What do you notice about what the teacher is doing and saying?
4. What surprises you?
5. What is familiar to you?
6. In what ways does this number talk differ from a traditional lesson teaching students how to multiply a whole number times a fraction?
7. What questions do you have after watching this number talk?

Why Number Talks?

The work-related challenges that most people face in today's world demand the best of creative thinking and problem-solving skills. To meet this call as teachers, we must develop our own conceptual understanding of mathematics. Specifically, teachers must be able to

- reason about quantitative information;
- utilize number sense;
- discern whether procedures make sense;
- identify which procedures are applicable to specific situations;

- check for reasonableness of solutions and answers; and
- communicate mathematically to others.

We must expect this not only of ourselves but also of our students. To summarize the previous statements, today's mathematics curricula and instruction must focus on preparing students to compute accurately, efficiently, and flexibly and to be mathematically proficient.

So what does it mean to reason and compute with accuracy, efficiency, and flexibility? *Accuracy* implies the ability to produce a correct answer; *efficiency* refers to the ability to choose an appropriate, expedient strategy for a specific problem; and *flexibility* refers to the ability to use number relationships with ease. Let's take a look at an example.

Sophia, a sixth grader, needs to compare $\frac{24}{50}$ and $\frac{33}{64}$. She chooses to use $\frac{1}{2}$ to prove that $\frac{33}{64}$ is greater than $\frac{24}{50}$. She explains that $\frac{25}{50}$ is exactly $\frac{1}{2}$, so $\frac{24}{50}$ would be a little less than $\frac{1}{2}$. She applies this same reasoning to note that $\frac{32}{64}$ is exactly $\frac{1}{2}$, so $\frac{33}{64}$ is a little more than $\frac{1}{2}$, which means it is greater than $\frac{24}{50}$.

Typically, students learn to use either the cross-multiplication algorithm or the common-denominator procedure to compare fractions, but as Sophia's example shows, using $\frac{1}{2}$ as a benchmark makes solving this problem much more efficient.

> **Number Talk Tip**
>
> Students need to be able to compute accurately, efficiently, and flexibly. *Accuracy* implies the ability to produce a correct answer; *efficiency* refers to the ability to choose an appropriate, expedient strategy for a specific problem; and *flexibility* refers to the ability to use number relationships with ease.

To help students become mathematically proficient, reason mathematically, and compute with accuracy, flexibility, and efficiency, teachers must provide opportunities for students to grapple with constructing number relationships, test these relationships, and analyze and discuss their reasoning. As educators, we want students to have strong number sense: "an awareness and understanding about what numbers are, their relationships, their magnitude, [and] the relative effect of operating on numbers, including the use of mental mathematics and estimation" (Fennell and Landis 1994, 187).

With this in mind, the use of classroom number talks is a powerful opportunity teachers can provide students. During a number talk, teachers ask students to mentally solve problems. These problems help students focus on number relationships, encourage and elicit students' individual strategies, and help students construct important mathematical ideas. The classroom conversations and discussions that ensue around these purposefully crafted problems are at the core of number

Number Talk Tip

Part of a successful number talk is encouraging students to solve problems mentally in various ways.

talks. As students share and defend their solutions and strategies, they have opportunities to collectively reason about numbers while building their mathematical understanding.

Number talks can be especially effective at helping students develop fractional reasoning. In particular, fraction number talks foster efficient, flexible, and accurate computation strategies that build on foundational ideas of rational numbers (e.g., part-to-whole relationships, equivalence, and partitioning). Consider the following "Inside the Classroom" excerpt.

Inside the Classroom

A Number Talk for $\frac{1}{2} + \frac{3}{4}$

Recently, we had the opportunity to visit Ms. Harris's fifth-grade classroom, where number talks are an integral component of mathematics instruction. Ms. Harris asked her fifth graders to gather on the rug without any paper or pencils. She then wrote $\frac{1}{2} + \frac{3}{4}$ where everyone could see it.

Ms. Harris: Show a thumb to your chest when you have a solution. *[Several students place their thumbs up to indicate they have one way to solve the problem.]*

If you find a second way to solve this problem, show you have another way by placing two fingers on your chest. *[Ms. Harris waits until a majority of the students show they have at least one way to think about the problem. Then she begins to request answers.]*

Who has an answer to share?

Leslie: $1\frac{1}{4}$.

Miguel: $\frac{5}{4}$.

Ms. Harris: Does anyone have a different answer?

Kevin: $\frac{4}{6}$.

Ms. Harris: Anyone else? *[Ms. Harris records all of the different answers, whether or not they are correct.]* Who would like to defend or prove one of the answers?

Susan: I want to defend $1\frac{1}{4}$. I thought about $\frac{3}{4}$ as $\frac{1}{2} + \frac{1}{4}$, so I put the two halves together to get one whole. Then I added in the other $\frac{1}{4}$ to get $1\frac{1}{4}$. *[As students explain their answers, Ms. Harris records each student's strategy where the whole class can see it. Ms. Harris records Susan's thinking as follows.]*

$$\frac{1}{2} + \frac{3}{4}$$

$$= \frac{1}{2} + \left(\frac{1}{2} + \frac{1}{4}\right)$$

$$= \left(\frac{1}{2} + \frac{1}{2}\right) + \frac{1}{4}$$

$$= 1 + \frac{1}{4}$$

$$= 1\frac{1}{4}$$

[Ms. Harris intentionally uses parentheses to highlight the associative property in Susan's strategy.]

Ms. Harris: So when Susan grouped addends together, she was using what mathematicians call the *associative property*.

Charlie: I got the same answer, but I did it differently. I changed the $\frac{1}{2}$ to $\frac{1}{4} + \frac{1}{4}$, so I added $\frac{1}{4} + \frac{3}{4}$ to get one whole, and then had $\frac{1}{4}$ left. I put that with the whole to get $1\frac{1}{4}$.

(continued)

Learn More...

Chapter 6, Chapter 8, and Chapter 10, discuss the importance of properties in developing computation strategies.

Blakely: I followed what Charlie did, but I got $\frac{5}{4}$ as my answer because $\frac{1}{4}+\frac{1}{4}+\frac{3}{4}=\frac{5}{4}$.

[Ms. Harris rewrites the original problem each time another student shares. She records Susan's, then Charlie's, and finally Blakely's solutions. All solutions and strategies for a given problem are recorded and left up so they are available for comparison.]

Susan	Charlie	Blakely
$\frac{1}{2}+\frac{3}{4}$	$\frac{1}{2}+\frac{3}{4}$	$\frac{1}{2}+\frac{3}{4}$
$=\frac{1}{2}+\left(\frac{1}{2}+\frac{1}{4}\right)$	$=\left(\frac{1}{4}+\frac{1}{4}\right)+\frac{3}{4}$	$=\left(\frac{1}{4}+\frac{1}{4}\right)+\frac{3}{4}$
$=\left(\frac{1}{2}+\frac{1}{2}\right)+\frac{1}{4}$	$=\frac{1}{4}+\left(\frac{1}{4}+\frac{3}{4}\right)$	$=\frac{1}{4}+\frac{1}{4}+\frac{3}{4}$
$=1+\frac{1}{4}$	$=1\frac{1}{4}$	$=\frac{5}{4}$
$=1\frac{1}{4}$		

Ms. Harris: So how could we get two answers, $1\frac{1}{4}$ and $\frac{5}{4}$? Could they both be correct?

Sara: I think $\frac{5}{4}$ and $1\frac{1}{4}$ are the same, because you could break $\frac{5}{4}$ apart into $\frac{4}{4}$ and $\frac{1}{4}$. Since $\frac{4}{4}$ is the same as one whole, it could be $1\frac{1}{4}$ or $\frac{5}{4}$. They mean the same thing.

Ms. Harris: Would you please turn and talk to someone near you about Sara's reasoning? Do you agree or disagree, and why? *[After about thirty seconds, Ms. Harris pulls the students back together to share their ideas with the whole group.]*

Miguel: Charlie and I agree with Sara. We pictured a rectangle divided into fourths and four fourths made a whole rectangle. If an extra fourth is added, that would be a whole and a fourth, or five fourths. Either way, it's the same. *[Ms. Harris captures Miguel's thinking by drawing an area model.]*

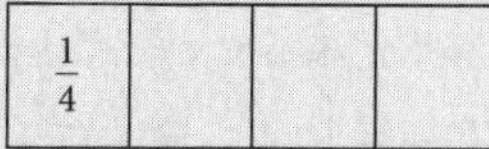

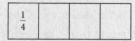

Kevin: I want to change my answer. When I first saw the problem, I added the numbers across the top and across the bottom. That's how I got $\frac{4}{6}$, but now I've changed my mind. I don't think there are sixths in this problem. Now I'm thinking about fourths, and I agree with $1\frac{1}{4}$ and $\frac{5}{4}$.

Understanding Number Talks: Four Foundational Principles

Let's take a few minutes to explore how Ms. Harris's classroom number talk contains four foundational principles that are inherent in every number talk. Keep in mind that while each of these principles is discussed separately on the following pages, they are interdependent and tightly interwoven.

Four Foundational Principles of Number Talks

1. Establish a safe learning community.
2. Use purposeful problems.
3. Record with purpose.
4. Know when to ask and when to tell.

Establish a Safe Learning Community

It's essential for teachers to build a cohesive classroom community and a safe, risk-free learning environment for effective number talks. The culture of the classroom should be based on mutual respect, and it should be driven by a common quest for learning and understanding. Students should be comfortable offering responses for discussion, questioning themselves and their peers, and investigating new strategies. Although it takes time to establish a community of learners built on mutual respect, if you consistently model and set this expectation from the beginning, students will respond.

The following are some key actions teachers can take to build a learning community prior to orchestrating a number talk.

- Be curious about what students think. Knowing that students have something important to contribute is an important first step.
- Ask open-ended questions like, "How did you know? Will it always work?"
- Wait for students to respond. Waiting even 15 seconds after you pose a problem or ask a question can make a big difference in the responses you get.
- Listen carefully to students' responses.
- Expect students to listen to and respect each other's ideas.

Number talks can be a powerful vehicle for promoting a safe learning environment. Let's highlight this by walking through how to facilitate a number talk.

As shown and discussed thus far, number talks start when teachers display a problem for the class and give students time to solve the problem mentally without paper or pencil. Students hold one fist to their chest as they think about the problem. Then, without moving their fist, they quietly put their thumb up to indicate that they have a solution. When teachers see that most students have found an answer—that is, when multiple students have raised a thumb—they encourage students to find additional efficient strategies while others continue thinking. Learners who find additional solutions raise a finger for each additional response. This finger-signal approach ensures that there is ample wait time for all

Number Talk Tip

Using finger signals in a number talk allows wait time for students to think, and it allows teachers to challenge and stretch the thinking of those who already have an answer.

students to think, and it simultaneously allows teachers to challenge and stretch the thinking of those students who already have an answer.

Once most of the students indicate they have a solution and strategy, teachers call for and record all answers—correct and incorrect—for everyone to see. It's important to do this without comment or change of facial expression. By acknowledging all answers, teachers communicate acceptance and a willingness to consider each student's reasoning.

Number Talk Tip

In a number talk, the teacher records all answers—correct and incorrect—for everyone to see. It's important to do this without comment or change of facial expression.

Next, students have the opportunity to share their strategies and justifications with their peers. There are several benefits of sharing and discussing strategies, summarized here.

Benefits of Sharing and Discussing Strategies

Students have the opportunity to

1. clarify their thinking;
2. consider and test other strategies to see if they are mathematically logical;
3. investigate and apply mathematical relationships;
4. build a repertoire of efficient strategies; and
5. make decisions about choosing efficient strategies for specific problems.

Encouraging social interaction, or the exchange of ideas, is an essential way that teachers build an effective learning community. In a number talk, when students exchange ideas they are explaining their thinking and deepening their own mathematical understanding. In turn, listening to others' ideas, considering how these ideas connect or conflict with their own ideas, and then adjusting their own thinking also gives students access to new ways to solve problems.

Do incorrect answers arise during a number talk? Absolutely. However, teachers may ask—and students may ask each other—to defend or justify their answers to prove their mathematical reasoning. When students participate in number talks, they have a sense of shared authority in determining whether an answer is accurate and students know they are expected to think carefully about the solutions and strategies presented.

$4 \times \frac{1}{2}$: Establishing a Safe Learning Community

Classroom Clip 1.2

To view this video clip, scan the QR code or access via mathsolutions .com/NTFDP1.2

Consider the following questions as you watch this number talk from a fifth-grade classroom:

1. How does the teacher elicit different answers?
2. How does the teacher react when different answers—both correct and incorrect—are given?
3. What does the teacher do to create a safe learning environment?
4. How does the teacher connect students' different strategies?
5. What mathematics do you notice the teacher focusing on during this number talk?
6. What else do you notice about the students and the teacher?

Learn More...

Chapter 2, pages 43–44, further explores the importance of accepting, respecting, and considering all answers when facilitating a number talk.

Wrong answers become opportunities to uncover misconceptions, investigate reasoning, and learn from mistakes. Teachers should emphasize that mistakes play an important role in learning. Mistakes provide opportunities for students to question and analyze thinking, bring misconceptions to the forefront, and solidify understanding. In fact, helping students view mistakes as opportunities for learning is an important cornerstone in building a learning community. This productive disposition fosters a growth mindset (Dweck 2006), which allows students to develop the attitude that "I may not understand this yet, but I'm capable of figuring this out."

Use Purposeful Problems

Careful planning before the number talk is essential. As teachers, we should take into account three considerations when choosing problems for number talks.

Three Considerations When Choosing Problems for Number Talks

1. Is the problem accessible to students?
2. Does the problem have potential for students to use multiple strategies?
3. What mathematical relationships might students construct while solving the problem?

For example, if we know that using $\frac{1}{2}$ as a benchmark is an important idea, we can help students consider this relationship by choosing a problem that naturally lends itself to using this benchmark while also providing the potential for students to use other strategies.

Consider the problem $\frac{1}{2}+\frac{7}{8}$. By decomposing the $\frac{7}{8}$ into $\frac{1}{2}+\frac{3}{8}$, students could combine the two halves to make 1 whole and then complete the strategy by adding the remaining $\frac{3}{8}$. Even though this problem could be solved in a number of ways, there is a strong likelihood that at least one student will use $\frac{1}{2}$ as a benchmark.

$$\begin{aligned}&\frac{1}{2}+\frac{7}{8}\\&=\frac{1}{2}+\left(\frac{1}{2}+\frac{3}{8}\right)\\&=\left(\frac{1}{2}+\frac{1}{2}\right)+\frac{3}{8}\\&=1+\frac{3}{8}\\&=1\frac{3}{8}\end{aligned}$$

Students could also solve $\frac{1}{2} + \frac{7}{8}$ by using common denominators, decomposing to make a benchmark, or rounding up to the nearest whole and then adjusting. (See Figure 1–1.)

Student's Strategy and Reasoning	Recording
Common Denominator Lilla: *I thought about $\frac{1}{2}$ as $\frac{4}{8}$ and I knew that $\frac{4}{8} + \frac{7}{8}$ would be $\frac{11}{8}$ or $1\frac{3}{8}$.*	$\frac{1}{2} + \frac{7}{8}$ $= \frac{4}{8} + \frac{7}{8}$ $= \frac{11}{8}$ or $1\frac{3}{8}$
Decomposing to Make a Benchmark Julian: *I broke apart $\frac{1}{2}$ into $\frac{3}{8}$ and $\frac{1}{8}$. Then I added $\frac{1}{8}$ to the $\frac{7}{8}$ to get one whole and then I added $\frac{3}{8} + 1$ to get $1\frac{3}{8}$.*	$\frac{1}{2} + \frac{7}{8}$ $= \left(\frac{3}{8} + \frac{1}{8}\right) + \frac{7}{8}$ $= \frac{3}{8} + \left(\frac{1}{8} + \frac{7}{8}\right)$ $= \frac{3}{8} + 1 = 1\frac{3}{8}$
Rounding to the Nearest Whole and Adjusting ReShana: *I added in an extra $\frac{1}{8}$ to the $\frac{7}{8}$ to make the problem $\frac{1}{2} + 1$. Then I took off the extra $\frac{1}{8}$ from $1\frac{1}{2}$ to get $1\frac{3}{8}$.*	$\frac{1}{2} + \frac{7}{8}$ $\frac{1}{2} + \left(\frac{7}{8} + \frac{1}{8}\right)$ $= \frac{1}{2} + 1$ $1\frac{1}{2} - \frac{1}{8} = 1\frac{3}{8}$

Figure 1–1. *Using Multiple Strategies to Solve $\frac{1}{2} + \frac{7}{8}$*

Of course, number talks don't always follow the path that teachers anticipate. Let's say that the teacher hopes that in a particular problem, students might use a benchmark, but none of the students use one to solve the problem. What then? In cases like this, teachers may decide to pose a carefully crafted sequence of separate but related problems to bring out that idea. This sequence of problems is called a *number talk string*, and its purpose is to provide more opportunities for students to make relationships between problems. The problems are still posed and solved one at a time, but because they are related, teachers can ask students if the previous problem and solutions could help them solve the next problem. For instance, the following number talk string could be used to help students consider the usefulness of benchmarks in computation.

Number Talk Tip

Use a number talk string, a carefully crafted sequence of separate but related problems, to bring out a particular idea with students.

Number Talk String

$\frac{1}{2} + \frac{1}{2}$

$\frac{1}{2} + \frac{3}{4}$

$\frac{1}{2} + \frac{7}{8}$

The first problem $\left(\frac{1}{2} + \frac{1}{2}\right)$ in the number talk string should be easily accessible for students and provide a springboard for solving other problems. Once students prove the solution for $\frac{1}{2} + \frac{1}{2}$, teachers keep that problem and solution on display so students may refer to it as they solve the second problem $\left(\frac{1}{2} + \frac{3}{4}\right)$. Specifically, students think about how they can use the solution from $\frac{1}{2} + \frac{1}{2}$ to help them solve $\frac{1}{2} + \frac{3}{4}$. Teachers then pose the next problem in this string $\left(\frac{1}{2} + \frac{7}{8}\right)$, using this same process, with the focus on the relationship between the new problem and the previous problems.

The goal of a number talk string is not to require all students to use one particular strategy, but rather to create an avenue that might help students make a relationship they have not previously considered. As teachers, we hope students' strategies will highlight certain big

Number Talk Tip

The goal of a number talk string is not to require all students to use one particular strategy, but rather to create an avenue that might help students make a relationship they have not previously considered.

mathematical ideas. Does this always happen? No. Numerous strategies exist for any given problem; however, specific types of problems often elicit certain strategies. This idea is explored further in the chapters to follow.

Record with Purpose

Purposeful, accurate recording—capturing and depicting in writing students' ideas for everyone to see—is an important part of number talks. Let's take a close look at two benefits for recording, which are summarized and then individually discussed in detail.

Learn More...

A third benefit of recording students' mathematical ideas is that when labeled with students' names and saved, the ideas give a written record of students' thinking over time, as well as provide visuals to share with parents. This is considered one of five ways to collect evidence of students' understanding (see Chapter 2, page 55).

Benefits of Purposeful Recording

Recording students' mathematical ideas provides opportunities to

1. make mathematical thinking public; and
2. focus on the mathematics.

When teachers record a student's thinking for everyone to see, they make that student's mathematical thinking public. This in turn gives students an opportunity to consider perspectives other than their own. Purposeful recording is a silent form of honoring and showing respect for student-generated ideas. It also offers a visual that students can use to analyze and critique each other's thinking, as well as to look for opportunities to make connections between different strategies.

An important part of recording student strategies is making sure those recordings are mathematically correct and highlight the mathematical ideas in an orderly, accessible way. Teachers often assume they must scribe verbatim what a student says; this is not necessarily true. Rather, we need to record a student's thinking in a way that (a) makes it easy for other students to follow and (b) purposely makes connections to the big mathematical ideas and structures. Teachers should anticipate how students will respond and take time beforehand to think through possible strategies for each problem. This key practice helps teachers listen to students and follow their thinking during the actual number talk.

Learn More...

Chapter 2, page 49, also looks at recording. Chapters 6, 7, 8, 9, and 10 highlight computation strategies commonly used by students, and include numerous additional examples of recording.

Consider two different recordings for a compensation strategy used with this problem: $0.48 + 0.37$. (See Figure 1–2.) The student who shared a solution said, "I took 0.02 from 0.37 and gave it to 0.48." Recording A mirrors the student's language but does not focus on the bigger mathematical ideas that are embedded in this strategy. Recording B captures the same reasoning but also highlights the underlying structure of decomposing and composing and the use of the associative property to "move" part of one addend to combine it with another addend.

Recording A	Recording B
$\begin{array}{rcl} 0.48 & + & 0.37 \\ \underline{+0.02} & & \underline{-0.02} \\ 0.50 & + & 0.35 = 0.85 \end{array}$	$0.48 + 0.37$ $= 0.48 + (0.02 + 0.35)$ $= (0.48 + 0.02) + 0.35$ $= 0.50 + 0.35$ $= 0.85$

Figure 1–2. *Which Recording Highlights the Student's Strategy and the Associative Property?*

Number Talk Tip

If you choose to use a model when recording, remember that the model itself is not a strategy but rather a representation of the student's thinking.

Teachers who notice that students are confused about a specific strategy can support a fragile idea by connecting the mathematics in the strategy to a model. For instance, let's say that Susanna shares that she added up to solve the problem *2.13 – 0.58* but other students are struggling to follow her thinking. Her teacher might record Susanna's step-by-step reasoning with a series of expressions and then represent her solution on an open number line. (See Figure 1–3.) Note that the

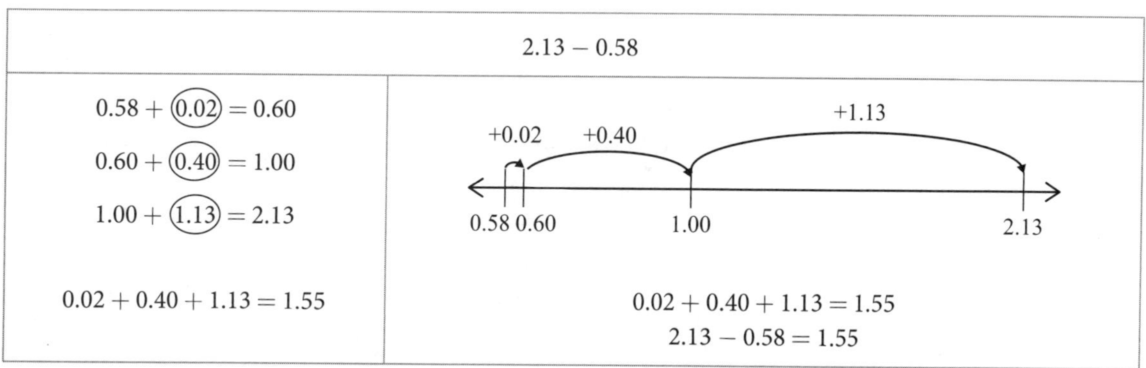

Figure 1–3. *Using "Adding Up" to Solve 2.13 – 0.58*

number line is not the strategy but is another way to represent Susanna's thinking.

Purposeful recordings—those that incorporate and highlight the use of properties, decomposition and composition of numbers, and place value—are highly beneficial in helping students understand mathematics that extends well beyond basic arithmetic.

Know When to Ask and When to Tell

Number talks are rooted in Jean Piaget's theory of learning, which states that not all knowledge is alike. Piaget (1971) distinguished among three types of knowledge according to their ultimate sources. Piaget's three types of knowledge are: physical, social, and logico-mathematical. Understanding the difference between each type of knowledge forms the basis for knowing when to ask our students questions and prompt them to form their own conclusions (e.g., "How did you think about solving this problem? How did you know . . . ?") and when to tell them things (e.g., the names of mathematical operations and how to write them). Let's briefly explore each of these knowledge types, one at a time.

Piaget's Three Types of Knowledge

1. Physical
2. Social
3. Logico-Mathematical

Physical Knowledge

Physical knowledge has its ultimate source in physical objects and their attributes. When artists mix red and blue paint, they get purple. If students connect a battery, wires and a bulb in a complete circuit, the bulb will light. As teachers, we can tell our class what happens when artists mix paint colors and how to make a light bulb light up, but the best way for students to construct these ideas is to personally work with the materials, observe, and test out their own theories.

Social Knowledge

The ultimate source of social knowledge is society. Social knowledge involves information we gain from other people through engaging in a conversation, listening to a lecture, reading, and so forth. It is knowledge that is impossible to figure out or construct independently because it is arbitrary and can change from society to society. For example, Americans celebrate the Fourth of July, but this is not a holiday celebrated in other countries. We each have a name, usually given to us by our parents, but we could be called by any name. We know our names and specific holidays because someone gave us this information.

The names for numbers and how we write them are social knowledge. In English, we say "one, two, three, four," but in Spanish we say "uno, dos, tres, quatro." The names of different operations or properties and how to write them are also examples of social knowledge in mathematics. Because all of these are conventions that have been established, students cannot build them for themselves; teachers need to convey this information directly to students.

When something that is considered social knowledge comes up in a number talk, teachers should *tell* students that information. This usually happens when there is a need for a "label" or a social convention to record an idea. For example, when students share a strategy and use the commutative property, teachers can supply the term *commutative property* during the recording. As another example, teachers might record "multiply four times five" as 4×5, $4(5)$, or $4 \cdot 5$, differently depending on the grade level they are teaching, but teachers may have to tell students what the symbols in the recording mean.

Many of us learned computation procedures by being told step by step what to do, memorizing these steps, and then practicing until we could recall these steps effortlessly. This type of teaching assumes that mathematics is all social knowledge.

Logico-Mathematical Knowledge

Logico-mathematical knowledge is the knowledge of relationships and has its ultimate source in each person's mind. Most of mathematics—the logical relationships we have to mentally construct for ourselves to understand something—is logico-mathematical knowledge. Consider the following collection of dots. How many dots do you see?

Some people know there are seven dots because they look at the three dots on each side and one in the middle and see this as $(3 + 3) + 1 = 7$. Others see a pattern of five dots in the middle, like on a die, and two dots on the outside, thus seeing the group of dots as $5 + 2 = 7$. Still others think about two dots on the top row, three dots on the middle row, and two more dots on the bottom row, combining the dots as $(2 + 3) + 2 = 7$. Even more approaches are possible. In each case, although the answer is the same, the way that people "see" the dots and mentally put them together to find out the answer is a relationship that individuals make for themselves. As teachers we can demonstrate how to count the dots and tell students how to "see" and find out how many dots there are, but ultimately, being sure and knowing "how many" is knowledge that each person constructs individually. That knowledge is logico-mathematical knowledge.

Since most of understanding mathematics fits into the realm of logico-mathematical knowledge and is about relationships that students have to construct for themselves, this means that we have to shift from being the source of information—telling students how to find an answer, or pre-teaching a strategy—to being facilitator, questioner, listener, and learner. Our primary role is to elicit student ideas through purposeful problems and questions, so that we are asking students how they can figure out a way to reason. In fact, since most of mathematics is about making relationships, the majority of our mathematics time should be spent in this role, helping students to solve problems on their own rather than telling them how to solve problems.

As educators, we are probably accustomed to assuming the role of telling and explaining. Teaching by telling is the method most of us experienced as students, and many of us have continued to emulate this model in our own practice. A shift from telling and showing to asking and listening can be challenging; however, if we allow students to construct their own ideas, we are helping them to become mathematically confident and proficient.

Number Talk Tip

As teachers, a shift from telling and showing to asking and listening can be challenging; however, if we allow students to construct their own ideas, we are helping them to become mathematically confident and proficient.

Realizing that students are capable of constructing mathematical understanding is an important first step in making the shift from teaching by telling to teaching by asking. Jo Boaler's work on growth mindsets versus fixed mindsets can also help us shift our beliefs about teaching and learning. In her book, *Mathematical Mindsets: Unleashing Students' Potential Through Creative Math, Inspiring Messages and Innovative Teaching* (2015), Boaler shares research indicating that mathematical ability is not predetermined or "fixed." Rather, mathematical ability needs to be considered with a "growth mindset," which maintains that all students are capable of doing and understanding mathematics; with hard work, every student can grow in their understanding.

Since classroom discourse is an expectation in a number talk, teachers must also move into the role of facilitator. It's our responsibility as facilitators to ask questions that focus the discussion on mathematical relationships—helping students to construct logico-mathematical knowledge. By posing questions like, "How does Joe's strategy connect to the ideas in Renee's strategy?" we can structure the conversation so that students have opportunities to focus on the big mathematical ideas, share strategies, listen to their peers, and ask questions.

Learn More...

Chapter 2, page 43, takes a closer look at encouraging student communication throughout a number talk.

When we as authors first began listening to our own students' reasoning, we realized we had a lot to learn about students' intuitions regarding numerical reasoning. Instead of concentrating only on a final, correct answer and one procedure for getting there, we broadened our scope to engage in listening to and learning about our students' thinking by asking open-ended questions. Our initial focus on "What answer did you get?" shifted to include "*How* did you get your answer?" We wanted to know *how* our students arrived at their answers and *why*. Did they find common denominators, visualize a model, compare the distance from the whole, or reason about the difference between unit fractions? By changing our questions from "What answer did you get?" to "How did you solve this problem?" we were able to identify and understand how our students were making sense of mathematics.

Mental Mathematics and Number Talks

Mental mathematics is a key component of number talks because it encourages students to construct numerical relationships and to develop their own strategies instead of relying on solely memorized procedures. When students approach problems without paper and pencil, they have to rely on what they know and understand about the numbers and subsequent relationships.

Mental mathematics can also help strengthen students' understanding of place value. When students look at numbers as whole quantities instead of discrete columns of digits, they have to use their knowledge of place value. During initial number talks, teachers often write problems horizontally to encourage students to think in this realm. For example, for a problem like *0.98 + 1.99*, teachers typically teach students to solve this problem by vertically lining up the addends, being careful to line up the decimal points, and treating each column as a column of ones. When students are mentally making relationships, however, they will likely think about 0.98 as 0.02 away from 1 whole, and 1.99 as 0.01 away from 2, so the answer is 0.03 away from 3, or 2.97. When students become consistent in their reasoning about the magnitude of numbers, using place value in their strategies and making mathematical relationships, teachers should present problems both horizontally and vertically so students are comfortable looking at problems in various formats.

Number Talks and the Standards for Mathematical Practice

Incorporating the use of number talks into our classroom practice provides an opportunity for students to develop the dispositions and processes of doing and reasoning with mathematics as outlined in the eight Standards for Mathematical Practice (National Governors Association Center for Best Practices [NGA], Council of Chief State School Officers [CCSSO] 2010). These standards are the culmination of NCTM's Process Standards (2000) and the National Research Council's Strands of Mathematical Proficiency (2001) and provide the impetus needed for students to move beyond passive learning to engage in building understanding with the mindset of a mathematician. (See Figure 1–4.)

NCTM Process Standards	**Strands of Mathematical Proficiency**
Problem Solving Reasoning and Proof Communication Representation Connections	Adaptive Reasoning Strategic Competence Conceptual Understanding Procedural Fluency Productive Disposition
Standards for Mathematical Practice MP1. Make sense of problems and persevere in solving them. MP2. Reason abstractly and quantitatively. MP3. Construct viable arguments and critique the reasoning of others. MP4. Model with mathematics. MP5. Use appropriate tools strategically. MP6. Attend to precision. MP7. Look for and make use of structure. MP8. Look for and express regularity in repeated reasoning.	

Figure 1–4. *The Standards for Mathematical Practice: A Culmination of NCTM's Process Standards and The National Research Council's Strands of Mathematical Proficiency*

Learn More...

Look back at Ms. Harris's number talk with fifth graders (pages 16–19). What Standards for Mathematical Practice (see Figure 1–4 on the previous page) are students using?

The Standards for Mathematical Practice describe what we hope to see students doing when they are doing mathematics. The very nature of a number talk provides opportunities for students to develop the mathematical practices. Let's look back at Ms. Harris's use of a number talk with her fifth graders (pages 16–19). The conversations during this number talk illustrate how students are engaged in *making sense of problems and persevering in solving them* (MP1), *reasoning abstractly and quantitatively* (MP2), and *constructing viable arguments and critiquing the reasoning of others* (MP3). As students shared their strategies and agreed on an accurate answer and the equivalence between $\frac{5}{4}$ and $1\frac{1}{4}$, they were *attending to precision* (MP6). The students used the standard *look for and make use of structure* (MP7) when they decomposed $\frac{1}{2}$ and $\frac{3}{4}$ and made use of the associative property to reach a solution.

When Miguel explained that he pictured a rectangle divided into fourths, he was *using appropriate tools strategically* (MP5). Tools might include paper and pencil, manipulatives, or models. In this case, Miguel's visualization of an area model was a tool he used to help access the problem.

Not all Standards for Mathematical Practice will be used in every number talk. In our fifth-grade example, two standards—*model with mathematics* (apply mathematics to solve problems arising in everyday life) (MP4) and *look for and express regularity in repeated reasoning* (MP8)—were not used. If Ms. Harris had given students an additional problem, they might have used the previous problem and strategies to apply to a new situation. This would be an example of *look for and express regularity in repeated reasoning* (MP8).

Number talks give teachers an opportunity to help students highlight the mathematical practices. Take, for example, *look for and make use of structure* (MP7). Here's how it might apply to a new problem: $8 \times \frac{3}{4}$. After collecting and recording student strategies for this problem, teachers can use the recordings to help students consider the structure of decomposing factors into factors or addends using the distributive or associative properties, or even the structure of doubling and halving. (See Figure 1–5.)

Student's Strategy and Reasoning	Recording
Decomposing Factors into Addends Henry: *I thought about $\frac{3}{4}$ as $\frac{1}{2}+\frac{1}{4}$ and then I multiplied both parts by 8. $8 \times \frac{1}{2} = 4$ and $8 \times \frac{1}{4} = 2$, and $4 + 2 = 6$*	$8 \times \frac{3}{4}$ $= 8 \times \left(\frac{1}{2}+\frac{1}{4}\right)$ $= \left(8 \times \frac{1}{2}\right) + \left(8 \times \frac{1}{4}\right)$ $= 4 + 2$ $= 6$
Decomposing Factors into Addends Brittany: *I knew that $\frac{1}{4}$ of 8 was 2 so I broke $\frac{3}{4}$ into $\frac{1}{4}+\frac{1}{4}+\frac{1}{4}$ and multiplied each $\frac{1}{4}$ by 8. That gave me $2 + 2 + 2$ which is 6.*	$8 \times \frac{3}{4}$ $= 8 \times \left(\frac{1}{4}+\frac{1}{4}+\frac{1}{4}\right)$ $= \left(8 \times \frac{1}{4}\right) + \left(8 \times \frac{1}{4}\right) + \left(8 \times \frac{1}{4}\right)$ $= 2 + 2 + 2$ $= 6$
Decomposing Factors into Factors Newana: *I made it an easier problem by thinking about 8 as 2×4. That was easier for me because I knew that $\frac{3}{4}$ of 4 was 3, so then I multiplied 2×3 and that's 6.*	$8 \times \frac{3}{4}$ $= (2 \times 4) \times \frac{3}{4}$ $= 2 \times \left(4 \times \frac{3}{4}\right)$ $= 2 \times 3$ $= 6$

Figure 1–5. *Using Multiple Strategies to Solve $8 \times \frac{3}{4}$ (continued)*

Student's Strategy and Reasoning	Recording
Doubling and Halving DeShawn: *I was trying to get to a whole number problem so I doubled $\frac{3}{4}$ and halved 8 and that gave $4 \times 1\frac{1}{2}$. Then I doubled and halved again and that gave me 2×3 so the answer is 6.*	$8 \times \frac{3}{4}$ $= \left(8 \times \frac{1}{2}\right) \times \left(\frac{3}{4} \times 2\right)$ $= 4 \times 1\frac{1}{2}$ $= \left(4 \times \frac{1}{2}\right) \times \left(1\frac{1}{2} \times 2\right)$ $= 2 \times 3$ $= 6$

Figure 1–5. *(continued)*

Teachers can also use this same number talk to begin conversations related to *attend to precision* (MP6) by having students turn and talk about not only accuracy but also efficiency with each of the strategies.

Placing 0.89 on the Number Line: Number Talks and the Standards for Mathematical Practice

Classroom Clip 1.3

Consider the following questions as you watch this number talk from a fourth-grade classroom:

1. Where do you see students *making sense of problems and persevering in solving them?*
2. What are some examples of students *constructing viable arguments and critiquing the reasoning of others?*
3. What evidence do you see of students *attending to precision or looking for and making use of structure?*
4. What else do you notice?
5. How can number talks help students become more proficient in using the Standards for Mathematical Practice?

To view this video clip, scan the QR code or access via mathsolutions .com/NTFDP1.3

Looking Ahead

In this chapter, we opened with answers to the questions, "What is a number talk?" and "Why number talks?" and explored the four foundational principles to using number talks in the classroom. In Chapter 2, we address ten essentials to getting started with number talks, followed by five ways to collect evidence of students' understanding.

Connecting the Chapter to Your Practice

1. When you read the "Inside the Classroom" scenario on pages 16–19 in this chapter, what do you notice about when Ms. Harris decided to ask a question and when she decided to tell?
2. Is there anything about the students' thinking in the above referenced scenario that surprises you?
3. What are some ways that you work to establish a safe learning environment in your classroom?
4. If you have already been using number talks with your students, how do you choose which problems to use?
5. What are some of the challenges related to recording students' strategies?
6. How does recognizing and paying attention to Piaget's three kinds of knowledge influence what we do as teachers?
7. What parts of your mathematics curriculum are social knowledge and which parts are logico-mathematical knowledge?
8. How can using number talks enhance students' proficiency as indicated in the Standards for Mathematical Practice?

CHAPTER 2

How Do I Get Started with Number Talks?

While a number talk is designed to be only five to fifteen minutes in duration, the potential for mathematical impact is significant. It is critical that students come ready to think, listen, share, and question themselves and their peers. This concentrated period should be a time of coming together as a community of learners with a common focus and purpose. Building this environment takes time, patience, and consistency. We have kept all this in mind and have designed this chapter to help you get started with using number talks with your students. This chapter encourages starting small, first introducing ten essentials to take into consideration when facilitating a number talk. Then, we conclude with five ways to develop student accountability with number talks.

OVERVIEW

Getting Started: Ten Essentials

Number talks can be a good way to start your math class. If the problems in your number talk are related to your lesson, you can continue to explore the mathematical ideas that surface during the number talk during your math lesson.

Other teachers do number talks when they have an extra few minutes during the day, or at the end of their class period. Doing number talks consistently—several times a week—is what makes the difference in students' number sense. Place number talks where it fits best for you and your students.

The conversations in number talks can be great launching points for discussions during the math lesson, but they don't always have to be directly related to what you are teaching that day. Even if you are teaching geometry or algebra, your students need number and logic to solve problems. Thinking from multiple perspectives is important in all areas of mathematics and doing a number talk problem several times a week can benefit your students' ability to think flexibly and logically.

In preparing for number talks, it's important to start small and establish procedures and expectations. As authors we've distilled this into "ten essentials"—a manageable list of teacher actions to support successful number talks implementation. Keep in mind that though each action is presented individually, many of these are interwoven. The following pages take a closer look at each.

Number Talk Tip

Keep in mind that though each of these ten essentials is presented individually, ultimately when facilitating a number talk, many of these are interwoven.

Ten Essentials for Number Talks

1. Organize your classroom space to foster student engagement.
2. Start with problems that give all students access and elicit thinking from multiple perspectives.
3. Insist on students solving problems mentally.
4. Provide appropriate wait time.
5. Accept, respect, and consider all answers.
6. Encourage student communication throughout the number talk.
7. Record strategies to make student thinking public.
8. Be prepared when the sharing of strategies doesn't go as anticipated.
9. Limit your number talks to five to fifteen minutes.
10. Be patient with yourself and your students.

Number Talk Tip

When students are gathered for a number talk, as teachers we should position ourselves to more easily observe and informally assess them. For more on what to observe during a number talk, see Essential 6.

Learn More...

One of the four foundational principles of number talks is "establish a safe learning community." Keep this in mind as you think about Essential 1. See Chapter 1 for more about this and the other foundational principles (it's recommended you read Chapter 1 first, then continue the discussion here).

Essential 1: Organize Your Classroom Space to Foster Student Engagement

When it's time for a number talk, we want students to be focused and ready to think. We also want them to talk to each other, and the way we set up our classrooms can impede or encourage this conversation. Some teachers set up their room with students' desks in pairs or small groups so students can easily turn and talk. Other teachers bring students closer during a number talk by giving students a choice of sitting on the floor, sitting on top of their desks, or finding a place closer to the front of the room.

Essential 2: Start with Problems That Give All Students Access and Elicit Thinking from Multiple Perspectives

In starting with number talks, use problems that you as the teacher think all students will be able to access. If you have never used number talks before, or if your students are not accustomed to solving problems in multiple ways, consider starting with whole number computation problems or dot images. It is important for students to be fluent with whole number strategies before incorporating number talks with fractions, because many whole number computation strategies also work with fractions.

When students are ready for number talks with fractions, it is important to start with fractions that are friendly and easy to think about such as $\frac{1}{2}$ or $\frac{1}{4}$ as opposed to $\frac{9}{11}$ or $\frac{13}{15}$. Using fractions that students often encounter in real life decreases the cognitive demand and allows students to focus on the mathematical relationships in the problem. Reasoning about $\frac{1}{2}+\frac{3}{4}$ gives the opportunity for students to make important mathematical relationships and investigate mathematical structures without having to deal with unfriendly fractions.

Essential 3: Insist on Students Solving Problems Mentally

Mentally is a key word in the definition of a number talk. As a teacher, it's critical to ensure that the focus be on ways that students solve problems mentally, without the use of paper and pencil, writing on mini whiteboard, tablets, or using calculators. When students write to solve problems, they often focus solely on memorized procedures and neglect to look for and use numerical relationships. This limits the strategies they will use, hinders their flexibility in thinking, and often fosters less efficient strategies. By requiring that problems be solved mentally, a number talk encourages rather than limits the use of multiple strategies.

Learn More...

It is important for students to be fluent with whole number strategies before incorporating number talks with fractions, because many whole number computation strategies also work with fractions. Number talks for whole number operations can be found in *Number Talks: Whole Number Computation* (2010, 2014).

Learn More...

Using purposeful problems is considered one of the four foundational principles of number talks; for more insight on this, see Chapter 1, page 23 (it's recommended you read Chapter 1 first, then continue the discussion here).

Learn More...

Chapter 4 provides ideas of places to start with number talks to build fractional reasoning.

Learn More...

Mental mathematics is a key means of helping students develop logico-mathematical knowledge. Explore this further in Chapter 1, pages 29–32.

Essential 4: Provide Appropriate Wait Time

Wait time is critical to ensure that the majority of students have accessed the problem. Many students have the misconception that they are not good at mathematics because they are not fast. As teachers we can easily reinforce this misconception if we begin gathering answers as soon as the first students are ready.

One way to help ensure we are providing enough wait time is to encourage students to use finger signals. The protocol is fairly simple: Students start with their fists held to their chests and indicate when they are ready with a solution by quietly putting their thumb up, still holding fist to chest. Once students have found an answer, they are encouraged to continue finding efficient strategies while others are thinking. To indicate that they have found other approaches, students raise a finger for each additional strategy (a thumb and finger indicates they have two strategies, a thumb and two fingers indicates they have three strategies, and so on). The teacher notes that enough wait time has been provided once most of the students indicate that they have at least one way to solve the problem.

Number Talk Tip

You and your students may choose to come up with your own hand signals to use during a number talk. For example, one teacher let us know that her students started tapping their heads to show when they heard somebody do something that they thought was really good thinking.

Using Hand Signals and Wait Time

Classroom Clip 2.1

Consider the following questions as you watch the beginning of this number talk from a sixth-grade classroom:

1. How can hand signals help students keep thinking after they have an answer to a problem?
2. How does using hand signals help a teacher facilitate wait time?
3. How does giving wait time benefit students?
4. How can using wait time help teachers?

To view this video clip, scan the QR code or access via mathsolutions .com/NTFDP2.1

Why not just have students raise their hands? Once students see several hands raised, they often stop thinking. They have become accustomed to the teacher calling on those students who already have an answer. One of the purposes of a number talk is to bring equity to the mathematics classroom. We want all students to have time to think.

Number Talk Tip

One of the purposes of a number talk is to bring equity to the mathematics classroom. As the teacher, make sure all students have time to think.

Benefits of Having Students Using Finger Signals During a Number Talk

- Allow quiet time for students to think.
- Challenge students who already have a solution and strategy to think of additional ones.
- Send the message that *all* students are expected to think and contribute during this time.
- Help us as teachers provide an appropriate amount of wait time.

The aim of wait time and finger signals is not to reward speed, but to help students focus on thinking about mathematical relationships. However, if the majority of students are slow to put their thumbs up, consider asking students to turn and talk to a partner about a way they could solve the problem. Thinking together can spark strategies and solutions and help give access into a problem that may be challenging at first.

Essential 5: Accept, Respect, and Consider All Answers

A first step toward establishing a respectful classroom learning community is acceptance of all ideas and answers—regardless of errors. This expectation must be in place for number talks and rich mathematical discussions to occur. Wrong answers are often rooted in misconceptions, and when these ideas are brought to the forefront, as teachers we can help students confront their misunderstandings. Students who are in safe learning environments are willing to risk sharing an incorrect answer with their peers in order to grow mathematically.

Learn More...

Establishing a safe learning community is one of the four foundational principles of number talks; see Chapter 1, page 20–22 (it's recommended you read Chapter 1 first, then continue the discussion here).

Students should refrain from derogatory comments when incorrect answers are shared. One way to help ensure appropriate responses to all

Number Talk Tip

All ideas and answers should be accepted, regardless of errors. Wrong answers are often rooted in misconceptions, and when these ideas are brought to the forefront, as teachers we can help students confront their misunderstandings.

answers (whether correct or incorrect) is for us as teachers to remain neutral as we collect answers and record strategies. When we record students' solutions and strategies, we should refrain from giving any verbal or facial expressions that indicate our agreement or disagreement. It is helpful to practice having a "blank face." Remember, students often look to teachers as the source of correct answers. Part of building a safe learning community is to shift this source of knowledge and equip students with the ability to own and defend the thinking behind their solutions and also change their reasoning once they have different information. Students will often initiate this by saying, "I disagree with myself," "I change my mind," or "Please erase my answer." This in-the-moment correction of wrong answers by students is much more powerful than when the teacher explains why an answer is incorrect.

If many of the answers shared are incorrect and unreasonable, consider having students turn and talk with a partner before processing specific solutions. In partners, students discuss which answers are reasonable and which answers could be ruled out based on logic and number sense. This not only continues to promote a safe learning community, but also provides an excellent opportunity for students to estimate and make further relationships between numbers.

Once all answers are collected, it then becomes time to consider each one. Begin by asking students "Who would like to share his/her strategy for solving the problem?" The student who volunteers should always first identify which answer he/she is defending, then proceed to share the strategy used to solve the problem. The goal is not necessarily to start with students who have the correct answer, but to let students volunteer to share their thinking until there is class consensus about the correct answer. Once the class decides on the right answer, the teacher crosses out or erases any other answers.

Learn More...

Encouraging student communication is a critical part of the number talks foundational principle, "establishing a safe learning community." See Chapter 1, page 20–22, for more on this principle and the benefits of sharing and discussing strategies. (It's recommended you read Chapter 1 first, then continue the discussion here.)

Essential 6: Encourage Student Communication Throughout the Number Talk

A successful number talk establishes productive conversations around mathematics, and is rooted in communication. Throughout number talks, ask students to share individual strategies and respond to others' strategies with partners and as a whole group. One way to ensure that everyone has an opportunity to share their thinking is to use the turn-and-talk technique.

Benefits of the Turn-and-Talk Technique

- Immediately involves and engages all students.
- Provides a more comfortable, smaller venue for students reluctant to speak in a whole group to still articulate their thinking.

$1\frac{1}{2} \times \frac{2}{5}$: Using Turn and Talk with a Number Talk

Classroom Clip 2.2

Consider the following questions as you watch this number talk from a sixth-grade classroom:

1. Why does the teacher implement a turn and talk at this point in the number talk?
2. How does using turn and talk benefit students?
3. How do teachers benefit when students turn and talk?
4. What do you notice about the solution both the boy in the small group and Samantha use to solve the problem?
5. What arithmetic property are they using?

To view this video clip, scan the QR code or access via mathsolutions .com/NTFDP2.2

Typically, the turn-and-talk technique is used after students have had time to think about their strategies and answers and offered, as a whole class, several answer possibilities (which, as the teacher, you've listed for everyone to see). Then have students pair up with a partner, asking them to share their thinking. If several answers are given, you can also ask students to think about which answers are reasonable and why. This use of turn and talk centers the conversation on ways to estimate and how to rule out answers that are unreasonable.

Another way to use turn and talk during a number talk is after an individual strategy has been offered by a student. Then have students turn and talk with a partner to state the strategy in their own words or discuss what they do and do not understand. You could also ask students, "Will this strategy work in every situation?" This allows students, in partners, to test other strategies.

Providing opportunities for students to articulate their thinking and reasoning with partners and as a whole group is important. Both allow students time to reconsider their own ideas, self-correct if needed, and clarify their understandings. Whether in partners or as a whole group, the role of the students who are not talking at the time is to listen carefully and consider the proposed strategies of their peers. Students tend to focus on their own ways of thinking, so considering strategies different from their own can be challenging; this is the same for teachers. Critiquing and analyzing other strategies strengthens both students' and our own mathematical foundation—and broadens our understanding.

Consider how you would mentally solve $\frac{3}{4}+\frac{5}{8}$. After you have solved this problem, look at the following strategies. (See Figure 2–1.)

Student's Strategy and Reasoning	Recording
Using $\frac{1}{2}$ as a Benchmark Francis: *I broke apart each number to get two halves and had $\frac{1}{4}$ and $\frac{1}{8}$ left. I put the two halves together to make 1 whole and then added the $\frac{1}{4}$ and $\frac{1}{8}$. I knew $\frac{1}{4}$ was the same as $\frac{2}{8}$, so $\frac{2}{8}$ plus $\frac{1}{8}$ gave me $\frac{3}{8}$. My answer is $1\frac{3}{8}$.*	$\frac{3}{4}+\frac{5}{8}$ $=\left(\frac{1}{2}+\frac{1}{4}\right)+\left(\frac{1}{2}+\frac{1}{8}\right)$ $=\left(\frac{1}{2}+\frac{1}{2}\right)+\left(\frac{1}{4}+\frac{1}{8}\right)$ $=1+\left(\frac{2}{8}+\frac{1}{8}\right)$ $=1\frac{3}{8}$

Figure 2–1. *Using Multiple Strategies to Solve* $\frac{3}{4}+\frac{5}{8}$

Student's Strategy and Reasoning	Recording
Compensation Sophie: *I decomposed $\frac{5}{8}$ into $\frac{2}{8}$ and $\frac{3}{8}$. I knew that $\frac{2}{8}$ was the same as $\frac{1}{4}$, so I grouped it with the $\frac{3}{4}$ to make 1 whole. The 1 whole plus the $\frac{3}{8}$ gave me $1\frac{3}{8}$.*	$\frac{3}{4}+\frac{5}{8}$ $=\frac{3}{4}+\left(\frac{2}{8}+\frac{3}{8}\right)$ $=\left(\frac{3}{4}+\frac{2}{8}\right)+\frac{3}{8}$ $=\left(\frac{3}{4}+\frac{1}{4}\right)+\frac{3}{8}$ $=1+\frac{3}{8}$ $=1\frac{3}{8}$
Common Denominators Lin: *I changed the $\frac{3}{4}$ to $\frac{6}{8}$ since they are equivalent fractions. Then I added all of the eighths to get a total of $\frac{11}{8}$. I knew that there were $\frac{8}{8}$s or 1 whole in $\frac{11}{8}$ with $\frac{3}{8}$ left. That gave me a total of $1\frac{3}{8}$.*	$\frac{3}{4}+\frac{5}{8}$ $=\frac{6}{8}+\frac{5}{8}$ $=\frac{11}{8}$ $=\frac{8}{8}+\frac{3}{8}$ $=1\frac{3}{8}$

Figure 2–1. *(continued)*

Are any of these strategies different from the one you used? If so, did you find them more difficult to follow? Flexibility in mathematical thinking develops as we push ourselves to reason through different approaches to problems. Asking students to test someone else's strategy with a new problem provides an opportunity for them to continue to add strategies to their mathematical toolbox.

We must repeatedly model appropriate ways to respond to other students' strategies. Displaying sample prompts to help students learn how to frame their questions and comments may help them learn how to share their thinking in a positive way. Possible prompts to consider are the following:

Sample Prompts for Students in Responding to Strategies

- I agree with _________ because _________.
- I don't understand _________. Can you explain it again?
- I disagree with _________ because _________.
- How did you decide to _________?

Consider posting prompts like this on a poster and permanently displaying it in your classroom. (See Figure 2–2.)

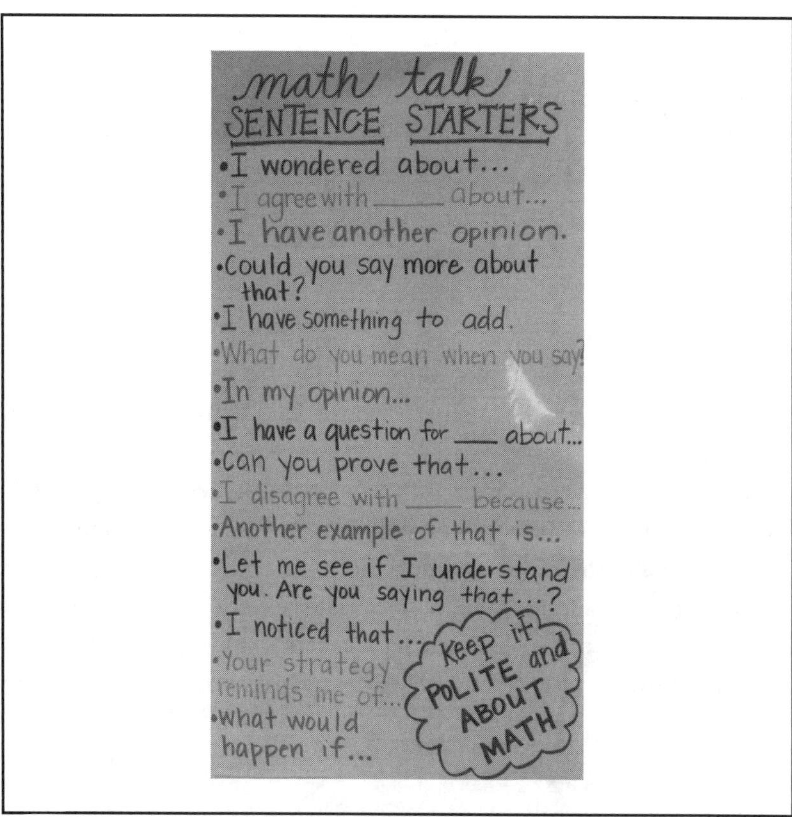

Figure 2–2. *A Poster of Sample Prompts Displayed in Ms. Alexander's Classroom*

However you choose to encourage student communication in a number talk, students should always clearly hear the message that they need to think continually about other strategies. It is a big idea for students to realize that there are always other possible approaches to solve a problem.

Observations to Make as Students Communicate During a Number Talk

As students communicate, we as teachers should observe and informally assess them. There are many possible situations to observe; are students

- engaged;
- struggling—or solving problems with ease;
- relying on certain tools during mental computation (for example, the use of fingers for calculation, or the use of a posted number line or hundreds chart); and/or
- relying on the standard U.S. algorithm by "writing" the problem on the floor or in the air with their fingers?

Observing students closely while they share strategies will also help in planning appropriate follow-up.

Essential 7: Record Strategies to Make Student Thinking Public

As first introduced in Chapter 1, recording—capturing and depicting in writing students' ideas for everyone to see—is an important part of number talks. A teacher's recording needs to be clear, concise, and capture the big mathematical ideas presented. A crucial step in successfully recording student strategies is to anticipate how students will respond.

Take a moment to think about what strategies students might use to solve the problem $1\frac{1}{4} - \frac{3}{4}$ and how you might record each strategy. Figure 2–3 shows some possible strategies, ways to record, and mathematical ideas that could come from this problem.

Learn More...

Purposeful recording is considered one of the four foundational principles of number talks, and is first introduced in Chapter 1 on page 26 (it's recommended you read Chapter 1 first, then continue the discussion here). Chapters 6–10 highlight computation strategies commonly used by students and are a valuable read for helping you anticipate how students may respond.

Student's Strategy and Reasoning	Recording	Mathematical Ideas
Decomposing the Minuend Candice: *First I broke apart $1\frac{1}{4}$ into 1 and $\frac{1}{4}$ so I could remove $\frac{3}{4}$ from the 1. That left me with $\frac{1}{4}$. I added it to the $\frac{1}{4}$ that was left and got $\frac{1}{2}$.*	$1\frac{1}{4}-\frac{3}{4}$ $=\left(1+\frac{1}{4}\right)-\frac{3}{4}$ $=\left(1-\frac{3}{4}\right)+\frac{1}{4}$ $=\frac{1}{4}+\frac{1}{4}$ $=\frac{1}{2}$	• Associative and Commutative Properties • Decomposing the Minuend
Decomposing the Subtrahend Jack: *I broke the $\frac{3}{4}$ into $\frac{1}{4}$ and $\frac{1}{2}$, so I could subtract $\frac{1}{4}$ from the $1\frac{1}{4}$ and get 1 whole. Then I subtracted $\frac{1}{2}$ from the 1 whole to get $\frac{1}{2}$.*	$1\frac{1}{4}-\frac{3}{4}$ $=1\frac{1}{4}-\left(\frac{1}{4}+\frac{1}{2}\right)$ $=\left(1\frac{1}{4}-\frac{1}{4}\right)-\frac{1}{2}$ $=1-\frac{1}{2}$ $=\frac{1}{2}$	• Associative and Distributive Properties • Decomposing the Subtrahend
Adding Up to Find the Difference Lars: *I thought about this problem as $\frac{3}{4}$ plus "something" equals $1\frac{1}{4}$. I first added $\frac{1}{4}$ to the $\frac{3}{4}$ to get 1 whole. Then I added $\frac{1}{4}$ to the 1 to get to $1\frac{1}{4}$. So I added two $\frac{1}{4}$s or $\frac{1}{2}$ to the $\frac{3}{4}$ to make $1\frac{1}{4}$.*	$\frac{3}{4}+\underline{\quad\quad}=1\frac{1}{4}$ $\frac{3}{4}+\circled{\frac{1}{4}}=1$ $1+\circled{\frac{1}{4}}=1\frac{1}{4}$ $\frac{1}{4}+\frac{1}{4}=\frac{1}{2}$ $\frac{3}{4}+\circled{\frac{1}{2}}=1\frac{1}{4}$	• Relationship between addition and subtraction • Interpreting subtraction as the difference between two numbers • Using benchmark numbers
Compensation Sal: *I added $\frac{1}{4}$ to $\frac{3}{4}$ to make a whole, because I knew it would be easier to subtract $1\frac{1}{4}$ minus 1. But since I took away $\frac{1}{4}$ too much, I had to add $\frac{1}{4}$ back to my answer.*	$1\frac{1}{4}-\frac{3}{4}$ $1\frac{1}{4}-\left(\frac{3}{4}+\circled{\frac{1}{4}}\right)$ $1\frac{1}{4}-1=\frac{1}{4}$ $1+\frac{1}{4}=\frac{1}{2}$	• Compensation (subtracting too much, then compensating) • Using benchmark numbers

Figure 2–3. *Using Multiple Strategies to Solve $1\frac{1}{4}-\frac{3}{4}$*

As you record student thinking, make sure your notation is mathematically correct. One symbol to watch carefully is the equals sign. The equals sign means that the quantities on each side of the sign are equivalent. If we are not careful with this convention, we can easily record mathematically incorrect statements. (See Figure 2–4.) The "Incorrect Recording" violates the equals sign because it suggests that $\frac{3}{4} + \frac{1}{4}$, $1 + \frac{1}{4}$, and $1\frac{1}{4}$ are all equivalent.

Student's Strategy and Reasoning	Incorrect Recording	Correct Recording
Adding Up to Find the Difference Angela: *I added $\frac{3}{4}$ plus $\frac{1}{4}$ and got 1. Then I added another $\frac{1}{4}$ to get $1\frac{1}{4}$. Since I added $\frac{1}{4}$ and another $\frac{1}{4}$, my answer is $\frac{2}{4}$ or $\frac{1}{2}$.*	$\frac{3}{4}+\frac{1}{4}=1+\frac{1}{4}=1\frac{1}{4}$ $\frac{1}{4}+\frac{1}{4}=\frac{1}{2}$	$\frac{3}{4}+\_\_\_\_\_=1\frac{1}{4}$ $\frac{3}{4}+\textcircled{\frac{1}{4}}=1$ $1+\textcircled{\frac{1}{4}}=1\frac{1}{4}$ $\frac{1}{4}+\frac{1}{4}=\frac{1}{2}$

Figure 2–4. *The Importance of Correct Notation (in This Case, the Equals Sign)*

Precise recording that helps all students make sense of the mathematics is crucial to successful number talks, and it takes practice and a willingness to grow and learn. There can be more than one correct way to record a student's thinking, but our recordings as teachers must be mathematically accurate and help make students' thinking accessible to the rest of the class.

While attending to mathematical precision when recording students' strategies is essential, we also want to record students' reasoning in an organized, accessible manner. Consider writing strategies from left to right on designated space to help students keep track of the strategies that are shared. Attention to this detail, along with numbering or labeling each strategy with a student's name, can help keep different strategies organized.

Number Talk Tip

Numbering or labeling a strategy with a student's name can help keep different strategies organized.

Essential 8: Be Prepared When the Sharing of Strategies Doesn't Go as Anticipated

When students begin to share strategies, the process is not always seamless. As a teacher, it helps to anticipate potential issues during this part of a number talk. Consider especially what to do if students don't offer a strategy, and/or if a student offers a strategy that is confusing and you aren't able to record it in the moment. Let's take a closer look at each of these scenarios.

Be Prepared to Offer a Part of a Strategy

When you begin number talks, you may have some students who have never been asked to think about numerical relationships or engage in mental mathematics. Even if you allow plenty of wait time after posing a problem, you may not have thumbs go up, or the only strategy students may be able to use is a standard algorithm. Your students may need help to know how to enter the conversation.

It is tempting to "rescue" students by telling them to use certain strategies, but it's important to give them the opportunity to productively struggle with finding a solution. When we tell students how to solve a problem, we send the message that we don't think they are capable of solving it for themselves, and students will look to you as the source of the answers and strategies. Instead, try sharing a small part of a strategy that you might have heard from a previous student. Ask students, "What do you think about this student's way to solve the problem?" If students think it is a viable strategy, ask, "Will it always work?" These questions help students know that they all have ideas and are capable of reasoning.

It Is Alright to Put a Student's Strategy on the Back Burner

One of the scariest things about leading a number talk is the fear that, as the teacher, you will not be able to follow students' thinking or pose the right questions to help them untangle their reasoning. If you find yourself struggling to follow a student's logic, first have the student restate the strategy. If this still doesn't help, facilitate a turn and talk, asking students to turn to a partner and talk about what they understand. Use this opportunity to listen in on their conversations. Is everyone as confused as you are, or is there a way to begin to build a conversation?

You can also simply tell the student who is sharing that you need time to think more about his or her ideas before continuing to think about this with the whole class. If you've already started recording his or her strategy, circle that strategy and then meet with the student privately to work through his thinking. This honors the student's reasoning while not slowing down the class conversation.

Essential 9: Limit Your Number Talks to Five to Fifteen Minutes

Stopping a number talk is difficult, but it should not become your whole math lesson. Be mindful of the pace of the number talk so as not to lose momentum and student interest. As teachers, we want our students to be thoroughly engaged and focused during a number talk, so we have to be aware of their attention and adjust accordingly. Many teachers set a timer to help stay within this time frame. It is tempting to hear from every student during a number talk, but after three or four students have shared their strategies for solving a problem and there is clear class consensus as to which answer is correct, move to a new problem or conclude the number talk.

Essential 10: Be Patient with Yourself and Your Students

The last essential, though perhaps the most important, is to be patient. Number talks require teaching for understanding, and making that shift can often be overwhelming. Many of us are comfortable with telling students how to solve a problem, but it may be foreign and intimidating not to provide procedures. When you first try number talks, you may be concentrating on how to ask open-ended questions to elicit students' thinking versus choosing words to demonstrate how to use a procedure. It can feel awkward not knowing in advance where students' conversations will go. You may worry about being able to follow your students' thinking if it is different from yours.

Learn More...

The majority of our mathematics time as teachers should be spent helping students problem solve on their own, rather than telling them how to solve problems. This is critical in order for students to develop logico-mathematical knowledge. For more on this, see Chapter 1, pages 29–32.

As you incorporate number talks into your regular math time, don't give up when things don't go perfectly well. Make adjustments and keep moving forward. You may face resistance initially, however as your students grow in their mathematical abilities, you'll find that there are significant payoffs in all areas of their mathematical learning. In turn, give yourself the license to be a learner along with your students. You will be surprised how you may grow in your own understanding of mathematics! Remember that you cannot change everything at once, so starting small (using the ten essentials just outlined) will be beneficial to you and your students.

Five Ways to Collect Evidence of Students' Understanding

Now that we've looked at ten essentials to getting started with number talks, it's important to think about ways to find out more about what each individual student understands. It is definitely possible for a student to give an illusion of understanding during number talks. As teachers, we not only want to keep the goals of accuracy, efficiency, and flexibility in the forefront, but we also want to ensure that each student is mentally participating and accessing other students' strategies. The very nature of a number talk lends itself to formative assessment. There are numerous ways to collect evidence about what individual students understand; the following pages take a closer look at five of these ways.

Learn More...

For more on the goals of accuracy, efficiency, and flexibility in number talks, see Chapter 1, page 15.

Five Ways to Collect Evidence of Students' Understanding

- Ask students to indicate which strategies are most efficient for them.
- Save recordings of the problems posed and corresponding student strategies.
- Hold small-group number talks throughout the week.
- Create and post classroom strategy charts.
- Give an occasional exit problem at the end of the number talk.

Ask Students to Indicate Which Strategies Are Most Efficient for Them

Finger signals can be used as a way for students to indicate which strategies are most efficient for them. For example, while strategies for a specific problem are still posted, label the strategies and have students indicate whether Strategy 1 or Strategy 2 and so on is the most efficient for them by signaling to you with their fingers. If a student thinks Strategy 3 was more efficient to use, then he would place

Number Talk Tip

So far we've learned that finger signals can be used for students to indicate how many strategies they have for solving a problem. Finger signals can also be used as a way for students to indicate which strategies are most efficient for them.

three fingers to his chest. The purpose of this is not to indicate that one specific strategy is better than another, but to provide an opportunity for students to evaluate their own reasoning. This procedure also allows you as the teacher to make a quick, informal assessment of where students are individually and collectively while also focusing the discussion back on your overarching mathematical goals.

$\frac{1}{2} + \frac{7}{8}$: Thinking About Efficient Strategies

Classroom Clip 2.3

To view this video clip, scan the QR code or access via mathsolutions .com/NTFDP2.3

Consider the following questions as you watch this number talk from a fourth-grade classroom:

1. Notice how the teacher spaces the different solutions on the board and labels the different strategies as Solution 1, 2, and 3. How does her recording help set up her goals of bringing out different solutions and being able to discuss efficiency?
2. What do you notice about the question the teacher asks as she sets up the turn and talk?
3. What is the benefit of using turn and talk at this point in the number talk?
4. How do you decide when to ask students to consider the idea of efficiency?

Save Recordings of the Problems Posed and Corresponding Student Strategies

When labeled with students' names and saved, recordings give a written record of students' thinking over time (especially allowing the teacher to keep track of which students are consistently voicing their strategies and which students are rarely participating), as well as provide visuals to share with parents.

Depending on the technological resources available (and ever-becoming available), there are several ways to save recordings. Some teachers capture student strategies using an interactive whiteboard and computer. Using this type of documentation, you can post number talks to a classroom Web page and provide access to parents. Other teachers prefer to use a whiteboard to record number talks and then take a picture with a smartphone and transfer the strategies to an electronic file. Some teachers record students' strategies in a composition notebook to keep an ongoing record of the progression of student reasoning over time.

Learn More...

Purposeful recording is considered one of the four foundational principles of number talks. See Chapter 1, pages 26–27, for more on recording.

Hold Small-Group Number Talks Throughout the Week

Incorporating small-group number talks throughout the week allows you to focus more carefully on individual strengths as well as factors interfering with understanding.

There are several ways that students can be grouped; see suggestions in the list here.

Ways to Group Students for Small-Group Number Talks

Group students according to:

- those who share a common mathematical need,
- those who need to be challenged beyond regular grade-level concepts,
- those who need additional support, or
- those who may be more reluctant to share in front of the whole group.

Create and Post Student-Generated Strategy Charts

As students collectively determine that certain strategies will always work for a specific operation or numbers, consider recording those generalized strategies on a *classroom strategy chart.* (See Figure 2–5.) This chart serves as an ongoing record of the ideas students have developed during number talks.

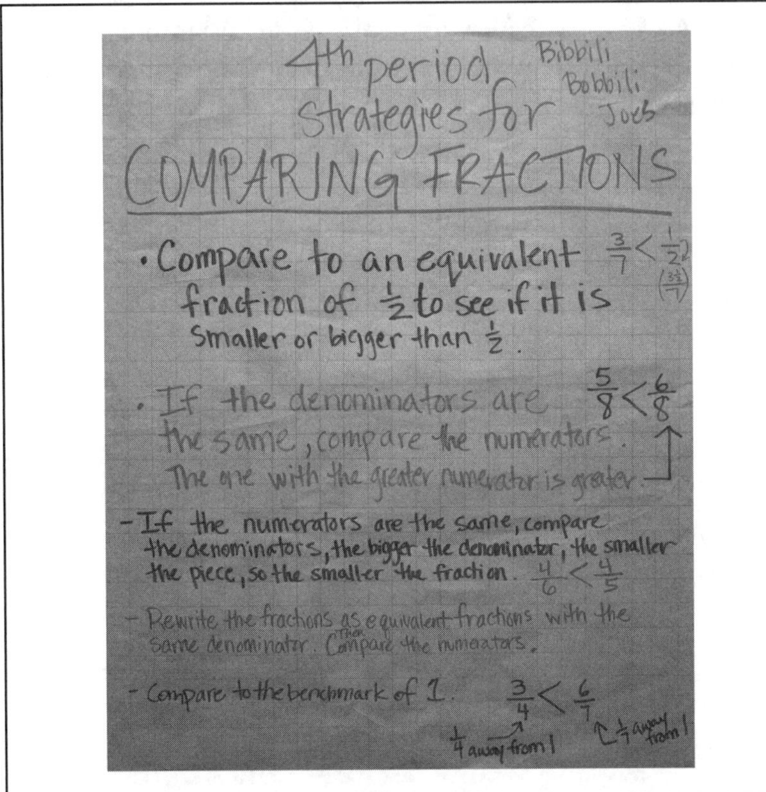

Figure 2–5. *A Classroom Strategy Chart Developed by Mrs. Laney's Students*

You should only post strategies that students have developed and are using, not ones that you as the teacher decide students should know. Classroom strategy charts provide a reference for students as they work, as well as support them in their continued investigation of new ideas. The charts should be living documents that can be added to throughout the year as new strategies are shared.

Give an Occasional Exit Problem at the End of the Number Talk

Another way to gather more individual information is to periodically have students complete an exit slip before transitioning to the rest of the lesson. Give students a problem to solve using a problem similar to one in the day's number talk. Give students an index card; ask them to solve the problem one way on one side of the card, and another way on the other side of the card. This type of exit card allows you to get a quick look at individual understandings and misconceptions. The exit slips are not graded. They are formative assessments that help us as teachers decide what problems to use in the next day's number talk or how to form small number talk groups based on common needs.

Looking Ahead

This chapter concludes "Section I, Understanding Number Talks." As authors, we hope that at this point you have read both Chapters 1 and 2 and are feeling comfortable with an initial understanding of number talks (if you've been using number talks, we hope that these chapters have served to refresh, enrich, and build on your use of them). The rest of the chapters delve into number talks with a focus on fractions, decimals, and percentages—looking at ways to build fractional reasoning and computation strategies for all operations. You'll encounter goals, example number talks, and student strategies to help you anticipate what might happen in your classroom.

Connecting the Chapter to Your Practice

1. If you have never tried number talks, how do you envision organizing your classroom space to foster student engagement?
2. If you have tried number talks, what does your classroom space look like during number talks? What do you like about your arrangement and what would you like to change?
3. What are some ways you could practice having a "blank face" when students give answers to a problem?
4. What are the benefits of allowing students to self-correct if they give a wrong answer?
5. Examine the "Observations to Make as Students Communicate During a Number Talk" on page 49 of this chapter. What evidence would you look for to know if students are engaged with a number talk, struggling with a number talk, or finding a number talk too easy?
6. Examine the figures on pages 50 and 51 of this chapter. Read each student's strategies and consider ways you might record that student's thinking. What mathematical ideas might you be able to highlight based on different recordings?
7. How might you balance having both small group and whole group number talks?
8. What kind of information would you look for on an exit slip?

Section II

Number Talks to Help Students Build Fractional Reasoning

CHAPTER 3

What Are the Big Ideas with Rational Numbers?

In the introductory chapter, we shared evidence of the ongoing struggle that most learners face as they reason and operate with rational numbers, as well as the cause of these difficulties. To build our students' understanding of and approach to working with fractions, we now must identify the essential ideas they need to understand so that they can reason and compute with accuracy, efficiency, and flexibility. In this chapter, we explore six big ideas essential in developing fractional reasoning. We look at these ideas through task examples and student work. It is our hope that by the end of this chapter, you will be ready to launch into your first number talk with fractions.

OVERVIEW

Big Idea 1: Fractions Are Distinct Numbers

Learn More...

Before reading this chapter, we recommend you read the introductory chapter (to learn of the evidence of students' struggles with rational numbers) and Chapter 1 (to learn more about what we mean when we ask students to compute with accuracy, efficiency, and flexibility).

One of the first ideas that students need to grapple with when they are beginning to understand fractions is that—like whole numbers—fractions represent distinct amounts. That means that fractions can be used to quantify situations. For example, it's possible to read $\frac{1}{2}$ the books on the shelf, run $2\frac{3}{4}$ miles, or eat $\frac{1}{3}$ of a pan of brownies. Fractions are numbers that represent specific quantities.

Since fractions are distinct numbers, they also have discrete places on the number line. When students are asked to place $\frac{1}{2}$ on a number line that stretches from 0 to 1, they are often successful, but when the number line stretches beyond 0 and 1, misconceptions are often revealed. Consider the following number line. Before reading further, think about where students might decide to place the number $\frac{1}{2}$.

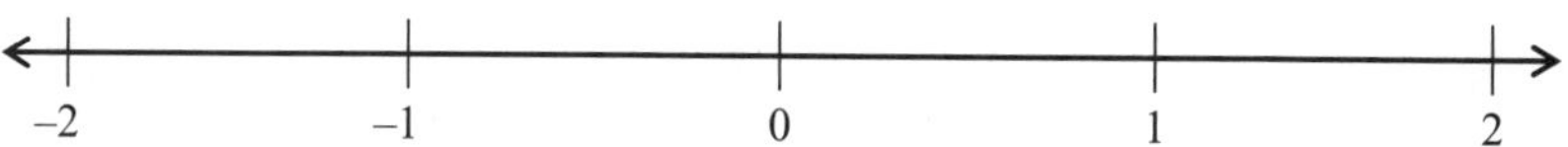

When we ask students, "Where does the number $\frac{1}{2}$ go on this number line?" we typically receive answers like these:

> *"I think $\frac{1}{2}$ goes on the 0 because that's half [of the line]."*
>
> *"I think it goes between the 1 and the 2 because those are the numbers in $\frac{1}{2}$."*
>
> *"It goes somewhere behind 0 because fractions are less than 0."*
>
> *"It goes between 0 and 1 because it's half of 1."*

When you collect answers from your own class, you might find that some students are convinced $\frac{1}{2}$ can be placed in more than one location on the number line. Keep in mind that as teachers we can tell students that fractions are numbers, and we can tell them where $\frac{1}{2}$ goes on the number line, but if we want them to truly develop this understanding, we have to create situations that require them to grapple with these ideas and justify their thinking.

One misconception that interferes with students' understanding of fractions as distinct numbers occurs when they view fractions through the lens of whole numbers and think about the numerator and denominators as whole numbers stacked on top of each other (Behr, Wachsmuth, and Post 1984; Petit, Laird, Marsden, and Ebby

2010; Saxe, Gearhart, and Seltzer 1999). For example, students may say, "One-half should be placed between the 1 and 2 on the number line because $\frac{1}{2}$ has a 1 and a 2 in it." These students are not thinking about the quantity of $\frac{1}{2}$, the part-to-whole relationship, or the relationship between the numerator and denominator. Instead, they are looking at the 1 and 2 in the numerator and denominator as two separate whole numbers. See Figure 3–1 for other common examples of inappropriate whole number reasoning (i.e., times when students inappropriately use what they know about whole numbers to try to make sense of fractions). How are students using whole number reasoning to solve these fraction problems?

Learn More...

For specific number talks using the number line to help students develop the idea of a fraction as a distinct number, see Chapter 4.

Example A

Circle $\frac{1}{5}$ of the bottles.

Example B

Add $\frac{1}{2} + \frac{5}{6}$.

$\frac{1}{2} + \frac{5}{6} = \frac{6}{8}$

Example C

Put $\frac{1}{2}$, $\frac{1}{4}$, and $\frac{1}{3}$ on the correct places on the number line.

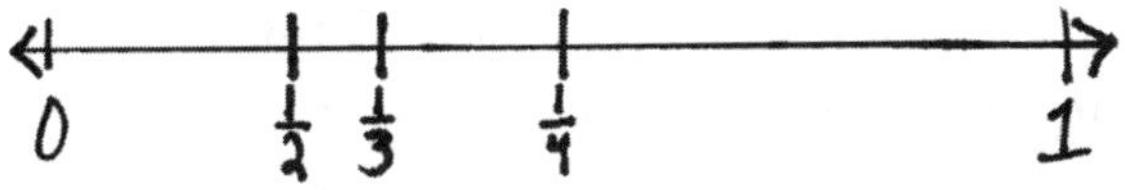

Figure 3–1. *How Are Students Using Inappropriate Whole Number Reasoning to Solve These Fraction Problems?*

In student work Example A, the student circles one bottle because she is focusing only on the 1 in the numerator. Other students might circle five bottles and ignore the 1 in the numerator. In either case, the students are thinking only about one part of the fraction as a whole number. In student work Example B, in adding these two fractions, the student treats the numerators and denominators as whole numbers and adds without thinking about the fractional relationships. In student work Example C, the student is ignoring the numerators and focusing only on the denominators to order these fractions. The student sequences the fractions according to the whole number sequence *2, 3, 4*.

Big Idea 2: A Fraction Is Part of a Whole

To develop fractional reasoning, students need to think about the whole and the parts of the whole *at the same time*. The complexity involved in holding on to more than one idea at a time is one of the reasons why understanding fractions can be challenging.

To begin to consider what a fraction of a whole is, students must first define the whole itself. In the model here, the box itself could be defined as the whole.

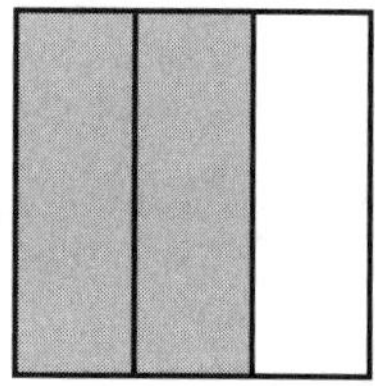

To think about two-thirds of the box being shaded, students must simultaneously identify the whole, determine that the whole is divided into three equal parts, and consider that two of those parts are shaded.

When dealing with a set of objects, the whole is defined as being all of the objects. Let's say students need to figure out if they have read half of the books on the classroom shelf. They must first determine how many books are on the shelf before they can decide how many books would be in a fraction of that amount.

Here's a similar dilemma. Would extremely thirsty students want to drink a whole bottle of water or a half bottle of water? If the goal is to get the most water, then the answer depends on the size of the whole. Half of a super-sized bottle is usually a lot more water than a whole mini-sized bottle. Defining the whole is essential to understanding what a fraction of that whole would be.

Big Idea 3: The Denominator Is a Divisor and Tells How Many Equal Parts the Whole Is Divided Into

Understanding what the denominator means is an essential part of understanding fractions. Telling students this information does not ensure that they understand these ideas. As teachers, we have to provide situations or tasks that encourage students to construct these critical understandings of what the denominator means. Tasks that focus on partitioning are especially helpful.

Partitioning fractions is a key element in thinking about the parts and the whole. As Behr and Post (1992) explain, "[Early] experiences with physically partitioning objects or sets of objects may be as important to a child's development of fraction concepts as counting is to their development of whole number concepts" (14).

The act of partitioning helps learners confront the idea that the parts of a fraction have to be equivalent. For example, "equal parts" of an area must be equivalent in size. "Equal parts" of a set must be equivalent in number. "Equal parts" of a linear model have to be equivalent in distance (Petit, Laird, Mardsen, and Ebby 2010). In this way, practice with partitioning is vital for students to develop an understanding of what the denominator means. To support students in making these relationships, teachers can also highlight the language about how the number of parts of the fraction is related to the name of the parts (e.g., four parts in a whole mean that each fractional part is called one *fourth*).

Learn More...

Giving students opportunities to partition area, set, and linear models is important for them to develop an understanding of what the denominator means; this is discussed in more depth in Chapter 4.

Students might partition an area model into halves in different ways. (See Figure 3–2.) Comparing different solutions can also provide a rich discussion about what dividing a whole into equal-sized parts means. In Figure 3–2, each area model is divided into two parts, and each of the parts is congruent to the other.

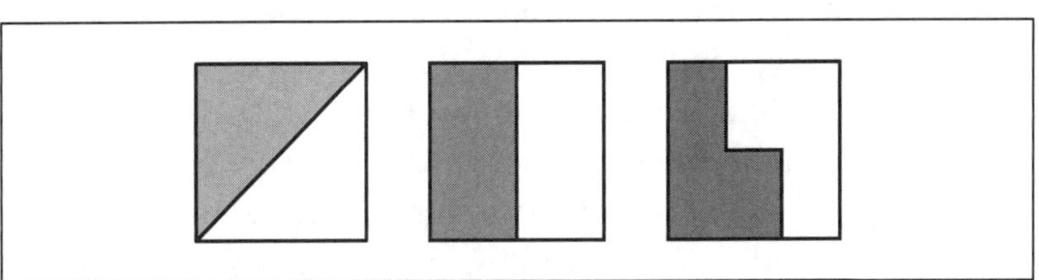

Figure 3–2. *Three Ways Students Might Partition an Area Model into Halves*

Big Idea 4: The Numerator Counts How Many Equal Parts There Are in the Fraction

The denominator tells how many equal parts the *whole* is divided into, and the numerator tells *how many* of those parts students are counting. For example, if students have $\frac{4}{5}$ of a pan of brownies, then they have four $\frac{1}{5}$s. They can also count that as $\frac{1}{5}$, $\frac{2}{5}$, $\frac{3}{5}$, and $\frac{4}{5}$ of a pan of brownies.

With an area model, students can count how many eighths are in $\frac{5}{8}$:

or with a linear model, they can count how many fourths are in $\frac{3}{4}$:

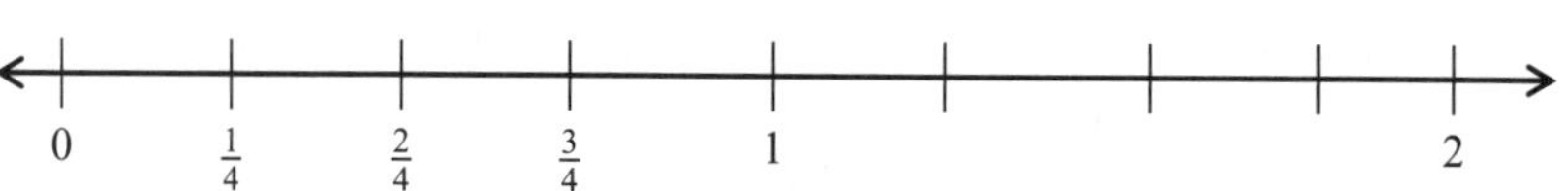

Learn More...

Chapter 4 provides number talks designed to help students develop an understanding of the meaning of the numerator and denominator.

Developing a deep understanding of what the numerator and denominator mean and how they relate is critical to understanding fractions.

Big Idea 5: There Is an Infinite Number of Fractions Between Any Two Given Fractions

When Olympic athletes compete, it is important for the officials to be able to measure the difference in the athletes' performances in increasingly small increments. Comparing their photo-finish times in minutes or even seconds would not distinguish many of the best athletes.

Being able to divide seconds into tenths, or hundredths, or thousandths relies on the density property that between any two given fractions there is an infinite number of fractions. For instance, if we ask students to think about fractions between $\frac{1}{4}$ and $\frac{1}{2}$, they may partition fourths into eighths and know that $\frac{3}{8}$ is between $\frac{2}{8}$ and $\frac{4}{8}$, or between $\frac{1}{4}$ and $\frac{1}{2}$. Continuing to partition means creating smaller and smaller increments between fractions. The notion that there are quantities in between quantities is a critical idea for students to consider in understanding fractions.

Big Idea 6: Equivalence Means That a Fraction Can Be Repartitioned and Renamed in an Infinite Number of Ways

Understanding that there can be an unlimited number of ways to repartition and describe the same number is a huge idea in fractions. The quantity $\frac{1}{2}$ can be described as $\frac{2}{4}, \frac{3}{8}, \frac{9}{18}, \frac{100}{200}$, and an infinite number of other ways. Understanding equivalence is essential to comparing, ordering, and operating with fractions.

Students often begin to develop an understanding of how fractions with two different names can be equivalent to each other by repartitioning models to "prove" their equivalence. (See Figure 3–3.)

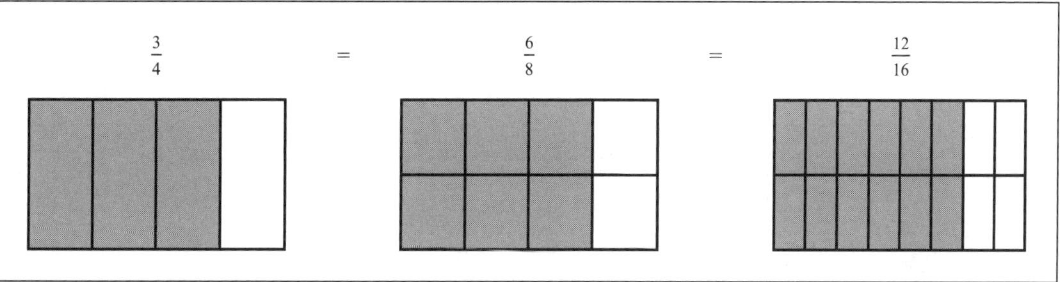

Figure 3–3. *Ways Students Might Repartition Area Models to "Prove" the Equivalence of* $\frac{3}{4}, \frac{6}{8},$ *and* $\frac{12}{16}$

This partitioning can also be done with a linear model. Figure 3–4 shows an example of a number line on which halves are repartitioned into fourths and eighths. The equivalent fractions are located at the same point on the number line even though they have different names.

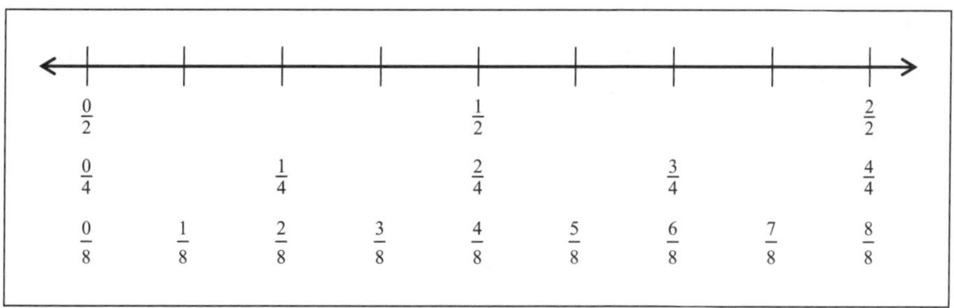

Figure 3–4. *How Students Might Repartition Halves into Fourths and Eighths Using a Linear Model*

Figure 3–5 gives an example of how partitioning can be done with a set model. In this example, a student partitioned the same set of stars into sixths as well as thirds which was how she justified that $\frac{1}{3}$ of the stars is equivalent to $\frac{2}{6}$ of the stars. Identifying the denominator is central to being able to consider that the different ways of representing a fraction are equivalent.

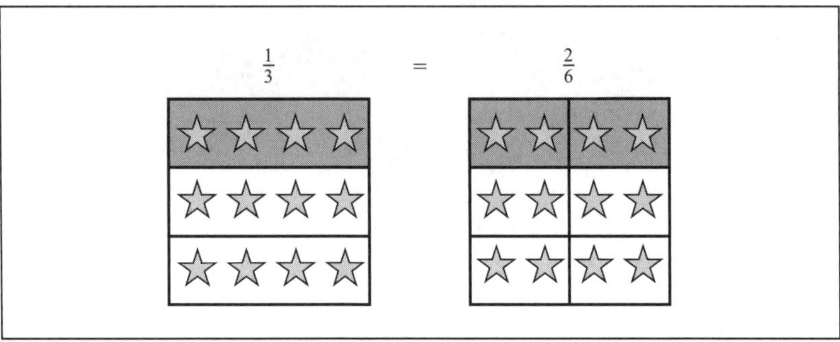

Figure 3–5. *How Students Might Partition Thirds into Sixths Using a Set Model*

A common error in thinking occurs when students say that to find equivalent fractions they multiply the numerator and the denominator by the same number. For instance, they might say that they take $\frac{1}{4}$ and multiply each numeral separately by 2 to get $\frac{2}{8}$. However, instead of multiplying the numerator and the denominator by whole numbers, they are really multiplying the fraction by 1 in the form of $\frac{2}{2}$, $\frac{3}{3}$, and so on. It is the identity property for multiplication—the concept that multiplying any number by 1 keeps its identity—that makes this algorithm work. However, to understand these important ideas, students have to reason through them for themselves. As we will show in the chapters that follow, number talks are an important venue for highlighting students' thinking and bringing their reasoning to the forefront of the classroom.

Learn More...

For specific number talks about equivalent fractions, see Chapter 4.

Looking Ahead

In this chapter, we have discussed six ideas related to developing fractional reasoning. What are some ways you might bring attention to some of these big ideas in your conversations with students?

In Chapter 4, we look at specific number talks teachers can use to build their students' conceptual understanding of fractions and help them develop fractional reasoning.

Connecting the Chapter to Your Practice

1. What surprises you about where students often misplace fractions when the number line is extended beyond 0–1?
2. What are some things we as teachers can do in the classroom to help students think about fractions as numbers?
3. How can we help highlight the importance of considering the whole when dealing with fractions?
4. How can our consideration of the complexity of understanding the density of fractions and the idea of equivalence help us as we listen to students to find their points of understanding and misunderstanding?
5. If a student is talking about making equivalent fractions and describes changing $\frac{1}{2}$ to $\frac{3}{6}$ by multiplying the numerator by 3 and the denominator by 3, how would you respond? How can our language help students attend to precision?

CHAPTER 4

Number Talks to Help Students Build Fractional Reasoning

What does a number talk look like when we initially begin to help students understand fractions? In this chapter, we discuss how to support student reasoning by framing number talks in a story context followed by suggestions of number talks that you can present to students to help them confront the big ideas discussed in Chapter 3. Two types of number talk structures to build students' fractional reasoning are offered: (1) number talks using area, set, and linear models, and (2) problems for comparing and ordering fractions.

OVERVIEW

(Continued)

Number Talks That Use Story Problems to Build Fractional Reasoning

We can support students who are just beginning to work with rational numbers by situating number talks within a story problem. A story problem helps provide learners with an entry point for

- making sense of the problem,
- giving meaning to the numbers, and
- discerning whether an answer is reasonable.

Consider the difference between posing the problem, "What is $\frac{3}{4}$ of 12?," as a stand-alone problem or presenting it framed as a story problem. (See Figure 4–1.)

Presenting a Problem in Isolation	Presenting a Problem in a Story Context
What is $\frac{3}{4}$ of 12?	*I have a dozen eggs and my family will eat $\frac{3}{4}$ of them for breakfast. How many eggs will we use?* *I had 12 brownies in a pan. If my friends ate $\frac{3}{4}$ of the brownies, how many brownies are left?* *If the bike race is 12 miles long, how long is $\frac{3}{4}$ of the race course?*

Figure 4–1. *Presenting a Problem in Isolation Versus in a Story Context*

In contrast to the problem presented in isolation, each example presented within a story context gives meaning to the $\frac{3}{4}$ and the 12 because students can visualize the action occurring in the problems. Note that framing a computation problem in a story context does not mean showing students a written version of the story problem. Instead, write the computation problem as you present the story context orally.

While it is not necessary to use a story context to frame every problem in a number talk, it can be especially helpful when we are first beginning to focus on fractions in our classroom or as we notice student confusion. When teachers embed fractions in real-world situations that are relevant to students, students have better access to making sense of the big ideas discussed in Chapter 3.

What is $\frac{3}{4}$ of 12? Using a Story Context
Classroom Clip 4.1

To view this video clip, scan the QR code or access via mathsolutions .com/NTFDP4.1

Consider the following questions as you watch this number talk from a third-grade classroom:

1. What role does context play in this number talk?
2. How does the story context of the eggs support students' reasoning about the numbers?
3. What is the source of Briana's misconception about this problem?
4. How does the teacher address Briana's misconception?
5. What Standards for Mathematical Practice do you see students exhibiting during this number talk?

Number Talks That Use Area Models to Build Fractional Reasoning

Students are often familiar with area models because most textbooks use them as the predominant representation for fractions. An area model focuses on part-to-whole relationships using a region or an area. The designated region defines the whole, which is divided into equal-sized parts. The parts must be equal in size, but they do not have to be congruent. For example, each patio is the same size and has $\frac{1}{4}$ shaded, but the fourths in the two patios are not the same shape. (See Figure 4–2.)

Learn More...

Developing understanding of the meaning of the numerator and denominator are two critical ideas first introduced in Chapter 3.

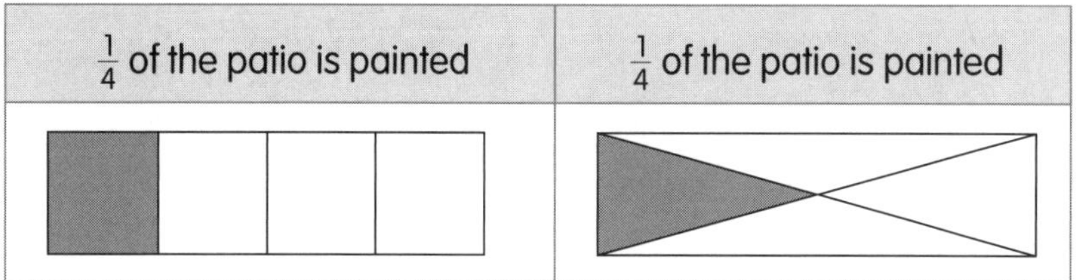

Figure 4–2. *In Area Models, Parts Must Be Equal in Size, But They Do Not Have to Be Congruent*

Area models are especially helpful as students reason about congruence and unit fractions. When students are introduced to fractions, they often experience problems that are based on two common misconceptions:

1. They focus only on the number of parts.
2. They ignore that the parts must be equal in size but not necessarily congruent, or the same shape.

For example, Ms. Egan presented the problems in Figure 4–3 (on page 76) to her students in a number talk and asked, "Which represents $\frac{1}{2}$ and how do you know?" Consider how students' misconceptions are revealed when presented with the three area models.

Number Talk Tip

Area models are one of three types of geometric models explored in this chapter (see later sections for insights on set and linear models). Each model has distinct characteristics. By using them interchangeably in number talks, teachers can give students more opportunities to deepen their understanding and think flexibly about fractional relationships.

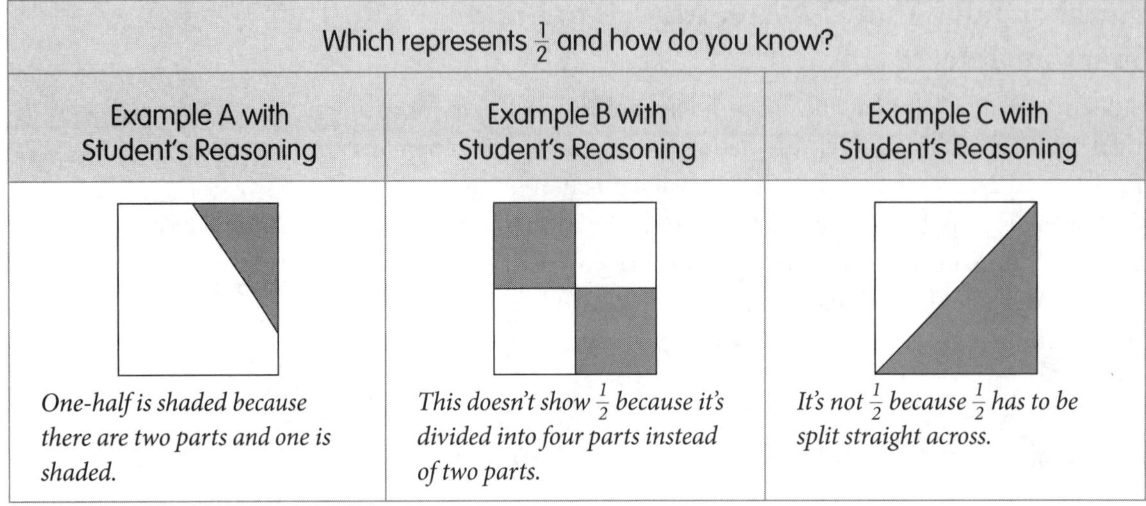

Which represents $\frac{1}{2}$ and how do you know?		
Example A with Student's Reasoning	Example B with Student's Reasoning	Example C with Student's Reasoning
One-half is shaded because there are two parts and one is shaded.	*This doesn't show $\frac{1}{2}$ because it's divided into four parts instead of two parts.*	*It's not $\frac{1}{2}$ because $\frac{1}{2}$ has to be split straight across.*

Figure 4–3. *Common Misconceptions When Interpreting Fractions Using an Area Model*

Category 1
Reasoning About Equal Parts of a Fraction

The number talks in this category are structured to help students confront the idea that a fraction is divided into equal, but not necessarily congruent, parts. They are designed to provide opportunities for discussions around students' common misconceptions (refer to Figure 4–3) that are likely to arise.

Instructions

These number talks use the unit fractions: $\frac{1}{2}, \frac{1}{4}, \frac{1}{8}, \frac{1}{3}, \frac{1}{6}$. There are four number talk sets for each unit fraction. Each set includes three area models that are already partitioned, some correctly and some incorrectly. The number talks progress in difficulty going from the first set to the next. Show students all three models in the set at the same time and ask, "*Which of these models represent _____ of the whole? How do you know?*" Feel free to start with the unit fraction that best meets your students' needs.

Which of these models represent $\frac{1}{2}$ of the whole? How do you know?

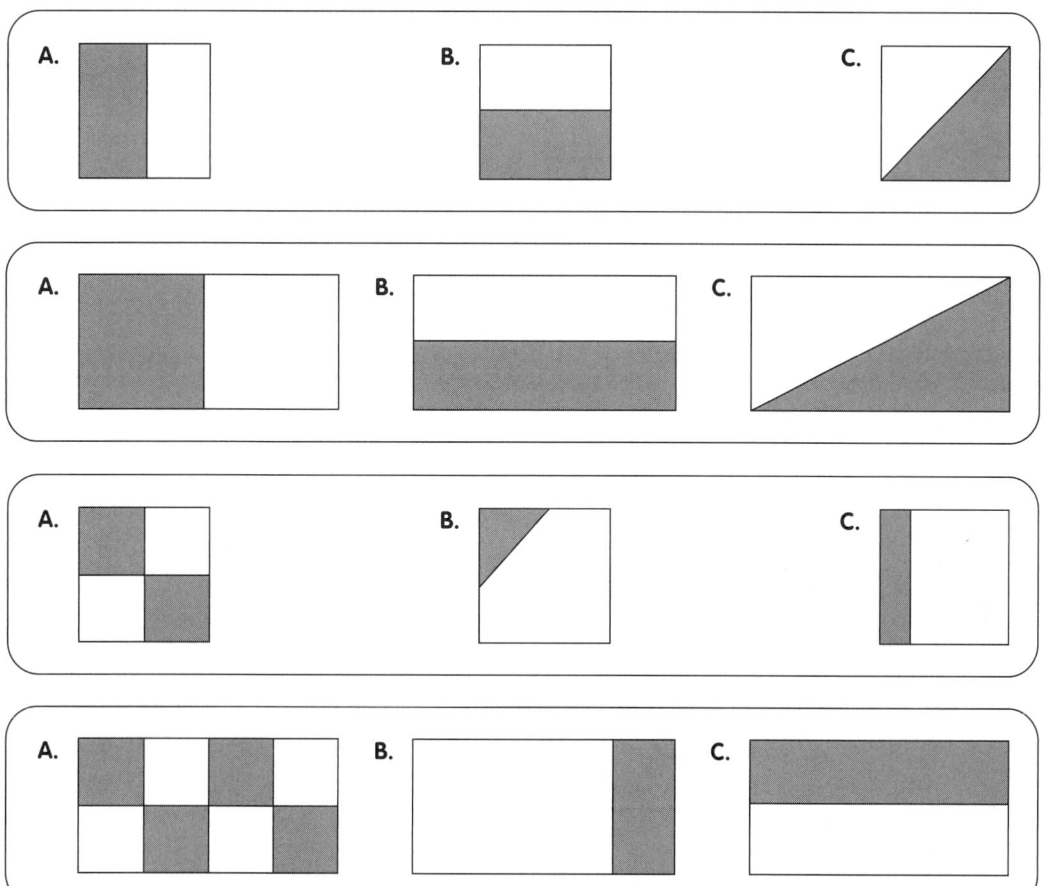

Reproducible 1

For reproducibles of these area models, visit www.mathsolutions.com/numbertalksfdp_reproducibles.

Which of these models represent $\frac{1}{4}$ of the whole? How do you know?

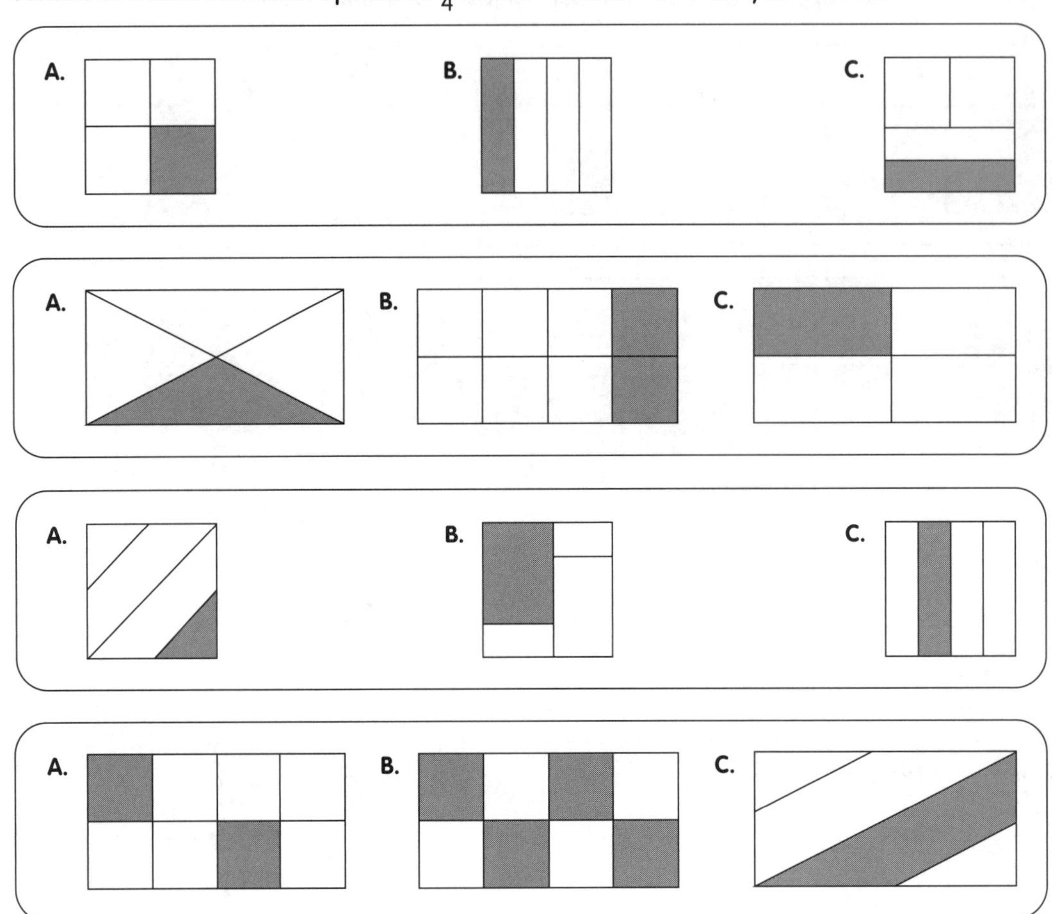

Which of these models represent $\frac{1}{8}$ of the whole? How do you know?

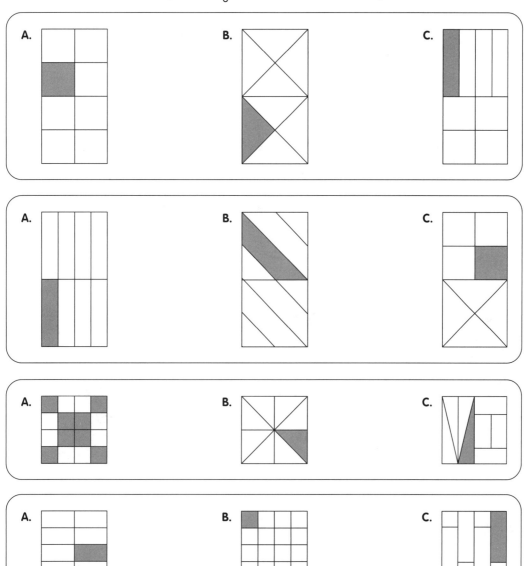

A.

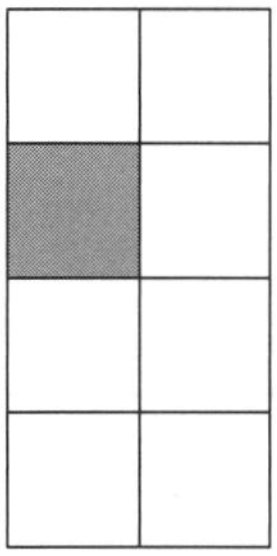

B.

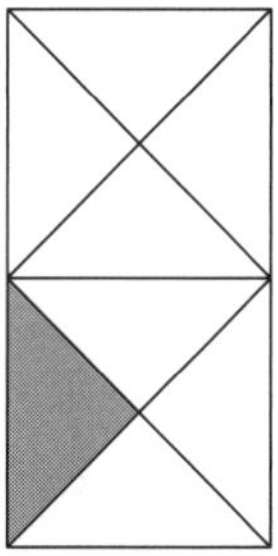

C.

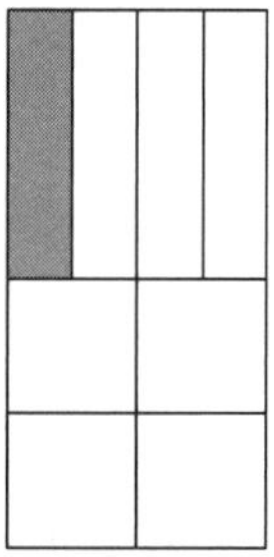

A.

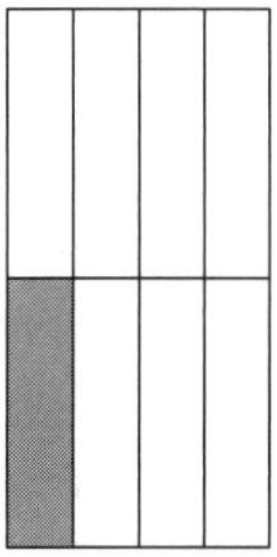

B.

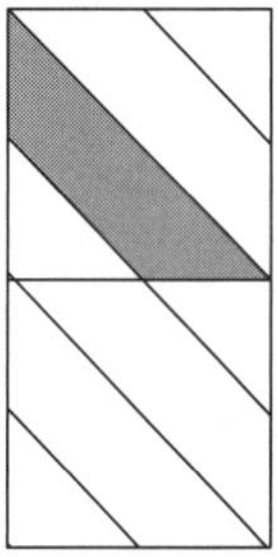

C.

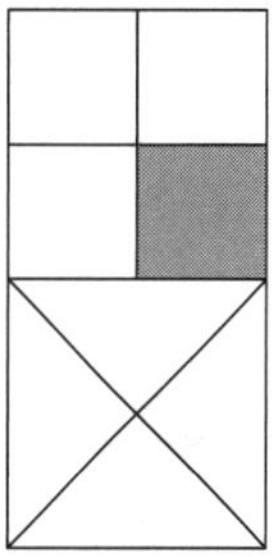

A.

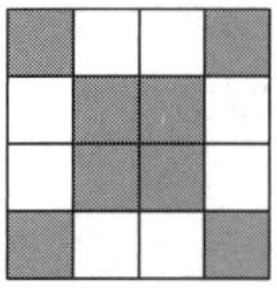

B.

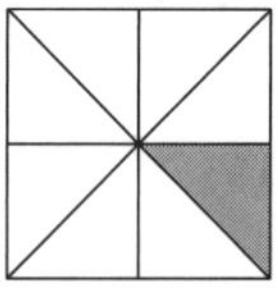

C.

A.

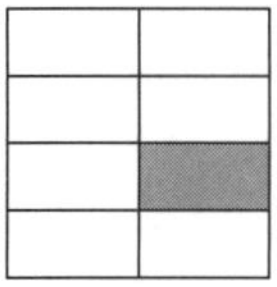

B.

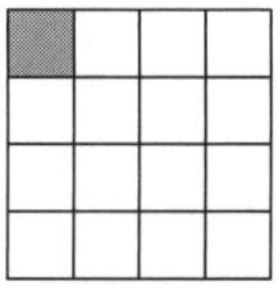

C.

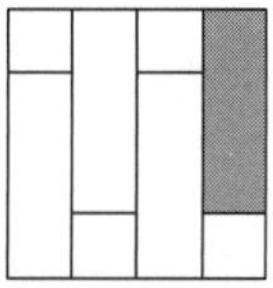

Which of these models represent $\frac{1}{3}$ of the whole? How do you know?

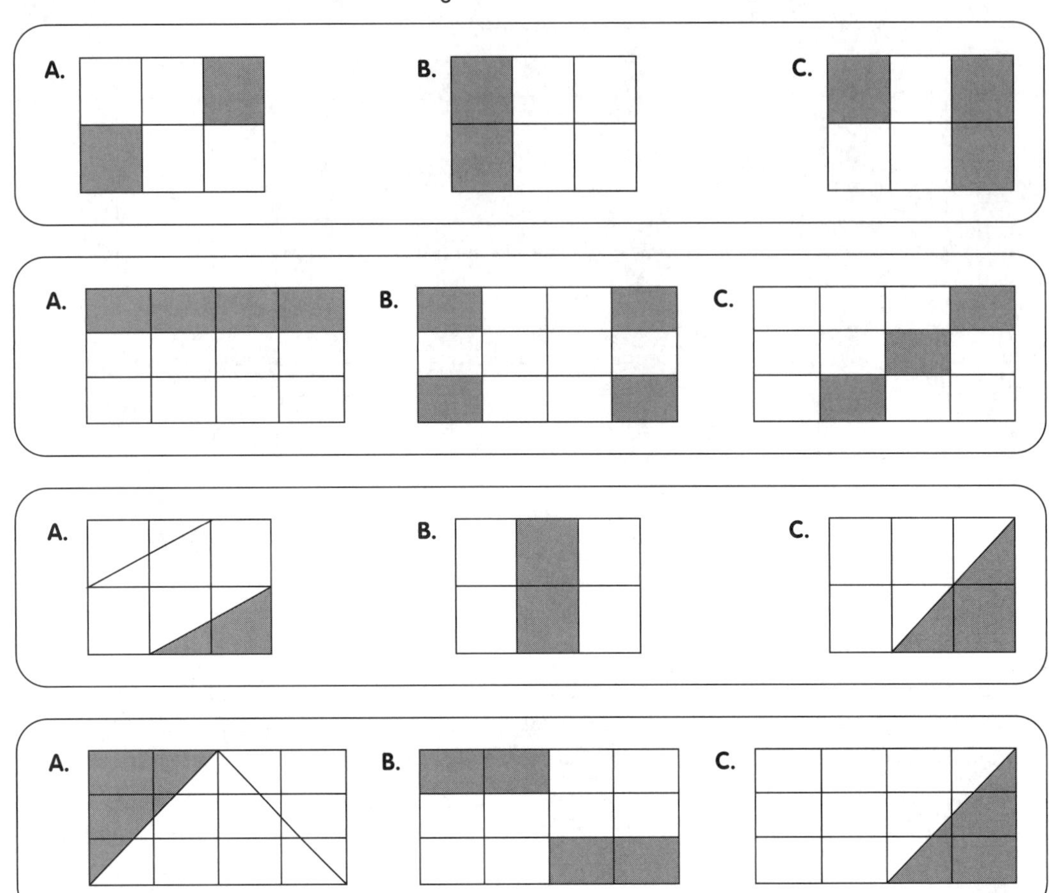

Which of these models represent $\frac{1}{6}$ of the whole? How do you know?

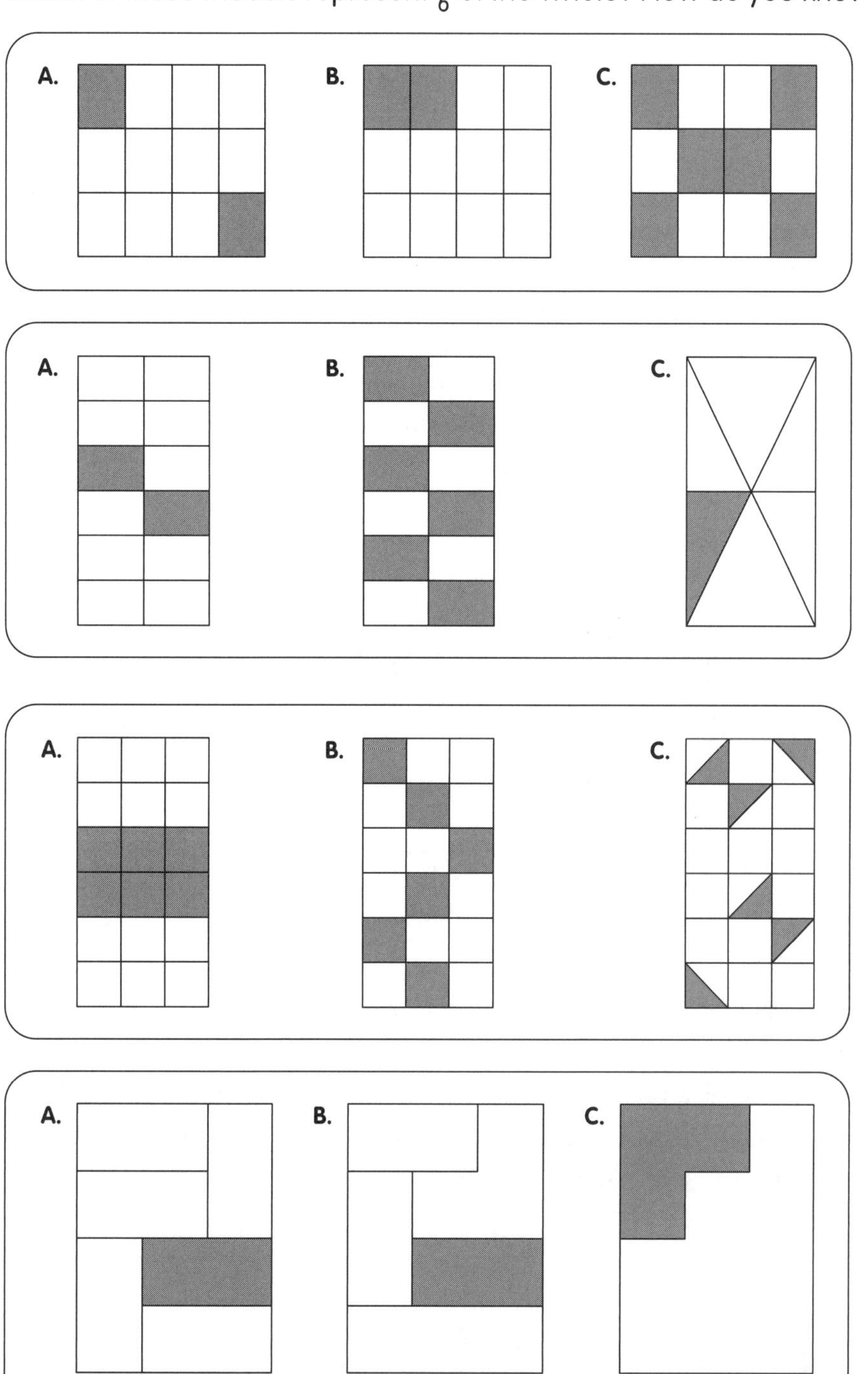

Category 2
Reasoning About Equivalence Among Fractions

Learn More...

Equivalence means that a fraction can be repartitioned and renamed in an infinite number of ways. See Chapter 3 pages 69–70 for more discussion about this essential understanding.

We can also use area models in number talks to help students develop an understanding of equivalence. The fact that multiple fractions can equal the same amount is an important idea and it impacts all facets of students' use of and operations with rational numbers. In order for learners to understand that $\frac{1}{4}$ can be represented as $\frac{2}{8}$, $\frac{4}{16}$, and so forth, they must be able to repartition the whole using a multiplicative relationship.

Consider the area model in Figure 4–4, which represents a whole using strips partitioned into halves, fourths, eighths, and sixteenths. To make fourths from halves, the halves are repartitioned by halving each half, which results in twice as many parts. This partitioning is a multiplicative relationship.

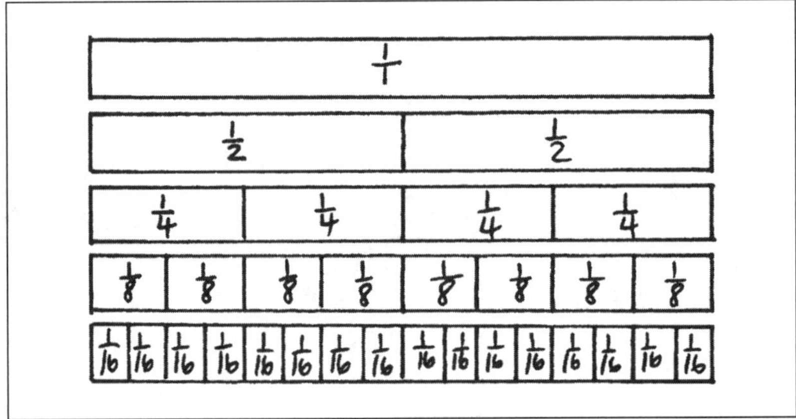

Figure 4–4. *Using Fraction Strips to Highlight Multiplicative Relationships*

We can use this fraction kit area model with students as a starting place for conversations around these big ideas. Consider the following "Inside the Classroom" excerpt.

Inside the Classroom

Using Fraction Strips to Discuss Equivalence

Ms. Rhodes's third graders recently made fraction kits and she has asked them to turn and talk with a partner about what they noticed.

Ms. Rhodes: I heard some interesting conversations during your turn and talk. Would someone be willing to share something you noticed about the fraction kit?

Will: Michael and I noticed that when we go from halves to fourths there are twice as many parts.

Abby: Elda and I noticed that too. When we go from fourths to eighths, it doubles and the same thing happens when we go from eighths to sixteenths.

Ms. Rhodes: Why do you think that's happening?

Cameron: I think it's because the parts get smaller every time, so you get more of them.

Brooke: I agree, but you get twice as many because you're splitting each piece into two parts. One-half split gives you $\frac{2}{4}$. One-fourth split gives you $\frac{2}{8}$. This keeps happening and the denominator doubles.

Ms. Rhodes: Did anybody notice something else?

Sam: We saw that $\frac{2}{4}$, $\frac{4}{8}$, and $\frac{8}{16}$ all make $\frac{1}{2}$.

Alisha: We noticed that $\frac{2}{8}$ and $\frac{4}{16}$ make $\frac{1}{4}$.

Ms. Rhodes: Why do you think that's happening?

Omar: They all have the same amount of space.

Ms. Rhodes: So are you saying that $\frac{1}{2} = \frac{2}{4} = \frac{4}{8} = \frac{8}{16}$? Can you think of any other fractions that would equal $\frac{1}{2}$?

The Fraction Kit: A Conversation About Equivalence

Classroom Clip 4.2

To view this video clip, scan the QR code or access via mathsolutions .com/NTFDP4.2

Consider the following questions as you watch this number talk from a third-grade classroom:

1. How does the arrangement of the fraction kit foster a discussion about equivalence?
2. Why does the teacher choose to use halves, fourths, eighths, and sixteenths (and not thirds, sixths, and twelfths) in her fraction kit as she is beginning discussions with her students around equivalence?
3. What do you notice about the questions the teacher is asking?
4. How does the teacher introduce the word *denominator* into the discussion?
5. What decisions do you see the teacher making about when to ask and when to tell?

As teachers, we can use the ideas that come from class discussions like the one in "Inside the Classroom" on the previous page as starting places for thinking about equivalence and understanding how that relates to making common denominators. Consider how students might change $\frac{4}{5}$ to $\frac{16}{20}$. Students often say, "I multiplied four times four and got sixteen, and then I multiplied five times four and got twenty, so my answer is sixteen over twenty." As we noted in Chapter 3, this inappropriate whole number reasoning—or thinking about multiplying by 4 instead of $\frac{4}{4}$ or 1—masks the bigger idea of the identity property of multiplication. To address this misconception and explore this idea, teachers can use an area model with students.

The following area model represents $\frac{4}{5}$ of the whole.

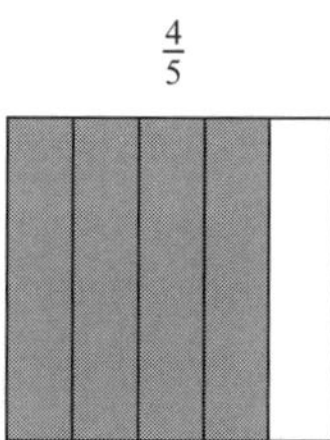

When students partition each fifth into fourths, they change the fifths into twentieths. The shaded section below represents $\frac{4}{5}$ now partitioned into $\frac{16}{20}$.

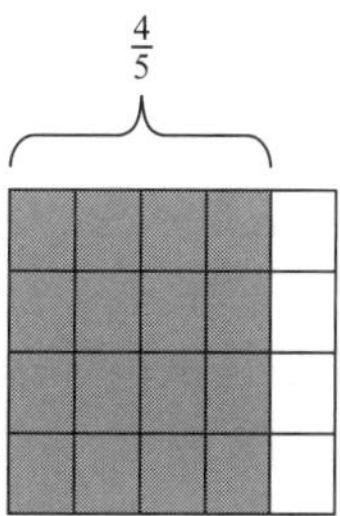

This idea can be represented numerically as $\frac{4}{4} \times \frac{4}{5}$ or $\frac{4 \times 4}{4 \times 5}$. Since $\frac{4}{4}$ is the same as 1, students are actually using the identity property of multiplication to represent that $\frac{4}{5} \times 1$ is equivalent to $\frac{16}{20}$. Reasoning about repartitioning numerically as well as geometrically helps learners develop an understanding of equivalent fractions.

Instructions

The following number talk strings include area models that are partitioned into multiples of the denominator. The number talks may be introduced individually or as a collection of problems that build on each other (from A to B to C, etc.). Feel free to work through each string in order or choose problems according to your students' needs. You may choose to pose one problem from the string each day, or do more than one as time allows. Let's walk through how we might use the number talk, *"Can you see $\frac{1}{2}$ of the whole?"* First show students model A and tell them, *"Put your thumb up when you can see $\frac{1}{2}$ of the whole."* Then say, *"Show a second finger if you can see one-half in a different way."* Once the majority of the students indicate that they have at least one way to see it, ask them to share their reasoning and proof, *"How can you prove your thinking?"*

Next show students model B and say, *"Put your thumb up when you can see $\frac{1}{2}$ of this whole."* Then say, *"Show a second finger if you can see $\frac{1}{2}$ in a different way."* Ask students to explain their thinking. *"Now can you see $\frac{2}{4}$ of the whole? Can you see it in a different way? How can you prove your thinking?"*

Can you see ______ of the whole? Can you see ______ in a different way? How can you prove your thinking?

A. $\frac{1}{2}$?

B. $\frac{1}{2}$? $\frac{2}{4}$?

C. $\frac{1}{2}$? $\frac{4}{8}$?

D. $\frac{1}{2}$? $\frac{8}{16}$?

Reproducible 2

For reproducibles of each of these area models, visit www.mathsolutions.com /numbertalksfdp_reproducibles.

A.

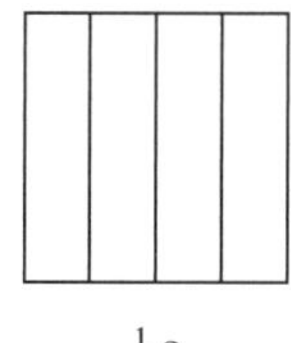

$\frac{1}{4}$?

B.

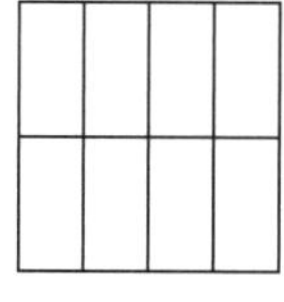

$\frac{1}{4}$? $\frac{2}{8}$?

C.

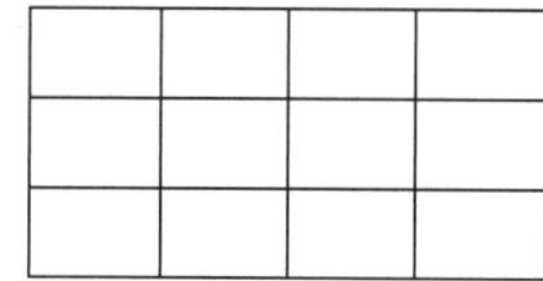

$\frac{1}{4}$? $\frac{3}{12}$?

D.

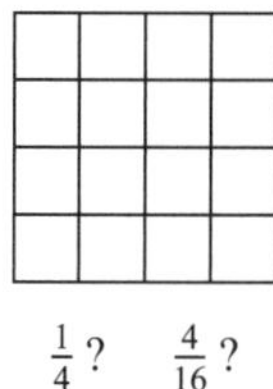

$\frac{1}{4}$? $\frac{4}{16}$?

E.

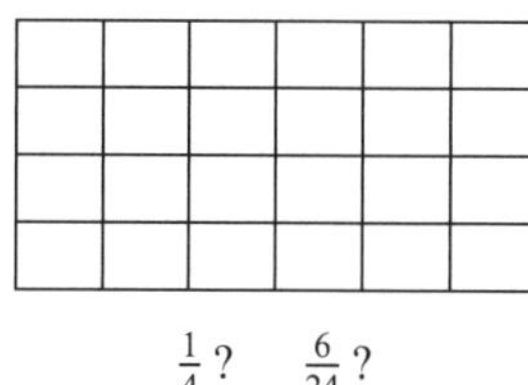

$\frac{1}{4}$? $\frac{6}{24}$?

F.

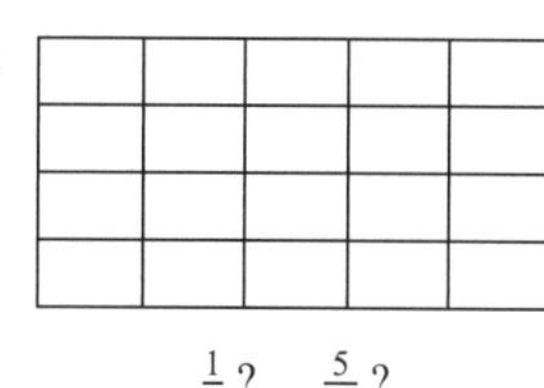

$\frac{1}{4}$? $\frac{5}{20}$?

A.

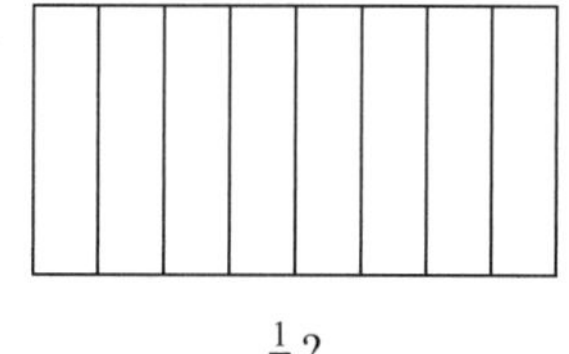

$\frac{1}{8}$?

B.

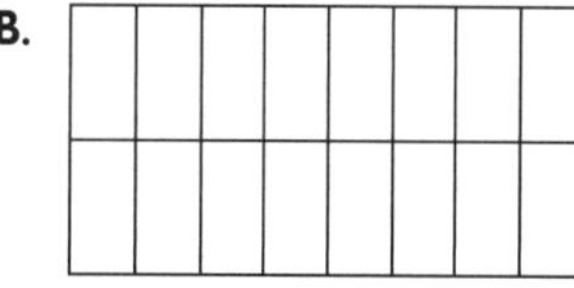

$\frac{1}{8}$? $\frac{2}{16}$?

C.

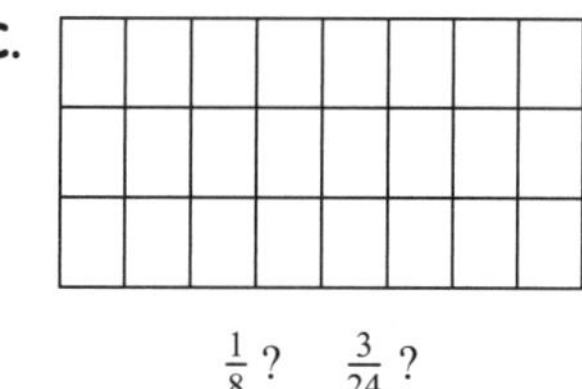

$\frac{1}{8}$? $\frac{3}{24}$?

D.

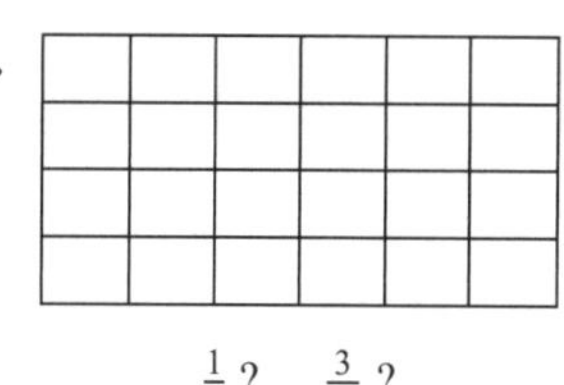

$\frac{1}{8}$? $\frac{3}{24}$?

(continued)

(Can you see ______ of the whole? Can you see ______ in a different way? How can you prove your thinking?, continued)

A.

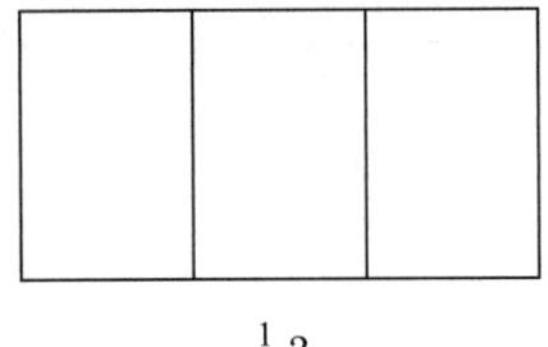

$\frac{1}{3}$?

B.

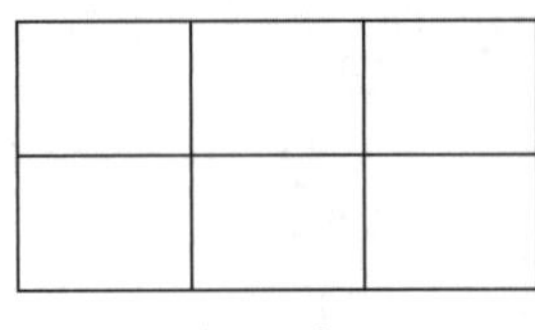

$\frac{1}{3}$? $\frac{2}{6}$?

C.

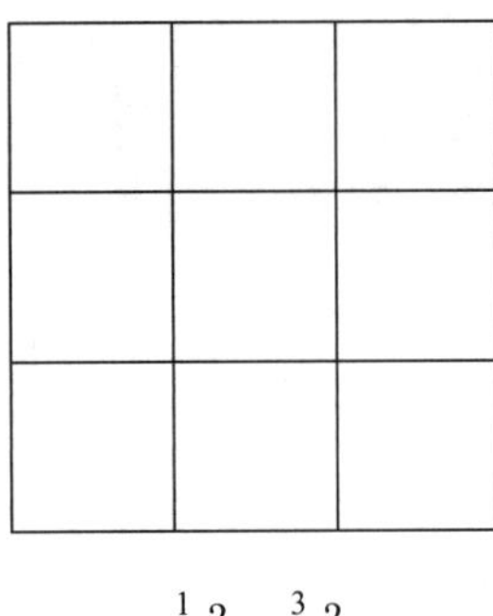

$\frac{1}{3}$? $\frac{3}{9}$?

D.

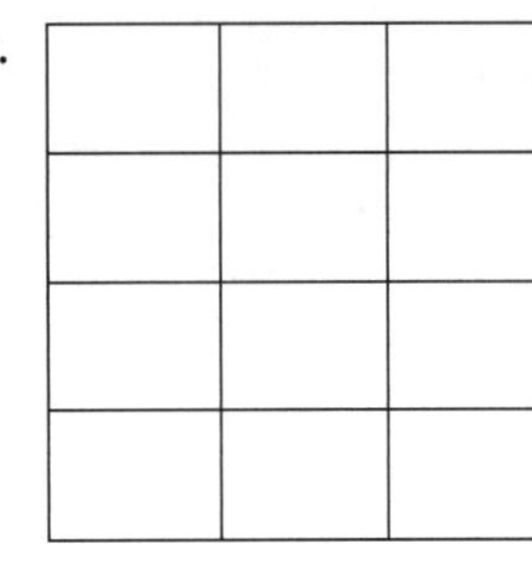

$\frac{1}{3}$? $\frac{4}{12}$?

A.

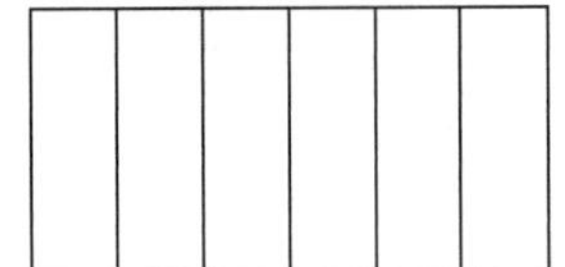

$\frac{1}{6}$?

B.

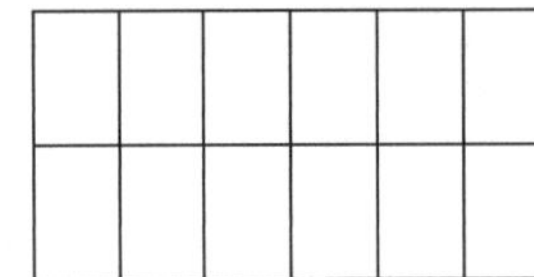

$\frac{1}{6}$? $\frac{2}{12}$?

C.

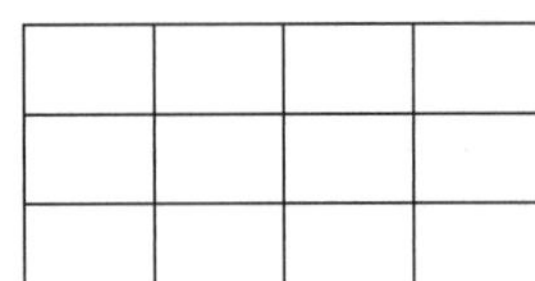

$\frac{1}{6}$? $\frac{2}{12}$?

D.

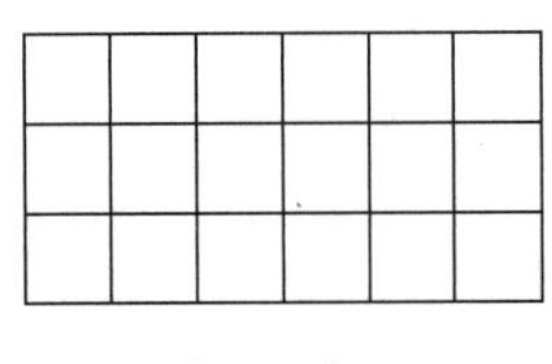

$\frac{1}{6}$? $\frac{3}{18}$?

E.

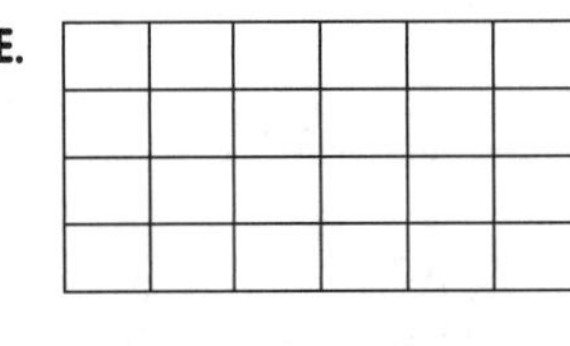

$\frac{1}{6}$? $\frac{4}{24}$?

F.

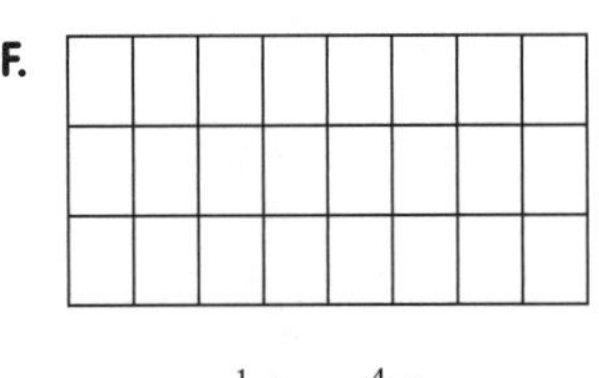

$\frac{1}{6}$? $\frac{4}{24}$?

Number Talks That Use Set Models to Build Fractional Reasoning

In a set model, the total number of objects in the set determines the whole, and how students partition or divide the total number of objects determines the number of parts. The objects do not need to be the exact same size or shape to be part of the whole just as if you ask what fraction of the students in your class wear glasses, not all of the students will look exactly alike. (See Figure 4–5.) This nuance makes the set model unique and sometimes more difficult for students. However, grappling with fractions in this context can serve as a vehicle for learners to deepen their understanding about part–whole relationships. As you work with your class, you can arrange the objects in a set model in an array formation or in a scattered group. (See Figure 4–5.) Each time you vary the presentation you also help stretch your students' thinking.

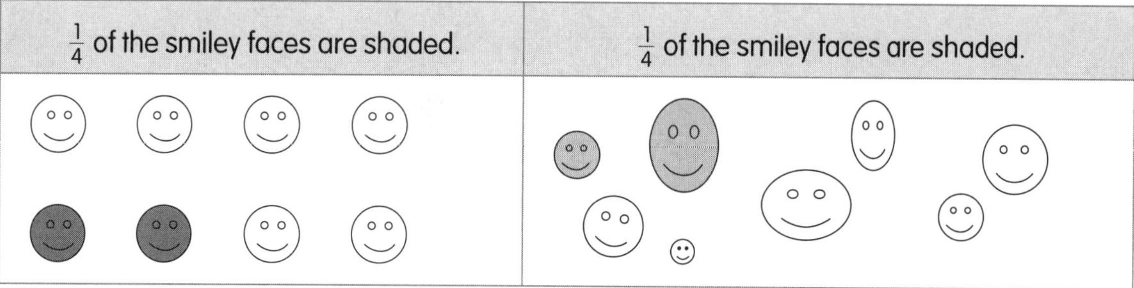

Figure 4–5. *In Set Models, Objects Do Not Need to Be the Exact Same Size or Shape*

These number talks are organized in groups that start by using a benchmark fraction $\left(\frac{1}{2}, \frac{1}{4}, \frac{1}{8}, \frac{1}{3}, \text{ or } \frac{1}{6}\right)$.

The strings are designed to help students think about equivalence. They are crafted in the same way as the previous area model number talk strings, only these use set models.

Learn More...

Remember that for most learners, thinking about $\frac{1}{2}$ in multiple ways can be more challenging than it looks; it is a big idea for students to realize that $\frac{1}{2}$ can be any of the parts that equal one-half of the set.

Instructions

These number talks are organized in groups that start by using a benchmark fraction $\left(\frac{1}{2}, \frac{1}{4}, \frac{1}{8}, \frac{1}{3}, \text{ or } \frac{1}{6}\right)$, progress in difficulty (from A to B to C, etc.), and may be introduced individually or as a collection of problems. Feel free to work through each string in order or choose problems according to your students' needs. You may choose to pose one problem each day, or do more than one as time allows. Let's walk through how we might use the number talk, *"Can you see $\frac{1}{2}$ of the whole?"* First show students model A and tell them, *"Put your thumb up when you can see $\frac{1}{2}$ of the whole."* Then say, *"Show a second finger when you can see $\frac{1}{2}$ in a different way."* Once the majority of the students indicate that they have at least one way to see it, ask them to share their reasoning and proof, *"How can you prove your thinking?"*

Can you see _____ of the whole? Can you see _____ in a different way? How can you prove your thinking?

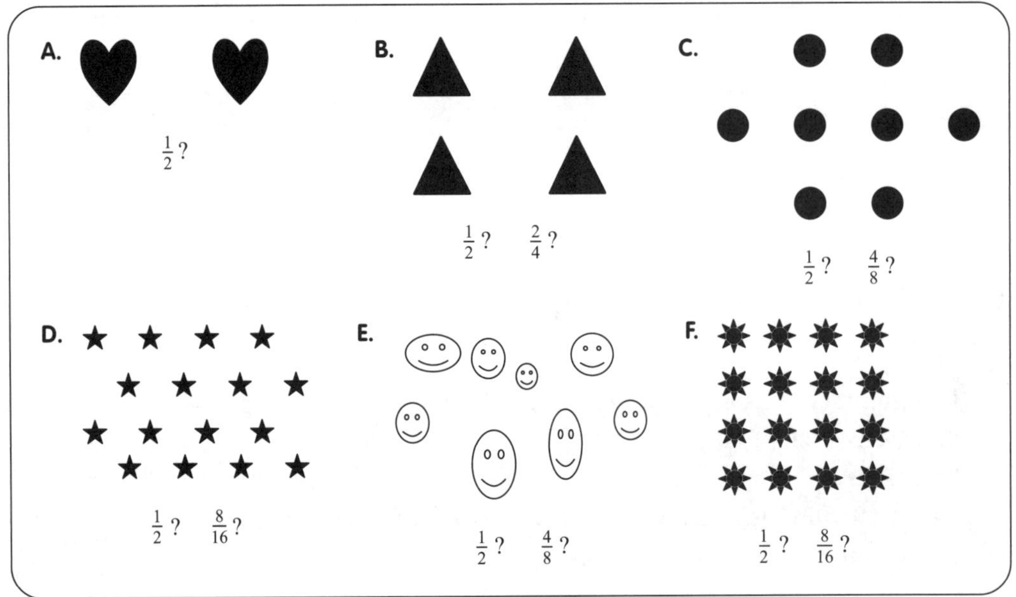

Reproducible 7

For reproducibles of each of these set models, visit www.mathsolutions.com/numbertalksfdp_reproducibles.

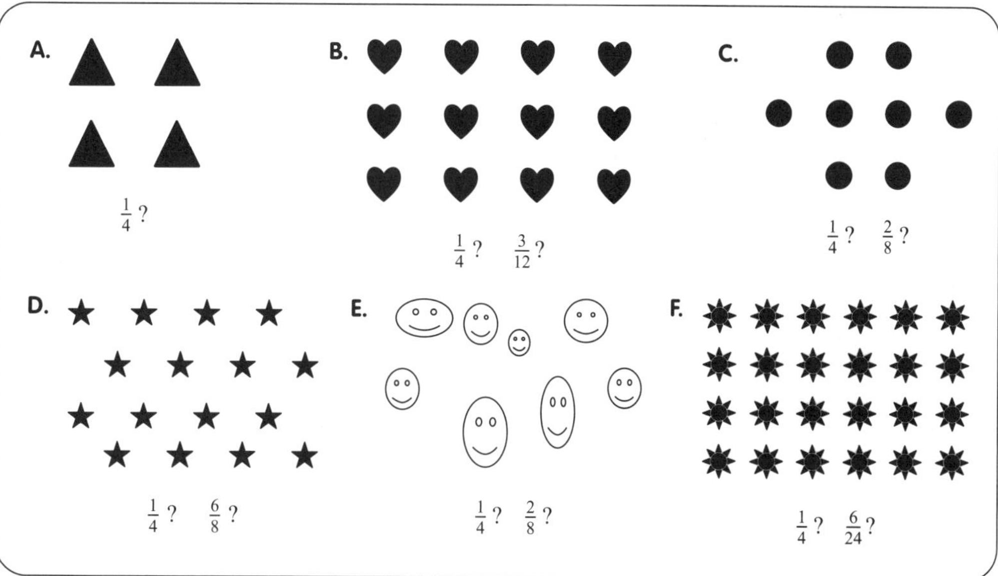
A.
$\frac{1}{4}$?
B.
$\frac{1}{4}$? $\frac{3}{12}$?
C.
$\frac{1}{4}$? $\frac{2}{8}$?
D.
$\frac{1}{4}$? $\frac{6}{8}$?
E.
$\frac{1}{4}$? $\frac{2}{8}$?
F.
$\frac{1}{4}$? $\frac{6}{24}$?

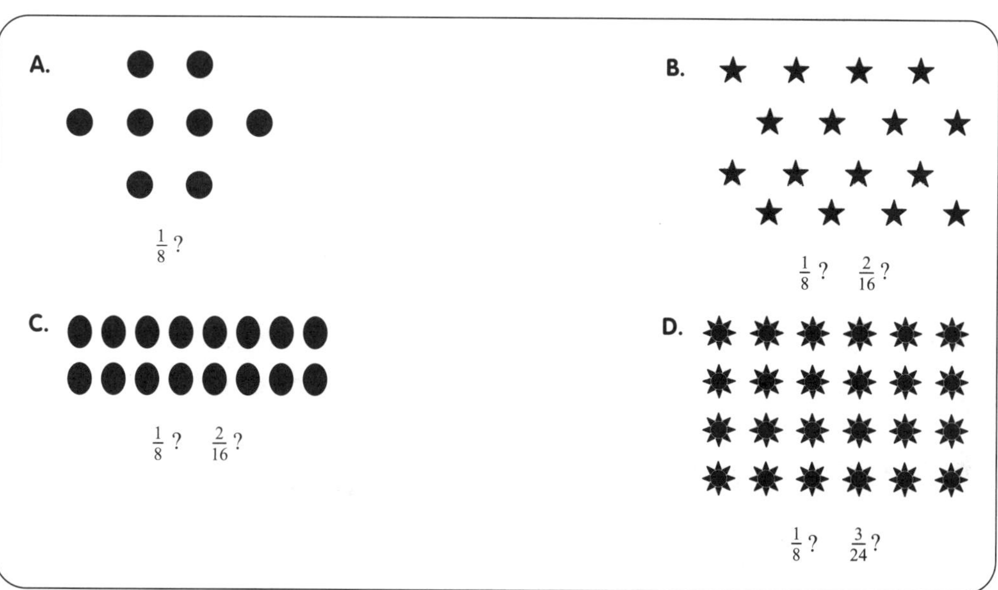
A.
$\frac{1}{8}$?
B.
$\frac{1}{8}$? $\frac{2}{16}$?
C.
$\frac{1}{8}$? $\frac{2}{16}$?
D.
$\frac{1}{8}$? $\frac{3}{24}$?

(continued)

(Can you see ______ of the whole? Can you see ______ in a different way? How can you prove your thinking?, continued)

A.

$\frac{1}{3}$?

B.

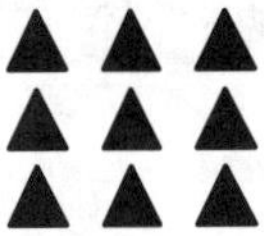

$\frac{1}{3}$? $\frac{3}{9}$?

C.

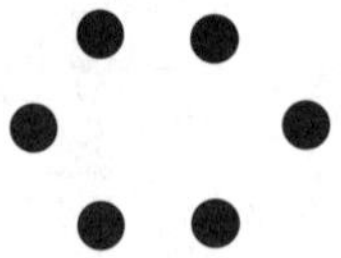

$\frac{1}{3}$? $\frac{2}{6}$?

D.

$\frac{1}{3}$? $\frac{4}{12}$?

E.

$\frac{1}{3}$? $\frac{6}{18}$?

F.

$\frac{1}{3}$? $\frac{8}{24}$?

A.

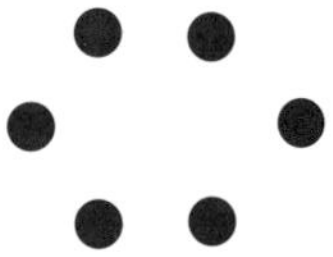

$\frac{1}{6}$?

B.

$\frac{1}{6}$? $\frac{2}{12}$?

C.

$\frac{1}{6}$? $\frac{3}{18}$?

D.

$\frac{1}{6}$? $\frac{4}{24}$?

Number Talks That Use Linear Models to Build Fractional Reasoning

Unlike an area or set model, in a linear model like a number line, the unit or whole is determined by the distance from 0 to 1. A linear model requires symbols or markings to indicate this distance. The parts of the whole in a linear model are determined by partitioning the length of the whole into equal distances. (See Figure 4–6.)

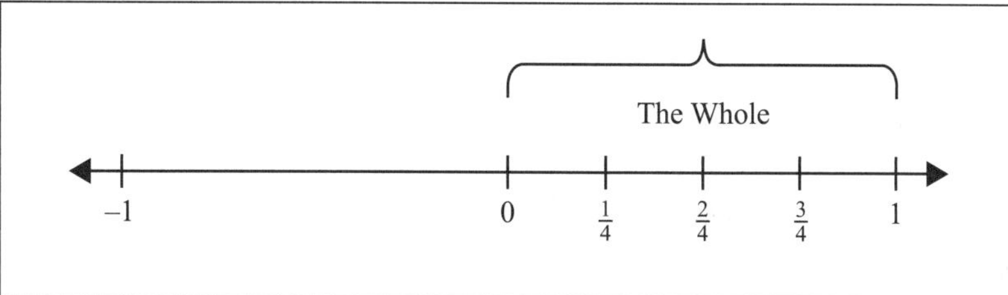

Figure 4–6. *In Linear Models, the Parts of the Whole Are Determined by Partitioning the Length of the Whole into Equal Parts*

To reduce the chance of unintentionally fostering misconceptions, number lines have been selected throughout this resource that extend beyond 0 and 1 and range from 0 to 2, 0 to 4, −1 to 1, and −2 to 2. Please use your judgment when deciding which of these number lines is most appropriate for your grade level.

Number Talk Tip

We suggest using number lines that extend beyond 0 to 1. When teachers use a 0 to 1 number line exclusively, they may miss these common student misconceptions:

- Students think the entire number line represents the whole.
- Students conclude that all fractions are less than one.
- Students believe that the same fraction can be placed at multiple places on the number line.

Number Talk Tip

An *integer* is any positive or negative whole number that is not a fraction or a decimal.

Reproducibles 9, 10, 12, 13

For reproducibles of each of these number lines, visit www.mathsolutions.com/numbertalksfdp_reproducibles.

Category 1
Using Integers as Benchmarks

Students need opportunities to use their understanding of unit fractions to place multiples of a unit fraction and the multiples' equivalents on a number line. For example, students might be asked to decide where to place $\frac{1}{4}$. Presented with this challenge, students often start with $\frac{1}{2}$ and then half each half to get fourths. Once they know where to place $\frac{1}{4}$, they use what they know about this unit fraction to partition the whole to find multiples. As students participate in discussions about $\frac{2}{4}$ sharing the same place as $\frac{1}{2}$, they begin to confront ideas around equivalence.

The number talk strings in this category use a linear model and require students to reason about the numerator and denominator, partitioning, and equivalence. Select one of the following number lines that extend beyond 0 to 1 to use with this collection of number talks.

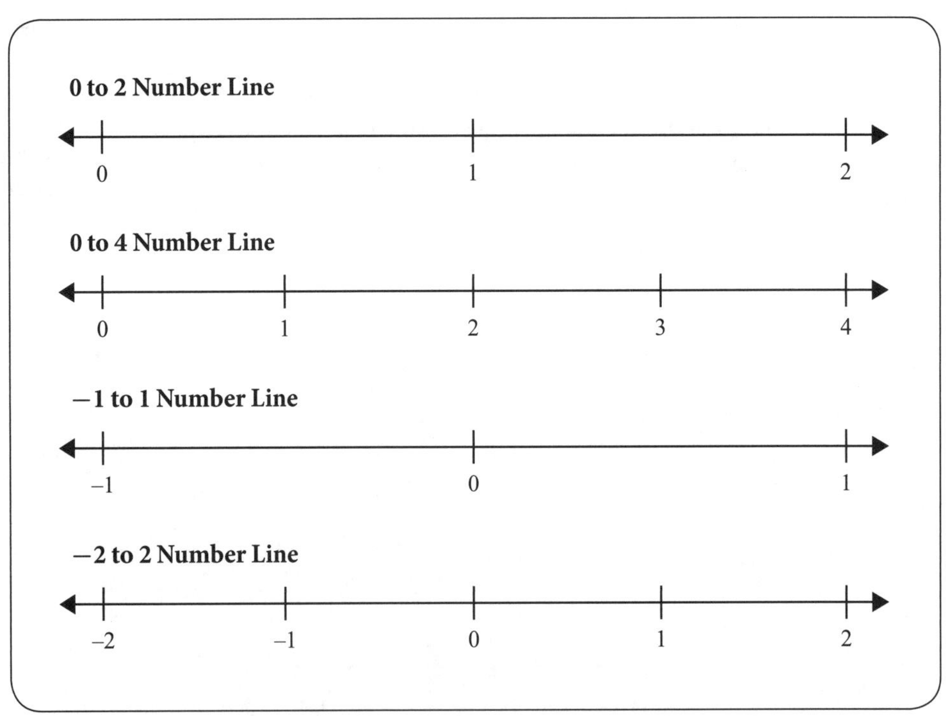

Instructions

These number talks may be introduced individually or as a collection of problems that build on each other (from A to B to C, etc.). Feel free to work through each string in order or choose problems according to your students' needs. You may choose to pose one problem each day, or do more than one as time allows. For each number talk string, choose an appropriate number line, post the first fraction, and ask students, *"Where should ____ be placed on the number line? How do you know?"* After students have reached a consensus, present the next fraction in the sequence. Be sure to present the fractions in each number talk one at a time, using the suggested sequence.

Number Talk Tip

If students put some of the fractions in the wrong place, do not be quick to correct them. Allow time for students to share their reasoning and let the proof come from the comparison of where other fractions should be placed.

Where should ______ be placed on the number line? How do you know?

A. $\frac{1}{2}, \frac{1}{4}, \frac{2}{4}, \frac{3}{4}$

B. $\frac{1}{2}, \frac{1}{4}, \frac{1}{8}, \frac{2}{8}, \frac{4}{8}, \frac{3}{4}, \frac{6}{8}$

C. $\frac{1}{3}, \frac{2}{3}$

D. $\frac{1}{3}, \frac{1}{6}, \frac{2}{6}, \frac{3}{6}, \frac{1}{2}, \frac{2}{3}$

E. $\frac{1}{2}, \frac{2}{2}, \frac{3}{2}, 1\frac{1}{2}, 2\frac{1}{2}, 3\frac{1}{2}$

F. $-1\frac{1}{2}, -\frac{1}{2}, -\frac{1}{4}, \frac{1}{2}, \frac{3}{4}$

Number Talk Tip

Reminder: For each number talk string shown here, first select a number line from page 94.

Category 2
Using Integers and Fractions as Benchmarks

Students also need the opportunity to consider the relationship between integers and fractions to determine how to partition the number line and accurately place a new fraction. For example, present a number line in which only 0 and $\frac{1}{4}$ are marked. Ask students, "Where should $\frac{5}{8}$ be placed?" To decide where $\frac{5}{8}$ should be placed, students might mentally partition the number line into fourths and then halve each fourth to find eighths.

The number talk strings in this category include a number line (linear model) and require students to reason about the numerator and denominator, partitioning, and equivalence. The number lines are purposefully crafted using only an integer and a fraction.

Instructions

These number talks are intended to be used as stand-alone problems and can be presented in any order according to your students' needs. You may choose to pose one problem each day, or do more than one as time allows. Show the accompanying number line for each problem and ask, *"Where should _____ be placed? How do you know?"*

Where should ______ be placed on the number line? How do you know?

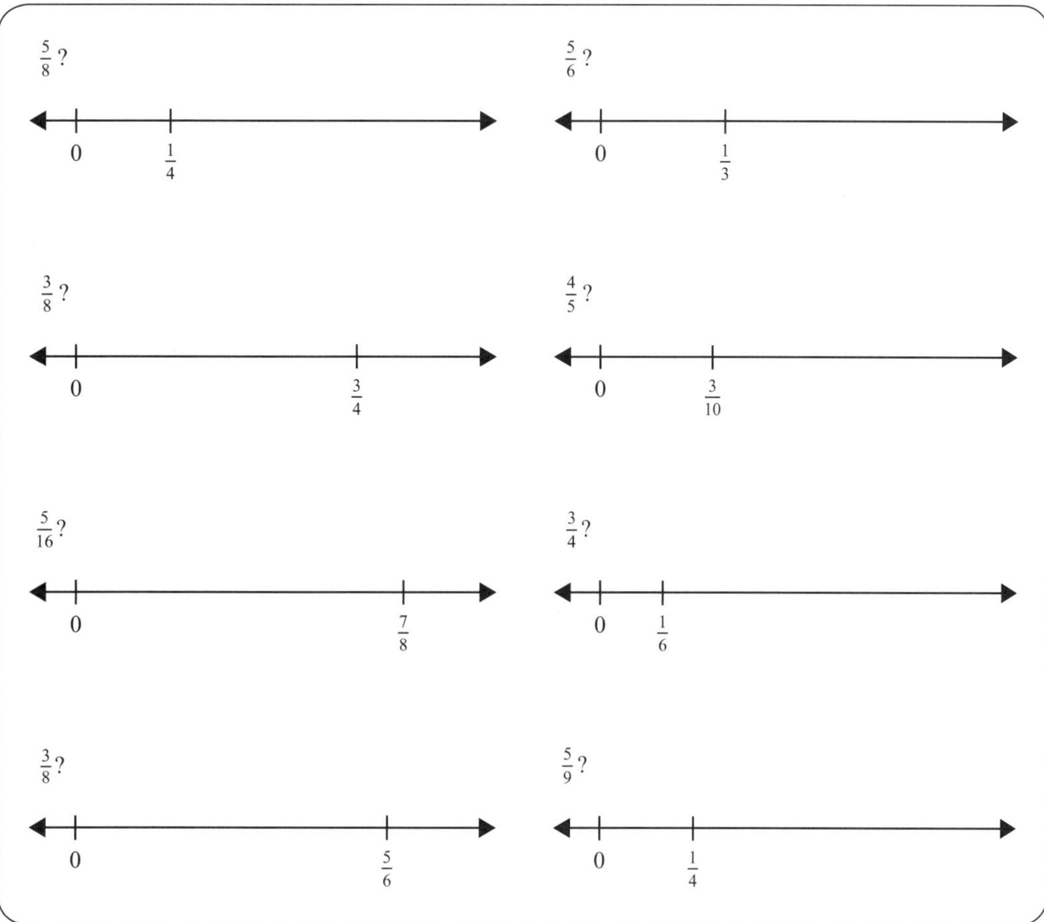

(continued)

Reproducible 14

For full-sized reproducibles of these number talks, visit www.mathsolutions.com /numbertalksfdp_reproducibles.

(Where should ________ be placed on the number line? How do you know?, continued)

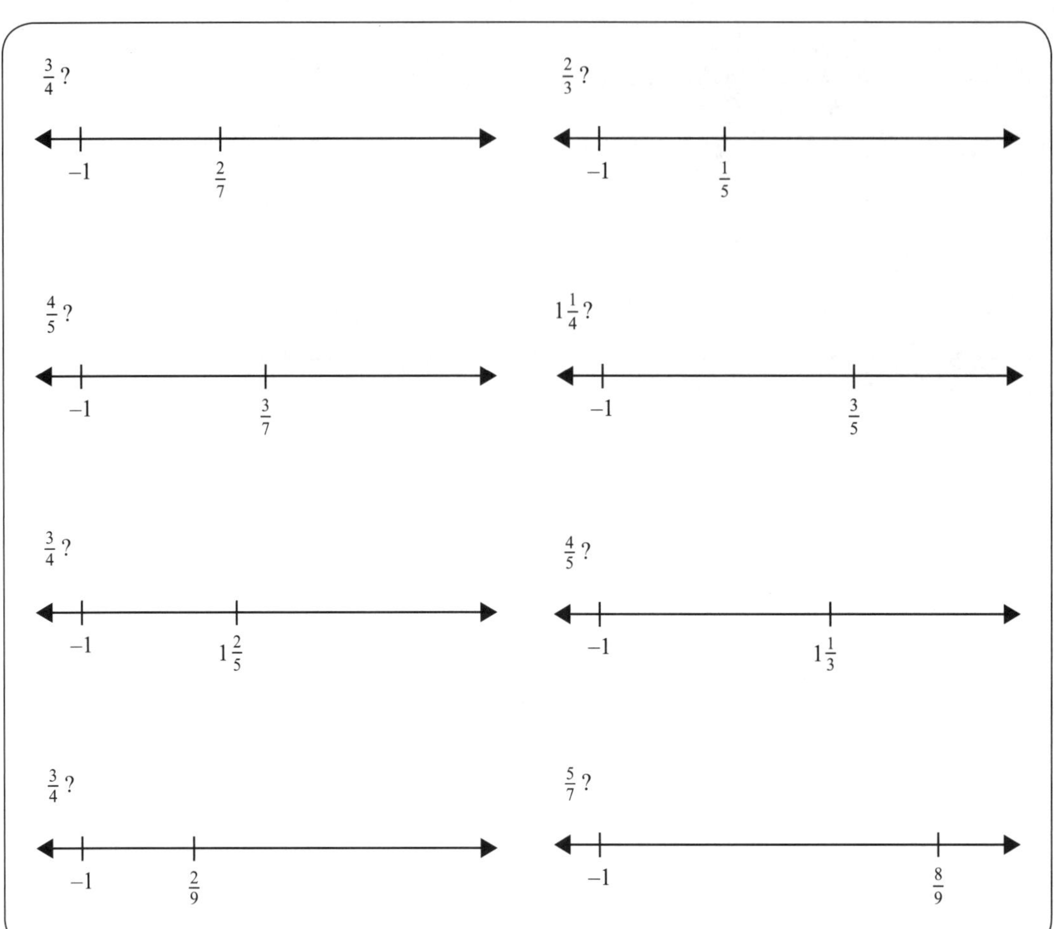

Number Talks That Use Comparing and Ordering to Build Fractional Reasoning

The ability to compare and order fractions is an essential component in fractional reasoning. Often students are taught to compare fractions by finding a common denominator and focusing solely on the difference in the numerators, or they are encouraged to cross multiply to compare. When either of these methods is taught from a procedural perspective, students frequently resort to inappropriate whole number reasoning and ignore the fractional relationships. This is illustrated in the following table. (See Figure 4–7.)

Learn More...

For more on inappropriate whole number reasoning, see Chapter 3, pages 64–66.

Comparing $\frac{2}{3}$ and $\frac{4}{5}$—Which is bigger?	
Student's Strategy and Reasoning	**Recording**
Finding a Common Denominator Conner: *I changed $\frac{2}{3}$ to $\frac{10}{15}$ and I changed $\frac{4}{5}$ to $\frac{12}{15}$. 12 is bigger than 10 so $\frac{4}{5}$ is greater than $\frac{2}{3}$.*	$\frac{2}{3} = \frac{10}{15}$ $\frac{4}{5} = \frac{12}{15}$ $12 > 10$ $\frac{4}{5} > \frac{2}{3}$
Cross Multiplication Debra: *I know I need to start with the denominators so I multiply 3 × 4 and then put 12 above the $\frac{4}{5}$. Then I multiply 5 × 2 and put 10 above the $\frac{2}{3}$. 12 is bigger than 10 so $\frac{4}{5}$ is bigger than $\frac{2}{3}$.*	$10 < 12$ $\frac{2}{3}$ ⤫ $\frac{4}{5}$ $3 \times 4 = 12$ $5 \times 2 = 10$ $\frac{4}{5} > \frac{2}{3}$

Figure 4–7. *Examples of Inappropriate Whole Number Reasoning When Comparing $\frac{2}{3}$ and $\frac{4}{5}$*

When students use either of these procedures (finding a common denominator or cross multiplication) with understanding, they are important and effective ways to compare fractions. However, there are other ways to compare and order fractions that teachers and students often overlook. Number talks can help students develop a variety of efficient ways to compare and order fractions as they reason using benchmarks, unit fractions, and relationships between and among numerators and denominators. As students reason about the relationship of individual fractions using benchmarks such as 0, $\frac{1}{2}$, 1, $1\frac{1}{2}$, and 2, they build a foundation for developing strategies when comparing one fraction to other fractions.

Number Talk Tip

You may want to post a linear model that includes the targeted benchmarks to provide a visual model of students' reasoning. For Category 1 problems, we suggest a 0 to 1 number line that has 0, $\frac{1}{2}$, and 1 marked. For a reproducible version of this number line, see www.mathsolutions.com/numbertalksfdp_reproducibles, Reproducible 8.

Category 1
Is the Fraction Closer to 0, $\frac{1}{2}$, or 1 Whole?

This category includes proper fractions that you can choose from for each problem. The teacher chooses a fraction and asks students whether they think it is closer to 0, $\frac{1}{2}$, or 1 and how they know. For example, let's say you choose $\frac{7}{8}$ and ask your students, "Is $\frac{7}{8}$ closer to 0, $\frac{1}{2}$, or 1?" One strategy you might anticipate students will use is, "$\frac{8}{8}$ is 1 whole, and $\frac{7}{8}$ is $\frac{1}{8}$ away from the whole, so $\frac{7}{8}$ is closer to 1 than it is to $\frac{1}{2}$ or 0."

As previously discussed, it is easier for students to partition a whole into an even number of parts, so fractions with even denominators may be an easier place to start if students are using partitioning as a strategy. Fractions that are closer to the benchmarks of 0, $\frac{1}{2}$, or 1 are also generally easier starting places. It is more difficult for students to partition a whole into an odd number of parts. Make sure they know that the fractions they are asked to compare have the same size wholes.

The following number talks use fractions with both even and odd denominators.

Instructions

These number talks are intended to be used as stand-alone problems and can be presented in any order according to your students' needs. You may choose to pose one problem each day, or do more than one as time allows. Select one fraction and ask, *"Is the fraction closer to 0, $\frac{1}{2}$, or 1 whole?"* Then ask students to justify their reasoning, *"How do you know?"* Be mindful that fractions with even-number denominators are a more accesible place to begin.

Is the fraction closer to 0, $\frac{1}{2}$, or 1 whole? How do you know?

$\frac{3}{8}$	$\frac{9}{10}$	$\frac{4}{6}$
$\frac{4}{10}$	$\frac{6}{10}$	$\frac{4}{12}$
$\frac{2}{6}$	$\frac{5}{8}$	$\frac{1}{4}$
$\frac{7}{8}$	$\frac{3}{4}$	$\frac{2}{8}$
$\frac{5}{6}$	$\frac{7}{10}$	$\frac{1}{6}$
$\frac{12}{16}$	$\frac{10}{16}$	$\frac{7}{12}$
$\frac{3}{5}$	$\frac{1}{3}$	$\frac{4}{7}$
$\frac{2}{5}$	$\frac{2}{3}$	$\frac{8}{9}$
$\frac{5}{9}$	$\frac{4}{5}$	$\frac{5}{7}$
$\frac{5}{11}$	$\frac{8}{11}$	$\frac{1}{5}$
$\frac{6}{7}$	$\frac{4}{9}$	$\frac{3}{11}$
$\frac{2}{9}$	$\frac{5}{9}$	$\frac{6}{11}$

Number Talk Tip

You may want to post a linear model that includes the targeted benchmarks to provide a visual model of students' reasoning. For Category 2 problems, use a number line that has 1, $1\frac{1}{2}$, and 2 marked (this number line is available as Reproducible 11; for more information, see mathsolutions.com/numbertalksfdp_reproducibles).

Category 2
Is the Fraction Closer to 1, $1\frac{1}{2}$, or 2 Wholes?

The number talks in this category include both improper fractions and mixed numbers. As a reminder, an *improper fraction* is a fraction where the numerator is greater than or equal to the denominator such as $\frac{4}{4}$ or $\frac{8}{7}$. A *mixed number* is a number consisting of a whole number and a fraction or decimal such as $3\frac{45}{100}$ or 3.45

Instructions

These number talks are intended to be used as stand-alone problems and can be presented in any order according to your students' needs. You may choose to pose one problem each day, or do more than one as time allows. Select one fraction and ask, *"Is the fraction closer to 1, $1\frac{1}{2}$, or 2 wholes?"* Then ask students to justify their reasoning, *"How do you know?"* Be mindful that fractions with even-number denominators are a more accessible place to begin.

Is the fraction closer to 1, $1\frac{1}{2}$, or 2 wholes? How do you know?

$1\frac{5}{8}$	$\frac{6}{4}$	$1\frac{9}{10}$
$\frac{11}{16}$	$\frac{14}{8}$	$1\frac{3}{4}$
$1\frac{5}{6}$	$\frac{5}{4}$	$1\frac{7}{8}$
$\frac{7}{4}$	$\frac{8}{6}$	$1\frac{1}{4}$
$1\frac{3}{8}$	$1\frac{6}{10}$	$\frac{18}{12}$
$1\frac{1}{10}$	$\frac{20}{14}$	$1\frac{9}{12}$
$\frac{4}{3}$	$1\frac{3}{7}$	$\frac{15}{9}$
$1\frac{2}{3}$	$\frac{6}{5}$	$\frac{9}{7}$
$\frac{9}{5}$	$1\frac{1}{3}$	$1\frac{3}{5}$
$\frac{11}{9}$	$1\frac{5}{9}$	$\frac{12}{7}$
$\frac{12}{11}$	$1\frac{6}{13}$	$\frac{18}{15}$
$\frac{7}{5}$	$\frac{6}{3}$	$1\frac{6}{11}$

Number Talks That Use Strategies for Comparing and Ordering Fractions

As students become more proficient in understanding and reasoning with fractions, they begin to develop strategies for comparing and ordering. These strategies often start with geometric justifications, but make sure to push for numerical reasoning as well. Take a moment to think about ways to compare $\frac{3}{4}$ and $\frac{2}{3}$ without using cross multiplication or finding a common denominator. What strategies did you come up with? See Figure 4–8 for a look at students' reasoning compared to benchmarks of 1 whole and $\frac{1}{2}$.

Comparing $\frac{3}{4}$ and $\frac{2}{3}$—Which is bigger?	
Student's Strategy and Reasoning	**Recording**
Comparing the Distance from the Whole Tami: *Three-fourths is $\frac{1}{4}$ less than the whole, and $\frac{2}{3}$ is $\frac{1}{3}$ less than the whole. I know that $\frac{1}{4}$ is a smaller fraction than $\frac{1}{3}$ so $\frac{3}{4}$ is closer to a whole and it's the bigger fraction.*	$\frac{3}{4}$ | $\frac{1}{4}$ *$\frac{3}{4}$ is $\frac{1}{4}$ less than the whole.* $\frac{2}{3}$ | $\frac{1}{3}$ *$\frac{2}{3}$ is $\frac{1}{3}$ less than the whole.*
Comparing the Distance to $\frac{1}{2}$ Jannette: *I thought about $\frac{3}{4}$ as $\frac{2}{4}+\frac{1}{4}$ and I thought about $\frac{2}{3}$ as $\frac{3}{6}+\frac{1}{6}$. Then I just compared $\frac{1}{4}$ and $\frac{1}{6}$. I know that $\frac{1}{4}$ is larger than $\frac{1}{6}$ so $\frac{3}{4}$ is larger than $\frac{2}{3}$.*	$\frac{1}{2}$ $\frac{2}{4}$ | $\frac{1}{4}$ $\frac{1}{2}$ $\frac{3}{6}$ | $\frac{1}{6}$

Figure 4–8. *Comparing $\frac{3}{4}$ and $\frac{2}{3}$ Using the Benchmarks $\frac{1}{2}$ and 1 Whole*

On the following pages, we offer number talk problems that are crafted around fractional relationships and organized by common strategies. However, this does not mean that the only way to compare the fraction pairs is to use the strategy under which they are listed. The categorization of problems by strategy is not meant to be limiting; it is meant to provide you with problems that have the potential to bring specific ideas forward from your students.

Learn More...

See pages 73–75 in this chapter for a more detailed discussion of the two types of context: story problems and geometric models.

Reminder: The Importance of Context

Keep in mind the importance of context, which helps students make sense of the problem. For instance, let's say you want students to compare $\frac{3}{4}$ and $\frac{5}{6}$. Note the difference in presenting the problem to students by using only numbers as opposed to including a story context. (See Figure 4–9.)

Presenting a Problem in Isolation	Presenting a Problem in a Story Context	Presenting Problems Using Models
Which is bigger $\frac{3}{4}$ or $\frac{5}{6}$?	*Sam and Theresa each bought the same size loaf of bread to make sandwiches for the week. On Wednesday, Sam had $\frac{3}{4}$ of his loaf left and Theresa had $\frac{5}{6}$ of her loaf. Who had more bread?*	$\frac{3}{4}$ of the loaf Sam's bread $\frac{5}{6}$ of the loaf Theresa's bread The bread problem suggests using an area model.
	The cross-country team is training for their next meet. Willa has run $\frac{3}{4}$ of a mile and Josiah has run $\frac{5}{6}$ of a mile. Who has run the farthest distance?	0 $\frac{3}{4}$ 1 Willa has run $\frac{3}{4}$ of a mile. 0 $\frac{5}{6}$ 1 Josiah has run $\frac{5}{6}$ of a mile. The track problem lends itself to using a linear model.

Figure 4–9. *Comparing $\frac{3}{4}$ and $\frac{5}{6}$ in Isolation Versus in a Context*

Each context implies a different geometric model. The bread problem suggests an area model and the track problem lends itself to a linear model.

Number Talk Tip

If students are already familiar with making common denominators or using the cross-multiplication method, consider asking them to set aside these approaches for now and instead think about how they could reason about fraction relationships to find a solution.

Category 1
Using Proximity to $\frac{1}{2}$

This strategy builds on the understanding of $\frac{1}{2}$ and reasoning about how far each additional fraction is from this benchmark. Take, for example the problem set $\frac{24}{50}$ and $\frac{25}{38}$. How might students reason to decide which one is greater? Knowing $\frac{25}{50}$ is exactly half of a whole, students can reason that $\frac{24}{50}$ would be a little less than a half (or $\frac{1}{50}$ less to be exact). Students can apply this same reasoning to $\frac{25}{38}$. If $\frac{19}{38}$ is exactly $\frac{1}{2}$, then $\frac{25}{38}$ would be greater than one half. Therefore, because $\frac{24}{50}$ is less than $\frac{1}{2}$ and $\frac{25}{38}$ is greater than $\frac{1}{2}$, $\frac{25}{38}$ is larger than $\frac{24}{50}$.

Instructions

Each of the following number talks consists of two fractions close to $\frac{1}{2}$. Feel free to work through each fraction pair in order (from A to B to C, etc.) or choose pairs according to your students' needs. You may choose to pose one problem each day, or do more than one as time allows. Present both fractions at the same time and ask students, *"Are the fractions equivalent or is one fraction greater? How do you know?"* Continue this format with each problem in the string.

Are the fractions equivalent or is one fraction greater? How do you know?

A. $\frac{4}{10}$ $\frac{7}{12}$
B. $\frac{3}{8}$ $\frac{6}{10}$
C. $\frac{5}{8}$ $\frac{3}{7}$
D. $\frac{5}{12}$ $\frac{7}{13}$
E. $\frac{4}{9}$ $\frac{5}{10}$

A. $\frac{9}{14}$ $\frac{6}{12}$
B. $\frac{3}{5}$ $\frac{4}{8}$
C. $\frac{7}{12}$ $\frac{6}{11}$
D. $\frac{6}{14}$ $\frac{5}{9}$
E. $\frac{2}{3}$ $\frac{3}{6}$

A. $\frac{24}{50}$ $\frac{24}{38}$
B. $\frac{18}{34}$ $\frac{12}{32}$
C. $\frac{19}{40}$ $\frac{17}{32}$
D. $\frac{9}{16}$ $\frac{3}{5}$
E. $\frac{17}{35}$ $\frac{18}{36}$

A. $\frac{15}{26}$ $\frac{14}{28}$
B. $\frac{32}{66}$ $\frac{21}{40}$
C. $\frac{26}{50}$ $\frac{19}{40}$
D. $\frac{16}{30}$ $\frac{30}{59}$
E. $\frac{19}{36}$ $\frac{15}{28}$

Comparing $\frac{24}{50}$ and $\frac{21}{40}$
Classroom Clip 4.3

Consider the following questions as you watch this number talk from a fourth-grade classroom:

1. What do you notice about the reasoning students use to solve this problem?
2. How does the teacher encourage students to "attend to precision"?
3. What is Pierce wondering about?
4. What might Pierce's question cause the teacher to consider as a topic for a future number talk?
5. What are you wondering about after watching this number talk?

To view this video clip, scan the QR code or access via mathsolutions .com/NTFDP4.3

Number Talk Tip

If students are already familiar with making common denominators or using the cross-multiplication method, consider asking them to set aside these approaches and instead think about how they could reason about fraction relationships to find a solution.

Category 2
Using Distance from the Whole

When students reason about how far a fraction is from one whole, they often use their understanding of unit fractions. Consider the fraction pair: $\frac{7}{8}$ and $\frac{8}{9}$. Note that $\frac{7}{8}$ is $\frac{1}{8}$ less than one whole, and $\frac{8}{9}$ is $\frac{1}{9}$ less than one whole. Since $\frac{1}{9}$ is a smaller distance to the whole, $\frac{8}{9}$ is larger. Some students may incorrectly generalize that these two fractions are equal, because they are both one unit-fraction away from the whole. A way to confront this misconception is to pose a counterquestion in which two fractions are still both one unit away from the whole, but the distance from the whole is magnified. Ask students whether $\frac{99}{100}$ and $\frac{3}{4}$ would be equal. In this example, both fractions are one unit away from the whole, but the difference between $\frac{1}{100}$ away from the whole and $\frac{1}{4}$ away from the whole is more obvious.

Instructions

Each of the following number talks consists of two fractions close to one whole. Feel free to work through each fraction pair in order (from A to B to C, etc.) or choose pairs according to your students' needs. You may choose to pose one problem each day, or do more than one as time allows. Present both fractions at the same time and ask students, *"Are the fractions equivalent or is one fraction greater? How do you know?"* Continue this format with each problem in the string.

Are the fractions equivalent or is one fraction greater? How do you know?

A. $\frac{7}{8}$ $\frac{8}{9}$
B. $\frac{3}{4}$ $\frac{2}{3}$
C. $\frac{4}{5}$ $\frac{3}{4}$
D. $\frac{9}{10}$ $\frac{10}{11}$
E. $\frac{3}{4}$ $\frac{8}{9}$

A. $\frac{11}{12}$ $\frac{15}{16}$
B. $\frac{8}{9}$ $\frac{4}{5}$
C. $\frac{6}{7}$ $\frac{4}{5}$
D. $\frac{3}{4}$ $\frac{5}{6}$
E. $\frac{12}{13}$ $\frac{9}{10}$

A. $\frac{13}{14}$ $\frac{15}{16}$
B. $\frac{9}{11}$ $\frac{7}{9}$
C. $\frac{11}{13}$ $\frac{13}{15}$
D. $\frac{12}{14}$ $\frac{15}{17}$
E. $\frac{15}{16}$ $\frac{5}{6}$

A. $\frac{23}{24}$ $\frac{37}{38}$
B. $\frac{17}{18}$ $\frac{21}{22}$
C. $\frac{18}{19}$ $\frac{34}{35}$
D. $\frac{31}{32}$ $\frac{43}{44}$
E. $\frac{29}{30}$ $\frac{45}{46}$

Category 3
Using Common Numerators

When the numerators in two fractions are the same, students can use the denominators to compare the fractions by reasoning about the size of the individual unit fractions. For instance, consider how students might reason about the problem: Is $\frac{7}{9}$ or $\frac{7}{11}$ of a candy bar greater? A student might reason, "A piece of candy from a bar divided into 9 pieces would be larger than a piece of candy from a bar divided into 11 pieces. Seven of the larger pieces (ninths) would be more than 7 of the smaller pieces (elevenths), so $\frac{7}{9}$ is larger than $\frac{7}{11}$."

Instructions

Each of the following number talks consists of two fractions with common numerators. Feel free to work through each fraction pair in order (from A to B to C, etc.) or choose pairs according to your students' needs. You may choose to pose one problem each day, or do more than one as time allows. Present both fractions at the same time and ask students, *"Are the fractions equivalent or is one fraction greater? How do you know?"* Continue this format with each problem in the string.

> **Number Talk Tip**
>
> If students are already familiar with making common denominators or using the cross-multiplication method, consider asking them to set aside these approaches and instead think about how they could reason about fraction relationships to find a solution.

Which fraction is greater? How do you know?

A.	$\frac{7}{9}$	$\frac{7}{11}$
B.	$\frac{8}{9}$	$\frac{8}{11}$
C.	$\frac{5}{6}$	$\frac{5}{7}$
D.	$\frac{2}{3}$	$\frac{2}{5}$
E.	$\frac{4}{5}$	$\frac{4}{7}$

A.	$\frac{3}{5}$	$\frac{3}{7}$
B.	$\frac{6}{11}$	$\frac{6}{15}$
C.	$\frac{4}{7}$	$\frac{4}{9}$
D.	$\frac{8}{13}$	$\frac{8}{14}$
E.	$\frac{7}{8}$	$\frac{7}{9}$

A.	$\frac{11}{12}$	$\frac{11}{13}$
B.	$\frac{9}{11}$	$\frac{9}{13}$
C.	$\frac{11}{15}$	$\frac{11}{16}$
D.	$\frac{12}{15}$	$\frac{12}{17}$
E.	$\frac{7}{11}$	$\frac{7}{13}$

A.	$\frac{25}{28}$	$\frac{25}{29}$
B.	$\frac{31}{33}$	$\frac{31}{35}$
C.	$\frac{35}{40}$	$\frac{35}{38}$
D.	$\frac{43}{50}$	$\frac{43}{47}$
E.	$\frac{51}{56}$	$\frac{51}{53}$

Number Talk Tip

If students are already familiar with making common denominators or using the cross-multiplication method, consider asking them to set aside these approaches for the time being and instead think about how they could reason about fraction relationships to find a solution.

Category 4
Using Proportional Reasoning

The number talk strings in this category are structured to help students compare fractions and reason about scale or proportionality. Consider the fractions $\frac{15}{38}$ and $\frac{5}{13}$. The number of parts in $\frac{15}{38}$ is about 3 times as much as in $\frac{5}{13}$. If students change $\frac{5}{13}$ to the equivalent fraction of $\frac{15}{39}$, the numerators will be the same (15), thus allowing students to focus on the size of the parts (38 parts versus 39 parts). Since $\frac{1}{39}$ is smaller than $\frac{1}{38}$, $\frac{15}{38}$ would be slightly larger than $\frac{15}{39}$ or $\frac{5}{13}$.

Each number talk string consists of two fractions crafted so that the numerators or denominators in the first fraction can be doubled or tripled to match the numerator or denominator in the second fraction.

Instructions

These number talks are organized into four columns and progress in difficulty (from A to B to C, etc.) going from the first column to the second column to the third column, and so on. Feel free to work through each fraction pair in order or choose pairs according to your students' needs. You may choose to pose one problem each day, or do more than as time allows. Present both fractions at the same time and ask students, *"Are the fractions equivalent or is one fraction greater? How do you know?"* Continue this format with each problem in the string.

Which fraction is greater? How do you know?

	Column 1		Column 2		Column 3		Column 4
A.	$\frac{2}{5}$ $\frac{4}{9}$	**A.**	$\frac{15}{38}$ $\frac{5}{13}$	**A.**	$\frac{2}{3}$ $\frac{5}{9}$	**A.**	$\frac{9}{15}$ $\frac{28}{45}$
B.	$\frac{3}{8}$ $\frac{6}{15}$	**B.**	$\frac{2}{3}$ $\frac{6}{7}$	**B.**	$\frac{4}{5}$ $\frac{9}{10}$	**B.**	$\frac{5}{7}$ $\frac{14}{21}$
C.	$\frac{6}{7}$ $\frac{12}{15}$	**C.**	$\frac{13}{20}$ $\frac{39}{19}$	**C.**	$\frac{11}{15}$ $\frac{34}{30}$	**C.**	$\frac{13}{30}$ $\frac{38}{60}$
D.	$\frac{10}{17}$ $\frac{20}{33}$	**D.**	$\frac{7}{15}$ $\frac{21}{44}$	**D.**	$\frac{11}{20}$ $\frac{21}{40}$	**D.**	$\frac{8}{13}$ $\frac{23}{39}$
E.	$\frac{5}{13}$ $\frac{10}{27}$	**E.**	$\frac{4}{11}$ $\frac{12}{34}$	**E.**	$\frac{8}{25}$ $\frac{15}{50}$	**E.**	$\frac{17}{20}$ $\frac{52}{60}$

Looking Ahead

Making sure students have strong fractional reasoning is essential before asking them to begin to operate with fractions. In this chapter, we discussed five number talk contexts to build students' fractional reasoning using: story problems, area models, set models, linear models, and comparing and ordering fractions. Which strategies are your "go-to" strategies? Which strategies do individual students gravitate toward? These strategies connect to the big ideas presented in Chapter 3. We now continue to Chapter 5, in which we investigate relationships among fractions, decimals, and percentages.

Connecting the Chapter to Your Practice

1. How do you think story contexts or geometric contexts with models impact students' understanding of fractions?
2. Most math textbooks rely heavily on area models for teaching fractions. How can using different types of models help students understand fractions?
3. Look back at Figure 4–3 on page 76. What parts of understanding numerators and denominators are social knowledge, or strictly a definition, and which parts are mental relationships that students have to make for themselves?
4. What evidence will you be listening for to know if students understand that parts of a fraction need to be equal even though not necessarily congruent?
5. What do you anticipate in your students' thinking as they use the "Can You See?" number talks on pages 86–92?
6. What strategies do you anticipate students might use to place fractions on the number line?
7. How do the numbers you choose to use in your number talks impact the strategies students might use to solve the problems?

CHAPTER 5

Number Talks to Help Students Connect Fractions, Decimals, and Percentages

In the first section of this chapter, we explore how a focus on fractions provides a natural connection for number talks with percentages and decimals. We then offer examples of number talks that help students develop an understanding of decimals and percentages as fractions.

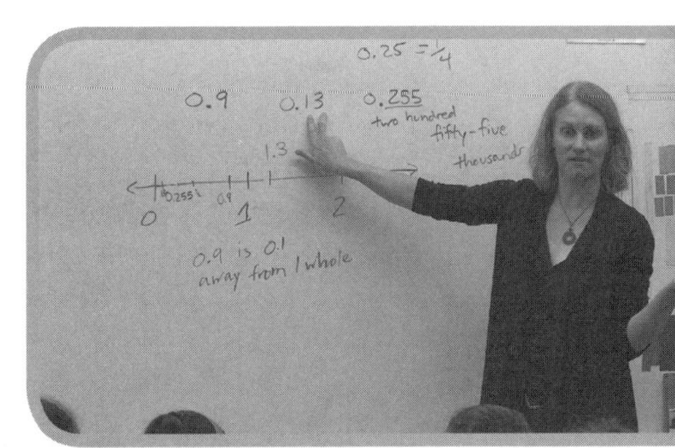

OVERVIEW

The Importance of Focusing on Fractions Before Decimals and Percentages

Though fractions, decimals, and percentages are all ways to represent parts of a whole, it's fractional reasoning that forms the basis of understanding for each of these rational number representations. Students often treat decimals and percentages as whole numbers in their reasoning, but in doing so they usually lose the relationship between the parts and the whole. Consider, for example when students are asked, "Which is greater: 0.25 or 0.125?" Students may ignore the decimal point and value and instead think about the decimals as whole numbers. This whole number reasoning results in an inaccurate answer of 0.125, because students view "125" as greater than "25." Likewise, this same inappropriate focus on whole number reasoning sometimes occurs when students are introduced to percentages before they develop a robust understanding of fractional relationships. For example, to add $\frac{1}{4} + \frac{1}{5}$, students may convert the fractions to percentages and change the problem to *25% + 20%.* While this may be efficient, and the answers of $\frac{9}{20}$ and 45% are correct because they are equivalent, students can easily ignore the part–whole relationship and the meaning of the fractions. These are all reasons why, as teachers, we should initially focus on fractions with learners before transitioning students to the study of decimals and percentages.

Number Talks That Connect Fractions to Percentages

Students are likely familiar with many real-world situations that refer to percentages. Here are a few examples.

- There is a 50% chance of rain.
- Eighty-five percent of the test questions are correct.
- Seventy-five percent of the computer program is downloaded.
- The diners left a 20% tip.
- Jeans are 40% off.

As teachers, we can use students' informal knowledge of percentages to help them make a connection to fractions. For example, we could ask students, "When have you heard the word *percent*?" Then take one of their examples, such as "I got 75% of the questions right on my test," and ask, "How could you also use a fraction to describe the percent of the test questions you answered correctly?"

The word *percent* comes from the Latin root *percentum*, which means one part in 100. A percentage represents a quantity out of 100 and connects to fractions with a denominator of 100. For example, 52% can also be represented as $\frac{52}{100}$. It's not usually a challenge for students to figure out the percent when the fraction is already presented in hundredths, but in order for students to find an equivalent percentage with other fractions, they need to think about the ratio of the fraction to hundredths.

Let's say we ask students to solve for x in this problem:

$$\frac{1}{4} = \frac{x}{100} = x\%$$

To find this ratio, students must repartition a whole that is in fourths into one that is in hundredths. One way students have represented their solution to this problem is to draw two candy bars with both "wholes" or candy bars the same size. (See Figure 5–1.) Candy Bar A uses fractions, while Candy Bar B uses percentages.

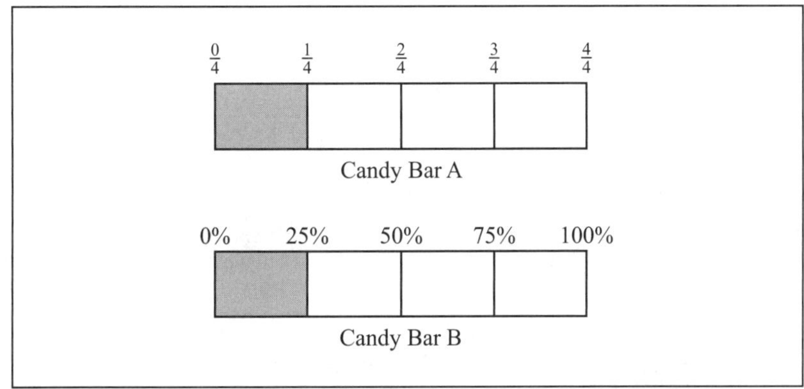

Figure 5–1. *Using Candy Bars to Represent Thinking About* $\frac{1}{4} = \frac{x}{100} = x\%$

As teachers, we can anticipate students may use their understanding that one-half of the candy bar would be the same as 50% and half of the half would be $\frac{1}{4}$ or 25%. Halves, fourths, and tenths are important benchmarks for fractions; these benchmarks serve as anchors for students as they think about percentages. Students can use these benchmarks to make relationships with common percentages such as 10%, 25%, and 50%. It is essential that we help students develop reasoning around benchmark fractions and the fractions' percent equivalents because this is a first step for learners in developing reasoning with percentages.

Let's look at how this reasoning may apply when we ask students to find a percentage of a whole number. Let's say we ask students to consider the following story problem.

The School Dance Problem

If the school needs $300 for the school dance and your class has to raise 25% of the money, how much money would your class need to raise?

Think about how students might divide 300 into fourths. Figure 5–2 shows a model students use to visualize how $300 can be partitioned into fourths and how $75 is equal to 25% of the money.

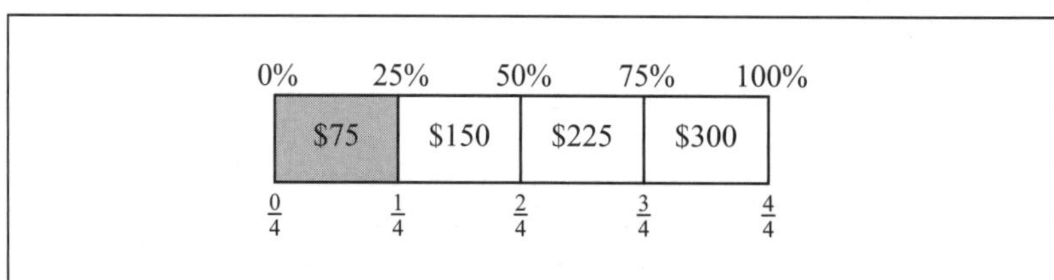

Figure 5–2. *Using an Area Model to Show Fraction and Percentage Equivalents for $300 ÷ 4*

The next example shows how benchmarks can be used to find 60% of $70. Students often reason that 50% of $70 would be $35 and 10% of

\$70 would be \$7, so 60% of \$70 would be \$35 + \$7 or \$42. In this way, students can use what they know (benchmarks) to figure out what they don't know. They could also represent their thinking using an area model. (See Figure 5–3.)

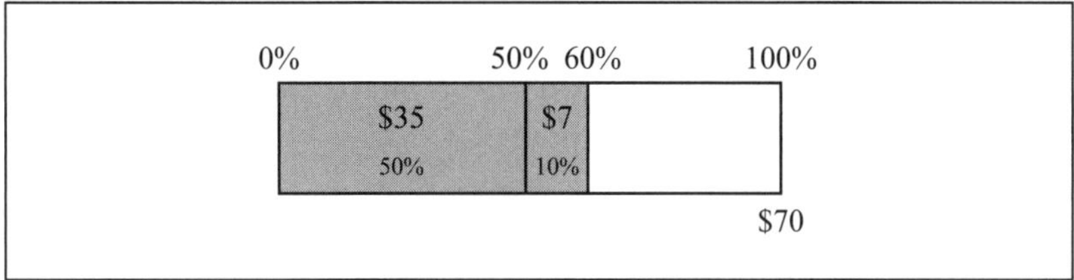

Figure 5–3. *Using an Area Model to Represent 60% of \$70*

This same strategy can be captured numerically to highlight the distributive property at work. (See Figure 5–4.)

$$
\begin{aligned}
&60\% \text{ of } \$70 \\
&= (50\% + 10\%) \times \$70 \\
&= (50\% \times \$70) + (10\% \times \$70) \\
&= \$35 + \$7 \\
&= \$42
\end{aligned}
$$

Figure 5–4. *Using the Distributive Property to Solve 60% of \$70*

Students also use unit fractions as benchmarks to find percentages. Think about how learners might write $\frac{4}{5}$ as a percentage. The standard procedure is to divide the 5 into the 4 until students have an answer in the hundredths place. By following this procedure, learners derive a quotient of 0.8, which converts into 0.80 or $\frac{80}{100}$ or 80%. In contrast, students who are fluent with unit fractions may solve this problem by thinking about how $\frac{1}{5}$ equals 20% and $\frac{4}{5}$ equals four times 20% or 80%. Figure 5–5 on the next page shows two ways students might explain their thinking for this problem.

Learn More...

Unit fractions are fractions where the numerator is 1. One-half, $\frac{1}{3}$, $\frac{1}{4}$, and $\frac{1}{10}$ are examples of unit fractions. Students often use unit fractions as benchmark numbers, or numbers that help them anchor their thinking and navigate through to a solution. See Chapter 4 for further discussion about unit and benchmark fractions.

What is the % equivalent of $\frac{4}{5}$?	
Student's Reasoning	**Recording**
Zoe: *I know $\frac{1}{5}$ of 100 is 20%. Since I need four $\frac{1}{5}$s, I need to multiply 20% times 4.*	$\frac{4}{5} = \_\_\_\_\_\%$ $\frac{1}{5} = 20\%$ $20\% \times 4 = 80\%$
Alice: *I thought about $\frac{4}{5}$ as four $\frac{1}{5}$s. Since $\frac{1}{5}$ is the same as 20%, I added 20% four times and got 80%.*	$\frac{4}{5} = \_\_\_\_\_\%$ $\frac{1}{5} + \frac{1}{5} + \frac{1}{5} + \frac{1}{5} = \frac{4}{5}$ $20\% + 20\% + 20\% + 20\% = 80\%$

Figure 5–5. *Using Unit Fractions to Solve $\frac{4}{5} = \_\_\_\_\_\%$*

$\frac{1}{4} \times \frac{1}{3}$: Connecting Fractions to Percentages

Classroom Clip 5.1

Consider the following questions as you watch this number talk from a fifth-grade classroom. The class just finished solving $\frac{1}{2} \times \frac{1}{3}$ and students arrived at $\frac{1}{6}$ and $16\frac{2}{3}\%$ as their answers.

1. What strategy is Ian using to solve $\frac{1}{4} \times \frac{1}{3}$?
2. What connections is Ian making between the two problems?
3. What connections is Ian making between percentages and fractions?
4. What is Seth's strategy for solving $\frac{1}{4} \times \frac{1}{3}$?
5. What does Seth know about multiplication of fractions?
6. What do you notice about the teacher's response when listening to and recording a student strategy that she had not thought of?

To view this video clip, scan the QR code or access via mathsolutions .com/NTFDP5.1

Category 1
Using Benchmark Fractions to Find Percentages

The number talk strings in this category are structured to help students compose and decompose benchmark numbers to make relationships between fractions and percentages. Each string is comprised of four problems.

Instructions

These number talks are organized into three columns and progress in difficulty going from the first column (from A to B to C) to the second column to the third column. Feel free to work through each string in order or choose problems according to your students' needs. You may choose to pose one problem or set of problems each day, or do more than one set of problems as time allows. Introduce the first problem in the string, collect solutions, then ask students to share their reasoning and proofs. Once the class reaches consensus, pose the second problem in the string and ask, *"How can you use what we already know to solve this next problem?"* Continue this format with each problem in the string.

What is the percentage equivalent of the fraction ______? How do you know?
How can you use what we already know to solve this next problem?

A. $\frac{1}{2}$ = ________%

$\frac{1}{4}$ = ________%

$\frac{3}{4}$ = ________%

$\frac{4}{4}$ = ________%

B. $\frac{1}{5}$ = ________%

$\frac{2}{5}$ = ________%

$\frac{4}{5}$ = ________%

$\frac{3}{5}$ = ________%

C. $\frac{1}{2}$ = ________%

$\frac{1}{4}$ = ________%

$\frac{1}{8}$ = ________%

$\frac{3}{8}$ = ________%

A. $\frac{1}{10}$ = ________%

$\frac{5}{10}$ = ________%

$\frac{3}{10}$ = ________%

$\frac{7}{10}$ = ________%

B. $\frac{1}{4}$ = ________%

$\frac{1}{8}$ = ________%

$\frac{5}{8}$ = ________%

$\frac{7}{8}$ = ________%

C. $\frac{1}{3}$ = ________%

$\frac{2}{3}$ = ________%

$\frac{1}{6}$ = ________%

$\frac{5}{6}$ = ________%

A. $\frac{2}{4}$ = ________%

$\frac{4}{4}$ = ________%

$\frac{5}{4}$ = ________%

$\frac{6}{4}$ = ________%

B. $\frac{1}{5}$ = ________%

$\frac{4}{5}$ = ________%

$\frac{6}{5}$ = ________%

$\frac{8}{5}$ = ________%

C. $\frac{1}{3}$ = ________%

$\frac{2}{3}$ = ________%

$\frac{4}{3}$ = ________%

$\frac{6}{3}$ = ________%

Category 2
Finding Percentages of Whole Numbers

The number talk strings in this category are structured to help students compose and decompose whole numbers to make relationships between fractions and percentages. Each string is comprised of four problems.

Instructions

These number talks progress in difficulty going from the first column (from A to B to C, etc.) to the second column to the third column. Feel free to work through each string in order or choose problems according to your students' needs. You may choose to pose one problem or set of problems each day, or do more than one set of problems as time allows. Introduce the first problem in the string, collect solutions, then ask students to share their reasoning and proofs. Once the class reaches consensus, pose the second problem in the string and ask, *"How can you use what we already know to solve this next problem?"* Continue this format with each problem in the string.

What is ______% of ______? How do you know? How can you use what we already know to solve this next problem?

A. 50% of 200

25% of 200

10% of 200

20% of 200

B. 10% of 50

20% of 50

50% of 50

75% of 50

C. 10% of 360

50% of 360

25% of 360

75% of 360

D. 10% of 72

50% of 72

25% of 72

$12\frac{1}{2}$% of 72

A. 1% of 200

10% of 200

12% of 200

15% of 200

B. 10% of 150

30% of 150

40% of 150

70% of 150

C. 20% of 240

40% of 240

60% of 240

80% of 240

D. 10% of 300

15% of 300

25% of 300

40% of 300

A. 100% of 75

200% of 75

300% of 75

400% of 75

B. 100% of 90

110% of 90

120% of 90

150% of 90

C. 100% of 50

125% of 50

150% of 50

200% of 50

D. 100% of 80

125% of 80

150% of 80

200% of 80

Number Talk Tip

You may choose to have students verbally share or physically place the numbers in order from least to greatest on a 0 to 2 number line. Determining the exact placement on a number line adds an additional challenge, because it requires students to repartition the number line and consider the relationship of the fraction or percentage to 0, 1, and 2. See Chapter 4, page 94, for number line suggestions.

Category 3
Comparing and Ordering Fractions and Percentages

Once students are comfortable moving flexibly between fractions and percentages, as teachers we should transition into comparing and ordering fractions and percentages. We can do this using number talks that incorporate both fractions and percentages.

Instructions

These number talks are organized into three columns. The first column uses several benchmark fractions and percentages. The second column provides numbers that are slightly removed from common benchmarks, and the third column uses numbers that are greater than one. Each number talk consists of four numbers, two fractions and two percentages. Feel free to work through each number talk in order (from A to B to C, etc.) or choose problems according to your students' needs. You may choose to pose one set of problems each day, or do more than one set of problems as time allows. Present all four numbers at the same time and ask students, *"How would you order these numbers from least to greatest? How do you know?"*

How would you order these numbers from least to greatest? How do you know?

A. $\frac{5}{6}$, 33%, 75%, $\frac{1}{2}$

B. $\frac{1}{3}$, 25%, $66\frac{2}{3}$%, $\frac{7}{8}$

C. $\frac{10}{16}$, 56%, $\frac{4}{5}$, 75%

D. 25%, $\frac{3}{4}$, 49%, $\frac{1}{5}$

A. $\frac{3}{8}$, 36%, $\frac{5}{16}$, 51%

B. 90%, $\frac{8}{9}$, $\frac{7}{8}$, 95%

C. $\frac{3}{5}$, 72%, $\frac{2}{3}$, 49%

D. $\frac{4}{5}$, 33%, $\frac{1}{8}$, 67%

A. $\frac{11}{9}$, 105%, $\frac{9}{11}$, 85%

B. 133%, $\frac{15}{12}$, 98%, $\frac{7}{8}$

C. 147%, $1\frac{6}{11}$, $\frac{11}{10}$, 155%

D. 180%, $1\frac{8}{9}$, $1\frac{3}{4}$, 99%

Number Talks That Connect Fractions to Decimals

The number talks in this section incorporate both fractions and decimals to keep the focus on fractional reasoning. When students reason with decimals as fractions, they are less likely to revert to whole number reasoning. Learners must have this understanding firmly in place before they transition to comparing decimals to decimals.

As teachers, we often give students several rules to follow when working with decimals. For example, we might ask students to compare decimals that have a different number of decimal places by just adding zeroes in order to make the number of decimal places equal. Similarly, we might tell students who are adding or subtracting decimals to "line up" the decimal points and "fill in" any gaps with zeros. Unfortunately, when we do this, students may then treat the computation as if all numbers are whole numbers. Consider the problem *0.5 – 0.064.*

$$\begin{array}{r} 0.5\underline{00} \\ -\ \underline{0.064} \end{array}$$

The shortcut of "just adding zeroes" masks the bigger ideas of place value and equivalence. Because of the identity property, 0.5 is actually being multiplied by $\frac{1000}{1000}$ to make an equivalent decimal fraction.

When students multiply and divide with decimals, they often learn to ignore the decimal points, treat everything as whole numbers, and then put the decimals back. Think about *0.7 ÷ 0.35*. Many of us were taught to move the decimal point in 0.35 over in order to divide by a whole number. Since we moved the decimal point over two places in the divisor, we also had to move the decimal over two places to the right in the dividend. Once we found the answer, we put the decimal point for the quotient in the same spot as the dividend. (See Figure 5–6.)

Step 1	Step 2
Change the number we are dividing by to a whole number by shifting the decimal point of both numbers to the right the same number of places. 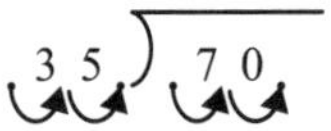 3 5) 7 0	*Put the decimal point for the quotient directly above the decimal point in the dividend.* 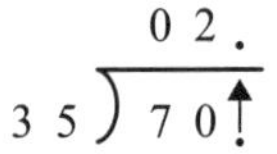 0 2 . 3 5) 7 0

Figure 5–6. *How Might These "Rules" Interfere with Students' Understanding of Dividing with Decimals?*

Following this rule for division of decimals works. However, it masks the bigger mathematical ideas of proportional reasoning and multiplying and dividing by powers of ten.

Learn More...

For more on social knowledge and logico-mathematical knowledge, see Chapter 1, pages 29–30.

The problem with asking students to memorize rules and follow procedures without developing their own understanding is that this approach treats these logical relationships as if they are social knowledge. Instead, because these relationships are based in logic, we have to help students construct these ideas for themselves. By posing questions such as "Will that always work? How are these two problems related? How did you know this was five-tenths instead of five?" we can help foster students' construction of those relationships.

Placing 0.9, 0.13, 0.255 on the Number Line: Connecting Fractions to Decimals

Classroom Clip 5.2

Consider the following questions as you watch this number talk from a sixth-grade classroom:

1. What strategy is Juli using to place 0.9 on the number line?
2. What strategy does the boy who disagrees with Makei use to decide where to place 0.255?
3. How would you characterize the exchange of ideas about where 0.255 belongs on the number line? What are the benefits of having students explain their thinking?
4. When Lauren is placing 0.255 on the board, why do you think the teacher asks, "Is there a way you could find out exactly what $\frac{1}{4}$ is?"
5. How does the teacher handle the incorrect placement of 0.13?
6. What do you notice about the use of precise mathematical language by the teacher and the students?

To view this video clip, scan the QR code or access via mathsolutions .com/NTFDP5.2

Number Talk Tip

You may choose to have students verbally share their solutions or physically place the numbers in order from least to greatest on a 0 to 2 number line. Determining the exact placement on a number line adds an additional challenge, because it requires students to repartition the number line and consider the relationship of the fraction or decimal to 0, 1, and 2. See Chapter 4, page 94, for number line suggestions.

Category 1
Comparing and Ordering Fractions and Decimals

Once students are comfortable moving flexibly between fractions and decimals, we should transition into comparing and ordering them interchangeably. We can do this using number talks that incorporate both fractions and decimals.

Instructions

These number talks are organized into three columns. The first column uses two benchmark numbers, each in fraction and decimal form; the second column provides numbers that are slightly removed from a common benchmark; and the third column uses numbers that are greater than one as well as less than one. Each number talk consists of four numbers, two decimals and two fractions. Feel free to work through the number talks in order (from A to B to C, etc.) or choose problems according to your students' needs. You may choose to pose one problem or set of problems each day, or do more than one set of problems as time allows. Write all four numbers on the board and ask students, *"How would you order these numbers from least to greatest? How do you know?"*

How would you order these numbers from least to greatest? How do you know?

A. $\frac{1}{4}$, 0.34, $\frac{7}{8}$, 0.75

B. $\frac{3}{4}$, 0.60, $\frac{2}{3}$, 0.48

C. $\frac{4}{5}$, 0.90, $\frac{5}{6}$, 0.78

D. $\frac{6}{10}$, 0.54, $\frac{2}{3}$, 0.06

E. $\frac{1}{4}$, 0.34, $\frac{7}{8}$, 0.75

F. $\frac{3}{4}$, 0.60, $\frac{2}{3}$, 0.48

A. $\frac{13}{14}$, 0.9, $\frac{5}{8}$, 0.7

B. $\frac{12}{15}$, 1.01, $\frac{9}{10}$, 0.88

C. $\frac{25}{75}$, 0.39, $\frac{1}{4}$, 0.28

D. $\frac{13}{15}$, 0.60, $\frac{8}{10}$, 0.89

E. $\frac{27}{50}$, 0.34, $\frac{30}{40}$, 0.66

F. $\frac{33}{60}$, 0.45, $\frac{22}{33}$, 0.6

A. $\frac{26}{25}$, 1.4, $\frac{8}{5}$, 1.38

B. $\frac{17}{16}$, 1.55, $\frac{15}{12}$, 1.06

C. $\frac{5}{12}$, 0.499, $\frac{6}{10}$, 0.5

D. $1\frac{5}{8}$, 1.62, $\frac{11}{7}$, 1.5

E. 1.09, $\frac{13}{11}$, 1.3, $\frac{7}{5}$

F. $1\frac{3}{10}$, 1.03, $\frac{12}{11}$, 1.15

Category 2
Comparing Decimals to Decimals

A challenge students face when comparing decimals is simultaneously considering density and equivalence. The number talks in this category use decimals that are close to common benchmark numbers to help students confront these ideas.

Number Talk Tip

You may choose to have students verbally share their solutions or physically place the numbers in order from least to greatest on a 0 to 2 number line. Determining the exact placement on a number line adds an additional challenge, because it requires students to repartition the number line and consider the relationship of each decimal to 0, 1, and 2. See Chapter 4, page 94, for number line suggestions.

Instructions

These number talks are organized into three columns. The first column uses decimals ranging from tenths to hundredths; the second column uses decimals ranging from tenths to thousandths; and the third column uses decimals ranging from thousandths to numbers greater than one. Each number talk consists of three decimals. Feel free to work through each number talk in order (from A to B to C, etc.) or choose problems according to your students' needs. You may choose to use one number talk each day, or more than one as time allows. Write all three decimals on the board and ask students, *"How would you order these numbers from least to greatest? How do you know?"*

How would you order these numbers from least to greatest? How do you know?

A.	0.1	0.10	0.01
B.	0.5	0.05	0.50
C.	0.5	0.48	0.06
D.	0.7	0.51	0.08
E.	0.16	0.4	0.08
F.	0.200	0.21	0.02

A.	0.340	0.5	0.042
B.	0.79	0.7	0.689
C.	0.125	0.3	0.205
D.	0.250	0.25	0.209
E.	0.38	0.4	0.291
F.	0.056	0.05	0.1

A.	1.500	1.5	1.50
B.	1.12	1.59	1.2
C.	1.08	1.092	1.1
D.	1.225	1.3	1.024
E.	1.8	1.753	1.64
F.	1.034	1.304	1.296

Number Talk Tip

You may choose to have students verbally share their solutions or physically place the numbers in order from least to greatest on a 0 to 2 number line. Determining the exact placement on a number line adds an additional challenge, because it requires students to repartition the number line and consider the relationship of each decimal to 0, 1, and 2. See Chapter 4, page 94, for number line suggestions.

Number Talks That Connect Fractions, Decimals, and Percentages

The final number talks in this chapter offer opportunities for students to think about fractions, decimals, and percentages collectively.

Instructions

These number talks are organized into three columns. The first column uses some benchmark numbers; the second column provides numbers that are slightly removed from a common benchmark; and the third column uses numbers that are greater than one. Each number talk consists of four numbers. Feel free to work through each number talk in order (from A to B to C, etc.) or choose problems according to your students' needs. You may choose to pose one problem each day, or more than one as time allows. Write all four numbers on the board and ask students, *"How would you order these numbers from least to greatest? How do you know?"*

How would you order these numbers from least to greatest? How do you know?

A. 10%, $\frac{1}{4}$, 0.1, 20%

B. 25%, $\frac{1}{3}$, 0.5, 36%

C. 0.7, $\frac{3}{4}$, 60%, 0.52

D. 0.75, $\frac{5}{6}$, $\frac{2}{3}$, 60%

E. 67%, $\frac{3}{4}$, 0.7, $\frac{3}{5}$

F. $\frac{4}{5}$, 0.7, 75%, $\frac{7}{8}$

A. $\frac{11}{12}$, 0.85, 8%, 0.9

B. 0.56, $\frac{6}{12}$, $\frac{2}{3}$, 0.8

C. 0.395, $\frac{3}{10}$, 31%, $\frac{1}{3}$

D. $\frac{25}{52}$, 0.9, $\frac{6}{7}$, 0.52

E. 0.625, 58%, $\frac{2}{3}$, 0.508

F. 39%, $\frac{3}{8}$, 0.315, $\frac{4}{9}$

A. 160%, $1\frac{3}{5}$, 1.4, $1\frac{5}{8}$

B. 115%, 1.2, $1\frac{1}{8}$, 133%

C. 1.9, 1.892, 189%, $1\frac{9}{10}$

D. 1.34, $1\frac{39}{80}$, 130%, 1.4

E. $1\frac{7}{8}$, 1.805, $1\frac{11}{12}$, 181%

F. 1.56, $1\frac{2}{3}$, 160%, 1.6

Looking Ahead

In this chapter, we have looked at ways to help students deepen their fractional reasoning by considering the relationships among fractions, decimals, and percentages. As you use fractions, decimals, and percentages in your number talks, what shifts in your students' thinking do you notice? How are they thinking flexibly and using fractional reasoning when they encounter decimals and percentages? In Chapter 6, we offer number talks for addition with fractions, explore big ideas to consider when adding fractions, and offer student-invented strategies for adding fractions.

Connecting the Chapter to Your Practice

1. What have you noticed about your students' thinking that gives you insight as to whether they use fractional understanding when they are working with decimals and percentages?
2. How do you think your students might solve some of the number talk problems on page 121?
3. What do you anticipate your students might do when comparing some of the fractions and percentages in the number talks on page 124?
4. Look at Figure 5–6 on page 126. How might "rules" for dividing decimals interfere with students' fractional understanding?
5. What evidence will you be listening for to know if a student is using the standard algorithm for dividing decimals with understanding?
6. What strategies do you anticipate students will use as they compare and order fractions, decimals, and percentages?

Section III

Number Talks to Help Students Operate with Fractions and Decimals

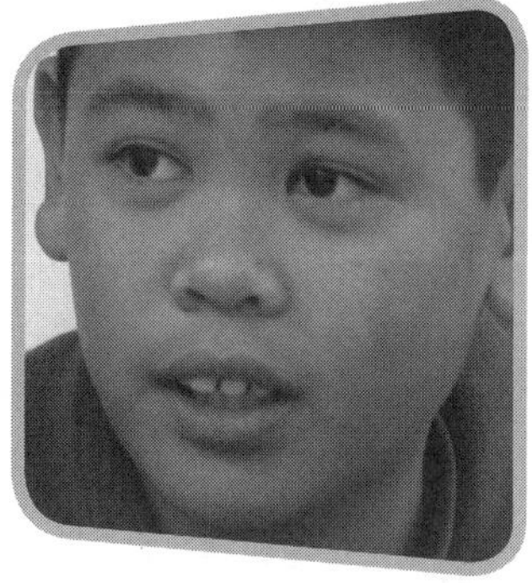

CHAPTER 6

Number Talks for Addition with Fractions

In this chapter, we offer a place for teachers to start when planning number talks around the addition of fractions. In the opening sections, we discuss how the use of number talks is helpful as students work to develop addition strategies. We then explore and offer number talks that are focused on helping learners build their understanding of adding fractions. We highly recommend that students are solid and flexible in their fractional reasoning (see Chapter 4) before using the number talks in this chapter.

OVERVIEW

(Continued)

How Number Talks Help the Development of Addition Strategies with Fractions

Three big ideas are key to understanding addition of fractions:

- Understanding fractions as distinct numbers,
- Knowing what it means for fractions to be equivalent to one another, and
- Recognizing what happens when fractions are combined.

Anticipating our students' strategies and potential misconceptions when they attempt to add fractions can help us facilitate discussions and guide our questions during number talks. One common misconception students have when adding fractions is that they treat the numerators and denominators as separate whole numbers. When they see an addition sign, they add the numerators together and then add the denominators together.

Learn More...

For more about inappropriate whole number reasoning, see Chapter 3, pages 64–66.

In a study of Algebra I students (N = 143) in a middle- to upper-class high school with 81 percent of the students having strong parent support, nearly 48 percent of the students tested could not find the sum of $\frac{5}{12}+\frac{3}{8}$. An analysis of their misconceptions showed that the most common errors were (1) not being able to find a common denominator, and (2) adding the numerators and adding the denominators (Brown and Quinn 2006).

Depending on what grade you teach, your students may already know the standard U.S. algorithm for adding fractions: make common denominators, add the numerators, and keep the common denominators. (Even without instruction in this algorithm, many students invent this strategy when they are fluent in making equivalent fractions.) In fact, using common denominators is an efficient, generalizable way of solving a problem. However, if we focus our efforts solely on teaching procedures, students can miss the big idea of reasoning with fractions. They may follow the "rules" without ever thinking about the fractional relationships involved, or they may simply wonder why keeping the denominators the same works for adding and subtracting fractions, but not for multiplying or dividing them. This is where the importance of number talks comes into play: Number talks help students focus on developing strategies to build their understanding of adding fractions.

Specifically, there are approaches we can take during a number talk to support students in inventing and developing strategies—and thus deepen their understanding of mathematics. These approaches include the following:

- Making connections to strategies for adding whole numbers
- Making connections to the arithmetic properties
- Using story problems
- Using models
- Connecting students' strategies

Each of these approaches is discussed in more detail in the sections that follow.

Learn More...

Students can invent their own strategies because of the mental relationships they make. Mental relationships are based on logico-mathematical knowledge, which is a foundational principle of number talks. See "Know When to Ask and When to Tell" in Chapter 1 for a more detailed explanation of Piaget's three types of knowledge.

Making Connections to Strategies for Adding Whole Numbers

Many of the strategies that students have developed for adding whole numbers also work for adding fractions. Before presenting your students with addition problems that include fractions, start with addition problems with whole numbers. This provides an opportunity for the class to confront misconceptions about addition and revisit effective addition strategies. The more fluent that students are with whole number strategies and the better they are at composing and decomposing fractions, the more flexible they will be in their strategies for adding fractions.

For example, during a number talk, one way a student might solve the problem $36 + 19$ is to make the second addend into a friendlier number, changing the problem to $36 + 20 = 56$. Then the student subtracts the extra 1 that was added on to 19 and gets a final answer of 55. Similarly, with the problem $\frac{4}{9} + \frac{8}{9}$, a student might change the problem to $\frac{4}{9} + 1 = 1\frac{4}{9}$ and then subtract the extra $\frac{1}{9}$ that was added to $\frac{8}{9}$ so the answer is $1\frac{3}{9}$. (See Figure 6–1.)

Using Benchmarks to Add Whole Numbers	Using Benchmarks to Add Fractions
$36 + 19$	$\frac{4}{9} + \frac{8}{9}$
$36 + 20 = 56$	$\frac{4}{9} + 1 = 1\frac{4}{9}$
$56 - 1 = 55$	$1\frac{4}{9} - \frac{1}{9} = 1\frac{3}{9}$

Figure 6–1. *Making Connections to Strategies for Computing with Whole Numbers*

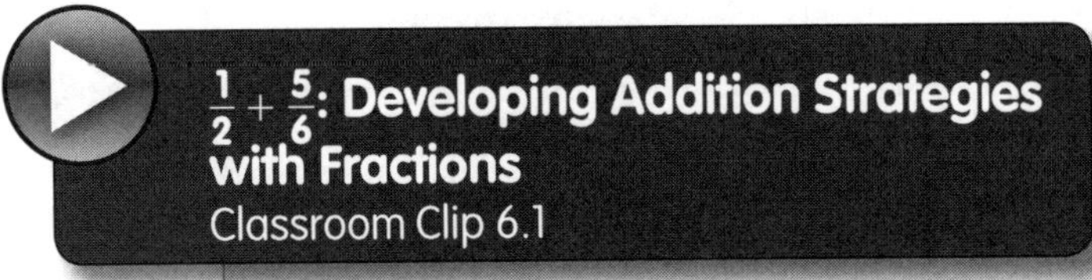

$\frac{1}{2} + \frac{5}{6}$: Developing Addition Strategies with Fractions
Classroom Clip 6.1

Consider the following questions as you watch this number talk from a fourth-grade classroom:

1. What are some advantages of collecting answers before asking students to explain their thinking?
2. What do you notice about the recording that the teacher uses for Mia's solution and Pierce's solution (Solutions 2 and 3)?
3. What questions might you ask if you wanted to help students notice the associative property at work in the solutions?
4. Where in this number talk do you notice the teacher helping students to think more about equivalence?

To view this video clip, scan the QR code or access via mathsolutions .com/NTFDP6.1

Making Connections to the Arithmetic Properties

Many of us learned about the arithmetic properties, including the commutative and associative properties, by memorizing definitions and matching vocabulary terms to examples. You may remember learning about the commutative property of addition as this:

for all real numbers a and b, $a + b = b + a$

When students rearrange the addends in a problem knowing they will still get the same answer, they are using the commutative property. For example, students might add $\frac{1}{8} + \frac{7}{8}$ to get 1, or they might think of the problem as $\frac{7}{8} + \frac{1}{8}$ and still get 1 as the answer.

Students who make a problem easier to solve by rearranging the way addends are originally grouped are using the associative property. We can represent the associative property of addition algebraically like this:

for all real numbers a, b, and c, $(a + b) + c = a + (b + c)$

For example, $\left(\frac{3}{4} + \frac{5}{8}\right) + \frac{3}{8}$ could also be solved as $\frac{3}{4} + \left(\frac{5}{8} + \frac{3}{8}\right) = \frac{3}{4} + 1 = 1\frac{3}{4}$. As students invent strategies, they are often using the properties of arithmetic. When as teachers we bring out the properties of mathematics in a number talk and connect it to the thinking students are already doing, we create opportunities to help them deepen their understanding of mathematics.

We can highlight the properties during number talks by thoughtfully recording and facilitating discussions that attach students' thinking to the properties. Consider the problem $\frac{5}{7} + \frac{4}{7}$. Some students will decompose the $\frac{4}{7}$ into $\frac{2}{7} + \frac{2}{7}$ and "give" one of the $\frac{2}{7}$ to the $\frac{5}{7}$ to make a whole. There could be two ways to record these students' strategies. (See Figure 6–2 on the next page.) While both are correct recordings, the second recording highlights the associative property.

Recording Without Highlighting the Associative Property	Recording to Highlight the Associative Property
$\frac{5}{7} + \frac{4}{7}$ $+\frac{2}{7} \quad -\frac{2}{7}$ $\frac{7}{7} + \frac{2}{7} = 1\frac{2}{7}$	$\frac{5}{7} + \frac{4}{7}$ $= \frac{5}{7} + \left(\frac{2}{7} + \frac{2}{7}\right)$ $= \left(\frac{5}{7} + \frac{2}{7}\right) + \frac{2}{7}$ $= \frac{7}{7} + \frac{2}{7}$ $= 1\frac{2}{7}$

Figure 6–2. *Recording to Highlight the Associative Property*

The strategy that students use to solve a problem is an example of logico-mathematical knowledge and is something students have to invent for themselves. What you call the strategy, how you might record it, and the name of the property that makes it work, however, are examples of social knowledge. The following dialogue shows a teacher distinguishing between logico-mathematical knowledge and social knowledge by the way he knows when to ask a question and when to tell during the number talk. He is connecting the mathematical term *associative property* (the social knowledge) to student thinking (logico-mathematical knowledge) as the class approaches the problem $\frac{5}{7} + \frac{4}{7}$. Because labels and symbols are social knowledge, we can tell students the names of properties, what mathematical symbols mean, and how to record their strategies.

Learn More...

Knowing when to ask and when to tell—based on what kind of knowledge you are dealing with—is one of the four foundational principals of number talks. For a more detailed explanation of Piaget's different kinds of knowledge, see Chapter 1.

Inside the Classroom

A Number Talk for $\frac{5}{7} + \frac{4}{7}$

Mr. Westbrook: What was it about Avery's strategy that made this an easier problem to solve?

Carla: She split the $\frac{4}{7}$ into $\left(\frac{2}{7} + \frac{2}{7}\right)$ and then moved one of the $\frac{2}{7}$ from the $\frac{4}{7}$ to the $\frac{5}{7}$. That changed the problem into $1 + \frac{2}{7}$ which is $1\frac{2}{7}$. It doesn't change the answer if you just change the way the numbers are grouped.

Mr. Westbrook: When we change the way the numbers are grouped in an addition problem, mathematicians call this the *associative property of addition.* Do you think it will always work? Let's do some more number talks so we can try this out on other problems.

Using Story Problems

Another way we can help learners develop a more complete understanding of what it means to add is to situate number talks within a story problem context. A context gives students an entry point for developing strategies and helps students make sense of the question the problem is asking and what the numbers mean in relationship to the problem. Consider the difference between posing the problem $\frac{1}{3} + \frac{1}{4}$ as a stand-alone problem or presenting it framed as a story problem. (See Figure 6–3 on the next page.)

Presenting a Problem in Isolation	Presenting a Problem in a Story Context
$\frac{1}{3}+\frac{1}{4}$	*There are 12 pieces of candy in a box. One-third of the candies have a cream filling and $\frac{1}{4}$ of the candies have caramel filling. The remaining candies have no filling. What fraction of the candies have filling?*
$\frac{1}{4}+\frac{1}{2}$	*Maleah gave $\frac{1}{4}$ of the pan of brownies to Rusty and $\frac{1}{2}$ of the pan of brownies to Taylor. What fraction of the pan of brownies did she give away?*
$1\frac{1}{2}+\frac{3}{10}$	*Esther walked $1\frac{1}{2}$ miles to the park and then $\frac{3}{10}$ of a mile to her friend's house. How far did Esther walk?*

Figure 6–3. *Presenting a Problem in Isolation Versus in a Story Context*

Learn More...

For more on the use of story problems in building fractional reasoning, see Chapter 4, page 73.

Framing a computation problem in a story context does not mean showing students a written version of the story problem. Instead, write the computation problem as you present the story context orally. It is the context that helps students bring meaning to the numbers in the problem and visualize the action of the operation, and it gives them a framework for evaluating the reasonableness of their answers.

Using Models

In addition to using a story problem, teachers can incorporate models during a number talk to (1) provide a visual context, (2) support a story problem, and (3) represent a student's strategy.

Using a model along with a story problem can provide additional support for students to understand what a problem is asking and to develop strategies to find a solution. It is one thing to talk about a box of candy or a carton of eggs, but it is another thing to be able to see a representation of the candy or the eggs to provide a framework for thinking. Consider the story problem in Figure 6–4 for $\frac{1}{3}+\frac{1}{4}$. If we use a set model to represent the candy along with giving the story problem verbally, this gives some students an additional entry point for partitioning the set into thirds and fourths and considering the result of combining these two fractions. (See Figure 6–4.)

Presenting a Problem in Isolation	Presenting a Problem in a Story Context	Presenting a Problem with a Set Model
$\frac{1}{3}+\frac{1}{4}$	*There are 12 pieces of candy in a box. One-third of the candies have cream filling and $\frac{1}{4}$ of the candies have caramel filling. The remaining candies have no filling. What fraction of the candies have filling?*	

Figure 6–4. *Presenting a Problem in Isolation Versus in a Story Context and with a Set Model*

During a number talk, we can record a student's mental strategy with both a model and a numerical recording. The following "Inside the Classroom" excerpt illustrates two examples of a teacher's recording to represent different ways students used the same mental strategy for adding $\frac{1}{2}+\frac{5}{6}$. Each student *decomposed to make a benchmark*, but one student thought about the problem using an area model, and the other student thought about using a linear model.

Inside the Classroom

A Number Talk for $\frac{1}{2}+\frac{5}{6}$

Gabriel: I pictured 2 rectangles divided into sixths. One-half was shaded in the first rectangle and $\frac{5}{6}$ of the second rectangle was shaded.

[Ms. Vu draws and shades $\frac{1}{2}$ and $\frac{5}{6}$.]

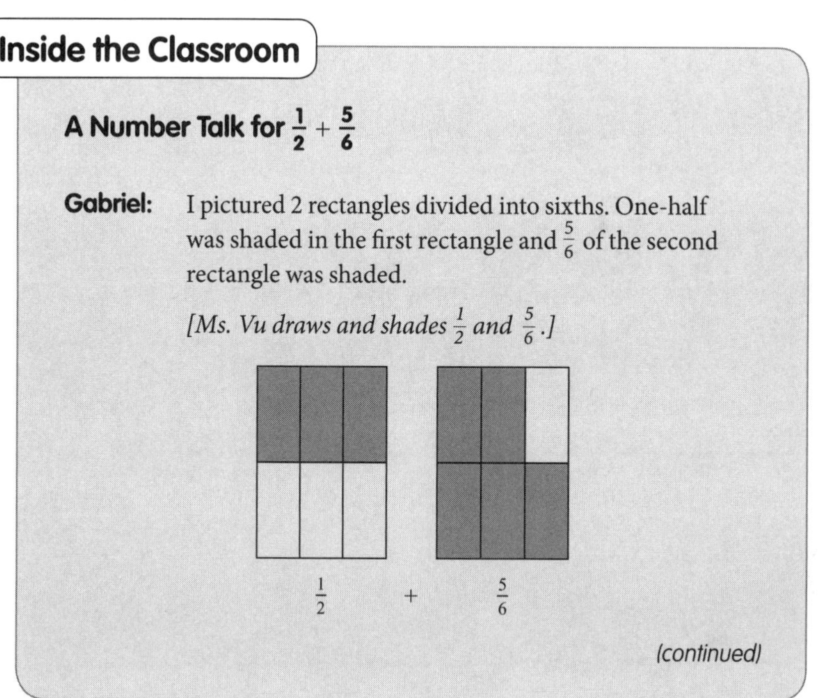

(continued)

Gabriel: Then I moved $\frac{3}{6}$ from the second rectangle to the first rectangle to make 1 whole.

[Ms. Vu circles the $\frac{3}{6}$ in $\frac{5}{6}$ and draws an arrow to indicate it is "moved" to the first rectangle to make 1 whole.]

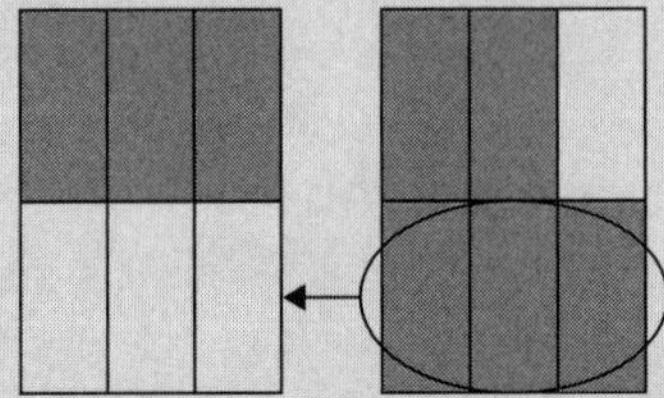

That left $\frac{2}{6}$ or $\frac{1}{3}$ in the second rectangle, so my answer was $1\frac{1}{3}$.

[Ms. Vu labels each rectangle accordingly.]

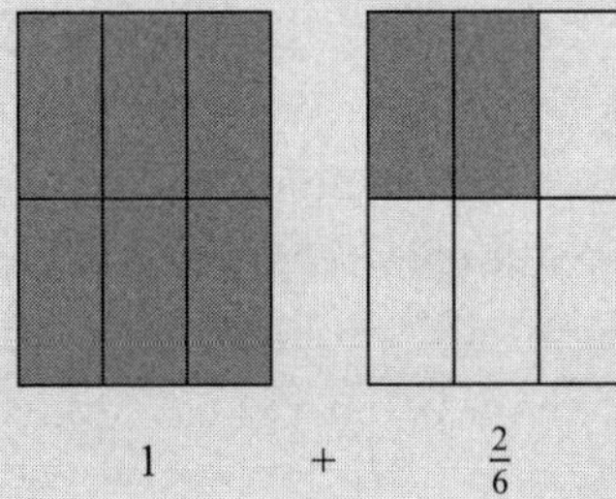

Ms. Vu: Gabriel, does this recording match your thinking?

$$\frac{1}{2} + \frac{5}{6}$$

$$= \frac{1}{2} + \left(\frac{3}{6} + \frac{2}{6}\right)$$

$$= \left(\frac{1}{2} + \frac{3}{6}\right) + \frac{2}{6}$$

$$= 1 + \frac{2}{6} = 1\frac{1}{3}$$

Jackie: I used the same strategy but I thought about the problem using a number line. I started at $\frac{1}{2}$, and I added $\frac{3}{6}$ or $\frac{1}{2}$ more to get 1 whole.

[Ms. Vu draws a 0 to 2 number line to show adding $\frac{3}{6}$ to $\frac{1}{2}$ to get to 1 whole.]

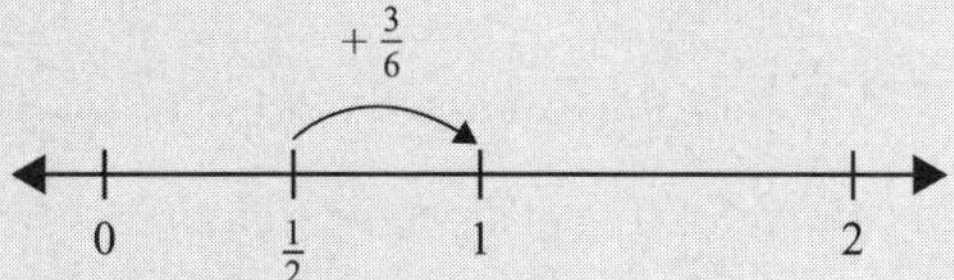

I had $\frac{2}{6}$ left to add, so I jumped $\frac{2}{6}$ more and got to $1\frac{2}{6}$. My answer is $1\frac{2}{6}$ or $1\frac{1}{3}$.

[Ms. Vu shows another jump of $\frac{2}{6}$.]

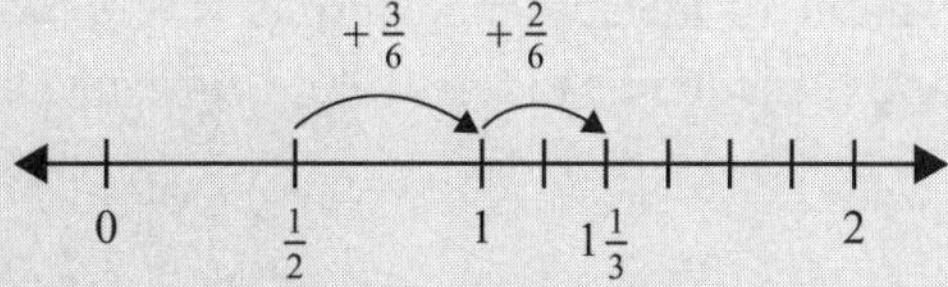

[Ms. Vu points to Gabriel's numerical recording:]

$$\frac{1}{2}+\frac{5}{6}$$

$$=\frac{1}{2}+\left(\frac{3}{6}+\frac{2}{6}\right)$$

$$=\left(\frac{1}{2}+\frac{3}{6}\right)+\frac{2}{6}$$

$$=1+\frac{2}{6}=1\frac{1}{3}$$

Ms. Vu (to the class): Does this recording show Jackie's thinking, too?

Connecting Students' Strategies

During number talks, if students have developed several different strategies for solving problems and are becoming confident in using different strategies, you can begin to include discussions about similarities and differences among strategies—and eventually, about which strategies different students find more efficient. Pose questions such as these.

- *How are Monique's strategy and Ty's strategy the same?*
- *What do you notice that is different about these two ideas?*
- *Is there a strategy that seems easier to you? Turn and talk to a partner about why it is easier for you.*

When students are listening to and discussing other students' strategies during a number talk, they are *constructing viable arguments and critiquing the reasoning of others* (MP3).

Try to make space to keep each strategy posted; this will help students compare strategies more easily. You can also label each strategy with a number or the name of the students who used it, which will make it easier for you and the students to refer to the different strategies.

Number Talks That Use Area Models for Addition with Fractions

As emphasized earlier, models give students an entry point for developing strategies and finding a solution. We can use area models in beginning number talks to support students as they think about equivalence, decomposing addends to compose benchmark fractions, and what it means to add fractions. For example, show students the following model and expression and ask, *"How could you combine these quantities to find the sum?"*

> **Number Talk Tip**
>
> An important part of a number talk involves making students' thinking public and accessible to other students. We can record a student's strategy numerically, but supporting the ideas with a model may help other students follow and understand another learner's thinking.

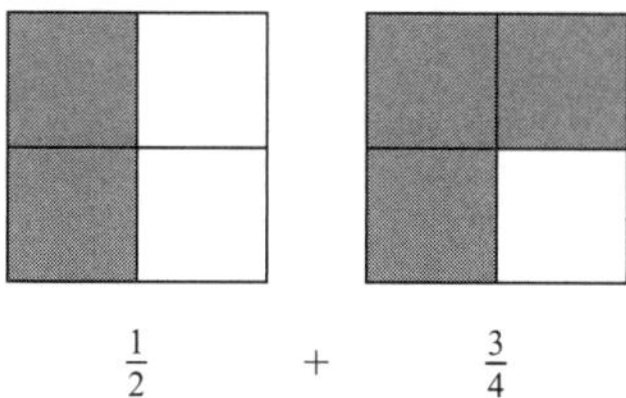

$$\frac{1}{2} \quad + \quad \frac{3}{4}$$

In addition to presenting the problem using the area model, you might also incorporate a story context, such as, *"Juan ate $\frac{1}{2}$ of a brownie and then ate $\frac{3}{4}$ of another brownie. How many brownies did Juan eat?"*

There are multiple ways the problem can be solved. Students might solve this problem and get an answer of $1\frac{1}{4}$ by taking any of the approaches shown in Figure 6–5.

Student's Strategy and Reasoning	Recording
Decomposing to Make a Benchmark Number Annie: *I moved $\frac{2}{4}$ over from $\frac{3}{4}$ and put it with the $\frac{1}{2}$ to make a whole brownie. Then I knew that Juan had eaten $1\frac{1}{4}$ brownies.*	$\frac{1}{2}+\frac{3}{4}$ $=\frac{1}{2}+\left(\frac{2}{4}+\frac{1}{4}\right)$ $=\left(\frac{1}{2}+\frac{2}{4}\right)+\frac{1}{4}$ $=1\frac{1}{4}$

Figure 6–5. *Using "Decomposing to Make a Benchmark Number" to Solve $\frac{1}{2}+\frac{3}{4}$ (continued)*

Student's Strategy and Reasoning	Recording
Decomposing to Make a Benchmark Number Jordan: *I counted the number of fourths and I got $\frac{5}{4}$ or 1 whole and $\frac{1}{4}$ brownies.*	$\frac{1}{2}+\frac{3}{4}$ $\left(\frac{1}{4}+\frac{1}{4}\right)+\left(\frac{1}{4}+\frac{1}{4}+\frac{1}{4}\right)$ $\frac{1}{4}+\frac{1}{4}+\frac{1}{4}+\frac{1}{4}+\frac{1}{4}=\frac{5}{4}=1\frac{1}{4}$
Decomposing to Make a Benchmark Number Kaj: *I moved $\frac{1}{4}$ over from $\frac{1}{2}$ to make a whole brownie and then I had $\frac{1}{4}$ left and so he ate $1\frac{1}{4}$ brownies.*	$\frac{1}{2}+\frac{3}{4}$ $=\left(\frac{1}{4}+\frac{1}{4}\right)+\frac{3}{4}$ $=\frac{1}{4}+\left(\frac{1}{4}+\frac{3}{4}\right)$ $=\frac{1}{4}+1$ $=1\frac{1}{4}$

Figure 6–5. *(continued)*

As students share solutions during the number talk, listen for any confusion around what the denominator means. For instance, some students might look at the model for the problem $\frac{1}{2}+\frac{3}{4}$ on the previous page and—rather than thinking about two wholes divided into fourths—may incorrectly think that each part represents $\frac{1}{8}$ and give an answer of $\frac{5}{8}$. You can bring the conversation back to a story problem (in this case, the brownie context) to help confront this misconception. Also consider asking students questions such as these:

- *How many parts is each brownie divided into?*
- *What if Juan ate $\frac{3}{4}$ of one brownie and then only $\frac{1}{4}$ of the other brownie? How many fourths would he have eaten?*

Asking students to consider key questions like these helps them redefine the "whole" in the problem.

Are the Addends Equal to 1? Using Area Models with Addition of Fractions

Classroom Clip 6.2

The problem in this video clip comes from a game called *Cover Up* that the students had played the day before. The previous day students generated problems that they thought would equal 1. As this clip begins, the teacher has put two of the problems on the board and is asking students to decide whether the addends are actually equal to 1.

Consider the following questions as you watch this number talk from a third-grade classroom:

1. What does Brittany know that is helping her to solve this problem?
2. What strategy is Brooke using to solve this problem?
3. What are some advantages of using a model as part of the context for this problem?
4. If you were going to record the strategy that the boy in the green shirt is using, what would you write?
5. What does Grace know that is helping her to solve this problem?
6. What mathematics do you notice in Avery's strategy?
7. What other mathematics could you pull from this number talk?

To view this video clip, scan the QR code or access via mathsolutions .com/NTFDP6.2

Category 1
Using Area Models Partitioned into Common Denominators

Each number talk string in this category is structured to help students think about equivalence, decomposing fractions to add, and the relationship between halves, fourths, and eighths. Each problem comprises two wholes that are partitioned into common denominators. The addition problems use fractions with denominators that are multiples of each other. The area models are partitioned into the larger denominator, and the models are shaded to represent each addend.

Instructions

These number talk strings progress in difficulty (from A to B to C, etc.). Feel free to work through each string in order or choose problems according to your students' needs. You may choose to pose one problem or set of problems each day, or do more than one set of problems as time allows. Introduce the first problem in the string, collect solutions, then ask students to share their reasoning and proofs. Once the class reaches consensus, pose the second problem in the string and ask, *"How can you use what we already know to solve this next problem?"* Continue this format with each problem in the string.

Number Talk Tip

As you present each problem, consider using various story contexts to deepen students' understanding of adding fractions. Using a model to represent students' ideas will also allow you to provide them with another layer of support.

How can you solve ______ + ______?
How can you use what we already know to solve this next problem?

A. $\frac{1}{2} + \frac{1}{2}$ $\frac{1}{4} + \frac{1}{4}$ $\frac{1}{2} + \frac{1}{4}$

B. $\frac{1}{2} + \frac{1}{4}$ $\frac{1}{2} + \frac{1}{8}$ $\frac{1}{4} + \frac{1}{8}$

C. $\frac{1}{8} + \frac{1}{8}$ $\frac{1}{8} + \frac{3}{8}$ $\frac{3}{8} + \frac{3}{8}$

D. $\frac{1}{2} + \frac{1}{4}$ $\frac{1}{2} + \frac{3}{4}$ $\frac{3}{4} + \frac{3}{4}$

(continued)

Reproducible 3

For full-sized reproducibles of these number talks, visit www.mathsolutions.com /numbertalksfdp_reproducibles.

(How can you solve _____ + _____? How can you use what we already know to solve this next problem?, continued)

E.

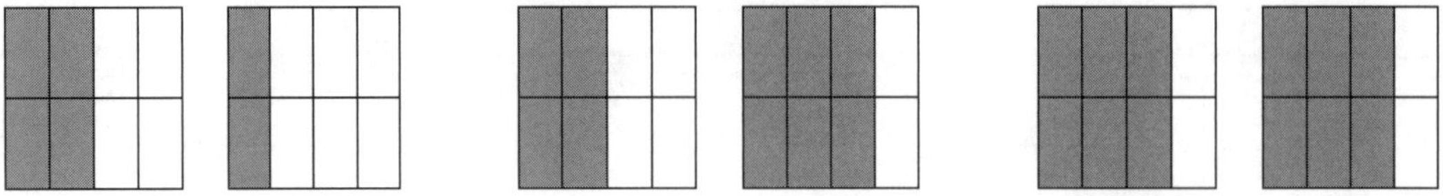

$\frac{1}{2} + \frac{1}{4}$ $\frac{1}{2} + \frac{3}{4}$ $\frac{6}{8} + \frac{3}{4}$

F.

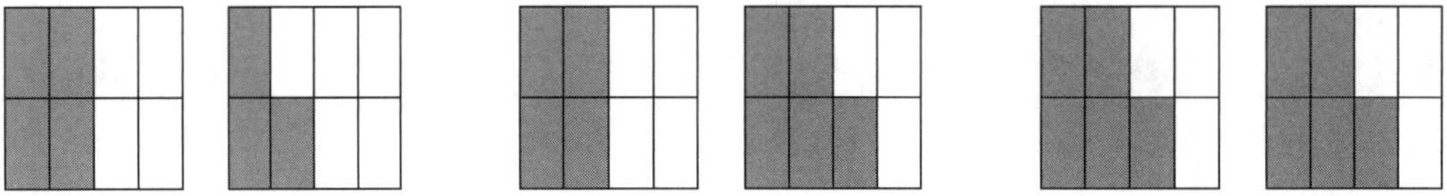

$\frac{1}{2} + \frac{3}{8}$ $\frac{1}{2} + \frac{5}{8}$ $\frac{5}{8} + \frac{5}{8}$

G.

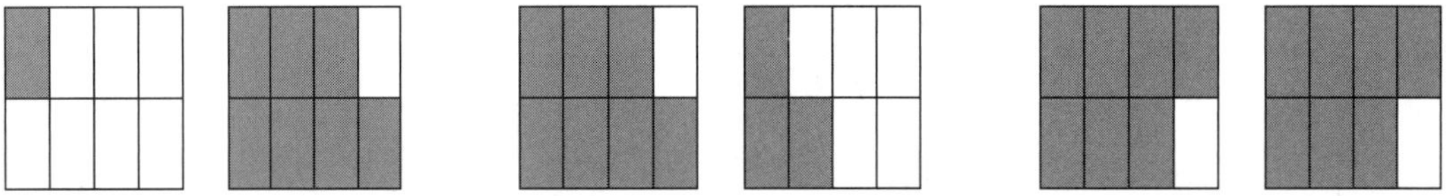

$\frac{1}{8} + \frac{7}{8}$ $\frac{7}{8} + \frac{3}{8}$ $\frac{7}{8} + \frac{7}{8}$

H.

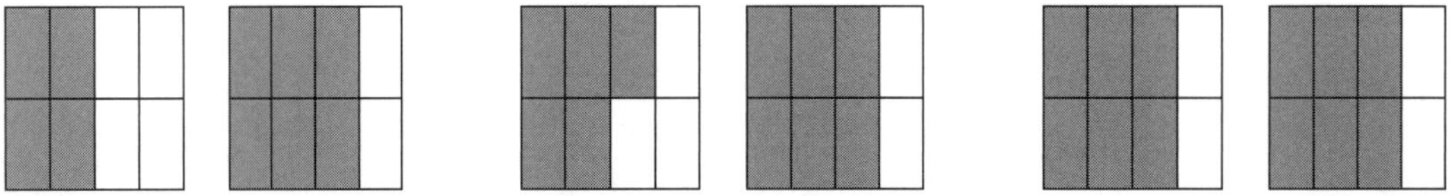

$\frac{4}{8} + \frac{6}{8}$ $\frac{5}{8} + \frac{6}{8}$ $\frac{6}{8} + \frac{6}{8}$

Category 2
Using Area Models Requiring Partitioning

The number talk strings in this category are structured to help students reason about equivalence and decomposing fractions to add. Each problem comprises two wholes that are partitioned into different denominators that have a multiplicative relationship.

Instructions

These number talk strings progress in difficulty (from A to B to C, etc.). Feel free to work through each string in order or choose problems according to your students' needs. You may choose to pose one problem or set of problems each day, or do more than one set of problems as time allows. Introduce the first problem in the string, collect solutions, then ask students to share their reasoning and proofs. Once the class reaches consensus, pose the second problem in the string and ask, *"How can you use what we already know to solve this next problem?"* Continue this format with each problem in the string.

Learn More . . .

An essential part of a number talk is accepting, respecting, and considering all answers whether correct or incorrect and allowing students to defend their thinking. For more information about the ten essentials for number talks, see Chapter 2.

How can you solve ______ + ______?
How can you use what we already know to solve this next problem?

> **Number Talk Tip**
>
> Using denominators that have a multiplicative relationship helps students focus on how the fractions are related. For instance, think about adding $\frac{5}{8}$ and $\frac{3}{16}$ compared to adding $\frac{5}{8}$ and $\frac{4}{7}$. It's easier to consider the relationships between eighths and sixteenths, because eighths can easily be partitioned into sixteenths, and only one of the fractions needs to be repartitioned. In contrast, with eighths and sevenths *both* fractions must be repartitioned.

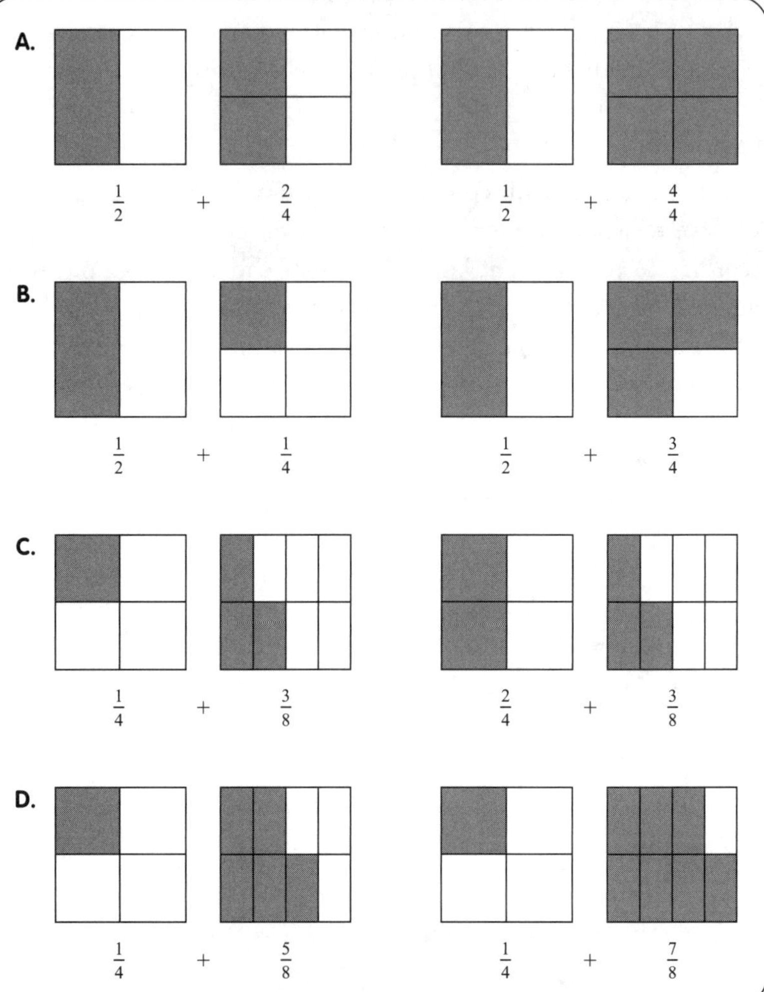

> **Reproducible 4**
>
> For full-sized reproducibles of these number talks, visit www.mathsolutions.com/numbertalksfdp_reproducibles.

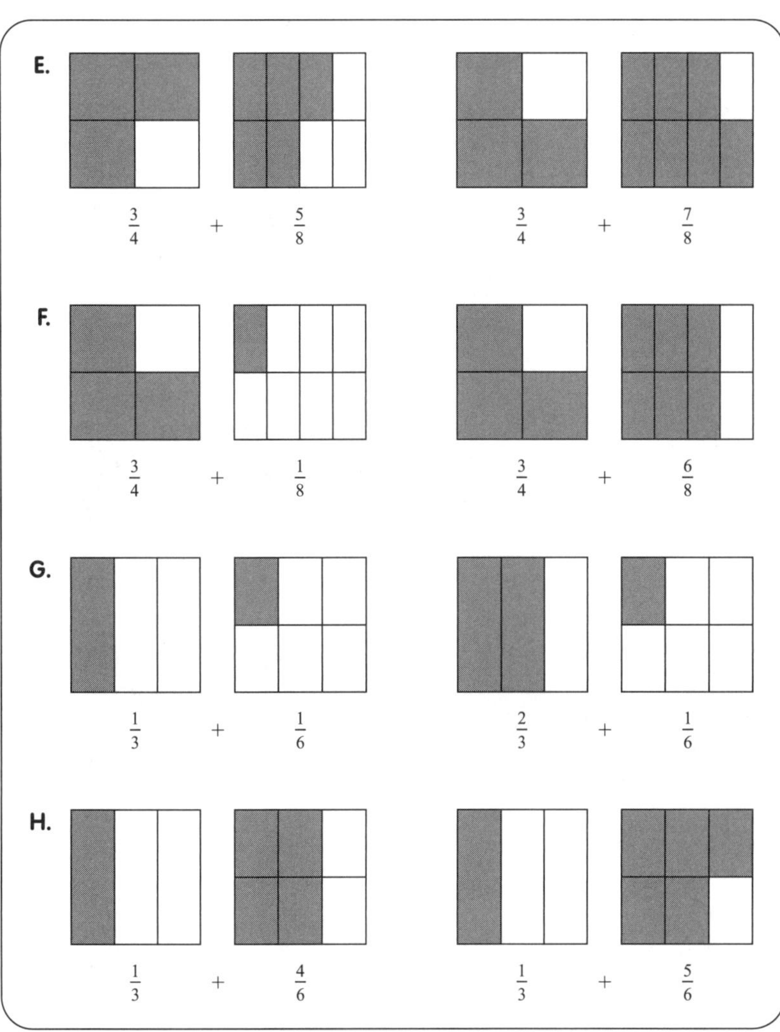
E.
$\frac{3}{4} + \frac{5}{8}$
$\frac{3}{4} + \frac{7}{8}$
F.
$\frac{3}{4} + \frac{1}{8}$
$\frac{3}{4} + \frac{6}{8}$
G.
$\frac{1}{3} + \frac{1}{6}$
$\frac{2}{3} + \frac{1}{6}$
H.
$\frac{1}{3} + \frac{4}{6}$
$\frac{1}{3} + \frac{5}{6}$

(continued)

(How can you solve ______ + ______? How can you use what we already know to solve this next problem?, continued)

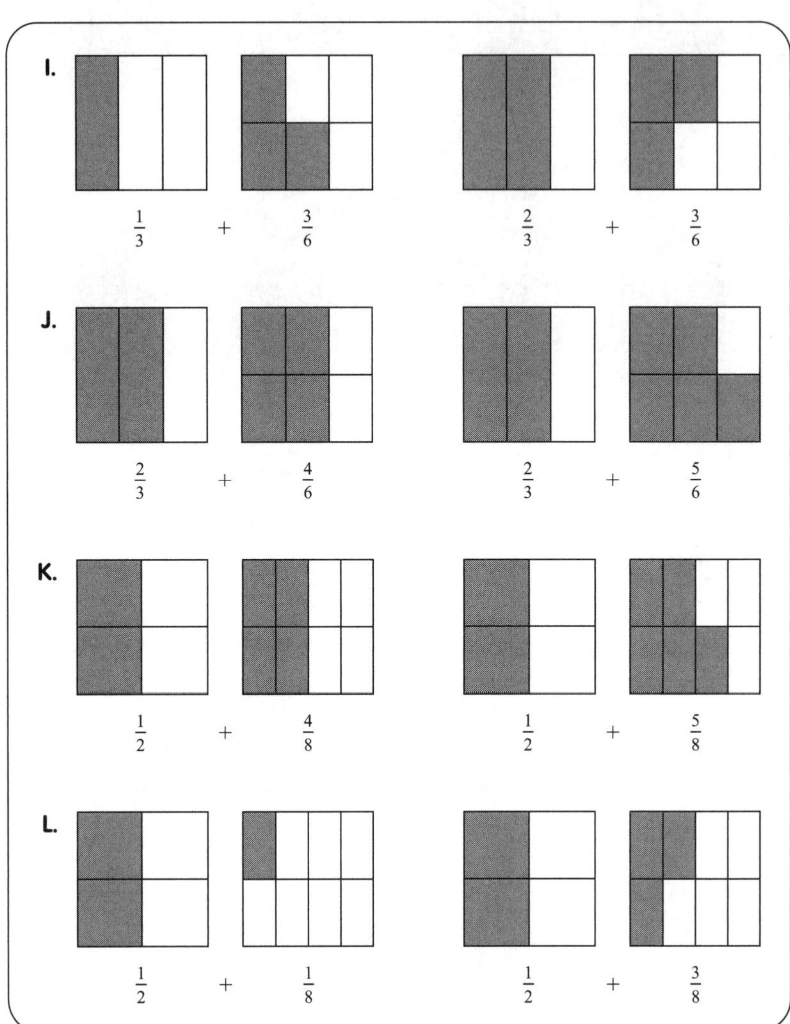

Number Talks That Use Set Models for Addition with Fractions

As we begin to help students construct strategies for adding fractions, using a model along with a computation problem can offer learners an entry point. Set models can support students as they think about equivalence, decomposing addends to compose benchmark fractions, and what it means to add fractions. For the following number talks, show students the two set models along with a computation problem and ask, "*How could you solve this problem?*" Collect and list all answers, and then ask, "*Who would like to defend their answer?*" As students share their strategies, make their thinking public by recording their strategies numerically. Some students may use the models and others may not. If students use the set models to describe their thinking, listen and record their reasoning by circling the dots to match their strategy. The following "Inside the Classroom" excerpt shows how you might capture a student's strategy for solving $\frac{1}{2} + \frac{5}{8}$ both numerically and using the set model shown here.

Inside the Classroom

A Number Talk for $\frac{1}{2} + \frac{5}{8}$

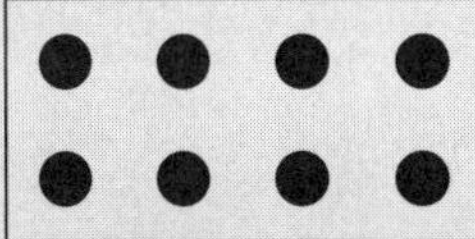
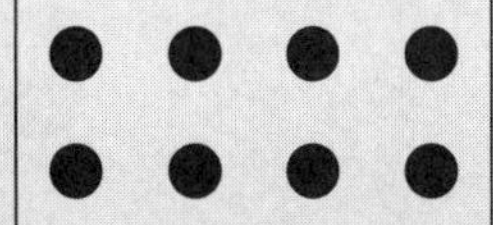

Simeon: I saw $\frac{1}{2}$ of the first set and $\frac{5}{8}$ of the second set.

Ms. Brewer: How did you see the $\frac{1}{2}$ and the $\frac{5}{8}$?

Simeon: I split the 8 dots down the middle and thought about $\frac{1}{2}$ as the first 4 dots. Then I looked at the second set as the first 4 dots and 1 more.

(continued)

Ms. Brewer: Like this?

Simeon: Yes. Then I put $\frac{1}{2}$ or 4 of the dots from the second set with the $\frac{1}{2}$ from the first set to make one whole. I had $\frac{1}{8}$ leftover from the second set, so the answer is $1\frac{1}{8}$.

[Ms. Brewer records numerically without speaking as the student is talking]:

$$\frac{1}{2}+\frac{5}{8}$$

$$=\frac{1}{2}+\left(\frac{1}{2}+\frac{1}{8}\right)$$

$$=\left(\frac{1}{2}+\frac{1}{2}\right)+\frac{1}{8}$$

$$=1+\frac{1}{8}$$

$$=1\frac{1}{8}$$

Category 1
Using Set Models with Eight Dots

The number talk strings in this category are structured to help students develop strategies for adding like and unlike denominators. Each string comprises three problems that purposefully use halves, fourths, and eighths because of their multiplicative relationship.

Instructions

These number talks are organized into three columns and progress in difficulty going from the first column (from A to B) to the second column to the third column. Feel free to work through each string in order or choose problems according to your students' needs. You may choose to pose one problem or set of problems each day, or do more than one set of problems as time allows. Display the two set models and pose the first addition problem in the string. Collect solutions, then ask students to share their reasoning and proofs. Once the class reaches consensus, pose the second problem in the string and ask, *"How can you use what we already know to solve this next problem?"* Continue this format with each problem in the string.

How can you solve _____ + _____?
How can you use what we already know to solve this next problem?

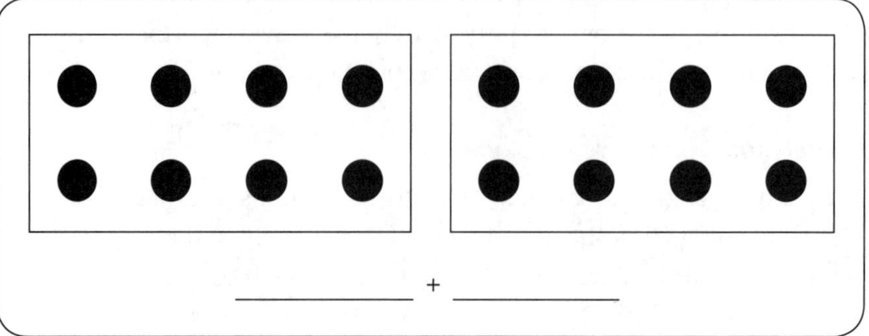

A. $\frac{3}{8}+\frac{3}{8}$	**A.** $\frac{1}{2}+\frac{1}{4}$	**A.** $\frac{1}{2}+\frac{3}{8}$
$\frac{3}{8}+\frac{5}{8}$	$\frac{1}{2}+\frac{2}{4}$	$\frac{1}{2}+\frac{5}{8}$
$\frac{3}{8}+\frac{6}{8}$	$\frac{1}{2}+\frac{3}{4}$	$\frac{1}{2}+\frac{6}{8}$
B. $\frac{1}{8}+\frac{5}{8}$	**B.** $\frac{1}{2}+\frac{1}{8}$	**B.** $\frac{1}{4}+\frac{1}{8}$
$\frac{2}{8}+\frac{5}{8}$	$\frac{1}{2}+\frac{2}{8}$	$\frac{1}{4}+\frac{2}{8}$
$\frac{2}{8}+\frac{7}{8}$	$\frac{1}{2}+\frac{7}{8}$	$\frac{1}{4}+\frac{5}{8}$

Category 2
Using Set Models with Twelve Dots

The number talk strings in this category are structured to help students develop strategies for adding like and unlike denominators. Each string comprises three problems that focus on the relationship between halves, fourths, thirds, sixths, and twelfths.

Instructions

These number talks are organized into three columns and progress in difficulty going from the first column (from A to B to C) to the second column to the third column. Feel free to work through each string in order or choose problems according to your students' needs. You may choose to pose one problem or set of problems each day, or do more than one set of problems as time allows. Display the two set models with the first addition problem. Collect solutions, then ask students to share their reasoning and proofs. Once the class reaches consensus, pose the second problem in the string and ask, *"How can you use what we already know to solve this next problem?"* Continue this format with each problem in the string.

How can you solve _____ + _____?

How can you use what we already know to solve this next problem?

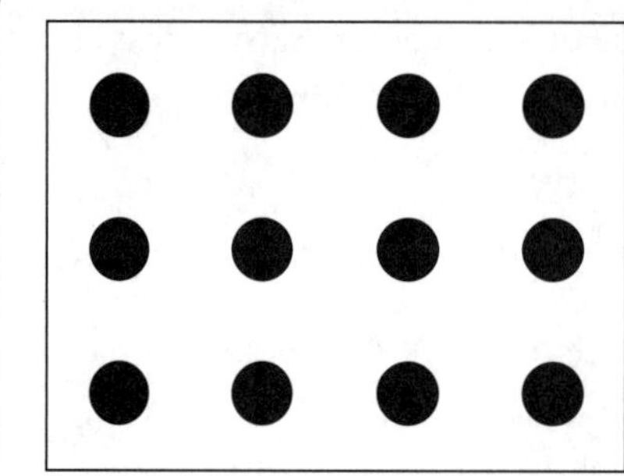

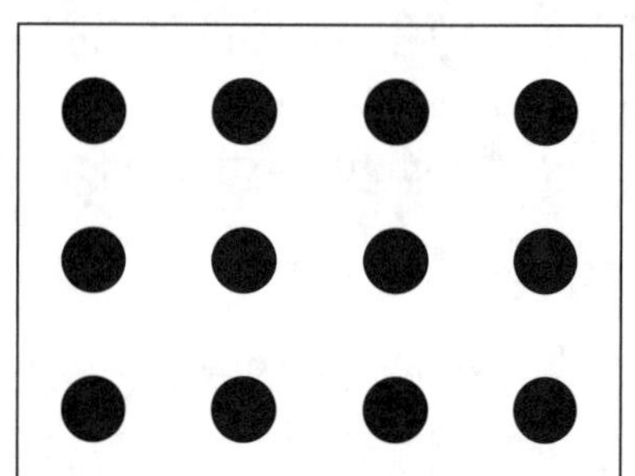

_____________ + _____________

A. $\frac{1}{2}+\frac{1}{2}$

$\frac{1}{2}+\frac{1}{4}$

$\frac{1}{2}+\frac{3}{4}$

B. $\frac{1}{2}+\frac{1}{6}$

$\frac{1}{2}+\frac{2}{6}$

$\frac{1}{2}+\frac{4}{6}$

C. $\frac{1}{2}+\frac{3}{3}$

$\frac{1}{2}+\frac{1}{3}$

$\frac{1}{2}+\frac{2}{3}$

A. $\frac{1}{2}+\frac{6}{12}$

$\frac{1}{2}+\frac{3}{12}$

$\frac{1}{2}+\frac{9}{12}$

B. $\frac{1}{6}+\frac{1}{12}$

$\frac{1}{6}+\frac{3}{12}$

$\frac{1}{6}+\frac{7}{12}$

C. $\frac{2}{6}+\frac{4}{12}$

$\frac{4}{6}+\frac{5}{12}$

$\frac{5}{6}+\frac{8}{12}$

A. $\frac{1}{4}+\frac{1}{12}$

$\frac{1}{4}+\frac{5}{12}$

$\frac{1}{4}+\frac{7}{12}$

B. $\frac{1}{4}+\frac{1}{3}$

$\frac{1}{4}+\frac{2}{3}$

$\frac{2}{4}+\frac{2}{3}$

C. $\frac{3}{4}+\frac{1}{3}$

$\frac{3}{4}+\frac{2}{3}$

$\frac{3}{4}+\frac{5}{6}$

Number Talks That Use Linear Models for Addition with Fractions

In the same way area and set models give students an entry point for developing strategies and finding a solution, we can also use linear models in beginning addition number talks to support students as they think about equivalence, decomposing addends to compose benchmark fractions, and what it means to add fractions. Because a number line can be a more difficult model for students, we might also include a story context for an additional layer of support. For example, we can write the problem $\frac{3}{4} + \frac{3}{4}$ along with a 0 to 2 number line partitioned into fourths, and say, "*I walked $\frac{3}{4}$ of a mile on Monday and another $\frac{3}{4}$ of a mile on Tuesday. How far have I walked?*" We might anticipate a student would start with $\frac{3}{4}$ and then decompose the second $\frac{3}{4}$ into $\frac{1}{4} + \frac{1}{2}$. (See Figure 6–6.)

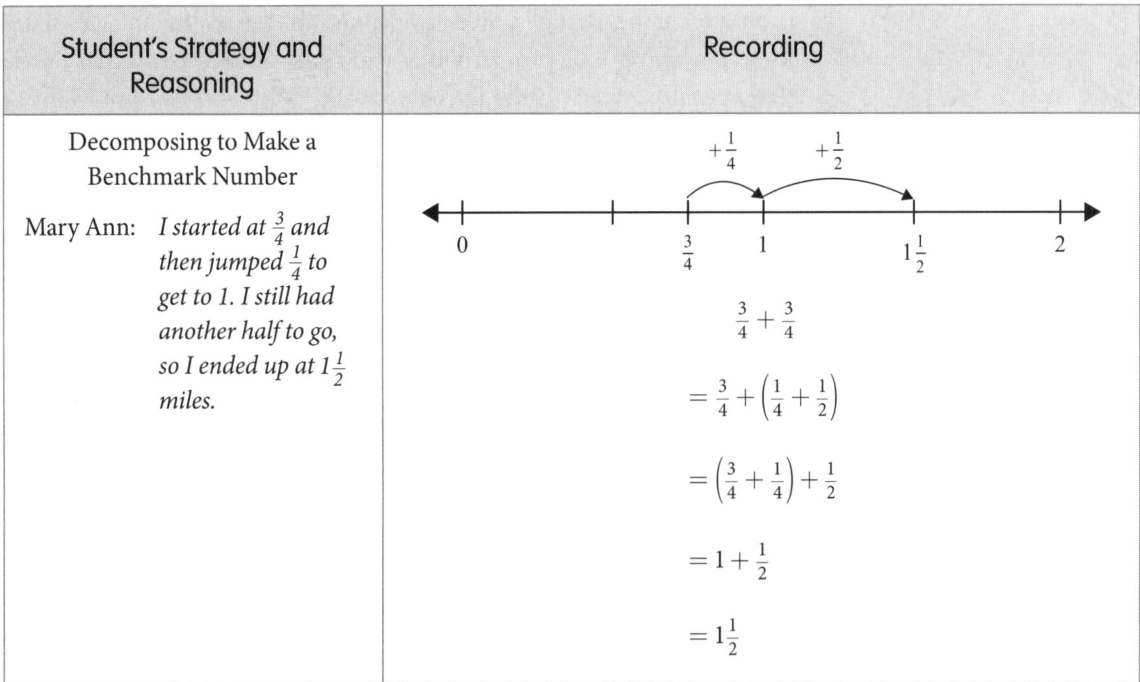

Student's Strategy and Reasoning	Recording
Decomposing to Make a Benchmark Number Mary Ann: *I started at $\frac{3}{4}$ and then jumped $\frac{1}{4}$ to get to 1. I still had another half to go, so I ended up at $1\frac{1}{2}$ miles.*	Number line: 0, $\frac{3}{4}$, 1, $1\frac{1}{2}$, 2; jumps $+\frac{1}{4}$, $+\frac{1}{2}$ $\frac{3}{4} + \frac{3}{4}$ $= \frac{3}{4} + \left(\frac{1}{4} + \frac{1}{2}\right)$ $= \left(\frac{3}{4} + \frac{1}{4}\right) + \frac{1}{2}$ $= 1 + \frac{1}{2}$ $= 1\frac{1}{2}$

Figure 6–6. *Using "Decomposing to Make a Benchmark Number" to Solve $\frac{3}{4} + \frac{3}{4}$*

Category 1
Using a Number Line Partitioned into Halves and Fourths

Reproducible 15

For a reproducible of the 0 to 2 number line, visit www.mathsolutions.com/numbertalksfdp_reproducibles.

The number talk strings in this category are structured to help students add fractions with like and unlike denominators. Each string comprises two problems that have denominators of halves, fourths, and eighths. The problems in the second and third columns require students to repartition the number line into eighths. We suggest using the 0 to 2 number line partitioned into fourths as you present each problem.

Instructions

These number talks are organized into three columns and progress in difficulty going from the first column (from A to B to C, etc.) to the second column to the third column. Feel free to work through each string in order or choose problems according to your students' needs. You may choose to pose one problem or set of problems each day, or do more than one set of problems as time allows. Introduce the first problem in the string, collect solutions, then ask students to share their reasoning and proofs. Once the class reaches consensus, pose the second problem in the string and ask, *"How can you use what we already know to solve this next problem?"* Continue this format with each problem in the string.

How can you solve ______ + ______?
How can you use what we already know to solve this next problem?

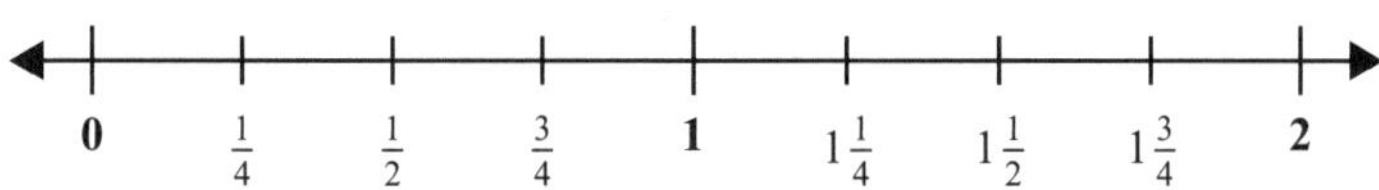

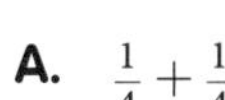

A. $\frac{1}{4} + \frac{1}{4}$

$\frac{1}{4} + \frac{3}{4}$

B. $\frac{1}{2} + \frac{1}{4}$

$\frac{1}{2} + \frac{3}{4}$

C. $\frac{1}{2} + \frac{1}{2}$

$\frac{1}{2} + \frac{3}{4}$

D. $\frac{3}{4} + \frac{2}{4}$

$\frac{3}{4} + \frac{3}{4}$

E. $\frac{1}{4} + 1\frac{1}{4}$

$\frac{3}{4} + 1\frac{1}{4}$

A. $\frac{1}{2} + \frac{1}{8}$

$\frac{1}{2} + \frac{2}{8}$

B. $\frac{1}{4} + \frac{1}{8}$

$\frac{1}{4} + \frac{3}{8}$

C. $\frac{1}{2} + \frac{4}{8}$

$\frac{1}{2} + \frac{5}{8}$

D. $\frac{3}{4} + \frac{1}{8}$

$\frac{3}{4} + \frac{3}{8}$

E. $\frac{1}{4} + \frac{4}{8}$

$\frac{1}{4} + \frac{5}{8}$

A. $\frac{4}{4} + \frac{1}{8}$

$\frac{6}{4} + \frac{1}{8}$

B. $\frac{5}{4} + \frac{1}{4}$

$\frac{5}{4} + \frac{1}{2}$

C. $1\frac{1}{4} + \frac{1}{8}$

$1\frac{1}{4} + \frac{2}{8}$

D. $\frac{5}{4} + \frac{3}{8}$

$\frac{5}{4} + \frac{5}{8}$

E. $\frac{1}{2} + \frac{7}{8}$

$\frac{1}{2} + \frac{9}{8}$

Category 2
Using a Number Line Partitioned into Halves and Thirds

Reproducible 16

For a reproducible of the 0 to 2 number line, visit www.mathsolutions.com/numbertalksfdp_reproducibles.

The number talk strings in this category are structured to help students consider adding fractions with like and unlike denominators. Each string comprises two problems that have denominators of halves, thirds, and sixths. The problems in the second and third columns require students to repartition the number line into sixths. We suggest using the 0 to 2 number line partitioned into halves and thirds as you present each problem.

Instructions

These number talks are organized into three columns and progress in difficulty going from the first column (from A to B to C, etc.) to the second column to the third column. Feel free to work through each string in order or choose problems according to your students' needs. You may choose to pose one problem or set of problems each day, or do more than one set of problems as time allows. Introduce the first problem in the string, collect solutions, then ask students to share their reasoning and proofs. Once the class reaches consensus, pose the second problem in the string and ask, *"How can you use what we already know to solve this next problem?"* Continue this format with each problem in the string.

How can you solve ______ + ______?
How can you use what we already know to solve this next problem?

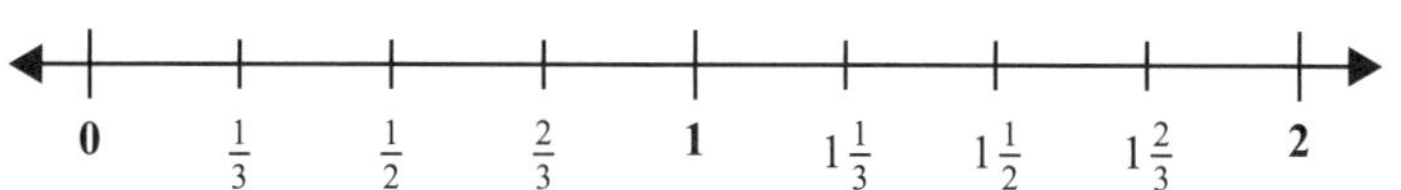

A. $\frac{1}{3} + \frac{1}{3}$

$\frac{1}{3} + \frac{3}{3}$

B. $\frac{2}{3} + \frac{2}{3}$

$\frac{2}{3} + \frac{4}{3}$

C. $\frac{1}{6} + \frac{2}{6}$

$\frac{3}{6} + \frac{4}{6}$

D. $\frac{3}{6} + \frac{3}{6}$

$\frac{3}{6} + \frac{5}{6}$

A. $\frac{1}{2} + \frac{3}{6}$

$\frac{1}{2} + \frac{5}{6}$

B. $\frac{1}{2} + \frac{1}{3}$

$\frac{1}{2} + \frac{2}{3}$

C. $\frac{1}{3} + \frac{3}{6}$

$\frac{1}{3} + \frac{5}{6}$

D. $\frac{1}{3} + \frac{1}{6}$

$\frac{1}{3} + \frac{2}{6}$

A. $\frac{2}{6} + \frac{1}{3}$

$\frac{2}{6} + \frac{2}{3}$

B. $\frac{2}{3} + \frac{6}{6}$

$\frac{2}{3} + \frac{7}{6}$

C. $\frac{1}{2} + \frac{3}{6}$

$\frac{1}{2} + \frac{1}{6}$

D. $\frac{2}{3} + \frac{1}{6}$

$\frac{2}{3} + \frac{4}{6}$

Number Talk Tip

Taking time to listen to students and honor their thinking creates a classroom environment where students are willing to take risks as they investigate complex ideas. Focusing on making sense of problems and justifying solutions helps students become confident in their ability to do mathematics.

Number Talk Tip

In this resource each strategy is named to represent the thinking involved (e.g., Adjusting an Addend). However, teachers often label a strategy with the name of the student who invented it. For example, if Joe offers the idea of decomposing a fraction to find and use benchmark numbers to add two fractions, the class might call this "Joe's Strategy." The name of the strategy is not as important as the mathematical ideas the students are using.

Number Talks That Highlight the Addition Strategy "Decomposing to Make a Benchmark Number"

Once students have worked with beginning number talks using models, transition into number talks that further emphasize numerical relationships and the development of strategies. In this section, the focus is on the addition strategy of decomposing to make a benchmark number.

Halves and wholes are benchmark numbers in fractions just like multiples of 10 and 25 are benchmarks for whole numbers. Benchmark numbers anchor students' thinking and give them access to solving problems mentally. When numbers in a fraction problem are close to a half or a whole, students often decompose the addends to make benchmarks and reason through to a solution. Decomposing to make a half or a whole and then rearranging the parts of the addends to make friendly numbers works because of the associative property of addition. As an example, Figure 6–7 shows two ways students might solve $\frac{1}{2}+\frac{3}{4}$.

Student's Strategy and Reasoning	Recording
Decomposing to Make a Benchmark Number Troxell: *I knew that $\frac{1}{2}+\frac{1}{2}$ was 1 whole so I split $\frac{3}{4}$ into $\frac{1}{2}+\frac{1}{4}$. Then I put the one halves together and I had $\frac{1}{4}$ left. That gave me $1+\frac{1}{4}$ which is $1\frac{1}{4}$.*	$\frac{1}{2}+\frac{3}{4}$ $=\frac{1}{2}+\left(\frac{1}{2}+\frac{1}{4}\right)$ $=\left(\frac{1}{2}+\frac{1}{2}\right)+\frac{1}{4}$ $=1+\frac{1}{4}=\mathbf{1\frac{1}{4}}$
Decomposing to Make a Benchmark Number Ginny: *I thought about $\frac{1}{2}$ as $\frac{1}{4}+\frac{1}{4}$ so I could make a whole. I put one of the one-fourths with the $\frac{3}{4}$ to get 1 so then I had $\frac{1}{4}+1$ which is $1\frac{1}{4}$.*	$\frac{1}{2}+\frac{3}{4}$ $=\left(\frac{1}{4}+\frac{1}{4}\right)+\frac{3}{4}$ $=\frac{1}{4}+\left(\frac{1}{4}+\frac{3}{4}\right)$ $=\frac{1}{4}+1=1\frac{1}{4}$

Figure 6–7. *Using "Decomposing to Make a Benchmark Number" to Solve $\frac{1}{2}+\frac{3}{4}$*

$\frac{1}{2}+\frac{1}{2}$, $\frac{1}{2}+\frac{3}{4}$: Developing Addition Strategies with Fractions

Classroom Clip 6.3

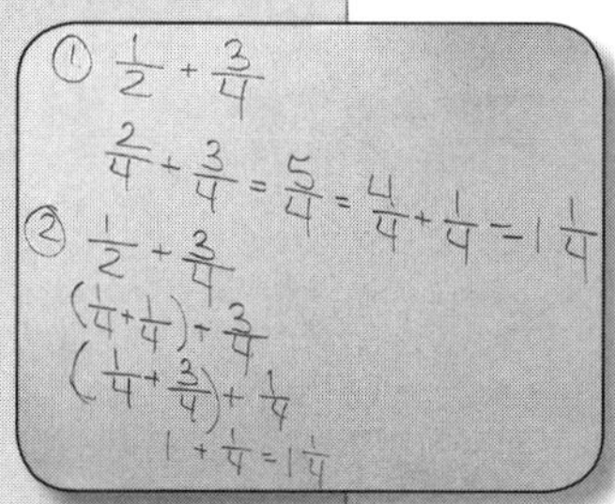

Consider the following questions as you watch this number talk from a fourth-grade classroom:

1. Why do you think the teacher starts with a problem she thinks most of the students will already be able to answer?
2. What do you notice about how the teacher collects answers for the first problem?
3. What does Havani know (Strategy 1) that helps her solve the problem?
4. What does Israel understand (Strategy 2) that helps him solve the problem?
5. How would you compare Strategies 2 and 3?
6. How do students use what they know about the first problem to solve the second problem?
7. Watch Classroom Clip 6.1 to see the third problem in this number talk string. How do the first and second problems in the string help students solve the third problem?

To view this video clip, scan the QR code or access via mathsolutions .com/NTFDP6.3

When students decompose an addend and use the associative property to make a benchmark number, they are *looking for and making use of structure* (MP7).

Category 1
Using Halves as Benchmarks

The number talk strings in this category are structured to help students develop reasoning using benchmark fractions. Addition number talks in this section begin with benchmark problems that students may "just know" and then transition to a second problem to encourage them to make relationships between the two problems to find a solution. As you progress through each problem, anticipate opportunities for conversations around equivalence and common denominators. Most of the problems use fractions with like denominators or denominators that are multiples of each other.

Instructions

These number talks are organized into three columns and progress in difficulty going from the first column (from A to B to C, etc.) to the second column to the third column. Feel free to work through each string in order or choose problems according to your students' needs. You may choose to pose one problem or set of problems each day, or do more than one set of problems as time allows.

Each pair of problems begins with the benchmark problem, $\frac{1}{2}+\frac{1}{2}$, followed by a second problem that uses addends equal to one-half or a fraction that is one unit fraction greater than one-half. As you introduce $\frac{1}{2}+\frac{1}{2}$, anticipate that students may just know this answer. If they quickly raise their thumbs, consider having students share their answers with a partner while you eavesdrop. If you hear "one" unanimously throughout the room, acknowledge that this is a solution everyone knows. If it is a solution that students "just know," move quickly to the next problem. If you hear any incorrect answers, collect solutions, then ask students to share their reasoning and proofs. Once the class reaches consensus, pose the second problem in the string and ask, *"How can you use what we already know to solve this next problem?"* Continue this format with each problem in the string.

What is ______ + ______? How do you know?
How can you use what we already know to solve this next problem?

A. $\frac{1}{2}+\frac{1}{2}$

$\frac{1}{2}+\frac{5}{8}$

B. $\frac{1}{2}+\frac{1}{2}$

$\frac{1}{2}+\frac{9}{16}$

C. $\frac{1}{2}+\frac{1}{2}$

$\frac{1}{2}+\frac{6}{10}$

D. $\frac{1}{2}+\frac{1}{2}$

$\frac{1}{2}+\frac{7}{12}$

E. $\frac{1}{2}+\frac{1}{2}$

$\frac{1}{2}+\frac{4}{6}$

F. $\frac{1}{2}+\frac{1}{2}$

$\frac{1}{2}+\frac{8}{14}$

A. $\frac{1}{2}+\frac{1}{2}$

$\frac{4}{8}+\frac{7}{12}$

B. $\frac{1}{2}+\frac{1}{2}$

$\frac{3}{6}+\frac{8}{14}$

C. $\frac{1}{2}+\frac{1}{2}$

$\frac{5}{10}+\frac{13}{24}$

D. $\frac{1}{2}+\frac{1}{2}$

$\frac{6}{12}+\frac{9}{16}$

E. $\frac{1}{2}+\frac{1}{2}$

$\frac{7}{14}+\frac{11}{20}$

F. $\frac{1}{2}+\frac{1}{2}$

$\frac{10}{20}+\frac{15}{28}$

A. $\frac{1}{2}+\frac{1}{2}$

$\frac{3}{4}+\frac{5}{8}$

B. $\frac{1}{2}+\frac{1}{2}$

$\frac{5}{8}+\frac{9}{16}$

C. $\frac{1}{2}+\frac{1}{2}$

$\frac{4}{6}+\frac{7}{12}$

D. $\frac{1}{2}+\frac{1}{2}$

$\frac{6}{10}+\frac{11}{20}$

E. $\frac{1}{2}+\frac{1}{2}$

$\frac{7}{12}+\frac{13}{24}$

F. $\frac{1}{2}+\frac{1}{2}$

$\frac{8}{14}+\frac{15}{28}$

Category 2
Using Wholes as Benchmarks

The number talk strings in this category are structured to help students develop reasoning using one whole as a benchmark number for fractions. The strings build on the relationship between one whole and a fraction that is one unit fraction away from a whole. Addition number talks in this section begin with benchmark problems that students may "just know" and then transition to a second problem to encourage them to make relationships between the two problems to find a solution. Most of the problems use fractions with like denominators or denominators that are multiples of each other.

Instructions

These number talks are organized into three columns and progress in difficulty going from the first column (from A to B to C, etc.) to the second column to the third column. The last column uses addends with different denominators, adding to the complexity of the sequence. Feel free to work through each string in order or choose problems according to your students' needs. You may choose to pose one problem or set of problems each day, or do more than one set of problems as time allows.

As you introduce the first problem, anticipate that students may just know this answer. If they quickly raise their thumbs, consider having students share their answers with a partner while you eavesdrop. If you hear the correct answer unanimously throughout the room, acknowledge that this is a solution everyone knows, and quickly pose the next problem. If you hear any incorrect answers, collect solutions, then ask students to share their reasoning and proofs. Once the class reaches consensus, pose the second problem in the string and ask, *"How can you use what we already know to solve this next problem?"* Continue this format with each problem in the string.

What is ______ + ______? How do you know?
How can you use what we already know to solve this next problem?

A. $1 + \frac{3}{8}$

$\frac{7}{8} + \frac{3}{8}$

B. $1 + \frac{2}{6}$

$\frac{5}{6} + \frac{2}{6}$

C. $1 + \frac{6}{7}$

$\frac{6}{7} + \frac{2}{7}$

D. $1 + \frac{3}{5}$

$\frac{4}{5} + \frac{3}{5}$

E. $1 + \frac{2}{10}$

$\frac{9}{10} + \frac{2}{10}$

F. $1 + \frac{3}{11}$

$\frac{10}{11} + \frac{3}{11}$

A. $1 + \frac{11}{12}$

$\frac{11}{12} + \frac{3}{12}$

B. $1 + \frac{3}{16}$

$\frac{15}{16} + \frac{3}{16}$

C. $1 + \frac{4}{13}$

$\frac{12}{13} + \frac{4}{13}$

D. $1 + \frac{4}{15}$

$\frac{14}{15} + \frac{4}{15}$

E. $2 + \frac{3}{9}$

$1\frac{8}{9} + \frac{3}{9}$

F. $2 + \frac{3}{5}$

$1\frac{4}{5} + \frac{3}{5}$

A. $1 + \frac{3}{10}$

$\frac{4}{5} + \frac{3}{10}$

B. $1 + \frac{5}{16}$

$\frac{7}{8} + \frac{5}{16}$

C. $1 + \frac{3}{12}$

$\frac{5}{6} + \frac{3}{12}$

D. $1 + \frac{4}{14}$

$\frac{6}{7} + \frac{4}{14}$

E. $2 + \frac{2}{5}$

$1\frac{9}{10} + \frac{2}{5}$

F. $2 + \frac{3}{14}$

$1\frac{6}{7} + \frac{3}{14}$

Number Talks That Highlight the Addition Strategy "Adjusting an Addend"

One form of compensation involves adding an additional amount to one or both addends to make a benchmark number and then readjusting the sum at the end to maintain the original quantity. Following are two ways students might adjust an addend to solve the problem $\frac{1}{2} + \frac{3}{4}$. (See Figure 6–8.)

Student's Strategy and Reasoning	Recording
Adjusting an Addend Millie: *I knew that $\frac{3}{4} + \frac{1}{4}$ was 1 whole so I added in an extra $\frac{1}{4}$ and that gave me 1 plus the $\frac{1}{2}$ I already had and that was $1\frac{1}{2}$. Then I took out the extra $\frac{1}{4}$ I added in at the beginning. $1\frac{1}{2} - \frac{1}{4} = 1\frac{1}{4}$.*	$\frac{1}{2} + \frac{3}{4}$ $\frac{1}{2} + \left(\frac{3}{4} + \frac{1}{4}\right)$ $\frac{1}{2} + 1 = 1\frac{1}{2}$ $1\frac{1}{2} - \frac{1}{4} = 1\frac{1}{4}$
Adjusting an Addend Isa: *I added in an extra $\frac{1}{2}$ to make the problem easier to solve. $\frac{1}{2} + \frac{1}{2} = 1$ so then I had $1 + \frac{3}{4}$ which is $1\frac{3}{4}$. Since I added in an extra $\frac{1}{2}$ to the problem, I took it back out and $1\frac{3}{4}$ minus $\frac{1}{2}$ or $\frac{2}{4}$ is $1\frac{1}{4}$.*	$\frac{1}{2} + \frac{3}{4}$ $\left(\frac{1}{2} + \frac{1}{2}\right) + \frac{3}{4}$ $1 + \frac{3}{4} = 1\frac{3}{4}$ $1\frac{3}{4} - \frac{1}{2} = 1\frac{1}{4}$

Figure 6–8. *Using "Adjusting an Addend" to Solve $\frac{1}{2} + \frac{3}{4}$*

The pairs of problems in the first column begin with $1+1$ followed by problems using like denominators and addends that are one unit fraction away from the whole. The pairs of problems in the second column also begin with $1+1$ and are followed by problems in which the addends are one unit fraction away from 1 whole but use unlike denominators that are multiples of each other. The pairs of problems in the third and fourth columns start with $\frac{1}{2}+\frac{1}{2}$ and then use problems in which one or both addends are one unit fraction away from $\frac{1}{2}$. They also use unlike denominators that are multiples of each other.

Instructions

These number talks are organized into four columns and progress in difficulty going from the first column (from A to B to C, etc.) to the second column and so on. Feel free to work through each pair of problems in order or choose problems according to your students' needs. You may choose to pose one problem or pair of problems each day, or do more than one pair of problems as time allows. As you introduce the first problem in each string, anticipate that students will "just know" the answer. If they quickly raise their thumbs, and you hear the correct answer unanimously throughout the room, acknowledge that this is a solution everyone knows, and quickly move to the next problem. If you hear any incorrect answers, collect solutions, then ask students to share their reasoning and proofs. Once the class reaches consensus, pose the second problem in the string and ask, *"How can you use what we already know to solve this next problem?"* Continue this format with each problem in the string.

What is ______ + ______? How do you know?
How can you use what we already know to solve this next problem?

A. $1 + 1$

$\frac{7}{8} + \frac{7}{8}$

B. $1 + 1$

$\frac{5}{6} + \frac{5}{6}$

C. $1 + 1$

$\frac{4}{5} + \frac{4}{5}$

D. $1 + 1$

$\frac{9}{10} + \frac{9}{10}$

E. $1 + 1$

$\frac{11}{12} + \frac{11}{12}$

A. $1 + 1$

$\frac{5}{6} + \frac{11}{12}$

B. $1 + 1$

$\frac{6}{7} + \frac{13}{14}$

C. $1 + 1$

$\frac{4}{5} + \frac{9}{10}$

D. $1 + 1$

$\frac{7}{8} + \frac{15}{16}$

E. $1 + 1$

$\frac{3}{4} + \frac{7}{8}$

A. $\frac{1}{2} + \frac{1}{2}$

$\frac{1}{2} + \frac{3}{8}$

B. $\frac{1}{2} + \frac{1}{2}$

$\frac{1}{2} + \frac{5}{12}$

C. $\frac{1}{2} + \frac{1}{2}$

$\frac{1}{2} + \frac{6}{14}$

D. $\frac{1}{2} + \frac{1}{2}$

$\frac{1}{2} + \frac{4}{10}$

E. $\frac{1}{2} + \frac{1}{2}$

$\frac{1}{2} + \frac{7}{16}$

A. $\frac{1}{2} + \frac{1}{2}$

$\frac{3}{8} + \frac{7}{16}$

B. $\frac{1}{2} + \frac{1}{2}$

$\frac{2}{6} + \frac{5}{12}$

C. $\frac{1}{2} + \frac{1}{2}$

$\frac{4}{10} + \frac{9}{20}$

D. $\frac{1}{2} + \frac{1}{2}$

$\frac{5}{12} + \frac{11}{24}$

E. $\frac{1}{2} + \frac{1}{2}$

$\frac{6}{14} + \frac{13}{28}$

Anticipating Student Thinking

The more regularly you use number talks with your students, the more confident you will become at anticipating your students' thinking and understanding the ways they solve problems. There are usually a limited number of strategies students actually use, so the more familiar you become with these strategies, the less challenging it will be to anticipate their thinking. As you plan your number talks, anticipate ways that students might solve each problem, and decide ahead of time how you might record their thinking so their strategies will be more accessible to others. Consider which mathematical ideas you want to highlight and how you might record strategies to emphasize those specific concepts.

Learn More...

Anticipating student strategies for subtracting, multiplying, and dividing fractions is discussed in Chapters 7, 8, and 9.

Looking Ahead

In this chapter we have looked at opportunities for students to begin thinking about what happens when they add fractions and how we can use number talks to help students develop their own addition strategies. Were there any addition strategies that surprised you as a teacher and helped you think more flexibly about fractions? What common misconceptions about adding fractions do you notice with your students, and how can you facilitate conversations to confront those misconceptions and help build understanding? In Chapter 7, we explore important ideas related to subtraction of fractions, examine student-invented strategies, and offer number talks to help students develop accuracy, efficiency, and flexibility with subtracting fractions.

Connecting the Chapter to Your Practice

1. What are some ways you might add 25 + 27? Can you use any of those same strategies to add $\frac{3}{4}+\frac{3}{4}$?
2. How would you record some of the strategies you discussed for adding $\frac{3}{4}+\frac{3}{4}$ to highlight the associative property of addition?
3. Look at the "Inside the Classroom" excerpt on page 141. Where do you see the teacher distinguishing between logico-mathematical knowledge and social knowledge?
4. How does distinguishing between different types of knowledge impact teaching practices?
5. How do you think your students might respond if you present problems using story problems and models in your number talks?
6. As you look at the number talks on pages 151–156, what student misconceptions do you anticipate?
7. What might you ask to help students confront their misconceptions and make sense of these problems?
8. What differences in your students' thinking do you anticipate as you use area, set, and linear models?
9. Which strategies for adding fractions do your students use most often?
10. What influences which strategies they use?

CHAPTER 7

Number Talks for Subtraction with Fractions

In this chapter, we offer a place for teachers to start when planning number talks around the subtraction of fractions. In the opening sections, we discuss how the use of number talks is helpful as students work to develop subtraction strategies with fractions. We then explore and offer number talks that are focused on helping students develop flexibility with decomposing fractions, deepen their understanding of equivalence, and understand what it means to subtract with fractions. We highly recommend that students are solid and flexible in their fractional reasoning (see Chapter 4) before using the number talks in this chapter.

OVERVIEW

(Continued)

How Number Talks Help the Development of Subtraction Strategies with Fractions

When we ask students to share their strategies for solving problems, we learn about their understandings as well as their misconceptions. Some common misconceptions related to subtracting fractions involve treating numerators and denominators as whole numbers, misapplying the commutative property to subtraction, and misunderstanding the procedure related to finding common denominators.

Examples of these misconceptions appear in the 2011 TIMSS study, which asked eighth-grade students to identify a correct method for solving $\frac{1}{3} - \frac{1}{4}$. Figure 7–1 shows the multiple-choice answers students had to select from, and the percentage of students in the United States who responded to each solution. A small percentage of the students either decided to leave the answer blank or did not get to this question on the test.

Which shows a correct method for finding $\frac{1}{3} - \frac{1}{4}$?	
Answers	Percentage of Responses
A. $\frac{(1-1)}{(4-3)}$	32.5%
B. $\frac{1}{(4-3)}$	26.1%
C. $\frac{(3-4)}{(3 \times 4)}$	10.7%
D. $\frac{(4-3)}{(3 \times 4)}$	29.1%

Figure 7–1. *U.S. Eighth-Grade 2011 TIMSS Responses*

Students who chose solutions A and B did not understand fractions as distinct quantities but rather viewed each numerator and denominator as a whole number. These solutions also imply that the original problem, $\frac{1}{3} - \frac{1}{4}$, can be changed to $\frac{1}{4} - \frac{1}{3}$, which suggests an overgeneralization of the commutative property. Solution C highlights some understanding of using a common denominator; however, the relationship between the subtrahend and the minuend has not been maintained. The correct answer, solution D, represents finding a common denominator to subtract fractions with unlike denominators.

Learn More...

For more about inappropriate whole number reasoning, see Chapter 3, pages 64–66.

If we were to ask a group of eighth graders to find an exact answer for $\frac{1}{3} - \frac{1}{4}$, it is likely that many would be able to give a correct solution. However, the TIMSS item reveals some of the widespread misunderstandings that students have about common denominators, equivalence, and subtraction as an operation.

We want students to become confident in finding and using common denominators as a strategy for solving fraction problems. However, it is equally important that students understand what fractions are, how fractions work, what happens when they operate with fractions, and how to use procedures with understanding. This is where the importance of number talks comes into play: Number talks help students focus on developing strategies to build their understanding of subtracting fractions.

Specifically, there are several approaches we can take during a number talk to support students in inventing and developing strategies—and thus deepen their understanding of mathematics. These approaches include the following:

- Making connections to strategies for subtracting whole numbers
- Using story problems
- Using models
- Connecting students' strategies

Each of these approaches is discussed in more detail in the sections that follow.

Making Connections to Strategies for Subtracting Whole Numbers

Many of the strategies that students have developed for subtracting whole numbers also work for subtracting fractions. Before presenting your students with subtraction problems that include fractions, start with subtraction problems with whole numbers. This provides an opportunity for the class to confront misconceptions about subtraction and revisit effective subtraction strategies. The more fluent that students are with whole number subtraction strategies and the better they are at composing and decomposing fractions, the more flexible they will be in their strategies for subtracting fractions.

For example, adding up to subtract is a strategy that works with both whole numbers and fractions. If you ask learners to try to solve *46 – 18*, some students might add up from 18 to 46 to find the difference between the two numbers. Since *18 + 2 = 20* and *20 + 26 = 46*, the difference between 18 and 46 is *2 + 26 = 28*. With fractions, a student could also add up to solve $1\frac{1}{8} - \frac{3}{8}$. In this case, a student might add $\frac{5}{8}$ to $\frac{3}{8}$ to get 1 whole and then add one more eighth to get to $1\frac{1}{8}$ (see Figure 7–2), correctly finding that the difference between $\frac{3}{8}$ and $1\frac{1}{8}$ is $\frac{5}{8} + \frac{1}{8}$ or $\frac{6}{8}$.

CCSS

When students are confident with a whole number subtraction strategy and find that it works to solve a subtraction problem with fractions, they are *looking for and expressing regularity in repeated reasoning* (MP8).

Adding Up to Find the Difference with Whole Numbers	Adding Up to Find the Difference with Fractions
$46 - 18$ $18 + \square = 46$ $18 + ⓶ = 20$ $20 + ㉖ = 46$ $2 + 26 = 28$ $18 + \boxed{28} = 46$	$1\frac{1}{8} - \frac{3}{8}$ $\frac{3}{8} + \square = 1\frac{1}{8}$ $\frac{3}{8} + \frac{5}{8} = \frac{8}{8} = 1$ (5/8 circled) $1 + \frac{1}{8} = 1\frac{1}{8}$ (1/8 circled) $\frac{5}{8} + \frac{1}{8} = \frac{6}{8}$ $\frac{3}{8} + \boxed{\frac{6}{8}} = 1\frac{1}{8}$

Figure 7–2. *Making Connections to Strategies for Computing with Whole Numbers*

Using Story Problems

Another way we can help learners develop a more complete understanding of what it means to subtract is to situate number talks within a story problem context. A context gives students an entry point for developing strategies and helps students make sense of the question the problem is asking and what the numbers mean in relationship to the problem.

For example, many students have learned that subtraction requires taking away an amount from a given quantity. However, while subtraction can involve removing or taking away an amount, subtraction can also mean finding the difference or distance between numbers. By situating subtraction problems in a context, we can help students develop a more complete understanding of this operation as well as build a toolbox of efficient strategies. Figure 7–3 shows examples of types of subtraction represented by specific contexts.

Presenting a Problem in Isolation	Presenting a Problem in a Story Context	Types of Subtraction
$5 - 3\frac{1}{4}$	*Stephano bought 5 pizzas for the birthday party. The guests ate $3\frac{1}{4}$ pizzas. How much pizza does Stephano have left?*	Removal
$57\frac{3}{4} - 52\frac{1}{2}$	*Eno is $52\frac{1}{2}$ inches tall. Lakea is $57\frac{3}{4}$ inches tall. How much taller is Lakea than Eno?*	Comparison
$2\frac{1}{2} - \frac{3}{4}$	*Michael walks $2\frac{1}{2}$ miles each day. He has already walked $\frac{3}{4}$ of a mile. How much further does Michael have to walk today?*	Difference/ Distance

Figure 7–3. *Presenting a Problem in Isolation Versus in a Story Context*

Learn More...

For more on the use of story problems in building fractional reasoning, see Chapter 4, pages 73–74.

The context can also influence which strategy students choose to use. Consider the last problem in Figure 7–3: $2\frac{1}{2} - \frac{3}{4}$. Figuring out how much farther Michael has to walk to make his distance may prompt students to think about adding up to find a solution.

Number Talk Tip

An important part of a number talk involves making students' thinking public and accessible to other students. We can record a student's strategy numerically, but also supporting the ideas with a model may help other learners follow and understand the student's thinking.

Using Models

In addition to using a story problem, we can incorporate a model during a number talk to give students an entry point for developing strategies and finding a solution. Different strategies lend themselves to different models. The following "Inside the Classroom" excerpt shows recordings and models to represent two strategies for the problem $1\frac{5}{12} - \frac{7}{12}$.

Inside the Classroom

A Number Talk for $1\frac{5}{12} - \frac{7}{12}$

Maria: I thought about 2 rectangles divided into twelfths with $1\frac{5}{12}$ shaded in.

[Ms. Muller draws and shades in two rectangles divided into twelfths.]

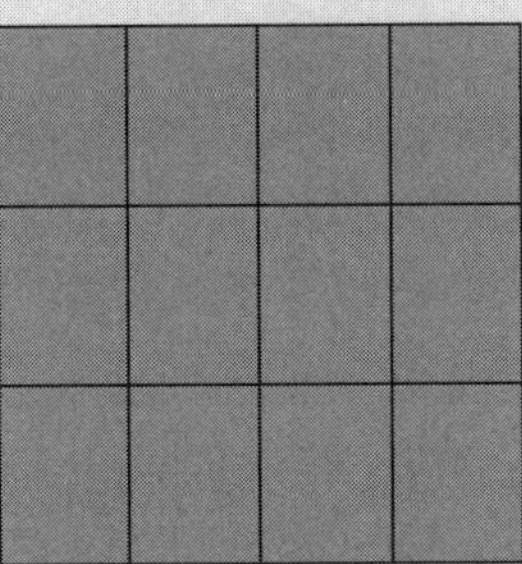

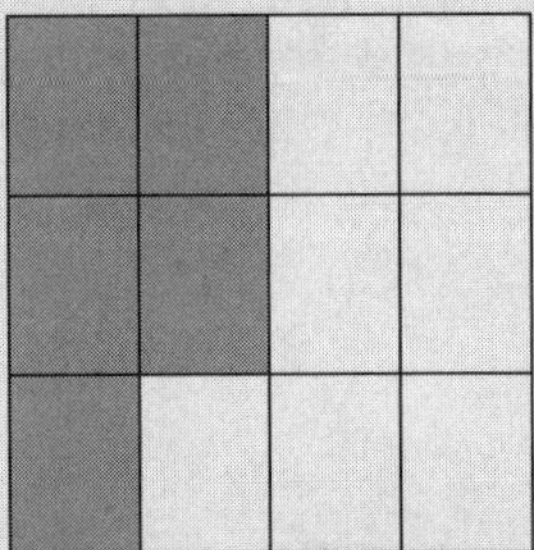

First I removed $\frac{5}{12}$ and that left me with 1 whole or $\frac{12}{12}$.

[Ms. Muller marks out $\frac{5}{12}$.]

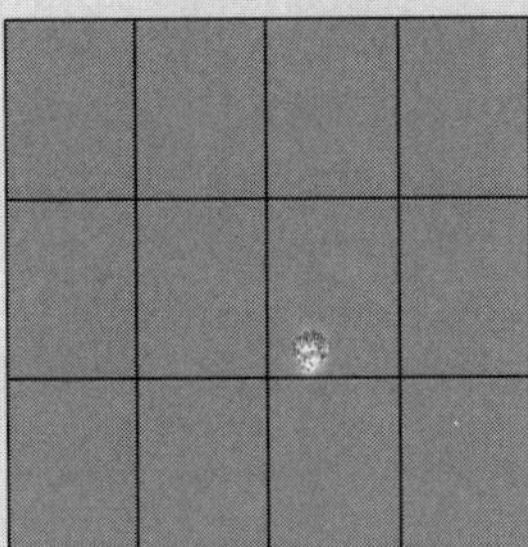

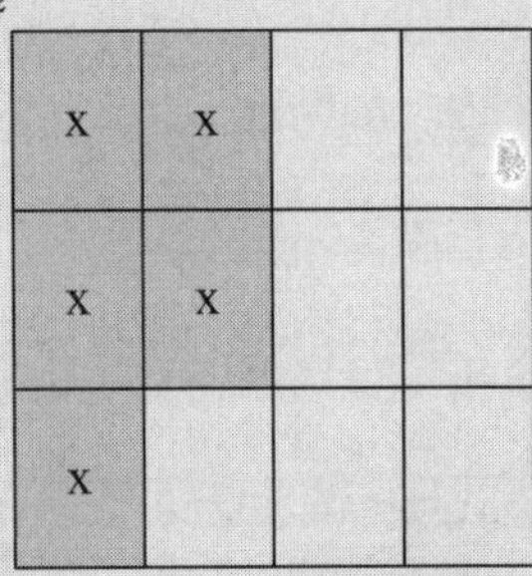

Then I took away the other $\frac{2}{12}$ from the 1 whole and had $\frac{10}{12}$ left.

[Ms. Muller marks out another $\frac{2}{12}$.]

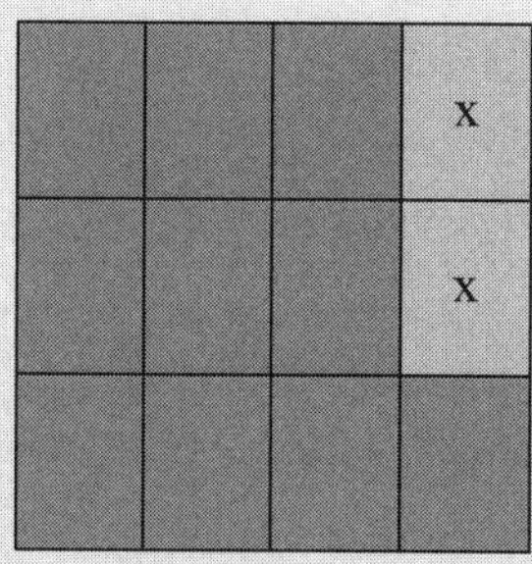

Ms. Muller: *[While writing.]*

We could also record your thinking numerically. You split $\frac{7}{12}$ into $\frac{5}{12}$ and $\frac{2}{12}$ and then you said first you removed $\frac{5}{12}$ and got 1, and then you took away the other $\frac{2}{12}$ and got $\frac{10}{12}$. Does this recording also match your thinking?

$$1\tfrac{5}{12} - \tfrac{7}{12}$$

$$= 1\tfrac{5}{12} - \left(\tfrac{5}{12} + \tfrac{2}{12}\right)$$

$$= \left(1\tfrac{5}{12} - \tfrac{5}{12}\right) - \tfrac{2}{12}$$

$$= 1 - \tfrac{2}{12} = \tfrac{10}{12}$$

Did anyone solve this problem another way?

Jaya: I added up to subtract. I know $\frac{7}{12}$ plus $\frac{5}{12}$ equals 1 whole. Then I added another $\frac{5}{12}$ to get to $1\frac{5}{12}$. Five-twelfths plus $\frac{5}{12}$ equals $\frac{10}{12}$.

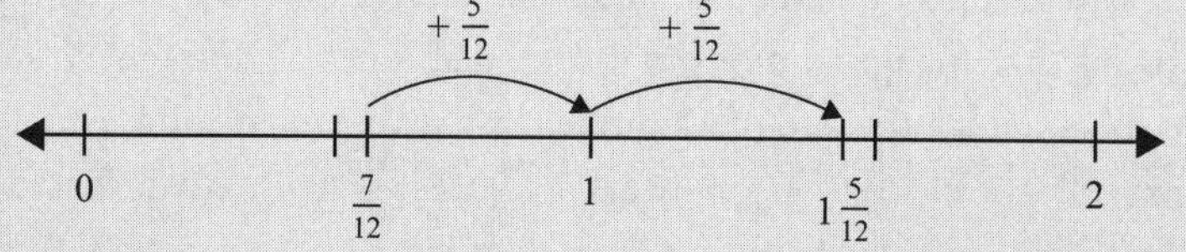

Ms. Muller: *[Ms. Muller records numerically as she speaks.]*

So to solve this problem you were thinking about what you needed to add to $\frac{7}{12}$ to get $1\frac{5}{12}$. You knew that $\frac{7}{12} + \frac{5}{12}$ would get you to 1 *[she circles the*

(continued)

Learn More...

For more on the use of models in building fractional reasoning, see Chapter 4.

first $\frac{5}{12}$*]*, and then you added the other $\frac{5}{12}$ to get to $1\frac{5}{12}$. *[She circles the next* $\frac{5}{12}$*.]* $\frac{5}{12}+\frac{5}{12}=\frac{10}{12}$, so that's how much you needed to add to $\frac{7}{12}$ to get $1\frac{5}{12}$; and that's how you knew that $1\frac{5}{12}-\frac{7}{12}=\frac{10}{12}$.

$$1\frac{5}{12}-\frac{7}{12}$$

$$\frac{7}{12}+\square=1\frac{5}{12}$$

$$\frac{7}{12}+\frac{5}{12}=1$$

$$1+\frac{5}{12}=1\frac{5}{12}$$

$$\frac{5}{12}+\frac{5}{12}=\frac{10}{12}$$

$$\frac{7}{12}+\boxed{\frac{10}{12}}=1\frac{5}{12}$$

$$1\frac{5}{12}+\frac{7}{12}=\frac{10}{12}$$

Connecting Students' Strategies

During a number talk, we want to honor all strategies and refrain from elevating one strategy over another. At the same time, we want to provide opportunities for students to reflect on their own thinking and refine their ideas. As students defend their solutions, look for opportunities to pose questions that engage students in thinking about how different strategies are connected. At the end of a number talk, you can encourage this process of reflection and revision by asking students to quietly indicate with a finger signal which shared strategy they view as the most efficient for them. This provides an opportunity for you to make a formative assessment, which you can use to guide the next day's number talk.

The following "Inside the Classroom" excerpt is from a classroom discussion about students' strategies for solving the problem $2\frac{3}{8}-\frac{5}{8}$. The first and third strategies are different ways of adding up, and the second uses the strategy of removing the subtrahend in parts.

Inside the Classroom

A Number Talk for $2\frac{3}{8} - \frac{5}{8}$

[Mr. Henry writes as each student explains their thinking. He numbers their strategies according to who shares first, second, and third.]

Mr. Henry: We have three strategies on the board. Use a quiet signal of 1, 2, or 3 fingers to show me which strategy is most efficient for you.

[Each student shares a quiet signal.]

Strategy 1	Strategy 2	Strategy 3
Gage: I started at $\frac{5}{8}$ and added on $\frac{1}{8}$ three times. That got me to $\frac{6}{8}$, then $\frac{7}{8}$, and then $\frac{8}{8}$ which is the same as 1. Then I added $1\frac{3}{8}$ more to get to $2\frac{3}{8}$. I added $\frac{1}{8} + \frac{1}{8} + \frac{1}{8} + 1\frac{3}{8}$ and that's $1\frac{6}{8}$ which is the difference between $\frac{5}{8}$ and $2\frac{3}{8}$.	Kevin: I thought about $\frac{5}{8}$ as $\frac{3}{8}$ and $\frac{2}{8}$. First I subtracted $\frac{3}{8}$ from $2\frac{3}{8}$ and got 2, and then I subtracted the other $\frac{2}{8}$ from the 2 and got $1\frac{6}{8}$ as my answer.	Leslie: I thought about this problem as $\frac{5}{8}$ + what would get me to $2\frac{3}{8}$. I knew that $\frac{5}{8} + \frac{3}{8}$ was $\frac{8}{8}$ or 1, and if I added $1\frac{3}{8}$ more to that, I would get $2\frac{3}{8}$. Three eighths + $1\frac{3}{8}$ is $1\frac{6}{8}$ and that's what I need to add to $\frac{5}{8}$ to get $2\frac{3}{8}$ so that's my answer.

(continued)

Strategy 1	Strategy 2	Strategy 3
$2\frac{3}{8} - \frac{5}{8}$	$2\frac{3}{8} - \frac{5}{8}$	$2\frac{3}{8} - \frac{5}{8}$
$\frac{5}{8} + \square = 2\frac{3}{8}$	$= 2\frac{3}{8} - \left(\frac{3}{8} + \frac{2}{8}\right)$	$\frac{5}{8} + \square = 2\frac{3}{8}$
$\frac{5}{8} + \left(\frac{1}{8}\right) = \frac{6}{8}$	$= \left(2\frac{3}{8} - \frac{3}{8}\right) - \frac{2}{8}$	
$\frac{6}{8} + \left(\frac{1}{8}\right) = \frac{7}{8}$	$= 2 - \frac{2}{8} = 1\frac{6}{8}$	$\frac{5}{8} + \left(\frac{3}{8}\right) = \frac{8}{8}$
$\frac{7}{8} + \left(\frac{1}{8}\right) = \frac{8}{8} = 1$		$1 + \left(1\frac{3}{8}\right) = 2\frac{3}{8}$
$1 + \left(1\frac{3}{8}\right) = 2\frac{3}{8}$		
$\frac{1}{8} + \frac{1}{8} + \frac{1}{8} + 1\frac{3}{8} = 1\frac{6}{8}$		$\frac{3}{8} + 1\frac{3}{8} = 1\frac{6}{8}$
$\frac{5}{8} + \boxed{1\frac{6}{8}} = 2\frac{3}{8}$		$\frac{5}{8} + \boxed{1\frac{6}{8}} = 2\frac{3}{8}$

Mr. Henry: I noticed several of you thought the third strategy was efficient. Could someone share why you thought this was an efficient strategy?

Blakely: Because it adds $\frac{3}{8}$ to get from $\frac{5}{8}$ to $\frac{8}{8}$ and then adds on $1\frac{3}{8}$ to get to $2\frac{3}{8}$. That makes it quicker.

Jose: I think number three and number one are alike, but the third strategy uses fewer jumps. Strategy one jumps $\frac{1}{8}$ and then another $\frac{1}{8}$ and then another $\frac{1}{8}$, but strategy three makes one jump of $\frac{3}{8}$ to get to 1 whole.

Mr. Henry: So are you saying that adding up in fewer jumps makes it a more efficient strategy?

Jose: Yes.

Mr. Henry: What about the second strategy?

Aaron: The $\frac{5}{8}$ was decomposed to $\frac{3}{8}$ and $\frac{2}{8}$. This made subtracting $\frac{3}{8}$ from $2\frac{3}{8}$ easy. Then they just subtracted $\frac{2}{8}$ from the 2.

Willa: That part seems fast, but I'm not sure why $\frac{2}{8}$ was subtracted at the end. It seems like you would add it.

Stephen: You have to subtract the $\frac{2}{8}$ because it was part of the $\frac{5}{8}$ from the original problem that had to be subtracted.

When students are listening to and thinking about other students' strategies during a number talk, they are *constructing viable arguments and critiquing the reasoning of others* (MP3).

$\frac{3}{4} - \frac{3}{8}$: Developing Subtraction Strategies with Fractions

Classroom Clip 7.1

Consider the following questions as you watch this number talk from a fourth-grade classroom:

1. What are some possible reasons that the teacher decides not to collect answers before asking students to turn and talk?
2. How do you decide when to use turn and talk in your classroom?
3. What does the student who uses Strategy 1 understand?
4. What do you notice about Israel's strategy?
5. What does Israel understand that helps him solve the problem?

To view this video clip, scan the QR code or access via mathsolutions.com/NTFDP7.1

Number Talks That Use Area Models for Subtraction with Fractions

As emphasized earlier in this chapter, models can give students an entry point for developing strategies and finding a solution. We can use area models in beginning number talks to support students as they think about subtraction, equivalence, and partitioning. Many students think in order to model a subtraction problem you have to use one model for the minuend and one for the subtrahend, but with subtraction problems, it is possible to use one model because the subtrahend is part of the minuend. As an example, think about the problem $\frac{5}{8} - \frac{1}{8}$. You might frame this problem in a story context, such as, "Five-eighths of Latoya's garden is planted with vegetables and rest is planted with flowers. One-eighth of the vegetable garden is planted with eggplant. How much of the garden is planted with other vegetables?" This context implies interpreting subtraction as removal. The $\frac{1}{8}$ can be removed from the $\frac{5}{8}$ because it is part of the $\frac{5}{8}$. This is the essence of the part–whole relationship in subtraction.

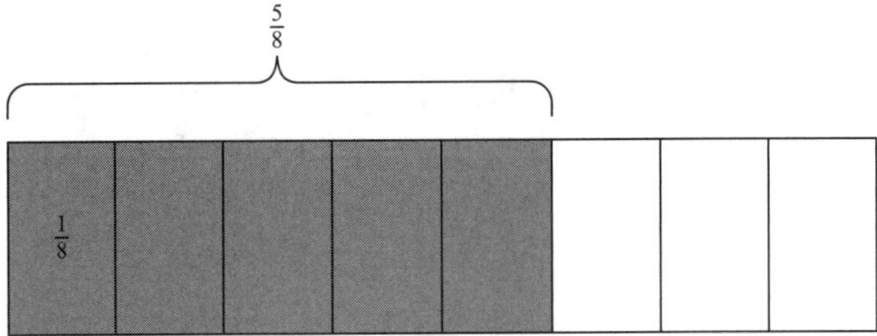

If we think about $\frac{5}{8} - \frac{1}{8}$ as a comparison problem, we can also use the same area model to represent this situation. For example, let's frame the problem in a different story context: "Melanie and Roberto each have candy bars of the same size. Melanie ate $\frac{5}{8}$ of her candy bar, and Roberto ate $\frac{1}{8}$ of his candy bar. How much more candy did Melanie eat than Roberto?" A student could represent this with one candy bar, since $\frac{5}{8}$ and $\frac{1}{8}$ are both parts of the same size whole.

Another student might use two separate candy bars to compare the difference between the two.

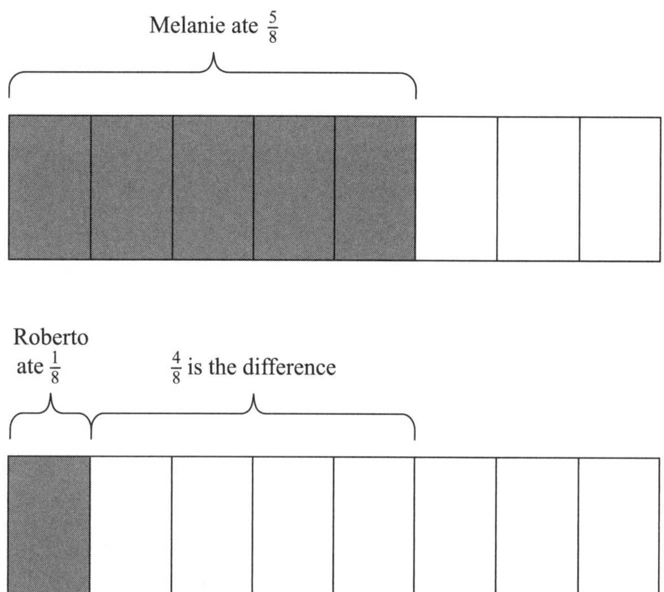

Each of the beginning number talks in this section use only one model. However, you may choose to incorporate a model for both the minuend and the subtrahend.

Using Area Models Partitioned into Eighths and Twelfths

The number talk strings in this category are structured to help students subtract fractions with like and unlike denominators. Each includes an area model showing the minuend shaded to provide an easier starting place; students only need to define the subtrahend. Each of the area models is partitioned into either eighths or twelfths. The models partitioned into eighths include problems using halves, fourths, and eighths. The models partitioned into twelfths use halves, thirds, fourths, sixths, and twelfths. This structure requires students to confront ideas of partitioning, equivalence, and common denominators. Each string is comprised of three problems designed to help students develop their reasoning by using the previous problems to build understanding.

Instructions

These number talk strings are organized into two columns and progress in difficulty (from A to B to C, etc.). Feel free to work through each string in order or choose problems according to your students' needs. You may choose to pose one problem or set of problems each day, or do more than one set of problems as time allows. For each number talk string, display the area model, introduce the first problem, collect solutions, then ask students to share their reasoning and proofs. Once the class reaches consensus, pose the second problem in the string and ask, *"How can you use what we already know to solve this next problem?"* Continue this format with each problem in the string.

What is _______ – _______? How do you know?
How can you use what we already know to solve the next problem?

A.

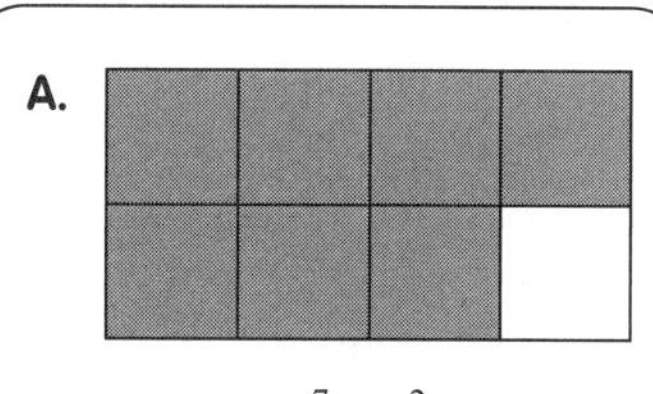

$\frac{7}{8} - \frac{2}{8}$

$\frac{7}{8} - \frac{3}{8}$

$\frac{7}{8} - \frac{5}{8}$

B.

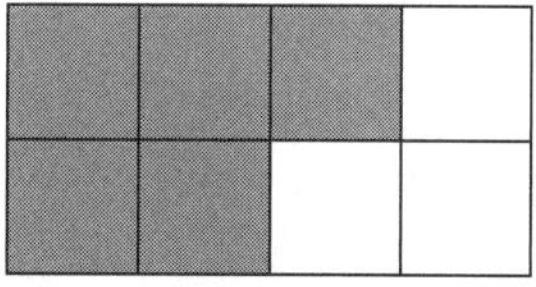

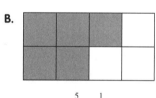

$\frac{5}{8} - \frac{1}{8}$

$\frac{5}{8} - \frac{1}{2}$

$\frac{5}{8} - \frac{1}{4}$

C.

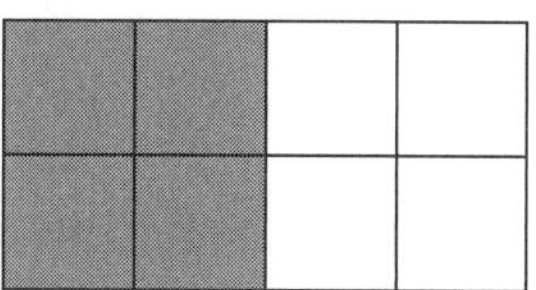

$\frac{1}{2} - \frac{1}{8}$

$\frac{1}{2} - \frac{3}{8}$

$\frac{1}{2} - \frac{1}{4}$

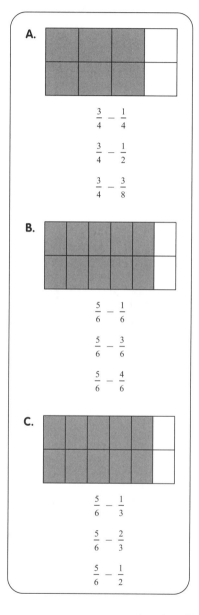

A.

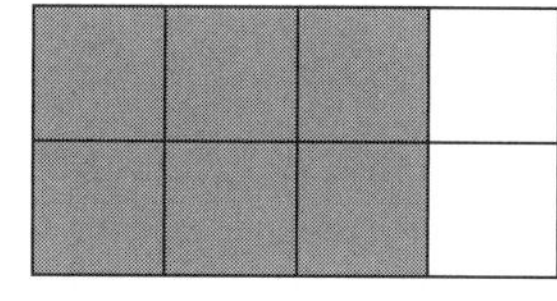

$\frac{3}{4} - \frac{1}{4}$

$\frac{3}{4} - \frac{1}{2}$

$\frac{3}{4} - \frac{3}{8}$

B.

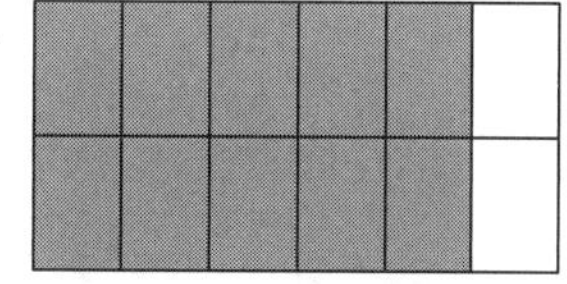

$\frac{5}{6} - \frac{1}{6}$

$\frac{5}{6} - \frac{3}{6}$

$\frac{5}{6} - \frac{4}{6}$

C.

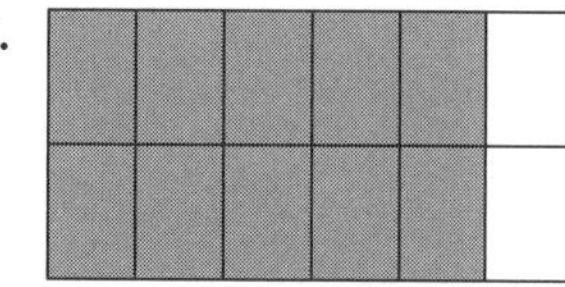

$\frac{5}{6} - \frac{1}{3}$

$\frac{5}{6} - \frac{2}{3}$

$\frac{5}{6} - \frac{1}{2}$

Number Talk Tip

As you present each problem, consider using various story contexts to deepen students' understanding of subtraction as removal, difference/comparison, and distance.

(continued)

Number Talk Tip

Using denominators that have a multiplicative relationship helps students focus on how the fractions are related. For instance, think about subtracting $\frac{2}{3} - \frac{1}{4}$ compared to subtracting $\frac{3}{4} - \frac{3}{8}$. It's easier to consider the relationships between fourths and eighths, because fourths can easily be partitioned into eighths, and only one of the fractions needs to be repartitioned. In contrast, with thirds and fourths *both* fractions must be repartitioned.

(What is _____ – _____? How do you know? How can you use what we already know to solve the next problem?, continued)

A.

$\frac{11}{12} - \frac{5}{12}$

$\frac{11}{12} - \frac{1}{2}$

$\frac{11}{12} - \frac{1}{4}$

B.

$\frac{3}{4} - \frac{1}{12}$

$\frac{3}{4} - \frac{1}{2}$

$\frac{3}{4} - \frac{1}{4}$

A.

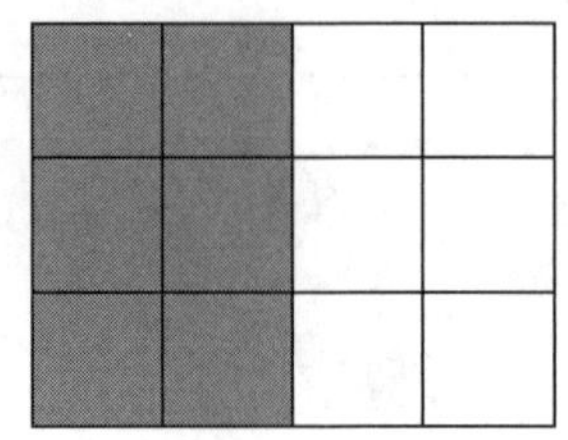

$\frac{1}{2} - \frac{1}{12}$

$\frac{1}{2} - \frac{1}{6}$

$\frac{1}{2} - \frac{1}{3}$

B.

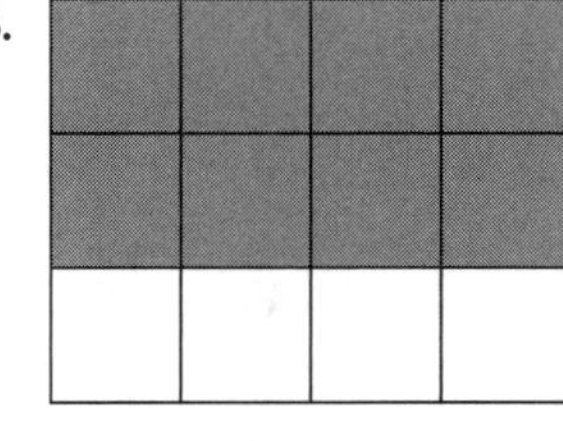

$\frac{2}{3} - \frac{1}{2}$

$\frac{2}{3} - \frac{1}{6}$

$\frac{2}{3} - \frac{1}{4}$

Reproducible 5

For full-sized reproducibles of the area models used in these number talks, visit www.mathsolutions.com/numbertalksfdp_reproducibles.

Number Talks That Use Set Models for Subtraction with Fractions

As emphasized earlier in this chapter, models give students an entry point for developing strategies and finding a solution. We can use set models in beginning number talks to support students as they think about equivalence, decomposing the minuend or subtrahend to make benchmark fractions, and what it means to subtract fractions. For the following number talks, show students the set model along with a computation problem and ask, *"How could you solve this problem?"* Collect and list all answers, and then ask, *"Who would like to defend their answer?"* As students share their strategies, make their thinking public by recording their strategies numerically. Some students may refer to the models and others may not. If students use the set models to defend their thinking, listen and record their reasoning by circling the dots or stars to match their strategy. The following "Inside the Classroom" excerpt shows how you might capture a student's thinking for solving $\frac{3}{4} - \frac{5}{8}$ numerically and using the set model.

Inside the Classroom

A Number Talk for $\frac{3}{4} - \frac{5}{8}$

☆ ☆ ☆ ☆
☆ ☆ ☆ ☆

$\frac{3}{4} - \frac{5}{8}$

Cameron: I knew that $\frac{3}{4}$ of the stars were 6 of them.

Ms. Corso: How did you know that?

Cameron: The stars are in four columns, so 3 of the 4 columns is $\frac{3}{4}$ of the stars.

[Ms. Corso partitions the set to show $\frac{3}{4}$ of the stars.]

☆ ☆ ☆ | ☆
☆ ☆ ☆ | ☆

(continued)

Cameron: I thought about $\frac{5}{8}$ as $\frac{1}{2}$ plus $\frac{1}{8}$. First I took away half of the stars and that left me with $\frac{1}{4}$.

[Ms. Corso crosses out half of the stars.]

Then I took away one more star and that left me with $\frac{1}{8}$ of the stars left from the $\frac{3}{4}$.

[Ms. Corso crosses out one more star and circles the $\frac{1}{8}$ that is left from $\frac{3}{4}$ of the stars.]

[Ms. Corso also records Cameron's thinking numerically]:

$$\frac{3}{4} - \frac{5}{8}$$

$$= \frac{3}{4} - \left(\frac{1}{2} + \frac{1}{8}\right)$$

$$= \left(\frac{3}{4} - \frac{1}{2}\right) - \frac{1}{8}$$

$$= \frac{1}{4} - \frac{1}{8}$$

$$= \frac{1}{8}$$

Ms. Corso: Does this recording match your thinking?

Number Talk Tip

Taking time to listen to students and honor their thinking creates a classroom environment where students are willing to take risks as they investigate complex ideas. Focusing on making sense of problems and justifying solutions helps students become confident in their ability to do mathematics.

These number talk strings are structured to help students think about composing and decomposing fractions and to consider equivalence when subtracting fractions. The set model offers opportunities for students to partition and consider the part–whole relationship. Each number talk string includes a set model with either eight stars or twelve dots. Problems using halves, fourths, and eighths are framed around the set model with eight stars. Problems using halves, thirds, fourths, sixths, and twelfths are designed to be used with the set of twelve dots. Each of the number talk strings use fractions with denominators that are multiples of each other.

Instructions

These number talks are organized into two columns and progress in difficulty (from A to B to C, etc.). Feel free to work through each string in order or choose problems according to your students' needs. You may choose to pose one problem or set of problems each day, or do more than one set of problems as time allows. For each number talk string, display the set model and introduce the first problem. Collect solutions, then ask students to share their reasoning and proofs. Once the class reaches consensus, pose the second problem in the string and ask, *"How can you use what we already know to solve this next problem?"* Continue this format with each problem in the string.

What is ______ – ______? How do you know?
How can you use what we already know to solve this next problem?

__________ – __________

A. $\frac{5}{8} - \frac{1}{8}$

$\frac{5}{8} - \frac{1}{2}$

$\frac{5}{8} - \frac{1}{4}$

B. $\frac{1}{2} - \frac{1}{8}$

$\frac{1}{2} - \frac{3}{8}$

$\frac{1}{2} - \frac{1}{4}$

A. $\frac{3}{4} - \frac{1}{4}$

$\frac{3}{4} - \frac{1}{2}$

$\frac{3}{4} - \frac{1}{8}$

B. $\frac{3}{4} - \frac{1}{8}$

$\frac{3}{4} - \frac{3}{8}$

$\frac{3}{4} - \frac{5}{8}$

(What is ______ – ______? How do you know? How can you use what we already know to solve this next problem?, continued)

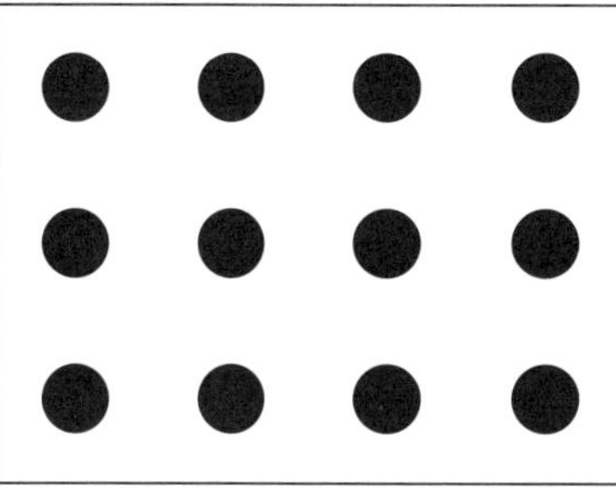

____________ – ____________

A. $\frac{11}{12} - \frac{1}{2}$

$\frac{11}{12} - \frac{4}{12}$

$\frac{11}{12} - \frac{1}{2}$

B. $\frac{1}{2} - \frac{1}{12}$

$\frac{1}{2} - \frac{3}{12}$

$\frac{1}{2} - \frac{1}{4}$

C. $\frac{3}{4} - \frac{1}{12}$

$\frac{3}{4} - \frac{1}{2}$

$\frac{3}{4} - \frac{3}{12}$

A. $\frac{3}{4} - \frac{1}{3}$

$\frac{3}{4} - \frac{2}{3}$

$\frac{3}{4} - \frac{1}{6}$

B. $\frac{5}{6} - \frac{1}{2}$

$\frac{5}{6} - \frac{1}{3}$

$\frac{5}{6} - \frac{1}{4}$

C. $\frac{5}{6} - \frac{5}{12}$

$\frac{5}{6} - \frac{2}{3}$

$\frac{5}{6} - \frac{3}{4}$

Number Talks That Use Linear Models for Subtraction with Fractions

As emphasized earlier in this chapter, models can give students an entry point for developing strategies and finding solutions. We can use linear models in beginning number talks to support students as they think about partitioning, equivalence, decomposing to make benchmark fractions, and what it means to subtract fractions. Including a story problem along with a number line adds another layer of support. For example, we can write the problem $1\frac{1}{2} - \frac{3}{4}$ with a 0 to 2 number line partitioned into fourths and say, *"Tamara had $1\frac{1}{2}$ yards of leather and used $\frac{3}{4}$ of a yard to make a belt. How much leather does she have left?"* We might anticipate that one way a student might solve this problem is to decompose $\frac{3}{4}$ into $\frac{1}{2}$ and $\frac{1}{4}$ and then subtract $1 - \frac{1}{4}$. (See Figure 7–4.)

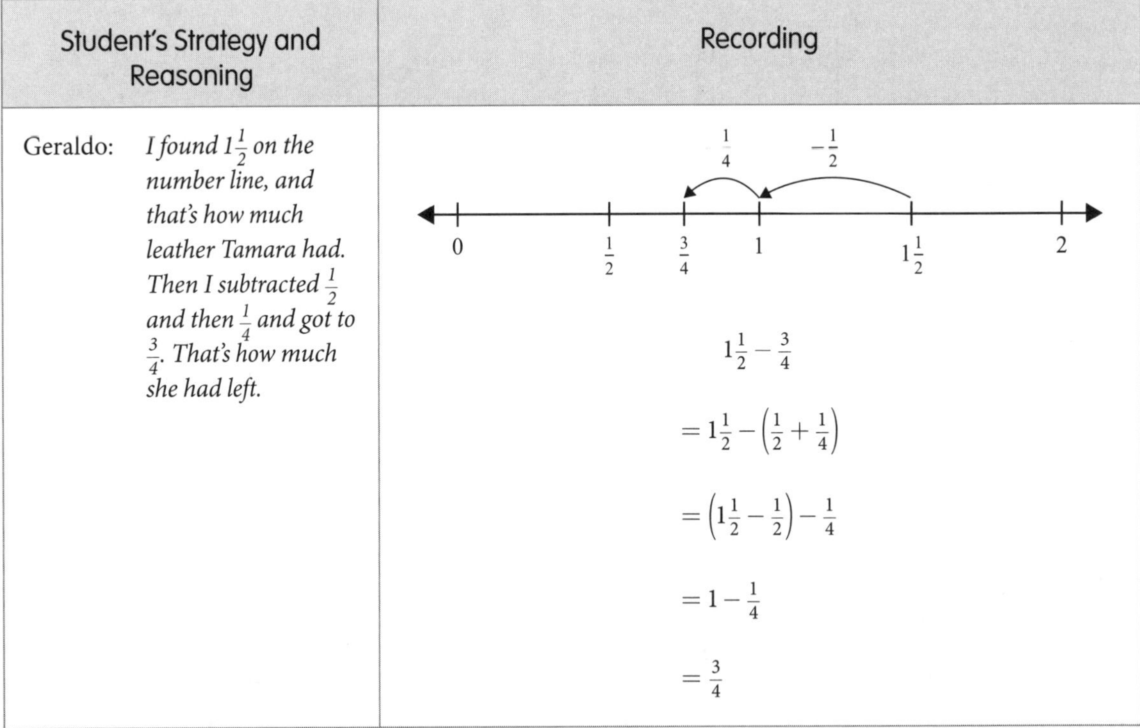

Student's Strategy and Reasoning	Recording
Geraldo: *I found $1\frac{1}{2}$ on the number line, and that's how much leather Tamara had. Then I subtracted $\frac{1}{2}$ and then $\frac{1}{4}$ and got to $\frac{3}{4}$. That's how much she had left.*	$\frac{1}{4}$ $-\frac{1}{2}$ 0 $\frac{1}{2}$ $\frac{3}{4}$ 1 $1\frac{1}{2}$ 2 $1\frac{1}{2} - \frac{3}{4}$ $= 1\frac{1}{2} - \left(\frac{1}{2} + \frac{1}{4}\right)$ $= \left(1\frac{1}{2} - \frac{1}{2}\right) - \frac{1}{4}$ $= 1 - \frac{1}{4}$ $= \frac{3}{4}$

Figure 7–4. *Using "Decomposing to Make a Benchmark Number" to Solve $1\frac{1}{2} - \frac{3}{4}$*

Category 1
Using a Number Line Partitioned into Halves and Fourths

The number talk strings in this category are structured to help students subtract fractions with like and unlike denominators. The strings include a number line partitioned into halves and fourths. This structure requires students to confront ideas of partitioning, equivalence, and common denominators. Each string is comprised of two problems that have denominators of halves, fourths, or eighths. We suggest using a 0 to 2 number line partitioned into fourths as you present each problem.

Instructions

These number talks are organized into three columns and progress in difficulty going from the first column (from A to B to C, etc.) to the second column to the third column. Feel free to work through each pair of problems in order or choose problems according to your students' needs. You may choose to pose one problem or set of problems each day, or do more than one set of problems as time allows. Introduce the first problem along with the 0 to 2 number line. Collect solutions, then ask students to share their reasoning and proofs. Once the class reaches consensus, pose the second problem in the string and ask, *"How can you use what we already know to solve this next problem?"* Continue this format with each problem in the string.

What is ______ – ______ ? How do you know?
How can you use what we already know to solve this next problem?

Number Talk Tip

Note that all subtraction problems can be represented using a number line. However, if you present the problems using a distance story problem, a number line is especially helpful to represent student thinking.

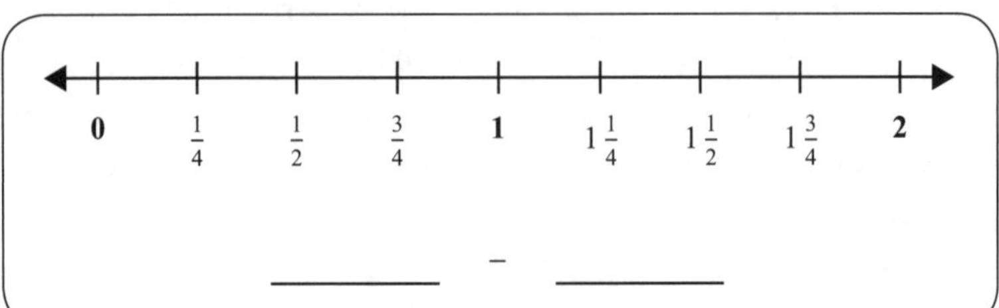

A. $\frac{3}{4} - \frac{1}{4}$

$\frac{3}{4} - \frac{1}{2}$

B. $1\frac{1}{2} - \frac{3}{4}$

$1\frac{1}{2} - 1\frac{1}{4}$

C. $2 - \frac{3}{4}$

$2 - 1\frac{1}{2}$

D. $\frac{6}{8} - \frac{2}{8}$

$\frac{6}{8} - \frac{1}{2}$

A. $2 - \frac{1}{2}$

$2 - \frac{3}{8}$

B. $2 - \frac{5}{8}$

$2 - \frac{3}{4}$

C. $1\frac{1}{4} - \frac{4}{8}$

$1\frac{1}{4} - \frac{6}{8}$

D. $1\frac{2}{8} - \frac{2}{4}$

$1\frac{2}{8} - \frac{3}{4}$

A. $\frac{3}{4} - \frac{2}{8}$

$\frac{3}{4} - \frac{4}{8}$

B. $\frac{5}{8} - \frac{1}{4}$

$\frac{5}{8} - \frac{1}{2}$

C. $1\frac{3}{8} - \frac{3}{4}$

$1\frac{3}{8} - 1\frac{1}{4}$

D. $1\frac{3}{4} - \frac{5}{8}$

$1\frac{3}{4} - \frac{3}{8}$

Reproducible 15

For a full-sized reproducible of the 0 to 2 number line used in these number talks, visit www.mathsolutions.com/numbertalksfdp_reproducibles.

Category 2
Using a Number Line Partitioned into Halves and Thirds

Reproducible 16

For a full-sized reproducible of the 0 to 2 number line used in these number talks, visit www.mathsolutions.com/numbertalksfdp_reproducibles.

The number talk strings in this category are structured to help students consider subtracting fractions with like and unlike denominators. The strings include a number line partitioned into halves and thirds. Each string is comprised of two problems that have denominators of halves, thirds, and sixths. We suggest using a 0 to 2 number line partitioned into halves and thirds as you present each problem.

Instructions

These number talks are organized into three columns and progress in difficulty going from the first column (from A to B to C, etc.) to the second column to the third column. Feel free to work through each pair of problems in order or choose problems according to your students' needs. You may choose to pose one problem or set of problems each day, or do more than one set of problems as time allows. Introduce the first problem in the pair along with a 0 to 2 number line, collect solutions, then ask students to share their reasoning and proofs. Once the class reaches consensus, pose the second problem and ask, *"How can you use what we already know to solve this next problem?"*

What is ______ – ______? How do you know?
How can you use what we already know to solve this next problem?

Number Talk Tip

Students can use the number line model to represent their thinking, but the number line itself is not a strategy for solving a problem. A strategy happens mentally and can be represented in various ways.

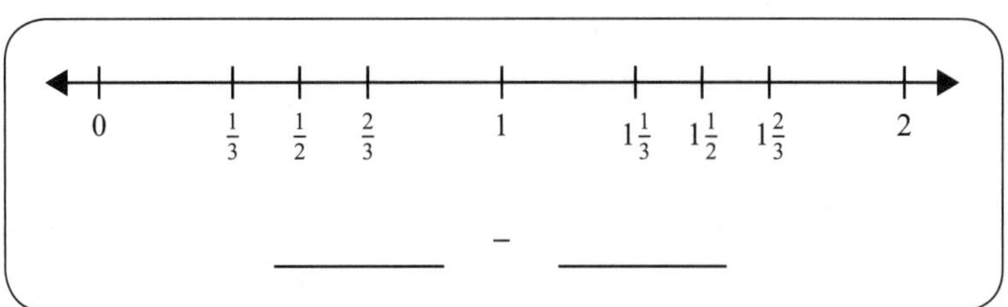

A. $\frac{5}{6} - \frac{3}{6}$

$\frac{5}{6} - \frac{2}{6}$

B. $1\frac{1}{3} - \frac{1}{3}$

$1\frac{1}{3} - \frac{2}{3}$

C. $2 - 1\frac{1}{3}$

$2 - 1\frac{2}{3}$

D. $\frac{5}{6} - \frac{1}{2}$

$\frac{5}{6} - \frac{1}{3}$

E. $1\frac{1}{3} - \frac{1}{6}$

$1\frac{1}{3} - \frac{3}{6}$

A. $2 - \frac{3}{6}$

$2 - \frac{5}{6}$

B. $\frac{2}{3} - \frac{1}{6}$

$\frac{2}{3} - \frac{2}{6}$

C. $1\frac{1}{2} - \frac{3}{6}$

$1\frac{1}{2} - \frac{5}{6}$

D. $2 - \frac{2}{3}$

$2 - 1\frac{1}{3}$

E. $\frac{4}{6} - \frac{1}{6}$

$\frac{4}{6} - \frac{2}{3}$

A. $1\frac{2}{3} - \frac{1}{2}$

$1\frac{2}{3} - \frac{4}{6}$

B. $2 - \frac{1}{3}$

$2 - \frac{2}{3}$

C. $\frac{1}{2} - \frac{1}{6}$

$\frac{1}{2} - \frac{1}{3}$

D. $1\frac{2}{3} - \frac{2}{6}$

$1\frac{2}{3} - \frac{5}{6}$

E. $2 - \frac{3}{3}$

$2 - \frac{4}{3}$

Number Talks That Highlight the Subtraction Strategy "Adding Up"

Once students have worked with beginning number talks using models, transition into number talks that further emphasize numerical relationships and the development of strategies. In this section the focus is on the subtraction strategy "Adding Up."

Because of the inverse relationship between addition and subtraction, any subtraction problem can be represented as a missing addend problem. When students understand this relationship and that subtraction involves finding the difference between two quantities, they realize they can add up to find the answer. Consider presenting the problem in a story context that looks at how much more is needed to get to an amount; this approach can help students understand that the goal is to find the difference between the numbers. Here are a few examples.

- *Margaret's goal is to run* $1\frac{3}{4}$ *miles. She has already run* $\frac{1}{4}$ *of a mile. How much further does she have to go to reach her goal?*
- *It takes* $3\frac{1}{2}$ *hours to drive to Grandma's house. We have been riding for an hour and 15 minutes. How much longer until we reach her house?*
- *The recipe needs* $2\frac{1}{2}$ *cups of flour. I have already put in* $\frac{3}{4}$ *of a cup. How much more flour do I need to add?*

Figure 7–5 on the next page shows how a teacher might record a student's thinking for the recipe problem, $2\frac{1}{2} - \frac{3}{4}$.

When students add up to subtract, they are relying on the relationship between addition and subtraction. As they use this strategy, they build up from the subtrahend to the minuend to find the difference between the two numbers and usually make jumps that get to the closest benchmark number. The larger and fewer the jumps, the more efficient this strategy becomes.

Number Talk Tip

Each strategy is labeled to represent the thinking involved; however, in our classrooms we often name the strategies according to the students who invent them. The name of the strategy is not as important as the mathematical ideas the students are using. Keep this in mind as you examine each strategy.

Student's Strategy and Reasoning	Recording
Adding Up Will: *I thought about this problem as $\frac{3}{4}$ plus what equals $2\frac{1}{2}$. I started at $\frac{3}{4}$ which was the amount of flour already in the recipe. Then I added $\frac{1}{4}$ cup more flour to get to 1 whole cup. Next I added $1\frac{1}{2}$ more cups of flour and got to $2\frac{1}{2}$ cups. So the amount I had to add to the $\frac{3}{4}$ I started with was $\frac{1}{4}$ + $1\frac{1}{2}$ or $1\frac{3}{4}$ cups. That's how much more flour I need to add to the recipe.* *[The teacher records Will's strategy on a number line as well as numerically to help make his thinking accessible to the rest of the class.]*	$2\frac{1}{2} - \frac{3}{4}$ $\frac{3}{4} + \square = 2\frac{1}{2}$ $\frac{3}{4} + \left(\frac{1}{4}\right) = 1$ $1 + \left(1\frac{1}{2}\right) = 2\frac{1}{2}$ $\frac{1}{4} + 1\frac{1}{2} = 1\frac{3}{4}$ $\frac{3}{4} + \boxed{1\frac{3}{4}} = 2\frac{1}{2}$ $2\frac{1}{2} - \frac{3}{4}$ Number line: 0, $\frac{3}{4}$, 1, 2, $2\frac{1}{2}$; jumps $+\frac{1}{4}$ and $+1\frac{1}{2}$

Figure 7–5. *Using "Adding Up" to Solve $2\frac{1}{2} - \frac{3}{4}$*

Category 1
Using Like Denominators

The number talk strings in this category are structured to help students decompose fractions to get to a benchmark number. Each string includes three problems in which the minuend is a whole number or the minuend and subtrahend have the same denominators. In either case, there is an inherent benchmark relationship that makes the numbers easier to hold on to mentally.

Number Talk Tip

You will notice that most of the problems use either common denominators or denominators that are multiples of each other. We deliberately chose these numbers to keep the focus on developing strategies, numerical relationships, and understanding subtraction with fractions.

Instructions

The number talks are organized into three columns and progress in difficulty going from the first column (from A to B to C) to the second column to the third column. Feel free to work through each string in order or choose problems according to your students' needs. You may choose to pose one problem or set of problems each day, or do more than one set of problems as time allows. For each number talk string, introduce the first problem, collect solutions, and then ask students to share their reasoning and proofs. Once the class reaches consensus, pose the next problem in the string and ask, *"How can you use what we just solved to help you with this next problem?"* or *"How does this new problem relate to the previous problem(s)?"* Continue this format with each problem in the string.

What is ______ – ______? How do you know?
How can you use what we already know to solve this next problem?

Number Talk Tip

Remember that there are multiple ways to solve a problem, and students may not always use the methods the problems in a given number talk are designed to elicit. The goal of the number talk is to help students make sense of the problems, notice relationships, and deepen their understanding of mathematics—not to try to force students to use any particular method for solving problems.

A. $4-1\frac{1}{2}$

$4-1\frac{1}{4}$

$4-1\frac{3}{4}$

B. $2-1\frac{4}{5}$

$2-1\frac{3}{5}$

$2-1\frac{2}{5}$

C. $3-\frac{2}{3}$

$3-1\frac{2}{3}$

$3-1\frac{1}{3}$

A. $3\frac{1}{6}-\frac{5}{6}$

$3\frac{1}{6}-\frac{3}{6}$

$3\frac{1}{6}-1\frac{2}{6}$

B. $5\frac{1}{3}-\frac{2}{3}$

$5\frac{1}{3}-2\frac{2}{3}$

$5\frac{1}{3}-4\frac{2}{3}$

C. $6\frac{1}{8}-3\frac{6}{8}$

$6\frac{1}{8}-2\frac{5}{8}$

$6\frac{1}{8}-4\frac{2}{8}$

A. $5\frac{2}{9}-3\frac{8}{9}$

$5\frac{2}{9}-2\frac{6}{9}$

$5\frac{2}{9}-1\frac{4}{9}$

B. $8\frac{2}{7}-6\frac{6}{7}$

$8\frac{2}{7}-4\frac{5}{7}$

$8\frac{2}{7}-5\frac{3}{7}$

C. $4\frac{2}{11}-3\frac{10}{11}$

$4\frac{2}{11}-3\frac{7}{11}$

$4\frac{1}{11}-3\frac{3}{11}$

Category 2
Using Unlike Denominators

The number talk strings in this category are structured to help students decompose fractions to get to a benchmark number. Each string includes three problems in which the minuend is a mixed number and the denominators in the subtrahend are multiples of the denominators in the minuend. In each problem, there is an inherent benchmark relationship that makes the numbers easier to hold on to mentally.

Instructions

The number talks are organized into three columns and progress in difficulty going from the first column (from A to B to C) to the second column to the third column. Feel free to work through each string in order or choose problems according to your students' needs. You may choose to pose one problem or set of problems each day, or do more than one set of problems as time allows. For each number talk string, introduce the first problem, collect solutions, and then ask students to share their reasoning and proofs. Once the class reaches consensus, pose the next problem in the string and ask, *"How can you use what we just solved to help you with this problem?"* Continue this format for each problem in the string.

What is ______ – ______? How do you know?
How can you use what we already know to solve the next problem?

Number Talk Tip

As you present each problem, consider using various story contexts to deepen students' understanding of subtracting fractions. Using a model to represent students' ideas will also provide them with another layer of support.

A. $2\frac{1}{2} - 1$

$2\frac{1}{2} - 1\frac{1}{4}$

$2\frac{1}{2} - 1\frac{3}{4}$

B. $1\frac{1}{2} - \frac{7}{8}$

$1\frac{1}{2} - \frac{5}{8}$

$1\frac{1}{2} - \frac{3}{8}$

C. $4\frac{1}{2} - 2\frac{5}{6}$

$4\frac{1}{2} - 2\frac{4}{6}$

$4\frac{1}{2} - 3\frac{1}{6}$

A. $5\frac{3}{8} - 4\frac{3}{4}$

$5\frac{3}{8} - 4\frac{1}{4}$

$5\frac{3}{8} - 4\frac{2}{4}$

B. $5\frac{3}{4} - 3\frac{7}{8}$

$5\frac{3}{4} - 2\frac{5}{8}$

$5\frac{3}{4} - 1\frac{1}{8}$

C. $5\frac{3}{10} - 2\frac{4}{5}$

$5\frac{3}{10} - 3\frac{3}{5}$

$5\frac{3}{10} - 1\frac{1}{5}$

A. $6\frac{2}{5} - 3\frac{9}{10}$

$6\frac{2}{5} - 2\frac{8}{10}$

$6\frac{2}{5} - 4\frac{3}{10}$

B. $5\frac{1}{3} - 4\frac{4}{6}$

$5\frac{1}{3} - 2\frac{5}{6}$

$5\frac{1}{3} - 1\frac{1}{6}$

C. $5\frac{1}{3} - 2\frac{8}{9}$

$5\frac{1}{3} - 3\frac{4}{9}$

$4\frac{2}{3} - 1\frac{5}{9}$

Number Talks That Highlight the Subtraction Strategy "Removing the Subtrahend in Parts"

Once students have worked with beginning number talks using models, transition into number talks that further emphasize numerical relationships and the development of strategies. In this section, the focus is on the subtraction strategy "Removing the Subtrahend in Parts."

Students who use this strategy keep the minuend whole and break down the subtrahend into parts to make a series of smaller and easier problems. They often decompose the subtrahend into benchmarks and/or unit fractions to make removal easier. For example, during a number talk, students might approach the problem $1\frac{1}{4} - \frac{3}{4}$ by breaking apart the subtrahend into $\frac{1}{4} + \frac{1}{4} + \frac{1}{4}$ and removing $\frac{1}{4}$ three times, or decomposing $\frac{3}{4}$ into $\frac{1}{4} + \frac{1}{2}$ and removing $\frac{3}{4}$ in two steps. Figure 7–6 on the next page shows how a teacher might record a student's thinking for this. For recording, it is important to help students keep track of how much they subtract to make sure they remove the correct amount. If students explain their thinking using a number line, we can represent their thinking with the number line but also include a numerical recording.

When students decompose the minuend, they are *looking for and making use of structure* (MP7) to subtract.

The following number talk strings use like and unlike denominators and are structured to help students develop reasoning using benchmark fractions.

Student's Strategy and Reasoning	Recording
Removing the Subtrahend in Parts Charlotta: *I knew there were 3 one-fourths in $\frac{3}{4}$. $1\frac{1}{4} - \frac{1}{4} = 1$, $1 - \frac{1}{4} = \frac{3}{4}$, and $\frac{3}{4} - \frac{1}{4} = \frac{1}{2}$.*	$1\frac{1}{4} - \frac{3}{4}$ $= 1\frac{1}{4} - \left(\frac{1}{4} + \frac{1}{4} + \frac{1}{4}\right)$ $= \left(1\frac{1}{4} - \frac{1}{4}\right) - \frac{1}{4} - \frac{1}{4}$ $= \left(1 - \frac{1}{4}\right) - \frac{1}{4}$ $= \frac{3}{4} - \frac{1}{4} = \frac{1}{2}$ $-\frac{1}{4}$ $-\frac{1}{4}$ $-\frac{1}{4}$ 0 $\frac{1}{2}$ $\frac{3}{4}$ 1 $1\frac{1}{4}$

Figure 7–6. *Using "Removing the Subtrahend in Parts" to Solve $1\frac{1}{4} - \frac{3}{4}$*

Instructions

These number talks are organized into three columns and progress in difficulty from the first column (from A to B to C), to the second column, to the third column. Feel free to work through each sting in order or choose problems according to your students' needs. You may choose to pose one problem or set of problems each day, or do more than one set as time allows. Introduce the first problem in the string, collect solutions, then ask students to share their reasoning and proofs. Once the class reaches consensus, pose the second problem in the string and ask, *"How can you use what we already know to solve this next problem?"* Continue this format with each problem in the string.

What is ______ – ______? How can you use the number line to justify your solution? How can you use what we already know to solve this next problem?

A. $1\frac{1}{2} - \frac{1}{2}$

$1\frac{1}{2} - \frac{1}{4}$

$1\frac{1}{2} - \frac{3}{4}$

B. $1 - \frac{1}{2}$

$1 - \frac{2}{6}$

$1 - \frac{5}{6}$

C. $1\frac{3}{4} - \frac{4}{8}$

$1\frac{3}{4} - \frac{1}{8}$

$1\frac{3}{4} - \frac{5}{8}$

A. $2\frac{1}{5} - \frac{1}{5}$

$2\frac{1}{5} - \frac{3}{5}$

$2\frac{1}{5} - \frac{4}{5}$

B. $4\frac{3}{8} - 1\frac{3}{8}$

$4\frac{3}{8} - \frac{2}{8}$

$4\frac{3}{8} - 1\frac{5}{8}$

C. $3\frac{1}{12} - \frac{1}{12}$

$3\frac{1}{12} - \frac{1}{12}$

$3\frac{1}{12} - \frac{7}{12}$

A. $2\frac{1}{7} - \frac{1}{7}$

$2\frac{1}{7} - \frac{2}{7}$

$2\frac{1}{7} - \frac{3}{7}$

B. $3\frac{1}{9} - \frac{1}{9}$

$3\frac{1}{9} - \frac{1}{3}$

$3\frac{1}{9} - \frac{4}{9}$

C. $3\frac{1}{10} - \frac{1}{10}$

$3\frac{1}{10} - \frac{3}{5}$

$3\frac{1}{10} - \frac{7}{10}$

Number Talks That Highlight the Subtraction Strategy "Partial Differences"

Once students have worked with beginning number talks using models, transition into number talks that further emphasize numerical relationships and the development of strategies. In this section, the focus is on the subtraction strategy "Partial Differences."

Students sometimes use this strategy when they subtract whole numbers. For example, for the problem *42 − 28*, a student might subtract 40 − 20 to get 20 and 2 − 8 to get −6. Then the student combines these differences to get 14.

$$\begin{array}{r} 42 \\ -\ \underline{28} \\ 20 + (-6) = 14 \end{array}$$

This is also a strategy that students sometimes use when subtracting mixed numbers. In lieu of regrouping or changing mixed numbers to improper fractions to subtract, they decompose the mixed numbers into whole numbers and fractions and subtract whole numbers from whole numbers and fractions from fractions. Sometimes subtracting a fraction from a fraction can result in a negative number. Students then combine the difference between the whole numbers and the difference between the fractions. Once students begin thinking about negative numbers, this is a strategy that many learners use. Figure 7–7 uses the problem $4\frac{3}{8} - 2\frac{7}{8}$ to illustrate this idea; different ways of recording this strategy can highlight different ideas. The first recording shows how both mixed numbers are decomposed. For many students, the second recording provides a clearer representation of subtracting whole numbers from whole numbers and fractions from fractions.

When we accurately record students' strategies to capture the mathematics, we are providing an example of *attending to precision* (MP6). The way we record will influence how students record.

The following number talk strings are designed so the fraction in the subtrahend is greater than the fraction in the minuend. This results in a negative difference.

Student's Strategy and Reasoning	Recording 1	Recording 2
Partial Differences Connor: *I split the mixed numbers into whole numbers and fractions.* *$4 - 2 = 2$, and* $\frac{3}{8} - \frac{7}{8} = -\frac{4}{8}$. *2 and* $-\frac{4}{8} = 1\frac{1}{2}$.	$4\frac{3}{8} - 2\frac{7}{8}$ $= \left(4 + \frac{3}{8}\right) - \left(2 + \frac{7}{8}\right)$ $= (4 - 2) + \left(\frac{3}{8} - \frac{7}{8}\right)$ $= 2 + \left(-\frac{4}{8}\right)$ $= 1\frac{1}{2}$	$\begin{array}{rr} 4 & \frac{3}{8} \\ -2 & \frac{7}{8} \\ \hline \end{array}$ $2 + \left(-\frac{4}{8}\right) = 1\frac{1}{2}$

Figure 7–7. *Two Ways to Record a Student Using "Partial Differences" with Negative Numbers*

Instructions

The number talks are organized into three columns and progress in difficulty from the first column (from A to B to C) to the second column to the third column. You may present the problems as a string or use them individually. Introduce the first problem, collect solutions, then ask students to share their reasoning and proofs. Once the class reaches consensus, pose the second problem in the string and ask, *"How can you use what we already know to solve this next problem?"*

What did you get for an answer to ______ – ______?
How do you know?
Can you use what we already know to solve this next problem?

A. $\frac{2}{7} - \frac{3}{7}$ $1\frac{2}{7} - \frac{3}{7}$	**A.** $\frac{6}{8} - \frac{7}{8}$ $6\frac{6}{8} - 2\frac{7}{8}$	**A.** $\frac{2}{5} - \frac{4}{5}$ $5\frac{2}{5} - 2\frac{4}{5}$
B. $\frac{2}{7} - \frac{5}{7}$ $3\frac{2}{7} - \frac{5}{7}$	**B.** $\frac{4}{9} - \frac{7}{9}$ $9\frac{4}{9} - 2\frac{7}{9}$	**B.** $\frac{12}{15} - \frac{14}{15}$ $8\frac{12}{15} - 4\frac{14}{15}$
C. $\frac{3}{8} - \frac{5}{8}$ $4\frac{3}{8} - 1\frac{5}{8}$	**C.** $\frac{6}{11} - \frac{8}{11}$ $5\frac{6}{11} - 3\frac{8}{11}$	**C.** $\frac{1}{2} - \frac{5}{6}$ $4\frac{1}{2} - 2\frac{5}{6}$

Anticipating Student Thinking

The more regularly you use number talks with your students, the more confident you will become at anticipating your students' thinking and understanding the ways they solve problems. There are usually a limited number of subtraction strategies students actually use, so the more familiar you become with these strategies, the less challenging it will be to anticipate their thinking. As you plan your number talks, anticipate ways students might solve each problem, and decide ahead of time how you might record their thinking so their strategies will be more accessible to others. Consider which mathematical ideas you want to highlight and how you might record strategies to emphasize those specific concepts.

Learn More...

Anticipating student strategies for adding, multiplying, and dividing fractions are discussed in Chapters 6, 8, and 9.

Looking Ahead

In this chapter, we have looked at opportunities for students to begin thinking about what happens when they subtract using fractions. Were some strategies more efficient for you as a teacher to use? Are there certain strategies that you think will be more accessible to your students? How do you think these number talks will help you know more about your students' understandings and misconceptions about subtracting fractions? In Chapter 8, we explore what it means to multiply with fractions, examine student-invented strategies, and offer number talks to help students develop strategies for multiplying with fractions.

Connecting the Chapter to Your Practice

1. Look at Figure 7–1 on page 180. What do you think eighth-grade students who chose each of those answers might have been thinking?
2. Examine Figure 7–3 on page 183. How might presenting subtraction problems in different types of contexts benefit your students?
3. When you read the "Inside the Classroom" excerpt on pages 187–189, what do you notice about Mr. Henry's questions to his students?
4. What are some ways teachers can foster a classroom environment in which students are willing to openly discuss their thinking?
5. The number talks on pages 190–204 use area, set, and linear models as a context for the problems. How do you anticipate your students might use some of the models in these number talks?
6. Which strategies for subtracting fractions do you anticipate your students might be most comfortable using?
7. Which strategies for subtracting fractions do your students tend to use most often?
8. If your students only know the standard algorithm for subtracting fractions, what are some questions you might ask to help them consider alternative strategies?
9. When would using an alternative strategy for subtracting fractions be useful?

CHAPTER 8

Number Talks for Multiplication with Fractions

In this chapter, we offer a place for teachers to start when planning number talks around the multiplication of fractions. In the opening sections, we discuss how the use of number talks is helpful as students work to develop multiplication strategies with fractions. We then explore and offer number talks that are focused on helping students build their understanding of multiplying fractions. We highly recommended that students are solid and flexible in their fractional reasoning (see Chapter 4) before using the number talks in this chapter.

OVERVIEW

How Number Talks Help the Development of Multiplication Strategies with Fractions

Students often overlook the complex ideas involved in multiplying fractions when teachers focus instruction on procedural steps before building students' understanding. Unfortunately, in an effort to help students arrive quickly at a correct answer, teachers sometimes sacrifice understanding for shortcuts. For example, teachers often tell students to multiply across the top (numerator × numerator) and across the bottom (denominator × denominator). This procedure produces a correct answer, but it treats the numerators and denominators as if they are whole numbers. This is where the importance of number talks comes into play: Number talks help learners focus on developing strategies to build their understanding of multiplying fractions. As they decompose fractions, use properties to solve problems, and make sense of relationships with fractions, students are not only building an understanding of fractions but they are also laying the foundation for algebraic reasoning.

Learn More...

For more about inappropriate whole number reasoning, see Chapter 3, page 64–66.

Specifically, there are approaches we can take during a number talk to support students in inventing and developing strategies—and thus deepen their understanding of mathematics. These approaches include:

- Making connections to strategies for multiplying whole numbers
- Making connections to arithmetic properties
- Highlighting the shifting whole
- Using story problems
- Using models
- Connecting students' strategies

Each of these approaches is discussed in more detail in the sections that follow.

Making Connections to Strategies for Multiplying Whole Numbers

Will the strategies used for multiplying whole numbers also work with fractions? This is an important question to pose to students as you transition into computing with fractions. This idea can be tested by starting with the whole number problem 16×25. First ask students, "What are some ways to solve this problem?" Once students have indicated that they have at least one way in mind, ask, "Now consider the strategies you used and test them with the problem $6 \times \frac{2}{3}$. Do your strategies still work?" Figure 8–1 on the next page shows three multiplication strategies for solving 16×25 and applies them to the problem $6 \times \frac{2}{3}$.

Multiplication Strategy	Recording	Recording
Partial Products Using the Distributive Property	16×25 $= (10 + 6) \times 25$ $= (10 \times 25) + (6 \times 25)$ $= 250 + 150$ $= 400$	$6 \times \frac{2}{3}$ $= 6 \times \left(\frac{1}{3} + \frac{1}{3}\right)$ $= \left(6 \times \frac{1}{3}\right) + \left(6 \times \frac{1}{3}\right)$ $= 2 + 2$ $= 4$
Decomposing Factors into Factors Using the Associative Property	16×25 $= (4 \times 4) \times 25$ $= 4 \times (4 \times 25)$ $= 4 \times 100$ $= 400$	$6 \times \frac{2}{3}$ $= (2 \times 3) \times \frac{2}{3}$ $= 2 \times \left(3 \times \frac{2}{3}\right)$ $= 2 \times 2$ $= 4$
Doubling and Halving Using Multiplicative Inverse Property	16×25 $= \left(16 \times \frac{1}{2}\right) \times (25 \times 2)$ $= 8 \times 50$ $= 400$	$6 \times \frac{2}{3}$ $= (6 \times 2) \times \left(\frac{2}{3} \times \frac{1}{2}\right)$ $= 12 \times \frac{1}{3}$ $= 4$

Figure 8–1. *Making Connections to Strategies for Computing with Whole Numbers*

Students may assume that if whole number multiplication strategies work with fractions, then other generalizations will also hold true. Be sure to take some time to explore these assumptions with students. For example, ask students, "What happens to the product when we multiply with numbers greater than one?" Consider putting it in a context such as, "If it takes 1 can of paint to paint a wall, and you need to keep painting walls, what does that do to the amount of paint you need? (The more walls you paint the more cans of paint you need.) As long as you have more than one wall to paint—even if it's a mixed number like $1\frac{1}{4}$ walls, or $1\frac{1}{2}$ walls—the number of cans of paint needed will still increase.

But what happens if we multiply with proper fractions—numbers between 0 and 1? What if we only need to paint $\frac{1}{2}$ a wall or $\frac{1}{3}$ of a wall? In this case we only need part of a can of paint to paint part of the wall. Multiplying with proper fractions is taking part of something. Figure 8–2 provides an opportunity to investigate this further.

When we ask students to consider whether whole number strategies will work with rational numbers, we are purposefully providing an opportunity for students to *look for and explore regularity in repeated reasoning* (MP8) and *look for and make use of structure* (MP7).

Look across the columns in Figure 8–2 and notice that the first factor is the same in each row and the second factor is what changes each time. In the first column, the second factor is a number greater than 1, and in the second column, the second factor is a proper fraction. Ask students what patterns they notice about the products compared to the first factor when the first factor is multiplied by a number greater than 1 as opposed to when the first factor is multiplied

Multiplying with Numbers Greater than 1 (Whole Numbers, Mixed Numbers, and Improper Fractions)	Multiplying with Numbers Between 0 and 1 (Proper Fractions)
$6 \times 4 = 24$	$6 \times \frac{1}{4} = 1\frac{1}{2}$
$25 \times 9 = 225$	$25 \times \frac{3}{5} = 15$
$12 \times 1\frac{1}{2} = 18$	$12 \times \frac{5}{6} = 10$
$18 \times 2\frac{1}{4} = 40\frac{1}{2}$	$18 \times \frac{1}{2} = 9$
$\frac{3}{4} \times \frac{5}{4} = \frac{15}{16}$	$\frac{3}{4} \times \frac{1}{4} = \frac{3}{16}$
$\frac{2}{3} \times \frac{6}{5} = \frac{12}{15} = \frac{4}{5}$	$\frac{2}{3} \times \frac{1}{5} = \frac{2}{15}$

Figure 8–2. *What Happens to the Product When We Multiply by Numbers Greater Than 1 Versus by Proper Fractions?*

by a proper fraction. Give students an opportunity to explore their gereralizations with other problems and test their findings. When we present the lesson in this way, students can independently develop important generalizations about what happens when they multiply by numbers greater than 1 versus by proper fractions.

Making Connections to Arithmetic Properties

Flexibility with composing and decomposing fractions is essential to developing computation strategies for multiplication using the associative, distributive, commutative, identity, and multiplicative inverse properties. Consider the problem $\frac{3}{8} \times 32$. Flexibility in decomposing $\frac{3}{8}$ into factors or addends provides opportunities for students to use smaller problems and apply the associative or distributive properties. A student who understands that $\frac{3}{8}$ can be decomposed into 3 times the unit fraction $\frac{1}{8}$, or $3 \times \frac{1}{8}$, can apply this relationship to solve $\frac{3}{8} \times 32$ using the associative property. (See Figure 8–3.)

Student's Strategy and Reasoning	Recording
Decomposing Factors into Factors Patty: *I knew that $\frac{3}{8}$ was $3 \times \frac{1}{8}$ and I knew that $\frac{1}{8}$ of 32 was 4, so $3 \times 4 = 12$.*	$\frac{3}{8} \times 32$ $= \left(3 \times \frac{1}{8}\right) \times 32$ $= 3 \times \left(\frac{1}{8} \times 32\right)$ $= 3 \times 4$ $= 12$

Figure 8–3. *Using "Decomposing Factors into Factors" to Solve $\frac{3}{8} \times 32$*

When students decompose factors into addends to multiply, they are using the distributive property of multiplication over addition. We can think about this idea using the same problem, $\frac{3}{8} \times 32$. Figure 8–4 shows two ways a student might decompose $\frac{3}{8}$ and use the distributive property to solve this problem.

Student's Strategy and Reasoning	Recording
Partial Products Ralph: *I thought about $\frac{3}{8}$ as $\frac{1}{8} + \frac{1}{8} + \frac{1}{8}$ because I knew that $\frac{1}{8} \times 32$ was 4; and $4 + 4 + 4 = 12$.*	$\frac{3}{8} \times 32$ $= \left(\frac{1}{8} + \frac{1}{8} + \frac{1}{8}\right) \times 32$ $= \left(\frac{1}{8} \times 32\right) + \left(\frac{1}{8} \times 32\right) + \left(\frac{1}{8} \times 32\right)$ $= 4 + 4 + 4$ $= 12$
Partial Products Gail: *I split $\frac{3}{8}$ into $\frac{1}{4}$ and $\frac{1}{8}$ to make it an easier problem to solve. One-fourth of 32 is 8 and $\frac{1}{8}$ of 32 is 4, and $8 + 4$ is 12 so 12 is the answer.*	$\frac{3}{8} \times 32$ $= \left(\frac{1}{4} + \frac{1}{8}\right) \times 32$ $= \left(\frac{1}{4} \times 32\right) + \left(\frac{1}{8} \times 32\right)$ $= 8 + 4$ $= 12$

Figure 8–4. *Using "Partial Products" to Solve $\frac{3}{8} \times 32$*

Highlighting the Shifting Whole

When adding, subtracting, or comparing fractions, students need to consider the relationship of the fractions to one specific whole. When multiplying fractions, however, they need to think about two wholes:

the original whole and then a "new" whole. We can use a multiplication story problem and area model to explore this idea. (See Figure 8–5.)

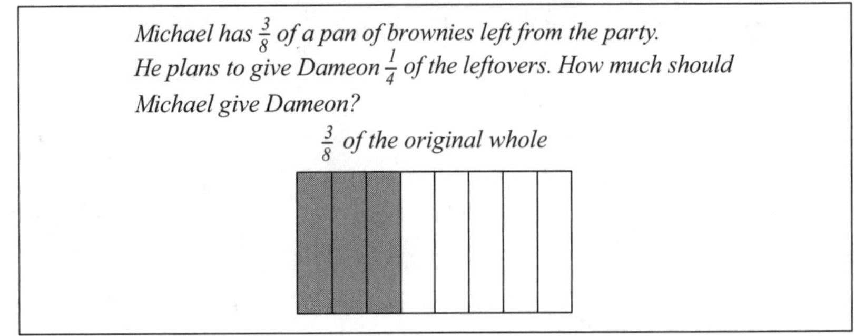

Figure 8–5. *The Shifting Whole: Thinking About the Original Whole and the "New" Whole*

The shaded part of this area model shows $\frac{3}{8}$ of Michael's pan of brownies. The initial whole is divided or partitioned into eighths. Michael wants to give his friend $\frac{1}{4}$ of the $\frac{3}{8}$ of the brownies left, so he partitions the $\frac{3}{8}$ into fourths to find out how much $\frac{1}{4}$ of the $\frac{3}{8}$ of the pan of brownies would be. The shaded $\frac{3}{8}$ becomes the "new" whole that Michael must divide into fourths. To understand the answer of $\frac{3}{32}$, the $\frac{1}{4}$ of the $\frac{3}{8}$ has to be related back to the original $\frac{8}{8}$ or whole pan, which has now been partitioned into thirty-seconds (see Figure 8–6).

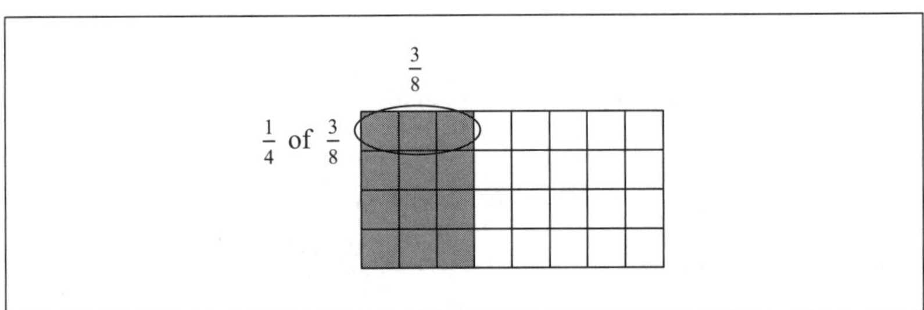

Figure 8–6. *Relating $\frac{1}{4}$ of $\frac{3}{8}$ to the Original Whole*

The shifting whole is often a point of confusion for students. For instance, with the example in Figure 8–6, a common misconception occurs when students reason that $\frac{1}{4}$ of $\frac{3}{8}$ is $\frac{3}{12}$ instead of $\frac{3}{32}$ because they think about $\frac{3}{8}$ as the whole and do not consider the relationship back to the original whole. When this misconception surfaces in your classroom, refer to the context and bring the conversation back to the original whole. In this case, you might ask, "What part of the whole pan of brownies did Michael give to his friend?"

$\frac{1}{4} \times \frac{1}{3}$: Developing Multiplication Strategies with Fractions

Classroom Clip 8.1

Consider the following questions as you watch this number talk from a fifth-grade classroom:

1. What does the girl who is talking during the turn and talk know about multiplication of fractions?
2. Why do you think the teacher chooses to collect more answers after the turn and talk?
3. What is the teacher's purpose in asking B.J. how the box he describes helps his numerical strategy make sense?
4. What does the teacher do to highlight B.J.'s strategy and maintain the focus on the shifting whole?

To view this video clip, scan the QR code or access via mathsolutions .com/NTFDP8.1

Using Story Problems

Another way we can help learners develop a more complete understanding of what it means to multiply with fractions is to situate number talks within a story problem context. A context gives students an entry point for developing strategies. It also helps students make sense of the question the problem is asking and what the numbers mean in relationship to the problem.

Consider the difference between the problems presented in isolation versus in a story context. (See Figure 8–7.)

Presenting a Problem in Isolation	Presenting a Problem in a Story Context
$\frac{1}{4} \times \frac{2}{3}$	*Madeline has $\frac{2}{3}$ of a yard of fabric and plans to take $\frac{1}{4}$ of her fabric to her grandmother. How much fabric does Madeline plan to bring to her grandmother?*
$\frac{1}{2} \times \frac{4}{5}$	*At Elizabeth's restaurant, $\frac{1}{2}$ of the dishes on the menu are vegetarian. Of the vegetarian dishes, $\frac{4}{5}$ are pasta dishes. What fraction of the dishes on the menu are vegetarian pasta dishes?*
$\frac{1}{3} \times \frac{3}{4}$	*A cookie recipe calls for $\frac{3}{4}$ of a cup of butter. Webb wants to make $\frac{1}{3}$ of the original recipe. How many cups of butter will Webb need?*

Figure 8–7. *Presenting a Problem in Isolation Versus in a Story Context*

The context gives a framework for understanding the problem and making sense of the solution. Consider incorporating either a story problem and/or a model as you introduce each number talk. For example, you might frame the problem $\frac{1}{3}$ *of 12* using the following story context and set model:

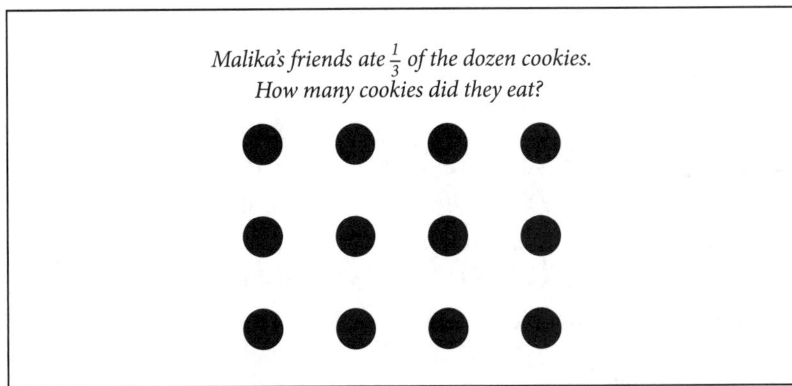

Malika's friends ate $\frac{1}{3}$ of the dozen cookies.
How many cookies did they eat?

Figure 8–8. *Using a Model and a Story Context to Present the Problem* $\frac{1}{3} \times 12$

Number Talk Tip

For more on the use of story problems in building fractional reasoning, see Chapter 4, page 75.

Using Models

In addition to using a story problem, teachers can incorporate a model during a number talk to give students an entry point for developing strategies and finding a solution. Different strategies lend themselves to different models. Consider, for example, how area, linear, and set models might each be used to represent several students' strategies for the problem $\frac{1}{2} \times \frac{3}{4}$. (See Figure 8–9.)

Number Talk Tip

An important part of a number talk involves making students' thinking public and accessible to other students. We can record a student's strategy numerically, but supporting their ideas with a model may help other learners follow and understand the student's thinking.

Student's Reasoning	Recording
Sara: *I thought about 1 whole divided into fourths with $\frac{3}{4}$ of the whole shaded.*	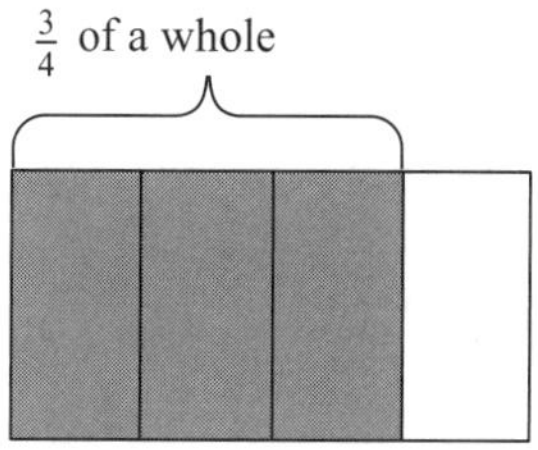 $\frac{3}{4}$ of a whole
I knew I needed $\frac{1}{2}$ of the $\frac{3}{4}$, so I drew a line to halve the $\frac{3}{4}$. This gave me eighths, but I needed only $\frac{1}{2}$ of the $\frac{6}{8}$, which would be $\frac{3}{8}$ of the whole.	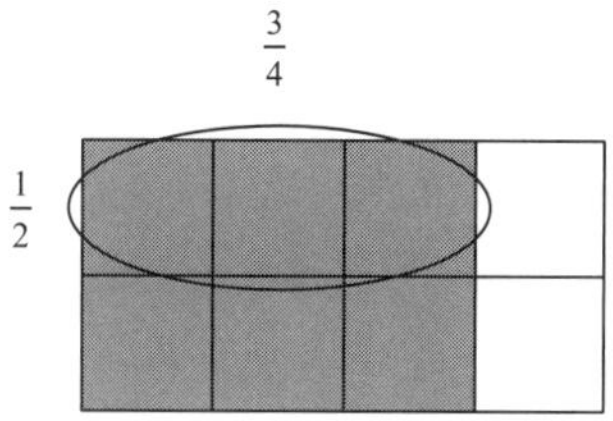 $\frac{3}{4}$ $\frac{1}{2}$
Olivia: *I used a number line to think about $\frac{1}{2}$ of $\frac{3}{4}$. First I divided my number line into fourths and marked where my $\frac{3}{4}$ would go.*	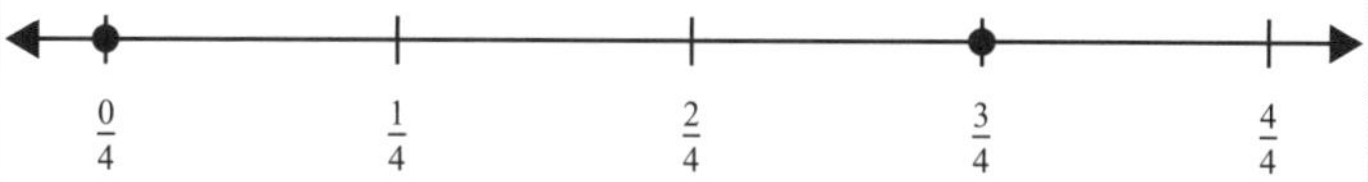 $\frac{0}{4}$ $\frac{1}{4}$ $\frac{2}{4}$ $\frac{3}{4}$ $\frac{4}{4}$
Then I halved each $\frac{1}{4}$, which divided my whole into eighths. Half of $\frac{3}{4}$ is $\frac{1}{2}$ of $\frac{6}{8}$ which is $\frac{3}{8}$.	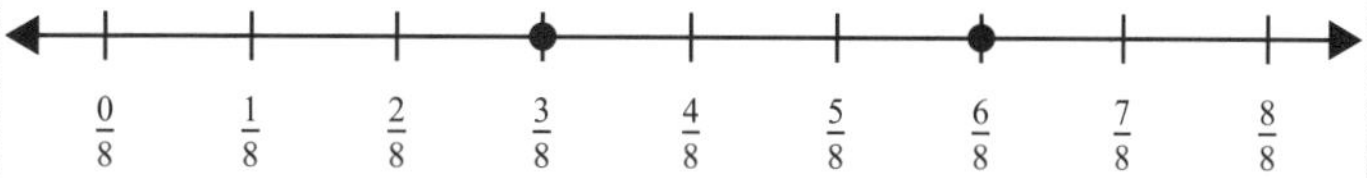 $\frac{0}{8}$ $\frac{1}{8}$ $\frac{2}{8}$ $\frac{3}{8}$ $\frac{4}{8}$ $\frac{5}{8}$ $\frac{6}{8}$ $\frac{7}{8}$ $\frac{8}{8}$

Figure 8–9. *Using Models to Record Students' Thinking to Solve $\frac{1}{2} \times \frac{3}{4}$ (continued)*

Student's Reasoning	Recording
Muhammad: *I thought about 8 pieces of candy divided into four groups or fourths. If each fourth has 2 pieces of candy, then $\frac{3}{4}$ would be 6 pieces, or $\frac{6}{8}$ of the candy. I need $\frac{1}{2}$ of $\frac{6}{8}$ of the candy, so my answer is $\frac{3}{8}$.*	

Figure 8–9. *Using Models to Record Students' Thinking to Solve $\frac{1}{2} \times \frac{3}{4}$ (continued)*

Number Talk Tip

For more on the use of models in building fractional reasoning, see Chapter 4.

Number talks offer the opportunity for teachers to use a variety of contexts to support students in developing conceptual understanding of multiplication of fractions and in developing strategies for this operation.

$\frac{1}{2}$ of 12, $\frac{1}{4}$ of 12: Developing Multiplication Strategies with Fractions

Classroom Clip 8.2

Consider the following questions as you watch this number talk from a third-grade classroom:

1. What does the teacher do to probe Avery for a more precise explanation of her thinking?
2. What does Avery understand about half?
3. How does the model help the second student justify his thinking that dividing 12 by 2 equates to half of the eggs?
4. What mathematical idea is the teacher pushing on when Ellie notices that the denominator in $\frac{1}{2}$ is 2 and they are dividing by 2?
5. How do the models support Drew's thinking?
6. What does the teacher do to further students' thinking about fractions as division in this number talk?

To view this video clip, scan the QR code or access via mathsolutions .com/NTFDP8.2

Connecting Students' Strategies

During a number talk, we want to honor all strategies and refrain from elevating one strategy over another. As students defend their solutions, first look for opportunities to pose questions that engage students in thinking about how different strategies are connected. For example, students might use the "Repeated Addition" and "Partial Products" strategies to solve $\frac{1}{4} \times 5$. (See Figure 8–10.) We can ask students, "How are these two strategies similar? Where is $\frac{1}{4} \times 4$ happening in the Repeated Addition strategy?" When we encourage students to compare strategies, we provide them with opportunities to think more deeply about the mathematics that makes each strategy work.

Student's Strategy and Reasoning	Recording
Repeated Addition Harper: *I knew I needed to add $\frac{1}{4}$ five times and that made $\frac{5}{4}$ or $1\frac{1}{4}$.*	$\frac{1}{4} \times 5$ $= \frac{1}{4} + \frac{1}{4} + \frac{1}{4} + \frac{1}{4} + \frac{1}{4}$ $= \frac{5}{4}$ $= 1\frac{1}{4}$
Partial Products José: *I already knew that $\frac{1}{4} \times 4$ was 1, so I broke up 5 into $4 + 1$. One-fourth $\times$ 4 equals 1 and $\frac{1}{4} \times 1 = \frac{1}{4}$. $1 + \frac{1}{4} = 1\frac{1}{4}$ so the answer is $1\frac{1}{4}$.*	$\frac{1}{4} \times 5$ $= \frac{1}{4} \times (4 + 1)$ $= \left(\frac{1}{4} \times 4\right) + \left(\frac{1}{4} \times 1\right)$ $= 1 + \frac{1}{4}$ $= 1\frac{1}{4}$

Figure 8–10. *Comparing "Repeated Addition" and "Partial Products" to Solve $\frac{1}{4} \times 5$*

Once students have started comparing strategies, begin looking for indications that they might be ready to consider the idea of efficiency. As teachers, we do not want to give the impression that one strategy is less valuable than another. However, we do want to help students consider the mathematical relationships among strategies. One way we can help students think about efficiency is by labeling each student's strategy with a number (e.g., Strategy 1, Strategy 2, and so forth). At the conclusion of the discussion, ask students to use a hand signal to quietly indicate which strategy is most efficient for them. This allows you to collect formative information about which strategies students are more readily using, and it helps students to consider whether there are more efficient ways to solve a problem than the strategies they are currently using.

When students are listening to and thinking about other students' strategies during a number talk, they are *constructing viable arguments and critiquing the reasoning of others* (MP3).

Inside the Classroom

A Number Talk for $\frac{3}{4} \times \frac{4}{5}$

Sixth graders Taylor and Meg have shared their strategies for solving the problem $\frac{3}{4} \times \frac{4}{5}$. (See Figure 8–11.) Review these strategies and then read the dialogue excerpt that follows; it was captured from a number talk discussion about efficiency.

Student's Strategy and Reasoning	Recording
Decomposing Factors into Factors Taylor: *I broke apart $\frac{3}{4}$ into $3 \times \frac{1}{4}$ because $\frac{1}{4}$ of $\frac{4}{5}$ was an easy problem. That gave me $3 \times \left(\frac{1}{4} \times \frac{4}{5}\right)$, which equals $3 \times \frac{1}{5}$ or $\frac{3}{5}$.*	$\frac{3}{4} \times \frac{4}{5}$ $= \left(3 \times \frac{1}{4}\right) \times \frac{4}{5}$ $= 3 \times \left(\frac{1}{4} \times \frac{4}{5}\right)$ $= 3 \times \frac{1}{5}$ $= \frac{3}{5}$

Figure 8–11. *Using "Decomposing Factors into Factors" and "Doubling and Halving" to Solve $\frac{3}{4} \times \frac{4}{5}$ (continued)*

(continued)

Student's Strategy and Reasoning	Recording
Doubling and Halving Meg: *I know that if I double one factor and halve the other I get the same answer, so I doubled $\frac{3}{4}$ and that gave me $1\frac{1}{2}$, and I halved $\frac{4}{5}$ and that gave me $\frac{2}{5}$. Then I did it again. I doubled $1\frac{1}{2}$ and got 3 and half of $\frac{2}{5}$ is $\frac{1}{5}$. $3 \times \frac{1}{5}$ is $\frac{3}{5}$.*	$\frac{3}{4} \times \frac{4}{5}$ $= \left(\frac{3}{4} \times 2\right) \times \left(\frac{4}{5} \times \frac{1}{2}\right)$ $= 1\frac{1}{2} \times \frac{2}{5}$ $= \left(1\frac{1}{2} \times 2\right) \times \left(\frac{2}{5} \times \frac{1}{2}\right)$ $= 3 \times \frac{1}{5}$ $= \frac{3}{5}$

Figure 8–11. *Using "Decomposing Factors into Factors" and "Doubling and Halving" to Solve $\frac{3}{4} \times \frac{4}{5}$ (continued)*

Ms. Puchta: I noticed that many of you indicated that Taylor's strategy was easier for you. Could someone share why you thought this was an efficient strategy?

Amy: Taylor decomposed the $\frac{3}{4}$ to $3 \times \frac{1}{4}$ and used the associative property to multiply $\frac{1}{4} \times \frac{4}{5}$. Finding $\frac{1}{4}$ of $\frac{4}{5}$ was easy, and then he needed three of the fifths.

Micah: I think it was quick, too, but finding $\frac{1}{4}$ of $\frac{4}{5}$ seems hard. How did you know that would be $\frac{1}{5}$, Taylor?

Taylor: You can think about a rectangle with $\frac{4}{5}$ shaded. If you circle $\frac{1}{4}$ of the $\frac{4}{5}$, that's $\frac{1}{5}$ of the whole. Since we need 3 of those parts, the answer is $\frac{3}{5}$.

[Ms. Puchta draws a model as Taylor explains.]

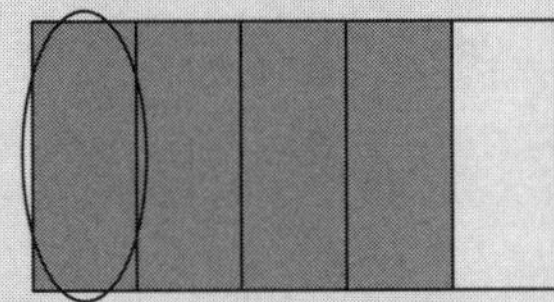

Ms. Puchta: Show me a quiet thumb if you follow Taylor's thinking. It looks like several people understand this strategy but others are still unsure. Even if a strategy seems to be quick, it may not be an efficient one to use if you are not sure why it works.

Shaun: Yes, but it makes me want to figure out how to use it. I thought Meg's way was really fast, because it changed the problem to a whole number times a fraction.

Jack: She changed the problem to $1\frac{1}{2} \times \frac{2}{5}$ and then $3 \times \frac{1}{5}$. Three times $\frac{1}{5}$ is an easy problem for me.

Ms. Puchta: It looks like many of you think this is also an efficient way. Let's try another problem to test Meg's and Taylor's strategies.

Learn More...

To learn more about other ways to foster conversations around efficiency, see Chapter 2, pages 55–56.

Number Talks That Use Unit Fractions and Whole Numbers with Multiplication

The following number talk strings use a unit fraction and a whole number as factors. The whole numbers are multiples of the denominators in the unit fractions to make it easier to partition.

If students have prior knowledge of the standard U.S. algorithms for multiplying fractions, many will use that procedure. Using that procedure with understanding is fine; however, we have designed the strings to provide challenges in which students will consider the relationships among problems and begin generalizing strategies that are grounded in fractional reasoning versus memorized procedures.

Number Talk Tip

As you present each problem, you may wish to provide a context, such as, "Marilee read $\frac{1}{10}$ of the 10 books on her shelf. How many books did she read?" or "Stephen has run $\frac{1}{10}$ of his goal of 10 miles. How far has he run?" Incorporating story or model contexts can provide another layer of support. See further discussion in the section "How Number Talks Help the Development of Multiplication Strategies with Fractions" in this chapter.

Instructions

These number talks are organized into three columns and progress in difficulty going from the first column (from A to B to C) to the second column to the third column. Feel free to work through each string in order or choose problems according to your students' needs. You may choose to pose one problem or set of problems each day, or do more than one set of problems as time allows. Introduce the first problem in the string, collect solutions, then ask students to share their reasoning and proofs. Once the class reaches consensus, pose the second problem in the string and ask, *"How can you use what we just solved to help you with this next problem?"* or *"How does this new problem relate to the previous problem(s)?"* Continue this format with each problem in the string.

What is ______ of ______? How do you know?
How can you use what we already know to solve this next problem?
How does this new problem relate to the previous problem(s)?

A. $\frac{1}{2}$ of 2

$\frac{1}{2}$ of 4

$\frac{1}{2}$ of 6

$\frac{1}{2}$ of 8

$\frac{1}{2}$ of 10

B. $\frac{1}{4}$ of 4

$\frac{1}{4}$ of 8

$\frac{1}{4}$ of 12

$\frac{1}{4}$ of 16

$\frac{1}{4}$ of 20

C. $\frac{1}{5}$ of 5

$\frac{1}{5}$ of 10

$\frac{1}{5}$ of 15

$\frac{1}{5}$ of 20

A. $\frac{1}{3}$ of 3

$\frac{1}{3}$ of 6

$\frac{1}{3}$ of 9

$\frac{1}{3}$ of 12

$\frac{1}{3}$ of 15

B. $\frac{1}{6}$ of 6

$\frac{1}{6}$ of 12

$\frac{1}{6}$ of 18

$\frac{1}{6}$ of 24

$\frac{1}{6}$ of 30

C. $\frac{1}{9}$ of 9

$\frac{1}{9}$ of 18

$\frac{1}{9}$ of 27

$\frac{1}{9}$ of 36

A. $\frac{1}{8}$ of 8

$\frac{1}{8}$ of 16

$\frac{1}{8}$ of 24

$\frac{1}{8}$ of 32

$\frac{1}{8}$ of 40

B. $\frac{1}{10}$ of 10

$\frac{1}{10}$ of 20

$\frac{1}{10}$ of 30

$\frac{1}{10}$ of 40

$\frac{1}{10}$ of 50

C. $\frac{1}{7}$ of 7

$\frac{1}{7}$ of 14

$\frac{1}{7}$ of 21

$\frac{1}{7}$ of 28

Number Talk Tip

It is important to note that in these beginning number talks, we substitute the word *of* for the multiplication sign to bring students' attention to what is happening in this operation. For example, in the same way that we can bring attention to what happens when you multiply 3×5 by talking about it as three groups of five, we can begin talking about $\frac{1}{2} \times 4$ as half "of" four to help students make sense of this operation.

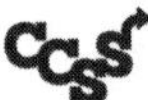

When students decompose a factor into other factors or addends, they are *looking for and making use of structure* (MP7).

Number Talks That Use Fractions and Whole Numbers with Multiplication

These number talks are structured to help students extend their reasoning with unit fractions to multiply with fractions and whole numbers. For example, students often use what they know about $\frac{1}{4} \times 8$ to solve $\frac{3}{4} \times 8$ by decomposing $\frac{3}{4}$ into factors $\left(3 \times \frac{1}{4}\right)$ or addends $\left(\frac{1}{4} + \frac{1}{4} + \frac{1}{4}\right)$ and using the associative or distributive properties. (See Figure 8–12.)

Student's Strategy and Reasoning	Recording
Decomposing Factors into Factors Lori: *I knew that $\frac{1}{4} \times 8$ was 2, so I broke down $\frac{3}{4}$ into $3 \times \frac{1}{4}$ and multiplied $\frac{1}{4} \times 8$ times 3. That was 3×2 which equals 6.*	$\frac{3}{4} \times 8$ $= \left(3 \times \frac{1}{4}\right) \times 8$ $= 3 \times \left(\frac{1}{4} \times 8\right)$ $= 3 \times 2$ $= 6$
Partial Products James: *I knew that $\frac{1}{4} \times 8$ was 2 so I broke down $\frac{3}{4}$ into $\frac{1}{4} + \frac{1}{4} + \frac{1}{4}$ and then multiplied $\frac{1}{4} \times 8$ three times. That gave me $2 + 2 + 2$, which is 6.*	$\frac{3}{4} \times 8$ $= \left(\frac{1}{4} + \frac{1}{4} + \frac{1}{4}\right) \times 8$ $= \left(\frac{1}{4} \times 8\right) + \left(\frac{1}{4} \times 8\right) + \left(\frac{1}{4} \times 8\right)$ $= 2 + 2 + 2$ $= 6$

Figure 8–12. *Using "Decomposing Factors into Factors" and "Partial Products" to Solve $\frac{3}{4} \times 8$*

Instructions

These number talks are organized into columns and progress in difficulty going from the first column (from A to B to C, etc.) to the second column to the third column. Feel free to work through each string in order or choose problems according to your students' needs. You may choose to pose one problem or set of problems each day, or do more than one set of problems as time allows. Introduce the first problem in each string, collect solutions, then ask students to share their reasoning and proofs. Once the class reaches consensus, pose the second problem in the string and ask, *"How can you use what we just solved to help you with this next problem?"* or *"How does this new problem relate to the previous problem(s)?"* Continue this format with each problem in the string.

What is ______ of ______? How do you know?
How can you use what we already know to solve this next problem?

A. $\frac{1}{10}$ of 10

$\frac{2}{10}$ of 10

$\frac{4}{10}$ of 10

$\frac{5}{10}$ of 10

$\frac{7}{10}$ of 10

B. $\frac{1}{4}$ of 8

$\frac{2}{4}$ of 8

$\frac{3}{4}$ of 8

$\frac{4}{4}$ of 8

$\frac{5}{4}$ of 8

A. $\frac{1}{9}$ of 18

$\frac{2}{9}$ of 18

$\frac{3}{9}$ of 18

$\frac{6}{9}$ of 18

$\frac{9}{9}$ of 18

B. $\frac{1}{6}$ of 12

$\frac{2}{6}$ of 12

$\frac{3}{6}$ of 12

$\frac{5}{6}$ of 12

$\frac{6}{6}$ of 12

A. $\frac{1}{4}$ of 4

$\frac{2}{4}$ of 4

$\frac{3}{4}$ of 4

$\frac{4}{4}$ of 4

$\frac{5}{4}$ of 4

B. $\frac{1}{2}$ of 8

$\frac{2}{2}$ of 8

$\frac{3}{2}$ of 8

$\frac{4}{2}$ of 8

$\frac{5}{2}$ of 8

C. $\frac{1}{5}$ of 20

$\frac{2}{5}$ of 20

$\frac{3}{5}$ of 20

$\frac{4}{5}$ of 20

$\frac{5}{5}$ of 20

D. $\frac{1}{10}$ of 20

$\frac{2}{10}$ of 20

$\frac{4}{10}$ of 20

$\frac{5}{10}$ of 20

$\frac{7}{10}$ of 20

C. $\frac{1}{12}$ of 24

$\frac{3}{12}$ of 24

$\frac{5}{12}$ of 24

$\frac{8}{12}$ of 24

$\frac{9}{12}$ of 24

D. $\frac{1}{8}$ of 24

$\frac{2}{8}$ of 24

$\frac{4}{8}$ of 24

$\frac{5}{8}$ of 24

$\frac{6}{8}$ of 24

C. $\frac{1}{3}$ of 9

$\frac{2}{3}$ of 9

$\frac{3}{3}$ of 9

$\frac{4}{3}$ of 9

$\frac{5}{3}$ of 9

D. $\frac{1}{16}$ of 16

$\frac{4}{16}$ of 16

$\frac{8}{16}$ of 16

$\frac{12}{16}$ of 16

$\frac{18}{16}$ of 16

Number Talks That Use Models to Focus on the Shifting Whole

The number talks in this section are structured to help students confront the idea of a shifting whole. Listen carefully to find out if students have formed the common misconception of not relating the part of the part back to the original whole. For example, consider the problem in the first string which asks students to find $\frac{1}{2}$ of $\frac{1}{2}$ of a 2×4 rectangle.

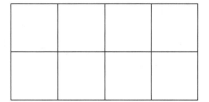

Number Talk Tip

Students can use models to support their thinking, but models themselves are not strategies for solving a problem. A strategy happens mentally and can be represented in various ways.

As students mentally partition the rectangle into halves and then reason about half of the half (or a part of a part), we can anticipate that some will think about fourths because of the four parts in half of the whole and say, "Half of a half is $\frac{2}{4}$." To confront this misconception, we can ask, "Two-fourths of what? What is the whole?"

Others might share that $\frac{1}{2}$ of $\frac{1}{2}$ is two squares. This is an excellent opportunity to push for accurate language and ask, "What fraction of the whole would two squares be?"

Instructions

These number talks are organized into three columns and progress in difficulty going from the first column (from A to B to C) to the second column to the third column. Feel free to work through each string in order or choose problems according to your students' needs. You may choose to pose one problem or set of problems each day, or do more than one set of problems as time allows. For each number talk string, show the model, introduce the first problem in the string, collect solutions, and then ask students to share their reasoning and proofs. Once the class reaches consensus, pose the second problem in the string and ask, *"How can you use what we just solved to help you with this next problem?"* or *"How does this new problem relate to the previous problem(s)?"* Continue this format with each problem in the string.

Reproducible 6

For full-sized reproducibles of the area models used in these number talks, visit www.mathsolutions.com/numbertalksfdp_reproducibles.

What is ______ of ______? How do you know?
How can you use what we already know to solve this next problem?

A.

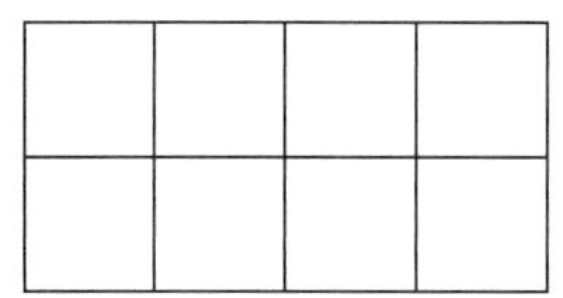

$\frac{1}{2}$ of the whole

$\frac{1}{2}$ of $\frac{1}{2}$

$\frac{1}{4}$ of $\frac{1}{2}$

B.

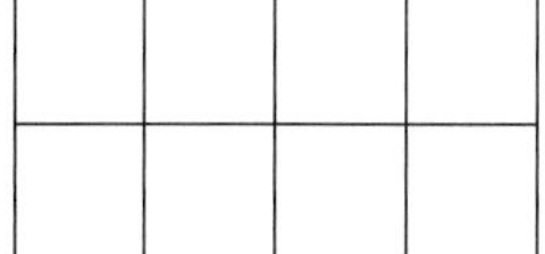

$\frac{1}{2}$ of $\frac{3}{4}$

$\frac{1}{3}$ of $\frac{3}{4}$

$\frac{2}{3}$ of $\frac{3}{4}$

C.

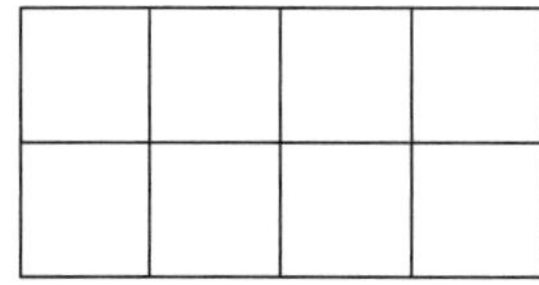

$\frac{1}{4}$ of $\frac{4}{8}$

$\frac{1}{3}$ of $\frac{3}{8}$

$\frac{2}{3}$ of $\frac{3}{8}$

A.

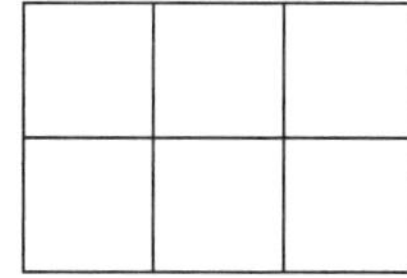

$\frac{1}{3}$ of the whole

$\frac{1}{2}$ of $\frac{1}{3}$

$\frac{1}{2}$ of $\frac{2}{3}$

B.

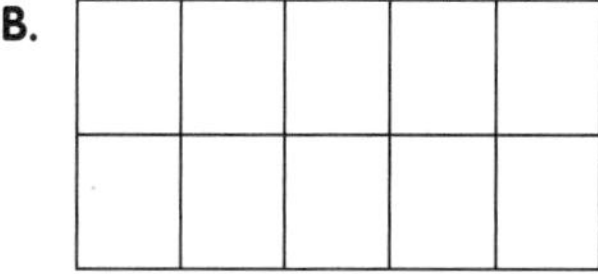

$\frac{1}{5}$ of $\frac{5}{10}$

$\frac{2}{5}$ of $\frac{5}{10}$

$\frac{3}{5}$ of $\frac{5}{10}$

C.

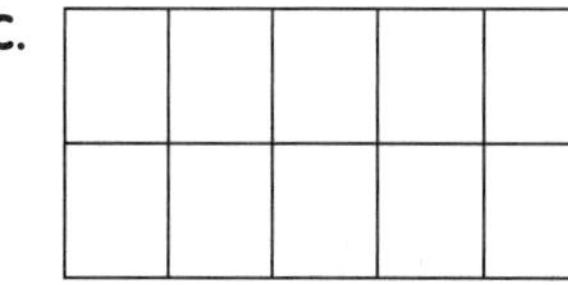

$\frac{1}{3}$ of $\frac{3}{5}$

$\frac{2}{3}$ of $\frac{3}{5}$

$\frac{1}{4}$ of $\frac{4}{5}$

A.

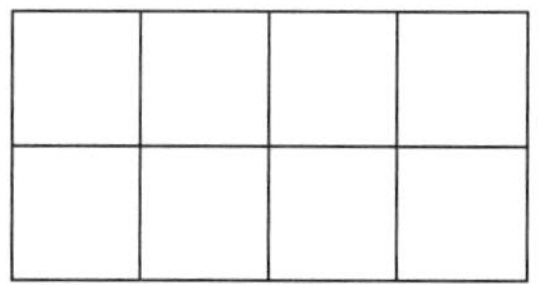

$\frac{1}{4}$ of the whole

$\frac{1}{2}$ of $\frac{1}{4}$

$\frac{1}{2}$ of $\frac{3}{4}$

B.

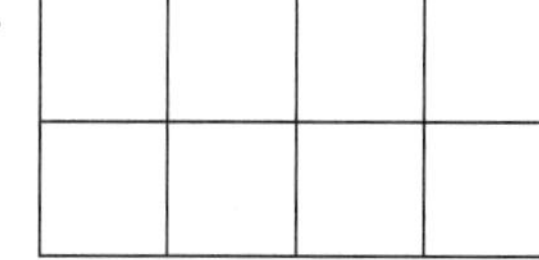

$\frac{1}{2}$ of $\frac{3}{4}$

$\frac{1}{3}$ of $\frac{3}{4}$

$\frac{1}{5}$ of $\frac{5}{8}$

C.

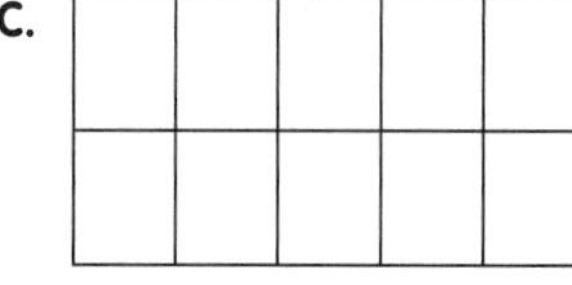

$\frac{1}{4}$ of $\frac{4}{10}$

$\frac{1}{2}$ of $\frac{4}{10}$

$\frac{3}{4}$ of $\frac{4}{10}$

Number Talks That Use Unit Fractions with Multiplication

The number talks in this section are crafted to foster discussions around what happens to the product when one of the factors is half of what it was in the previous problem. The first factor in each string continues to be halved in subsequent problems. This algorithmic halving also makes the product half of what it was in the previous answer. This sequence of problems provides opportunities for students to reflect on the relationships between problems and consider how the magnitude of the product is affected when a factor is halved. For example, the first string begins with $\frac{1}{2}$ of $\frac{1}{2}$ and results in the following products:

$$\frac{1}{2} \text{ of } \frac{1}{2} = \frac{1}{4}$$

$$\frac{1}{4} \text{ of } \frac{1}{2} = \frac{1}{8}$$

$$\frac{1}{8} \text{ of } \frac{1}{2} = \frac{1}{16}$$

$$\frac{1}{16} \text{ of } \frac{1}{2} = \frac{1}{32}$$

Notice how as the factors in the progression halve, so do the products.

Instructions

These number talks are organized into three columns and progress in difficulty going from the first column (from A to B to C) to the second column to the third column. Feel free to work through each string in order or choose problems according to your students' needs. You may choose to pose one problem or set of problems each day, or do more than one set of problems as time allows. Introduce the first problem in the string, collect solutions, then ask students to share their reasoning and proofs. Once the class reaches consensus, pose the next problem in the string and ask, *"How can you use what we just solved to help you with this next problem?"* or *"How does this new problem relate to the previous problem(s)?"* Continue this format with each problem in the string.

What is ______ of ______? How do you know?
How can you use what we already know to solve this next problem?

A. $\frac{1}{2}$ of $\frac{1}{2}$

$\frac{1}{4}$ of $\frac{1}{2}$

$\frac{1}{8}$ of $\frac{1}{2}$

$\frac{1}{16}$ of $\frac{1}{2}$

B. $\frac{1}{3}$ of $\frac{1}{2}$

$\frac{1}{6}$ of $\frac{1}{2}$

$\frac{1}{12}$ of $\frac{1}{2}$

$\frac{1}{24}$ of $\frac{1}{2}$

C. $\frac{1}{5}$ of $\frac{1}{2}$

$\frac{1}{10}$ of $\frac{1}{2}$

$\frac{1}{20}$ of $\frac{1}{2}$

A. $\frac{1}{2}$ of $\frac{1}{4}$

$\frac{1}{4}$ of $\frac{1}{4}$

$\frac{1}{8}$ of $\frac{1}{4}$

$\frac{1}{16}$ of $\frac{1}{4}$

B. $\frac{1}{3}$ of $\frac{1}{4}$

$\frac{1}{6}$ of $\frac{1}{4}$

$\frac{1}{12}$ of $\frac{1}{4}$

$\frac{1}{24}$ of $\frac{1}{4}$

C. $\frac{1}{5}$ of $\frac{1}{4}$

$\frac{1}{10}$ of $\frac{1}{4}$

$\frac{1}{20}$ of $\frac{1}{4}$

A. $\frac{1}{2}$ of $\frac{1}{3}$

$\frac{1}{4}$ of $\frac{1}{3}$

$\frac{1}{8}$ of $\frac{1}{3}$

$\frac{1}{16}$ of $\frac{1}{3}$

B. $\frac{1}{3}$ of $\frac{1}{4}$

$\frac{1}{6}$ of $\frac{1}{4}$

$\frac{1}{12}$ of $\frac{1}{4}$

$\frac{1}{24}$ of $\frac{1}{4}$

C. $\frac{1}{5}$ of $\frac{1}{3}$

$\frac{1}{10}$ of $\frac{1}{3}$

$\frac{1}{20}$ of $\frac{1}{3}$

Number Talks That Highlight the Multiplication Strategy "Partial Products"

Number Talk Tip

Once students have worked with the beginning number talks on pages 237–245 of this chapter and have an understanding of what it means to multiply with fractions, transition into number talks that further emphasize numerical relationships and the development of strategies. The following number talks are organized around four strategies for multiplying fractions: partial products, switching numerators or denominators, decomposing factors, and doubling and halving.

With the Partial Products strategy, students decompose one or both factors into addends to create smaller problems. This strategy works because of the distributive property of multiplication over addition. While decomposing both factors will give a correct solution, it is often more efficient to keep one factor intact. Notice how the factors are decomposed in the two following problems, $8 \times \frac{3}{4}$ (shown in Figure 8–13) and $\frac{1}{2} \times \frac{3}{4}$ (shown in Figure 8–14 on the next page).

Student's Strategy and Reasoning	Recording
Partial Products Barrett: *I broke $\frac{3}{4}$ into $\frac{1}{4} + \frac{1}{2}$ and then multiplied each part by 8. Eight times $\frac{1}{4}$ equals 2 and $8 \times \frac{1}{2} = 4$ and $2 + 4 = 6$.*	$8 \times \frac{3}{4}$ $= 8 \times \left(\frac{1}{4} + \frac{1}{2}\right)$ $= \left(8 \times \frac{1}{4}\right) + \left(8 \times \frac{1}{2}\right)$ $= 2 + 4$ $= 6$
Partial Products Bella: *I thought about $\frac{3}{4}$ as $\frac{1}{4} + \frac{1}{4} + \frac{1}{4}$ and then multiplied each part by 8. I know that $8 \times \frac{1}{4} = 2$ and $2 + 2 + 2 = 6$.*	$8 \times \frac{3}{4}$ $= 8 \times \left(\frac{1}{4} + \frac{1}{4} + \frac{1}{4}\right)$ $= \left(8 \times \frac{1}{4}\right) + \left(8 \times \frac{1}{4}\right) + \left(8 \times \frac{1}{4}\right)$ $= 2 + 2 + 2$ $= 6$

Figure 8–13. *Using "Partial Products" to Solve $8 \times \frac{3}{4}$*

An area model can also be used to represent the partial products strategy. For example, with the problem $\frac{1}{2} \times \frac{3}{4}$, the shaded part of the model represents how $\frac{3}{4}$ is decomposed into $\frac{1}{4} + \frac{1}{4} + \frac{1}{4}$. One-half of each of the shaded one-fourths is circled for a total of $\frac{3}{8}$. (See Figure 8–14 on the next page.)

Student's Strategy and Reasoning	Recording
Partial Products Derrick: *I thought about $\frac{3}{4}$ as $\frac{1}{4}+\frac{1}{4}+\frac{1}{4}$. Half of each of the 3 one-fourths is $\frac{1}{8}$ so the answer is $\frac{1}{8}+\frac{1}{8}+\frac{1}{8}$ or $\frac{3}{8}$.*	$\frac{1}{2}\times\frac{3}{4}$ $=\frac{1}{2}\times\left(\frac{1}{4}+\frac{1}{4}+\frac{1}{4}\right)$ $=\left(\frac{1}{2}\times\frac{1}{4}\right)+\left(\frac{1}{2}\times\frac{1}{4}\right)+\left(\frac{1}{2}\times\frac{1}{4}\right)$ $=\frac{1}{8}+\frac{1}{8}+\frac{1}{8}$ $=\frac{3}{8}$ $\frac{1}{4}$ $\frac{1}{4}$ $\frac{1}{4}$ $\frac{1}{2}$ [$\frac{1}{8}$ $\frac{1}{8}$ $\frac{1}{8}$]

Figure 8–14. *Using "Partial Products" to Solve $\frac{1}{2}\times\frac{3}{4}$*

$1\frac{1}{3}\times\frac{3}{4}$: Developing Multiplication Strategies with Fractions

Classroom Clip 8.3

Consider the following questions as you watch this number talk from a sixth-grade classroom:

1. What strategy is Khalil using to solve this problem?
2. What is ReSean thinking?
3. What is the benefit of having students defend wrong answers?
4. How does the teacher foster a classroom community to accept and discuss both correct and incorrect answers?
5. How does the teacher help students resolve the dilemma of having two answers?

To view this video clip, scan the QR code or access via mathsolutions.com/NTFDP8.3

Category 1
Multiplying a Fraction by a Whole Number

The number talks in this category are structured to help students use prior problems to solve new problems. Each string begins with multiplying a whole number by a unit fraction to offer students a more accessible starting point. This first problem can be used to solve all other problems in the string. For example, the first string begins with $\frac{1}{4} \times 8$. This problem can be used to solve the remaining problems in the string, $\frac{1}{2} \times 8$ and $\frac{3}{4} \times 8$, by decomposing the $\frac{1}{2}$ into $\frac{1}{4} + \frac{1}{4}$ and decomposing the $\frac{3}{4}$ into $\frac{1}{4} + \frac{1}{4} + \frac{1}{4}$. The final problem in each number talk string can be solved using previous problems in the sequence.

Number Talk Tip

In this book, each strategy is labeled to represent the thinking involved; however, in our classrooms we often name a strategy with a number or according to the name of the student who invented it. For example, if Kira offered the idea of using "Partial Products" to solve a multiplication of fractions problem, the class might call this "Kira's strategy." The name of the strategy is not as important as the mathematical ideas the students are using. Keep this in mind as you examine each strategy.

Instructions

These number talks are organized into three columns and progress in difficulty going from the first column (from A to B to C) to the second column to the third column. Feel free to work through each string in order or choose problems according to your students' needs. You may choose to pose one problem or set of problems each day, or do more than one set of problems as time allows. Introduce the first problem in the string, collect solutions, then ask students to share their reasoning and proofs. Once the class reaches consensus, pose the next problem in the string and ask, *"How can you use what we just solved to help you with this next problem?"* or *"How does this new problem relate to the previous problem(s)?"* Continue this format with each problem in the string.

What is ______ × ______? How do you know?
How can you use what we already know to solve this next problem?

A. $\frac{1}{4} \times 8$

$\frac{1}{2} \times 8$

$\frac{3}{4} \times 8$

B. $\frac{1}{4} \times 16$

$\frac{1}{2} \times 16$

$\frac{3}{4} \times 16$

C. $\frac{1}{4} \times 20$

$\frac{1}{2} \times 20$

$\frac{3}{4} \times 20$

A. $\frac{1}{5} \times 10$

$\frac{2}{5} \times 10$

$\frac{3}{5} \times 10$

$\frac{4}{5} \times 10$

B. $\frac{1}{5} \times 15$

$\frac{2}{5} \times 15$

$\frac{3}{5} \times 15$

$\frac{4}{5} \times 15$

C. $\frac{1}{5} \times 20$

$\frac{2}{5} \times 20$

$\frac{3}{5} \times 20$

$\frac{4}{5} \times 20$

A. $\frac{1}{6} \times 12$

$\frac{2}{6} \times 12$

$\frac{3}{6} \times 12$

$\frac{5}{6} \times 12$

B. $\frac{1}{6} \times 18$

$\frac{2}{6} \times 18$

$\frac{3}{6} \times 18$

$\frac{5}{6} \times 18$

C. $\frac{1}{6} \times 24$

$\frac{2}{6} \times 24$

$\frac{3}{6} \times 24$

$\frac{5}{6} \times 24$

Category 2
Multiplying a Mixed Number by a Fraction

The number talk strings in this category continue to build on the idea that factors can be decomposed into addends. They are structured for students to use previous problems to solve new problems. Each string begins with multiplying a unit fraction by another fraction. In subsequent problems, the second factor remains the same; this helps students consider how the first factor can be used to solve all other problems in the progression. The final problem in each number talk string involves multiplying a mixed number by a fraction and can be solved using previous problems in the sequence.

Instructions

These number talks are organized into three columns and progress in difficulty going from the first column (from A to B to C) to the second column to the third column. Feel free to work through each string in order or choose problems according to your students' needs. You may choose to pose one problem or set of problems each day, or do more than one set of problems as time allows. Introduce the first problem in the string, collect solutions, then ask students to share their reasoning and proofs. Once the class reaches consensus, pose the next problem in the string and ask, *"How can you use what we just solved to help you with this next problem?"* or *"How does this new problem relate to the previous problem(s)?"* Continue this format with each problem in the string.

What is ______ × ______? How do you know?
How can you use what we already know to solve this next problem?

A. $\frac{1}{4} \times \frac{1}{2}$

$1 \times \frac{1}{2}$

$1\frac{1}{4} \times \frac{1}{2}$

B. $\frac{1}{4} \times \frac{3}{4}$

$1 \times \frac{3}{4}$

$1\frac{1}{4} \times \frac{3}{4}$

C. $\frac{1}{3} \times \frac{1}{2}$

$\frac{2}{3} \times \frac{1}{2}$

$1 \times \frac{1}{2}$

$1\frac{2}{3} \times \frac{1}{2}$

A. $\frac{1}{6} \times \frac{1}{2}$

$\frac{3}{6} \times \frac{1}{2}$

$1 \times \frac{1}{2}$

$1\frac{4}{6} \times \frac{1}{2}$

B. $\frac{1}{4} \times \frac{1}{4}$

$\frac{2}{4} \times \frac{1}{4}$

$1 \times \frac{1}{4}$

$1\frac{3}{4} \times \frac{1}{4}$

C. $\frac{1}{5} \times \frac{1}{2}$

$\frac{2}{5} \times \frac{1}{2}$

$\frac{4}{5} \times \frac{1}{2}$

$1\frac{4}{5} \times \frac{1}{2}$

A. $\frac{1}{2} \times \frac{4}{5}$

$\frac{1}{4} \times \frac{4}{5}$

$\frac{3}{4} \times \frac{4}{5}$

$1\frac{3}{4} \times \frac{4}{5}$

B. $\frac{1}{2} \times \frac{2}{3}$

$\frac{1}{4} \times \frac{2}{3}$

$\frac{3}{4} \times \frac{2}{3}$

$1\frac{3}{4} \times \frac{2}{3}$

C. $\frac{1}{8} \times \frac{1}{2}$

$\frac{2}{8} \times \frac{1}{2}$

$\frac{3}{8} \times \frac{1}{2}$

$1\frac{6}{8} \times \frac{1}{2}$

Category 3
Multiplying a Fraction by a Fraction

These number talk strings are structured to help students think about decomposing a fraction into smaller fractions and using the distributive property to multiply. Each of the number talk strings begin with multiplying a fraction by a unit fraction to offer students a more accessible starting point. This first problem can be used to solve all other problems in the string. For example, the first string begins with $\frac{1}{4} \times \frac{4}{5}$. This problem can be used to solve the remaining problems in the string, $\frac{1}{2} \times \frac{4}{5}$ and $\frac{3}{4} \times \frac{4}{5}$, by decomposing the $\frac{1}{2}$ into $\frac{1}{4} + \frac{1}{4}$ and decomposing the $\frac{3}{4}$ into $\frac{1}{4} + \frac{1}{4} + \frac{1}{4}$ or $\frac{1}{2} + \frac{1}{4}$. The final problem in each number talk string can be solved using previous problems in the sequence.

Instructions

These number talks are organized into three columns and progress in difficulty going from the first column (from A to B to C) to the second column to the third column. Feel free to work through each string in order or choose problems according to your students' needs. You may choose to pose one problem or set of problems each day, or do more than one set of problems as time allows. Introduce the first problem in the string, collect solutions, then ask students to share their reasoning and proofs. Once the class reaches consensus, pose the next problem in the string and ask, *"How can you use what we just solved to help you with this next problem?"* or *"How does this new problem relate to the previous problem(s)?"* Continue this format with each problem in the string.

What is ______ × ______? How do you know?
How can you use what we already know to solve this next problem?

A. $\frac{1}{4} \times \frac{4}{5}$

$\frac{1}{2} \times \frac{4}{5}$

$\frac{3}{4} \times \frac{4}{5}$

B. $\frac{1}{4} \times \frac{4}{7}$

$\frac{1}{2} \times \frac{4}{7}$

$\frac{3}{4} \times \frac{4}{7}$

C. $\frac{1}{4} \times \frac{4}{9}$

$\frac{1}{2} \times \frac{4}{9}$

$\frac{3}{4} \times \frac{4}{9}$

A. $\frac{1}{5} \times \frac{5}{6}$

$\frac{2}{5} \times \frac{5}{6}$

$\frac{4}{5} \times \frac{5}{6}$

B. $\frac{1}{5} \times \frac{5}{8}$

$\frac{2}{5} \times \frac{5}{8}$

$\frac{4}{5} \times \frac{5}{8}$

C. $\frac{1}{5} \times \frac{5}{10}$

$\frac{2}{5} \times \frac{5}{10}$

$\frac{4}{5} \times \frac{5}{10}$

A. $\frac{1}{3} \times \frac{3}{7}$

$\frac{2}{3} \times \frac{3}{7}$

$\frac{4}{3} \times \frac{3}{7}$

B. $\frac{1}{3} \times \frac{3}{4}$

$\frac{2}{3} \times \frac{3}{4}$

$\frac{4}{3} \times \frac{3}{4}$

C. $\frac{1}{6} \times \frac{6}{13}$

$\frac{2}{6} \times \frac{6}{13}$

$\frac{4}{6} \times \frac{6}{13}$

Number Talks That Highlight the Multiplication Strategy "Switching Numerators or Denominators"

These number talks provide an opportunity for students to discuss why the products for each problem are the same. The factors in a multiplication problem can be multiplied in any order because of the commutative property. For example, $\frac{3}{4} \times \frac{1}{2}$ can be changed to $\frac{1}{2} \times \frac{3}{4}$. Thinking about $\frac{1}{2}$ of $\frac{3}{4}$ is easier than considering $\frac{3}{4}$ of $\frac{1}{2}$. Because the denominator indicates the size of the parts and the numerator represents how many of those parts, we can also use the commutative property with only the numerators or the denominators. For example, in the problem $\frac{2}{3} \times \frac{3}{4}$ the commutative property can be used to "swap" the numerators, which changes the problem to $\frac{3}{3} \times \frac{2}{4}$, or to "swap" the denominators which changes the problem to $\frac{2}{4} \times \frac{3}{3}$. In each case, students create an easier problem to solve because of the multiplicative identity property. Swapping the numerators or denominators in a multiplication of fractions problem works because the commutative and associative properties are working together, as seen in the numerical recording in Figure 8–15 on the next page.

Number Talk Tip

The Multiplicative Identity Property states that a number does not change when it is multiplied by 1.

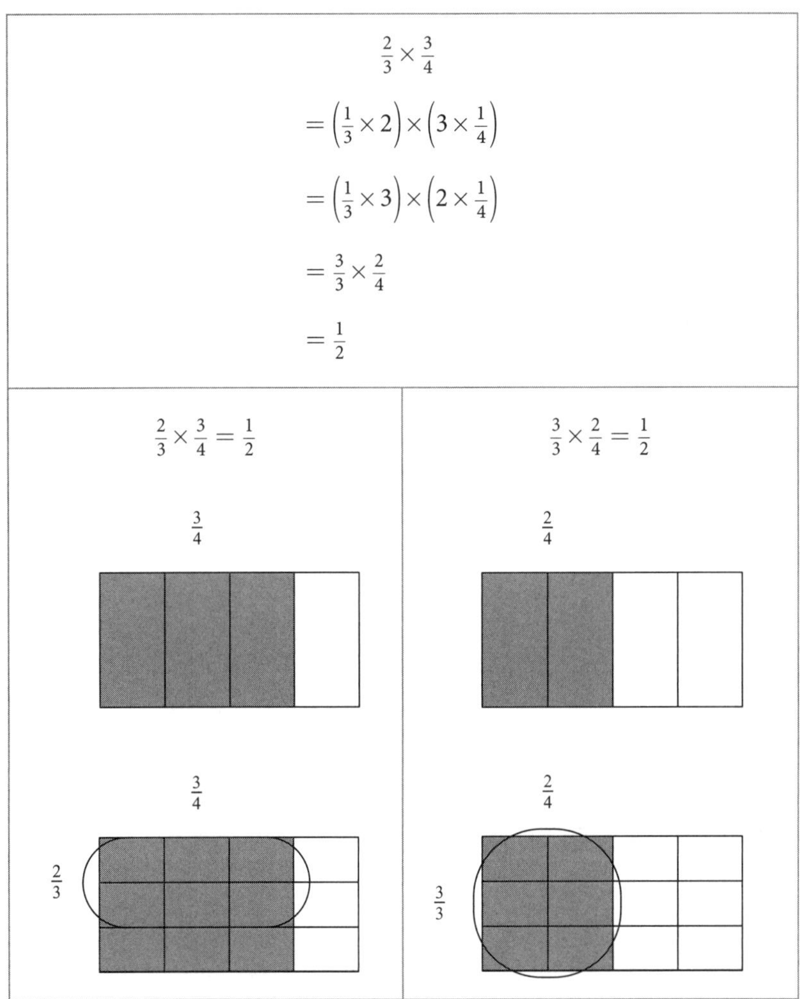

$\frac{2}{3} \times \frac{3}{4}$
$= \left(\frac{1}{3} \times 2\right) \times \left(3 \times \frac{1}{4}\right)$
$= \left(\frac{1}{3} \times 3\right) \times \left(2 \times \frac{1}{4}\right)$
$= \frac{3}{3} \times \frac{2}{4}$
$= \frac{1}{2}$
$\frac{2}{3} \times \frac{3}{4} = \frac{1}{2}$
$\frac{3}{4}$
$\frac{3}{4}$
$\frac{2}{3}$
$\frac{3}{3} \times \frac{2}{4} = \frac{1}{2}$
$\frac{2}{4}$
$\frac{2}{4}$
$\frac{3}{3}$

Figure 8–15. *Using "Switching Numerators or Denominators" to Solve* $\frac{2}{3} \times \frac{3}{4}$

Learn More...

Students can invent their own strategies because of the mental relationships they make. Mental relationships are based on logico-mathematical knowledge, which is a foundational principle of number talks. See "Logico-Mathematical Knowledge" in Chapter 1, on pages 29–31, for a more detailed explanation of the three types of knowledge.

In Figure 8–16, we can continue to test this strategy using the problems $\frac{2}{3} \times \frac{3}{5}$ and $\frac{1}{2} \times \frac{3}{4}$. While this idea works for both problems, notice how switching the numerators or denominators for $\frac{2}{3} \times \frac{3}{5}$ results in an easier problem. Switching the numerators or denominators for $\frac{1}{2} \times \frac{3}{4}$ makes the problem harder to solve. As with any strategy, students need to choose the strategy that makes a particular problem easier to solve.

Recording for $\frac{2}{3} \times \frac{3}{5}$	Recording for $\frac{1}{2} \times \frac{3}{4}$
$\frac{2}{3} \times \frac{3}{5}$	$\frac{1}{2} \times \frac{3}{4}$
$= \left(2 \times \frac{1}{3}\right) \times \left(3 \times \frac{1}{5}\right)$	$= \left(1 \times \frac{1}{2}\right) \times \left(3 \times \frac{1}{4}\right)$
$= \left(3 \times \frac{1}{3}\right) \times \left(2 \times \frac{1}{5}\right)$	$= \left(3 \times \frac{1}{2}\right) \times \left(1 \times \frac{1}{4}\right)$
$= \frac{3}{3} \times \frac{2}{5}$	$= \frac{3}{2} \times \frac{1}{4}$
$= \frac{2}{5}$	$= \frac{3}{8}$

Figure 8–16. *When Does "Switching Numerators or Denominators" Make a Problem Easier or Harder to Solve?*

Instructions

These number strings are organized into three columns and progress in difficulty going from the first column (from A to B to C, etc.) to the second column to the third column. Feel free to work through each string in order or choose problems according to your students' needs. You may choose to pose a pair of problems each day or multiple pairs as time allows. Introduce the first problem in each string, collect solutions, and then ask students to share their reasoning and proofs. Once the class reaches consensus, pose the next problem in the string. After students have shared their strategies and reached agreement on a solution, ask them, *"Why are the answers the same for each problem? What relationships do you notice between these two problems?"* As students notice that the numerators or denominators have been switched, ask, *"Can anyone help us think about whether this will always work?"*

What is ______ × ______? How do you know?
Why are the answers the same for each problem?
What relationships do you notice between these two problems?

A. $\frac{2}{2} \times \frac{1}{5}$

$\frac{1}{2} \times \frac{2}{5}$

B. $\frac{3}{2} \times \frac{2}{4}$

$\frac{2}{2} \times \frac{3}{4}$

C. $\frac{1}{3} \times \frac{3}{5}$

$\frac{3}{3} \times \frac{1}{5}$

D. $\frac{2}{3} \times \frac{3}{5}$

$\frac{3}{3} \times \frac{2}{5}$

E. $\frac{1}{4} \times \frac{4}{5}$

$\frac{4}{4} \times \frac{1}{5}$

F. $\frac{2}{4} \times \frac{4}{5}$

$\frac{4}{4} \times \frac{2}{5}$

A. $\frac{3}{4} \times \frac{4}{5}$

$\frac{3}{5} \times \frac{4}{4}$

B. $\frac{3}{5} \times \frac{5}{8}$

$\frac{3}{8} \times \frac{5}{5}$

C. $\frac{3}{4} \times \frac{4}{7}$

$\frac{3}{7} \times \frac{4}{4}$

D. $\frac{3}{5} \times \frac{5}{7}$

$\frac{3}{7} \times \frac{5}{5}$

E. $\frac{2}{3} \times \frac{3}{6}$

$\frac{2}{6} \times \frac{3}{3}$

F. $\frac{2}{3} \times \frac{3}{8}$

$\frac{2}{8} \times \frac{3}{3}$

A. $\frac{3}{8} \times \frac{8}{4}$

$\frac{8}{8} \times \frac{3}{4}$

B. $\frac{5}{8} \times \frac{8}{9}$

$\frac{5}{9} \times \frac{8}{8}$

C. $\frac{5}{6} \times \frac{6}{7}$

$\frac{6}{6} \times \frac{5}{7}$

D. $\frac{2}{5} \times \frac{5}{8}$

$\frac{2}{8} \times \frac{5}{5}$

E. $\frac{3}{7} \times \frac{7}{8}$

$\frac{3}{8} \times \frac{7}{7}$

F. $\frac{4}{9} \times \frac{9}{11}$

$\frac{9}{9} \times \frac{4}{11}$

Number Talks That Highlight the Multiplication Strategy "Decomposing Factors into Factors"

Decomposing factors into factors can create easier multiplication problems. This strategy works because of the associative property. This can be an especially efficient strategy when students break down factors into unit fractions or use numerators or denominators that are multiples of one another. See, for example, the recordings for $8 \times \frac{3}{4}$ and $\frac{1}{2} \times \frac{3}{4}$. (See Figures 8–17 and 8–18.) In each of these recordings, one of the factors is decomposed into other factors. Choosing which factor or factors to decompose affects the efficiency of this strategy.

Student's Strategy and Reasoning	Recording
Decomposing Factors Into Factors Bo: *I knew that* $4 \times \frac{3}{4}$ *was 3, so I broke up 8 into* 2×4. *Then I multiplied* $2 \times \left(4 \times \frac{3}{4}\right)$ *and that equals* 2×3, *which is 6.*	$8 \times \frac{3}{4}$ $= (2 \times 4) \times \frac{3}{4}$ $= 2 \times \left(4 \times \frac{3}{4}\right)$ $= 2 \times 3$ $= 6$

Figure 8–17. *Using the "Decomposing Factors into Factors" to Solve* $8 \times \frac{3}{4}$

Student's Strategy and Reasoning	Recording
Decomposing Factors into Factors Sue: *I broke* $\frac{3}{4}$ *into* $3 \times \frac{1}{4}$. *I know that* $\frac{1}{2}$ *of* $\frac{1}{4}$ *is* $\frac{1}{8}$ *so then I multiplied* $\frac{1}{8}$ *by 3 and that gave me* $\frac{1}{8} \times 3 = \frac{3}{8}$.	$\frac{1}{2} \times \frac{3}{4}$ $= \frac{1}{2} \times \left(3 \times \frac{1}{4}\right)$ $= \left(\frac{1}{2} \times \frac{1}{4}\right) \times 3$ $= \frac{1}{8} \times 3$ $= \frac{3}{8}$

Figure 8–18. *Using "Decomposing Factors into Factors" to Solve* $\frac{1}{2} \times \frac{3}{4}$

Category 1
Multiplying a Fraction by a Whole Number

The number talk strings in this category consist of three problems and are structured to help students consider decomposing a factor into other factors to make a multiplication problem easier to solve. At least one factor in each problem is a whole number to provide a beginning place to investigate this strategy. The first two problems represent different ways to decompose the factors of the third problem in each string.

Instructions

These number talks are organized into three columns and progress in difficulty going from the first column (from A to B to C) to the second column to the third column. Feel free to work through each string in order or choose problems according to your students' needs. You may choose to pose one problem or set of problems each day, or do more than one set of problems as time allows. Introduce the first problem in the string, collect solutions, then ask students to share their reasoning and proofs. Once the class reaches consensus, pose the next problem in the string and ask, *"How can you use what we just solved to help you with this next problem?"* or *"How does this new problem relate to the previous problem(s)?"* Continue this format with each problem in the string.

What is ______ × ______? How do you know?
How can you use what we already know to solve this next problem?
How does this new problem relate to the previous problem(s)?

A. $3 \times \frac{1}{4} \times 8$

$2 \times 4 \times \frac{3}{4}$

$\frac{3}{4} \times 8$

B. $5 \times \frac{1}{8} \times 8$

$\frac{5}{8} \times 2 \times 4$

$\frac{5}{8} \times 8$

C. $3 \times \frac{1}{4} \times 12$

$\frac{3}{4} \times 4 \times 3$

$12 \times \frac{3}{4}$

A. $2 \times \frac{1}{3} \times 15$

$\frac{2}{3} \times 3 \times 5$

$15 \times \frac{2}{3}$

B. $3 \times \frac{1}{7} \times 14$

$\frac{3}{7} \times 7 \times 2$

$\frac{3}{7} \times 14$

C. $5 \times \frac{1}{8} \times 4$

$\frac{5}{8} \times 2 \times 2$

$4 \times \frac{5}{8}$

A. $3 \times \frac{1}{5} \times 10$

$\frac{3}{5} \times 5 \times 2$

$\frac{3}{5} \times 10$

B. $5 \times \frac{1}{10} \times 20$

$\frac{5}{10} \times 10 \times 2$

$\frac{5}{10} \times 20$

C. $3 \times \frac{1}{8} \times 24$

$\frac{3}{8} \times 8 \times 3$

$\frac{3}{8} \times 24$

Category 2
Multiplying a Fraction by a Fraction

The following number talks consist of different ways to break apart the factors of the final problem in each string into other factors. The first two problems represent different ways to decompose the factors of the third problem in each string.

Instructions

These number talks are organized into three columns and progress in difficulty going from the first column (from A to B to C) to the second column to the third column. Feel free to work through each string in order or choose problems according to your students' needs. You may choose to pose one problem or set of problems each day, or do more than one set of problems as time allows. Introduce the first problem in the string, collect solutions, then ask students to share their reasoning and proofs. Once the class reaches consensus, pose the next problem in the string and ask, *"How can you use what we just solved to help you with this next problem?"* or *"How does this new problem relate to the previous problem(s)?"* Continue this format with each problem in the string.

What is ______ × ______? How do you know?
How can you use what we already know to solve this next problem?
How does this new problem relate to the previous problem(s)?

A. $3 \times \frac{1}{4} \times \frac{4}{8}$

$\frac{3}{4} \times 4 \times \frac{1}{8}$

$\frac{3}{4} \times \frac{4}{8}$

B. $3 \times \frac{1}{4} \times \frac{4}{12}$

$\frac{3}{4} \times 4 \times \frac{1}{12}$

$\frac{3}{4} \times \frac{4}{12}$

C. $2 \times \frac{1}{3} \times \frac{3}{5}$

$\frac{2}{3} \times 3 \times \frac{1}{5}$

$\frac{2}{3} \times \frac{3}{5}$

A. $5 \times \frac{1}{6} \times \frac{6}{15}$

$\frac{5}{6} \times 6 \times \frac{1}{15}$

$\frac{5}{6} \times \frac{6}{15}$

B. $2 \times \frac{1}{5} \times \frac{5}{8}$

$\frac{2}{5} \times 5 \times \frac{1}{8}$

$\frac{2}{5} \times \frac{5}{8}$

C. $3 \times \frac{1}{8} \times \frac{16}{15}$

$\frac{3}{8} \times 16 \times \frac{1}{15}$

$\frac{3}{8} \times \frac{16}{15}$

A. $2 \times \frac{1}{3} \times \frac{6}{8}$

$\frac{2}{3} \times 6 \times \frac{1}{8}$

$\frac{2}{3} \times \frac{6}{8}$

B. $2 \times \frac{1}{3} \times \frac{6}{9}$

$\frac{2}{3} \times 6 \times \frac{1}{9}$

$\frac{2}{3} \times \frac{6}{9}$

C. $2 \times \frac{1}{3} \times \frac{9}{15}$

$\frac{2}{3} \times 9 \times \frac{1}{15}$

$\frac{2}{3} \times \frac{9}{15}$

Number Talks That Highlight the Multiplication Strategy "Doubling and Halving"

When factors in a multiplication problem are changed by dividing one factor by a quantity and multiplying the other factor by that same amount, the product will always remain the same. This idea holds true whether students double and halve, triple and third, quadruple and quarter, and so forth. The foundation for this idea is the multiplicative inverse property, which states that for every number x that is not zero, x multiplied by $\frac{1}{x}$ will equal 1. For example, $\frac{7}{1} \times \frac{1}{7} = \frac{7}{7} = 1$.

Consider the idea of doubling and halving using the multiplicative inverse property with the problem 6×5. If we halve the 6 and double the 5, the result will be 3×10. Thirding and tripling will also work. (See Figure 8–19.)

Student's Strategy and Reasoning	Recording
Doubling and Halving Ellie: *I halved 6 to make 3 and I doubled 5 to make 10. That changed the problem to 3 × 10 which equals 30.*	6×5 $= \left(6 \times \frac{1}{2}\right) \times \left(5 \times \frac{2}{1}\right)$ $= 3 \times 10$ $= 30$
Thirding and Tripling Rafael: *I thirded 6 to make 2 and I tripled 5 to make 15. That changed the problem to 2 × 15 which is 30.*	6×5 $= \left(6 \times \frac{1}{3}\right) \times \left(5 \times \frac{3}{1}\right)$ $= 2 \times 15$ $= 30$

Figure 8–19. *Using the Multiplicative Inverse to Solve 6 × 5*

We can continue to test the doubling and halving strategy using the problems $8 \times \frac{3}{4}$ and $\frac{1}{2} \times \frac{3}{4}$. (See Figures 8–20 and 8–21.)

Student's Strategy and Reasoning	Recording
Doubling and Halving Clair: *Half of 8 is 4 and $\frac{3}{4} \times 2$ is $1\frac{1}{2}$ so that changes the problem to $4 \times 1\frac{1}{2}$*, which is 6.	$8 \times \frac{3}{4}$ $= \left(8 \times \frac{1}{2}\right) \times \left(\frac{3}{4} \times 2\right)$ $= 4 \times 1\frac{1}{2}$ $= 6$

Figure 8–20. *Using "Doubling and Halving" to Solve $8 \times \frac{3}{4}$*

Student's Strategy and Reasoning	Recording
Doubling and Halving Carmen: *I doubled $\frac{1}{2}$ and that gave me 1. Half of $\frac{3}{4}$ is $\frac{3}{8}$ so that makes the new problem $1 \times \frac{3}{8}$* which equals $\frac{3}{8}$.	$\frac{1}{2} \times \frac{3}{4}$ $= \left(\frac{1}{2} \times \frac{2}{1}\right) \times \left(\frac{3}{4} \times \frac{1}{2}\right)$ $= 1 \times \frac{3}{8}$ $= \frac{3}{8}$

Figure 8–21. *Using "Doubling and Halving" to Solve $\frac{1}{2} \times \frac{3}{4}$*

Doubling and Halving to Solve $\frac{1}{4} \times \frac{2}{3}$

Classroom Clip 8.4

Consider the following questions as you watch this number talk from a fifth-grade classroom:

1. What do you notice about MaKaya's strategy?
2. What questions would you ask if you wanted to highlight the mathematical properties underlying this strategy?
3. What makes this a useful strategy for solving this problem?
4. What are some cases in which Doubling and Halving would be an inefficient strategy?
5. What might the teacher have done prior to this number talk that helped give MaKaya confidence in using this strategy?

To view this video clip, scan the QR code or access via mathsolutions .com/NTFDP8.4

Category 1
Multiplying Whole Numbers and Fractions

This category of "Doubling and Halving" number talks are structured to begin with whole numbers and progress into fractions. Each string is comprised of four or more sequential problems that offer students opportunities to investigate relationships between problems when one factor is doubled and the other is halved.

Instructions

These number talks are organized into three columns and progress in difficulty going from the first column (from A to B to C) to the second column to the third column. Feel free to work through each string in order or choose problems according to your students' needs. You may choose to pose one set of problems each day or do more than one set as time allows. Introduce the first problem, collect solutions, then ask students to share their reasoning and proofs. Once the class reaches consensus, pose the next problem in the string. As students agree on the solution, ask, "*How does this problem relate to the previous problem(s)*?" When students begin to notice that each problem in the string has the same product, ask, "*Why do you think we are getting the same answer each time*?"

What is ______ × ______? How do you know?
How does this problem relate to the previous problem(s)?
Why do you think we are getting the same answer each time?

A. 2×5

1×10

$\frac{1}{2} \times 20$

$\frac{1}{4} \times 40$

B. 2×10

1×20

$\frac{1}{2} \times 40$

$\frac{1}{4} \times 80$

C. 6×5

3×10

$1\frac{1}{2} \times 20$

$\frac{3}{4} \times 40$

A. 20×2

40×1

$80 \times \frac{1}{2}$

$160 \times \frac{1}{4}$

B. 1×6

$\frac{1}{2} \times 12$

$\frac{1}{4} \times 24$

$\frac{1}{8} \times 48$

C. 2×6

1×12

$\frac{1}{2} \times 24$

$\frac{1}{4} \times 48$

A. 3×5

$1\frac{1}{2} \times 10$

$\frac{3}{4} \times 20$

$\frac{3}{8} \times 40$

B. 3×4

$1\frac{1}{2} \times 8$

$\frac{3}{4} \times 16$

$\frac{3}{8} \times 32$

C. 3×2

$1\frac{1}{2} \times 4$

$\frac{3}{4} \times 8$

$\frac{3}{8} \times 16$

Category 2
Multiplying a Fraction by a Fraction

The number talk strings in this category are comprised of strings of four sequential problems. The first multiplication problem in each string uses two fractions, and the final problem uses a whole number and a fraction. They are structured to give students opportunities to investigate relationships between problems when one factor is doubled and the other is halved.

Instructions

These number talk strings are organized into three columns and progress in difficulty going from the first column (from A to B to C) to the second column to the third column. Feel free to work through each string in order or choose problems according to your students' needs. You may choose to pose one set of problems each day, or do more than one set of problems as time allows. Introduce the first problem, collect solutions, then ask students to share their reasoning and proofs. Once the class reaches consensus, pose the next problem in the string. As students agree on the solution, ask, *"How does this problem relate to the previous problem(s)?"* When students begin to notice that each problem in the string has the same product ask, *"Why do you think we are getting the same answer each time?"*

What is ______ × ______? How do you know?
How does this problem relate to the previous problem(s)?
Why do you think we are getting the same answer each time?"

A. $\frac{1}{2}\times\frac{1}{2}$	**A.** $\frac{1}{2}\times\frac{4}{5}$	**A.** $\frac{1}{4}\times\frac{2}{8}$
$\frac{1}{4}\times 1$	$1\times\frac{2}{5}$	$\frac{1}{2}\times\frac{1}{8}$
$\frac{1}{8}\times 2$	$2\times\frac{1}{5}$	$1\times\frac{1}{16}$
$\frac{1}{16}\times 4$	$4\times\frac{1}{10}$	$2\times\frac{1}{32}$
B. $\frac{2}{5}\times\frac{1}{2}$	**B.** $\frac{2}{3}\times\frac{1}{2}$	**B.** $\frac{1}{4}\times\frac{4}{5}$
$\frac{1}{5}\times 1$	$\frac{1}{3}\times 1$	$\frac{1}{2}\times\frac{2}{5}$
$\frac{1}{10}\times 2$	$\frac{1}{6}\times 2$	$1\times\frac{1}{5}$
$\frac{1}{20}\times 4$	$\frac{1}{12}\times 4$	$2\times\frac{1}{10}$
C. $\frac{4}{3}\times\frac{1}{2}$	**C.** $\frac{3}{4}\times\frac{1}{2}$	**C.** $\frac{1}{4}\times\frac{8}{12}$
$\frac{2}{3}\times 1$	$1\frac{1}{2}\times\frac{1}{4}$	$\frac{1}{2}\times\frac{4}{12}$
$\frac{1}{3}\times 2$	$3\times\frac{1}{8}$	$1\times\frac{2}{12}$
$\frac{1}{6}\times 4$	$6\times\frac{1}{16}$	$2\times\frac{1}{12}$

Anticipating Student Thinking

Do not be discouraged if you do not immediately follow a student's thinking. It takes time to understand a learner's strategy, especially when you hear it for the first time. However, students commonly use a limited number of strategies to solve different types of problems, and taking time to think through possible strategies for each problem beforehand will help you gain confidence in listening to and following students' thinking. As you become more familiar with these strategies, you will find yourself anticipating your students' thinking and becoming more comfortable in understanding the approaches they have selected.

As you select problems for your number talks, anticipate potential student strategies and think about which mathematical properties you might highlight based on their thinking. Consider how you might record each strategy as well as how you will deal with student misconceptions such as the "shifting whole."

Learn More...

For a more detailed look at the "shifting whole" see "Highlighting the Shifting Whole" on pages 225–227 earlier in this chapter.

Looking Ahead

In this chapter, we have looked at opportunities for students to begin thinking about what happens when they multiply fractions. We have also examined some of the common misconceptions that may arise during a number talk.

Shifting from following a procedure to making relationships with fractions can be challenging for us as teachers as well as for our students. Are there certain multiplication strategies that are more comfortable for you as a teacher than others? Which strategies seem to be most efficient for you to use? How do the strategies you are using for multiplying fractions relate to strategies for multiplying whole numbers?

As we help our students investigate and develop understanding in this operation, we also see them make connections between multiplication and division. In Chapter 9, we explore what it means to divide fractions, examine student-invented strategies, and offer number talks to help students develop strategies for dividing fractions with understanding.

Connecting the Chapter to Your Practice

1. In what ways might using some of the number talks in this chapter help your students deepen their understanding of arithmetic properties?
2. What understandings do you anticipate your students might bring to the exploration of ideas in Figure 8–2 on page 223?
3. What have you noticed about your students' thinking regarding the "shifting whole"?
4. How can you help students who are confused about the idea of the "shifting whole" begin to confront their misunderstandings?
5. Look at the "Inside the Classroom" excerpt on pages 233–235. What do you notice about the strategies students found to be most efficient?
6. What do you anticipate your students' reactions might be if you present beginning multiplication of fractions problems by substituting the word *of* for the multiplication sign?
7. What do your students do that helps strengthen their understanding of multiplication of fractions?

CHAPTER 9

Number Talks for Division with Fractions

In this chapter, we offer a place for teachers to start when planning number talks around the division of fractions. In the opening sections, we discuss how the use of number talks is helpful as students work to develop division strategies with fractions. We then explore and offer number talks that are focused on helping students build their understanding of dividing fractions. We highly recommended that students are solid and flexible in their fractional reasoning (see Chapter 4) before using the number talks in this chapter.

OVERVIEW

How Number Talks Help the Development of Division Strategies with Fractions

Learn More...

For more insights on procedural versus conceptual understanding, see the section "Procedural Knowledge Linked to Students' Difficulties with Fractions" in the Introduction, pages 7–9.

Division with fractions is a complex part of mathematics that requires multiplicative reasoning and a thorough understanding of what it means to divide. Many students are familiar with the interpretation of division with whole numbers as a "sharing" situation but have not developed a complete understanding of division. When we teach division with fractions from a procedural perspective without developing students' conceptual understanding first, they struggle to make sense of the operation.

Let's say someone asked you to solve the problem $\frac{7}{9} \div \frac{2}{3}$. Would you automatically think, "Keep, change, flip," or "Yours is not to reason why, just invert and multiply?" When researchers gave this problem to prospective middle school teachers, 93 percent could accurately solve this problem using procedural knowledge. However, when the researchers asked them, "How many $\frac{1}{2}$s are in $\frac{2}{3}$?"—which requires conceptual understanding—only 52 percent gave a correct answer. The prospective teachers could think about division of fractions procedurally, but many lacked conceptual understanding (Li and Smith 2007).

This lack of conceptual understanding affects students' interpretation of what it means to divide with fractions. One common misconception is that students often think dividing by 2 and dividing by $\frac{1}{2}$ are synonymous (Mack 1995; Rizvi 2007; Isik, Cemalettin, and Tugrul 2012). Consider how your students might interpret the following two story problems. Which scenario represents $1\frac{1}{4} \div \frac{1}{2}$?

- *Malika has $1\frac{1}{4}$ cakes left from the party. She shared this amount with a friend. How much cake will they each get?*
- *Roberto has $1\frac{1}{4}$ yards of bubble wrap. It takes $\frac{1}{2}$ of a yard to wrap a package for shipping. How many packages can Roberto wrap?*

Because Malika is sharing the cake between two people, this situation is actually about dividing by 2 rather than dividing by $\frac{1}{2}$. Many students mistakenly interpret dividing by $\frac{1}{2}$ as splitting something into two equal parts. The second scenario is asking, "How many halves are in $1\frac{1}{4}$?" which is a quotative interpretation of division and matches the expression $1\frac{1}{4} \div \frac{1}{2}$.

This is where the importance of number talks comes into play. Number talks help students focus on developing strategies to build their conceptual understanding of dividing fractions. Specifically, there are approaches that we can take during a number talk to support students in inventing and developing strategies—and thus deepen their understanding of mathematics. These approaches include:

- Making connections to strategies for dividing whole numbers
- Highlighting the shifting whole
- Using story problems
- Using models
- Connecting students' strategies

Each of these approaches is discussed in more detail in the sections that follow.

Making Connections to Strategies for Dividing Whole Numbers

Will the strategies used for dividing whole numbers also work with fractions? This is an important question to pose to your students as they transition into division with fractions. You can help them test this idea by starting with the whole number problem $300 \div 25$. Ask students, "What are some ways we can solve this problem without using the U.S. standard algorithm?" Once students have indicated that they have at least one way in mind, ask, "Now consider the strategies you used and test them with the problem $\frac{3}{4} \div \frac{1}{2}$. Do your strategies still work?" Figure 9–1 on the next page shows three whole number division strategies and applies them to the problem $\frac{3}{4} \div \frac{1}{2}$.

Learn More . . .

For more about how the standard algorithm for dividing fractions is based on proportional reasoning see page 297–298 in this chapter.

Division Strategy	Dividing with Whole Numbers	Dividing with Decimals
Proportional Reasoning	$300 \div 25$ $= (300 \times 4) \div (25 \times 4)$ $= 1200 \div 100$ $= 12$	$\frac{3}{4} \div \frac{1}{2}$ $= \left(\frac{3}{4} \times 2\right) \div \left(\frac{1}{2} \times 2\right)$ $= 1\frac{1}{2} \div 1$ $= 1\frac{1}{2}$
Partial Quotients	$300 \div 25$ $= (100 + 100 + 100) \div 25$ $= (100 \div 25) + (100 \div 25) + (100 \div 25)$ $= 4 + 4 + 4$ $= 12$	$\frac{3}{4} \div \frac{1}{2}$ $= \left(\frac{1}{2} + \frac{1}{4}\right) \div \frac{1}{2}$ $= \left(\frac{1}{2} \div \frac{1}{2}\right) + \left(\frac{1}{4} \div \frac{1}{2}\right)$ $= 1 + \frac{1}{2}$ $= 1\frac{1}{2}$
Multiplying Up	$300 \div 25$ $25 \times \square = 300$ $25 \times 4 = 100$ $25 \times 4 = 100$ $25 \times 4 = 100$ $25 \times \boxed{12} = 300$	$\frac{3}{4} \div \frac{1}{2}$ $= \frac{1}{2} \times \square = \frac{3}{4}$ $\frac{1}{2} \times 1 = \frac{1}{2}$ $\frac{1}{2} \times \frac{1}{2} = \frac{1}{4}$ $\frac{1}{2} \times \boxed{1\frac{1}{2}} = \frac{3}{4}$

Figure 9–1. *Making Connections to Strategies for Computing with Whole Numbers*

Students may assume that if whole number division strategies work with fractions, then other generalizations will also hold true. For example, when dividing a positive number by a number greater than 1, the quotient is always smaller than the dividend. Ask students, "Does this generalization hold true when dividing by fractions?" You can use the examples in Figure 9–2 to help students investigate this idea.

Dividing by Numbers Greater Than 1 (Whole Numbers, Mixed Numbers, and Improper Fractions)	Dividing by Numbers Between 0 and 1 (Proper Fractions)
$6 \div 3 = 2$	$6 \div \frac{1}{2} = 12$
$\frac{1}{5} \div 2 = \frac{1}{10}$	$\frac{1}{5} \div \frac{1}{2} = \frac{2}{5}$
$\frac{7}{8} \div 1\frac{1}{4} = \frac{7}{10}$	$\frac{7}{8} \div \frac{3}{4} = 1\frac{1}{6}$
$8 \div 2\frac{1}{8} = 5$	$8 \div \frac{1}{8} = 64$
$\frac{2}{3} \div \frac{4}{3} = \frac{1}{2}$	$\frac{2}{3} \div \frac{1}{3} = 2$
$\frac{3}{4} \div \frac{5}{4} = \frac{3}{5}$	$\frac{3}{4} \div \frac{1}{4} = 3$

Figure 9–2. *What Happens to the Quotient When We Divide by Numbers Greater Than 1 Versus by Proper Fractions?*

When we divide a positive number by another number greater than 1, the quotient is always *smaller* than the dividend because the whole amount is being divided into groups. Using the quotative model for division, we partition the dividend into groups of a given size and determine how many groups there are. When the size of each group is greater than 1, the number of groups will be smaller than the dividend. For example, if we have 12 candies and put them into groups of equal size, as long as each group contains more than one piece, we will have fewer than 12 groups.

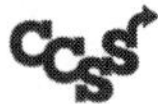

When we ask students to consider whether whole number strategies will work with rational numbers, we are purposefully providing an opportunity for students to *look for regularity in repeated reasoning* (MP8) and *look for and make use of structure* (MP7).

In contrast, when we divide a positive number by a proper fraction, the quotient is *larger* than the dividend. For example, for $\frac{4}{5} \div \frac{1}{2}$, we are asking how many groups of size $\frac{1}{2}$ are in $\frac{4}{5}$. When the size of each group is less than 1, the number of groups will be larger than the dividend.

These are important generalizations that students can construct for themselves without being told. To help learners develop these key ideas, ask what they notice when they investigate and explore relationships between factors and products, and among dividends, divisors, and quotients.

Highlighting the Shifting Whole

Just as the idea of the shifting whole occurs with multiplication of fractions, it also occurs with division of fractions. Consider this idea through the story context and area model. (See Figure 9–3.)

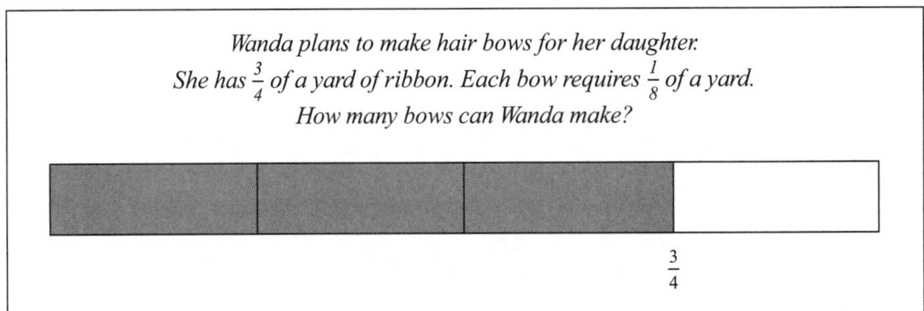

Wanda plans to make hair bows for her daughter.
She has $\frac{3}{4}$ of a yard of ribbon. Each bow requires $\frac{1}{8}$ of a yard.
How many bows can Wanda make?
$\frac{3}{4}$

Figure 9–3. *The Shifting Whole: Thinking About the Original Whole and the "New" Whole*

This question is asking how many one-eighths of a yard are in $\frac{3}{4}$ of a yard. One yard of fabric is the original whole, and the $\frac{3}{4}$ of a yard that is shaded becomes the "new" whole. To find how many eighths are in $\frac{3}{4}$ of a yard, we can repartition the original whole yard into eighths. Six-eighths of a yard are in $\frac{3}{4}$ of a yard. (See Figure 9–4.)

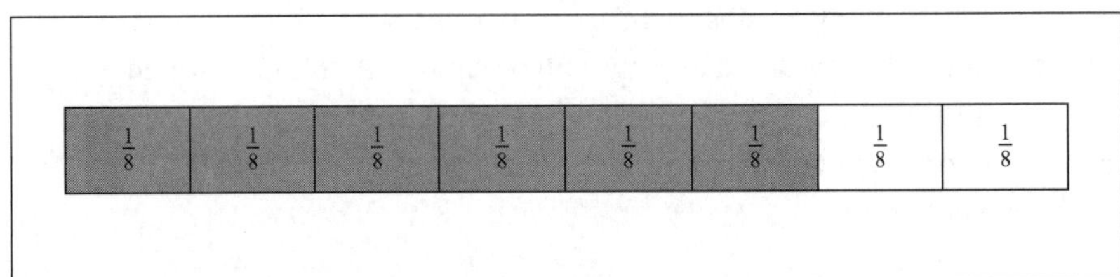

Figure 9–4. *Repartitioning the Whole to Find How Many Eighths Are in $\frac{3}{4}$ of a Yard*

Thinking about the relationship between the original whole and the "new" whole created when considering $\frac{3}{4}$ of the yard of fabric is a complex idea. It should not be surprising that this shifting whole can be problematic for many students.

It is also essential for teachers to anticipate possible misconceptions and incorrect answers. The following classroom scenario describes a number talk in which students are discussing their solutions for $2 \div \frac{3}{4}$. For this problem, learners will often correctly respond that there are two complete groups of $\frac{3}{4}$ in 2 but then they are unsure how to interpret the remaining $\frac{1}{2}$. This is especially true with the Common Denominator strategy. What do you notice about the way the teacher in the following "Inside the Classroom" excerpt navigates her students' common misunderstanding about the remainder in this problem?

When students are listening to and thinking about other students' strategies during a number talk, they are *constructing viable arguments and critiquing the reasoning of others* (MP3).

Inside the Classroom

A Number Talk for $2 \div \frac{3}{4}$

Ms. Rodriguez: We have some strategies justifying $2\frac{2}{3}$ as the answer for the problem $2 \div \frac{3}{4}$, but we also have $2\frac{1}{2}$ as a possible answer. Would someone like to share your reasoning for this answer?

Martin: I think the answer is $2\frac{1}{2}$. I changed 2 into $\frac{8}{4}$ so that I could think about how many $\frac{3}{4}$ were in $\frac{8}{4}$. Two groups of $\frac{3}{4}$ would be $\frac{6}{4}$, and that left $\frac{2}{4}$, which is the same as $\frac{1}{2}$, so my answer is $2\frac{1}{2}$.

Sumari: I follow your idea and see how you have $\frac{1}{2}$ left, but I don't think you answered the question.

Ms. Rodriguez: What do you mean, Sumari?

Sumari: Martin still needs to find how many $\frac{3}{4}$ are in the $\frac{1}{2}$ that is left. I think it would be $\frac{2}{3}$ of a $\frac{3}{4}$.

Martin: I hear what you're saying, but I'm not sure why it would be $\frac{2}{3}$.

Ms. Rodriguez: Can someone convince us?

(continued)

Ben: I think I can. Martin took the 2 wholes and divided them into fourths, which gave him 8 fourths.

[Ben draws two area models to represent his thinking.]

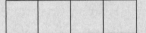

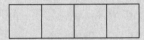

We can circle 2 complete groups of $\frac{3}{4}$ and that leaves us with $\frac{2}{4}$.

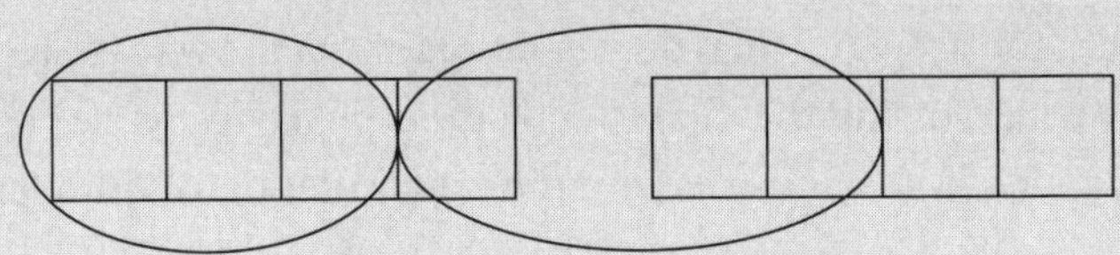

We still have to think about how much of a group of $\frac{3}{4}$ we can get out of $\frac{2}{4}$, and that is $\frac{2}{3}$ of a $\frac{3}{4}$. I can see this because if we had $\frac{3}{4}$ shaded, it would look like this.

[Ben draws and shades $\frac{3}{4}$ of a rectangle.]

$\frac{3}{4}$ shaded

But we don't have a complete $\frac{3}{4}$; we only have $\frac{2}{3}$ of it.

$\frac{2}{3}$ of the $\frac{3}{4}$ shaded

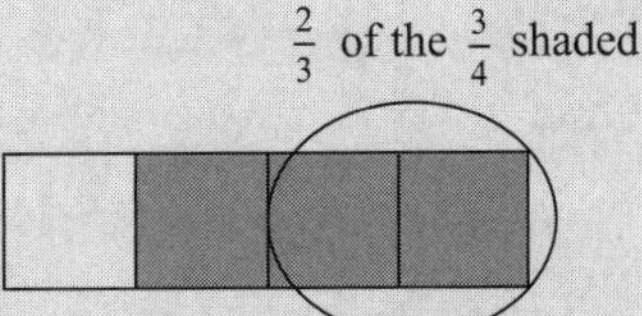

Martin: Oh, now I see. I still need to think about the remainder in terms of how much of a $\frac{3}{4}$ it is.

The problem $2 \div \frac{3}{4}$ is purposeful because it creates a situation for students to grapple with how to interpret the remainder and how it relates to $\frac{3}{4}$. As teachers, we can benefit from anticipating our students' potential struggles because it allows us to be prepared with questions to help students confront their misconceptions. Being prepared also helps us avoid resorting to telling.

Number Talk Tip

Knowing when to ask and when to tell is a foundational principle of number talks. To learn more about this, see Chapter 1, page 28.

$1 \div \frac{3}{8}$: Developing Division Strategies with Fractions

Classroom Clip 9.1

Consider the following questions as you watch this number talk from a sixth-grade classroom:

1. The problems in this number talk string are: $1 \div \frac{1}{2}$; $1 \div \frac{1}{4}$; $1 \div \frac{1}{8}$, and $1 \div \frac{3}{8}$. What makes the last problem the most challenging?
2. What are some ways the teacher supports students in thinking about the shifting whole in the remainder?
3. What are some possible numerical recordings for Lauva's strategy?
4. How does the use of models in Lauva's explanation support students' discussion of her ideas?
5. What do you notice about how students think about this problem?

To view this video clip, scan the QR code or access via mathsolutions.com/NTFDP9.1

Using Story Problems

Another way we can help learners develop a more complete understanding of what it means to divide is to situate number talks within a story problem context. A context gives students an entry point for developing strategies. It also helps them make sense of the question the problem is asking and what the numbers mean in relationship to the problem.

Think about the problem $8 \div 2$. This problem can be interpreted as either how many groups of 2 are in 8 (quotative), or if 8 is divided into 2 groups, then how many are in each group (partitive). Both types of division have unique characteristics and require different reasoning.

Students tend to be more familiar with partitive division with whole numbers, which is often described as a sharing or "dealing out" situation. In this division structure, students know the number of groups, and they are trying to find out how much is in each group. With quotative or measurement division, students know the size of the group, and they are trying to find out how many groups there are. Figure 9–5 on the next page shows examples of the two types of division represented by specific story contexts.

Presenting a Problem in Isolation	Presenting a Problem in a Story Context	Types of Division
$3\frac{1}{2} \div 4$	*LeShawn brought $3\frac{1}{2}$ brownies to share equally with 4 friends. What fraction of a brownie does each friend get?*	Partitive
$\frac{3}{4} \div \frac{1}{4}$	*Elda has $\frac{3}{4}$ of a cup of chocolate chips. This is enough to make $\frac{1}{4}$ of a batch of cookies. How many cups of chocolate chips does she need to make 1 batch?*	Partitive
$\frac{3}{5} \div \frac{1}{3}$	*Michelle can paint $\frac{3}{5}$ of the room using $\frac{1}{3}$ of a gallon of paint. How much paint will she need to paint the whole room?*	Partitive
$1\frac{1}{2} \div \frac{1}{2}$	*Suzanne made $1\frac{1}{2}$ pounds of trail mix. If she puts $\frac{1}{2}$ of a pound in each bag, how many bags can she make?*	Quotative
$\frac{3}{4} \div \frac{1}{4}$	*I have $\frac{3}{4}$ of a cup of cheese. I need $\frac{1}{4}$ of a cup of cheese for each quesadilla. How many quesadillas can I make?*	Quotative
$12 \div 1\frac{1}{2}$	*Michael's goal is to walk 12 miles. If he walks $1\frac{1}{2}$ miles each day, how many days will it take him to reach his goal?*	Quotative

Figure 9–5. *Presenting a Problem in Isolation Versus in a Story Context*

Framing a number talk problem in a story context helps students make sense of the two types of division and supports their understanding of division with fractions.

Learn More . . .

For more on the use of story problems in building fractional reasoning, see Chapter 4, page 73.

Number Talk Tip

An important part of a number talk involves making students' thinking public and accessible to other students. We can record a student's strategy numerically, but supporting their ideas with a model may help other learners follow and understand the student's thinking.

Using Models

In addition to using a story problem, teachers can incorporate a model during a number talk to give students an entry point for developing strategies and finding a solution. Different strategies lend themselves to different models. Consider, for example, how area, linear, and set models might each be used to represent three strategies for the problem $\frac{3}{4} \div \frac{1}{2}$. (See Figure 9–6.)

Student's Strategy and Reasoning	Recording
Common Denominators John: *I thought about a rectangle divided into fourths and shaded in $\frac{3}{4}$ of the whole.* *Then I changed the $\frac{1}{2}$ to $\frac{2}{4}$ and thought about how many $\frac{2}{4}$ were in the $\frac{3}{4}$. I could get one group of $\frac{2}{4}$ and then half of another $\frac{2}{4}$, so I knew there were $1\frac{1}{2}$ groups of $\frac{2}{4}$ in $\frac{3}{4}$.*	$\frac{3}{4} \div \frac{1}{2}$ $\frac{3}{4}$ of 1 whole 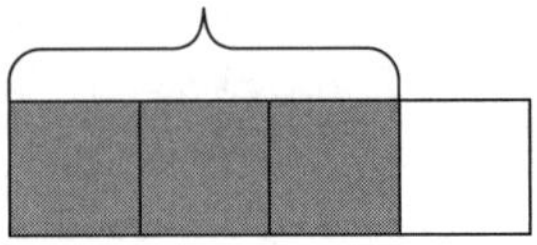 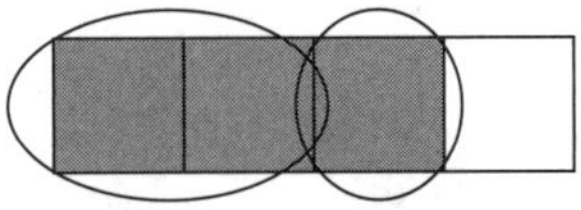 1 group of $\frac{2}{4}$ $\frac{1}{2}$ of a group of $\frac{2}{4}$ *[As John describes his thinking, Mr. Gilchrist records with models and then numerically.]* $\frac{3}{4} \div \frac{1}{2}$ $= \frac{3}{4} \div \frac{2}{4}$ $= 1\frac{1}{2}$

Figure 9–6. *Using Models to Represent Students' Thinking for Solving $\frac{3}{4} \div \frac{1}{2}$*

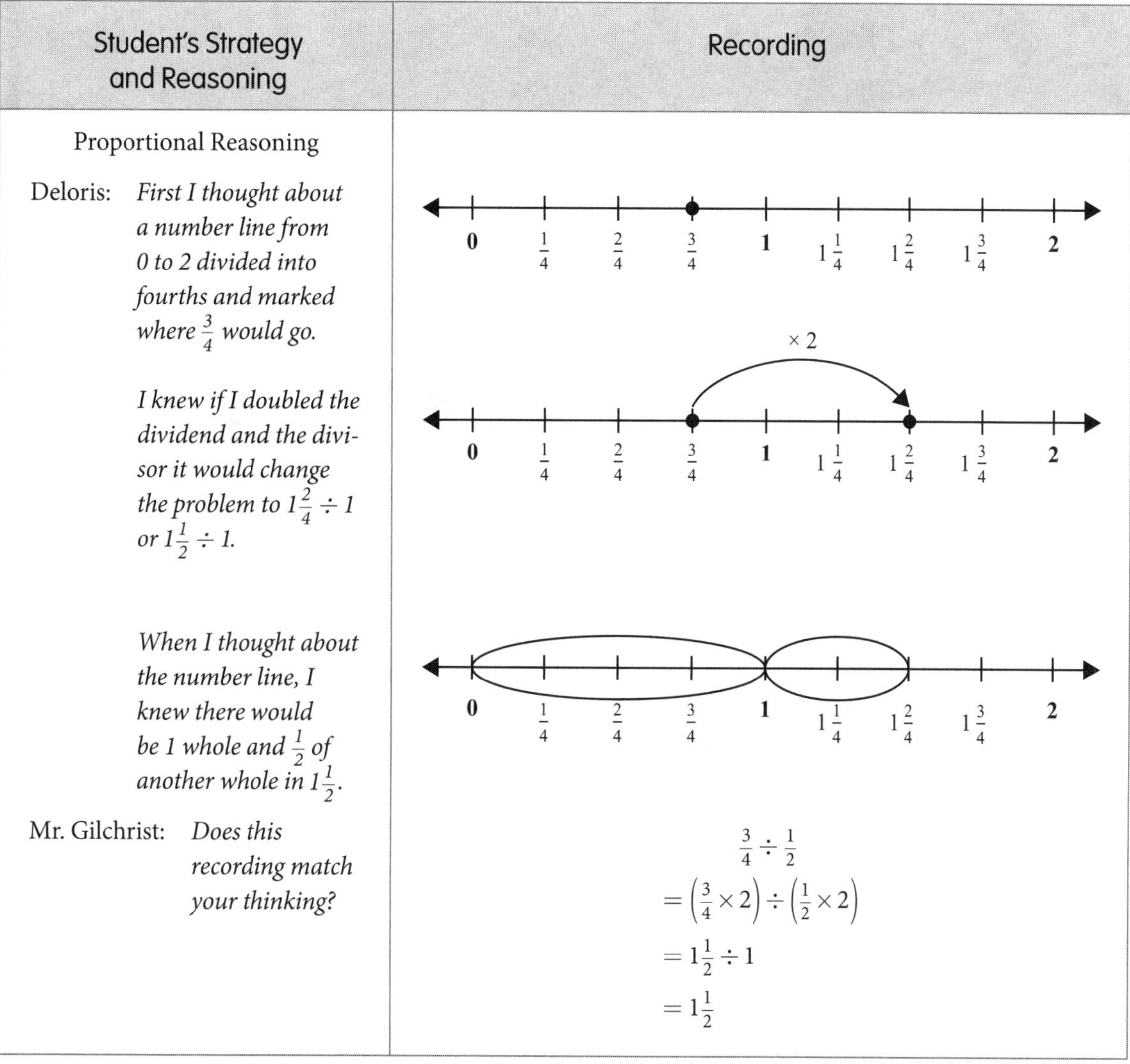

Student's Strategy and Reasoning	Recording
Proportional Reasoning	
Deloris: *First I thought about a number line from 0 to 2 divided into fourths and marked where $\frac{3}{4}$ would go.*	0, $\frac{1}{4}$, $\frac{2}{4}$, $\frac{3}{4}$, 1, $1\frac{1}{4}$, $1\frac{2}{4}$, $1\frac{3}{4}$, 2
I knew if I doubled the dividend and the divisor it would change the problem to $1\frac{2}{4} \div 1$ or $1\frac{1}{2} \div 1$.	× 2 0, $\frac{1}{4}$, $\frac{2}{4}$, $\frac{3}{4}$, 1, $1\frac{1}{4}$, $1\frac{2}{4}$, $1\frac{3}{4}$, 2
When I thought about the number line, I knew there would be 1 whole and $\frac{1}{2}$ of another whole in $1\frac{1}{2}$.	0, $\frac{1}{4}$, $\frac{2}{4}$, $\frac{3}{4}$, 1, $1\frac{1}{4}$, $1\frac{2}{4}$, $1\frac{3}{4}$, 2
Mr. Gilchrist: *Does this recording match your thinking?*	$\frac{3}{4} \div \frac{1}{2}$ $= \left(\frac{3}{4} \times 2\right) \div \left(\frac{1}{2} \times 2\right)$ $= 1\frac{1}{2} \div 1$ $= 1\frac{1}{2}$

Figure 9–6. *(continued)*

Student's Strategy and Reasoning	Recording
Partial Quotients Liam: *I thought about a package of 8 cans of soda, and $\frac{3}{4}$ of the cans would give me 6 cans.* *Since $\frac{1}{2}$ of all of the cans would be 4, I knew I could get 4 cans or one group of $\frac{1}{2}$ a out of the $\frac{3}{4}$ but then I would have 2 cans left. Those 2 cans are a half of a group of $\frac{1}{2}$, so I could get $1\frac{1}{2}$ halves out of $\frac{3}{4}$.* *[Mr. Gilchrist records numerically as he talks.] You were thinking about how many groups of $\frac{1}{2}$ were in $\frac{3}{4}$ of the cans, so you thought about $\frac{3}{4}$ of the cans as $\frac{1}{2}$ and $\frac{1}{4}$. You knew that there was 1 group of $\frac{1}{2}$ in $\frac{1}{2}$, and $\frac{1}{2}$ of a group of $\frac{1}{2}$ in $\frac{1}{4}$, so that was $1\frac{1}{2}$ groups of $\frac{1}{2}$ in $\frac{3}{4}$ of the cans.*	6 cans = $\frac{3}{4}$ of 8 cans $\frac{3}{4} \div \frac{1}{2}$ $= \left(\frac{1}{2} + \frac{1}{4}\right) \div \frac{1}{2}$ $= \left(\frac{1}{2} \div \frac{1}{2}\right) + \left(\frac{1}{4} \div \frac{1}{2}\right)$ $= 1 + \frac{1}{2}$ $= 1\frac{1}{2}$

Figure 9–6. *Using Models to Represent Students' Thinking for Solving $\frac{3}{4} \div \frac{1}{2}$ (continued)*

Learn More . . .

For more on the use of models in building fractional reasoning, see Chapter 4.

By presenting problems in different contexts that incorporate partitive and quotative division, teachers can help students deepen their understanding of the big ideas in these operations. Number talks offer the opportunity for teachers to use a variety of contexts, including story problems and models, to support students in developing conceptual understanding of division of fractions and in developing strategies for this operation.

Connecting Students' Strategies

During a number talk, we want to honor all strategies and refrain from elevating one strategy over another. As students defend their solutions, first look for opportunities to pose questions that engage students in thinking about how different strategies are connected. Comparing strategies provides opportunities for students to think more deeply about the relationships between them.

Inside the Classroom

A Number Talk for $6 \div \frac{2}{3}$

Figure 9–7 below highlights two strategies that students, Tonya and Emma, have shared for solving the problem $6 \div \frac{2}{3}$. Review these strategies and then read the dialogue excerpt that follows; it was captured from a number talk discussion about how the strategies are related.

Student's Strategy and Reasoning	Recording
Multiplying Up Tonya: *I thought about the problem as what times $\frac{2}{3}$ equals 6. Since $3 \times \frac{2}{3}$ would be 2, I need three times this amount — or 9 groups of $\frac{2}{3}$ — to make 6.*	$6 \div \frac{2}{3}$ $\square \times \frac{2}{3} = 6$ $3 \times \frac{2}{3} = \frac{6}{3} = 2$ $3 \times \left(3 \times \frac{2}{3}\right)$ $(3 \times 3) \times \frac{2}{3}$ $\boxed{9} \times \frac{2}{3} = 6$

Figure 9–7. *Comparing "Multiplying Up" and "Partial Quotients" to Solve $6 \div \frac{2}{3}$ (continued)*

(continued)

Student's Strategy and Reasoning	Recording
Partial Quotients Emma: *I already knew that $2 \div \frac{2}{3}$ was 3 because we had solved it earlier, so I broke apart the 6 into three 2s and divided each one by $\frac{2}{3}$. This gave me three 3s which was 9.*	$6 \div \frac{2}{3}$ $= (2 + 2 + 2) \div \frac{2}{3}$ $= \left(2 \div \frac{2}{3}\right) + \left(2 \div \frac{2}{3}\right) + \left(2 \div \frac{2}{3}\right)$ $= 3 + 3 + 3$ $= 9$

Figure 9–7. *Comparing "Multiplying Up" and "Partial Quotients" to Solve $6 \div \frac{2}{3}$ (continued)*

Mr. Laney: I'd like us to focus on Tonya's and Emma's strategies for a moment. Turn and talk to someone about how you think their strategies are related. *[As the students turn and talk, Mr. Laney eavesdrops on several conversations to anticipate the ideas being shared. After about 25 seconds, he asks the students to finish their last thoughts and be prepared to share what they noticed.]* Would someone be willing to share your thinking about how these two strategies are related?

Cecelia: I noticed that they both got the same answer, 9.

Matthew: Brian and I agree that the answer is 9, but we also talked about if you had 3 groups of $\frac{2}{3}$ that would be 2, which is the same thing as breaking apart the 6 into 3 groups of 2.

Mr. Laney: Can someone add on to Matthew's idea?

Maggie: I think I can show what Matthew is saying. I thought about a rectangle divided into 6 columns and I grouped the columns by 2s.

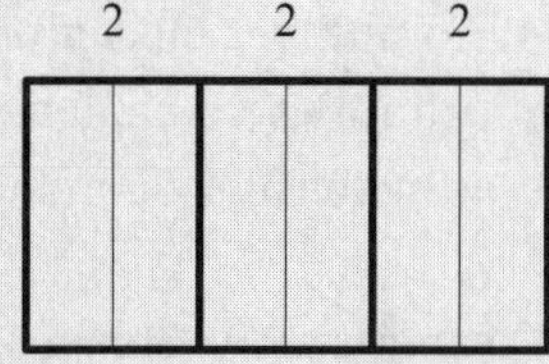

Then I divided each column into thirds. Two squares would be $\frac{2}{3}$ of 1 column. So for 2 columns, I would have 3 groups of $\frac{2}{3}$.

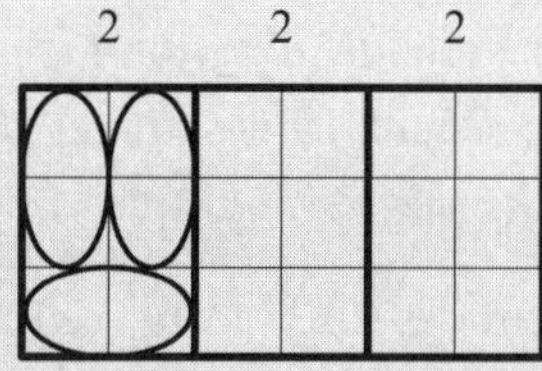

Xavi: Oh, I see how the strategies are related! It takes 9 groups of $\frac{2}{3}$ to make 6 columns. That's the same as $2 \div \frac{2}{3}$ three times.

Mr. Laney: Turn and talk to your partner again about this idea and what you understand as well as what is confusing.

As teachers, it's important for us to pay attention to how different strategies are related and to look for opportunities to take students deeper into the mathematics.

When we ask students to analyze and compare strategies, we are offering opportunities for them to *look for and make use of structure* (MP7).

Number Talks That Use Whole Numbers and Unit Fractions with Division

The number talks in this section offer a way to begin building your students' understanding of what it means to divide with fractions before transitioning to number talks around specific strategies. Their structure offers opportunities for students to think about partitioning the dividend or whole by the divisor and why the answer always results in a fraction.

Learn More...

As you present each problem, consider using various story contexts to deepen students' understanding of division. The contexts will likely influence whether students think about the problems as partitive (how many in each group) or quotative (how many groups of the divisor are in the dividend) division. Using a model along with a context will also provide another layer of support.

Consider introducing each problem in these number talk strings with a story context that fosters a "fair share" approach to help students make sense of the remainder and how it relates to the dividend. For example, for $3 \div 2$, the following story context suggests a partitive interpretation of division:

- *There are 3 brownies left from the party. Hosea and Micah plan to share them. How can they share the brownies so they each have the same amount?*

This context encourages students to continue to partition the "leftover" or remainder into a fraction. If students respond that each boy received 1 brownie and 1 was left, counter this solution by asking, "How could they share the 3 brownies so there were none left?"

Category 1
Using Whole Number Divisors with Mixed Number Quotients

The number talk strings in this category are structured to help students interpret remainders when using whole number divisors. Each string consists of three problems; the answer to each problem will result in a quotient that can be represented as a fraction or a mixed number.

Instructions

These number talks are organized into three columns and progress in difficulty going from the first column (from A to B to C) to the second column to the third column. Feel free to work through each string in order or choose problems according to your students' needs. You may choose to pose one problem or set of problems each day, or do more than one set of problems as time allows. Introduce the first problem in each string using a partitive division story context. For instance, the story might be:

- *There are ____ brownies left from the party. ____ friends plan to share them. How can they share the brownies so they each have the same amount?*

Then collect all solutions and ask students to share their reasoning and proofs. Once the class reaches consensus, pose the next problem in the string and ask, *"How can you use what we just solved to help you with this next problem?"* or *"How does this new problem relate to the previous problem(s)?"* You can use the same story context for all of the problems in a string.

There are ______ brownies left from the party. ______ friends plan to share them.
How can they share the brownies so they each have the same amount?
How do you know?
How can you use what we already know to solve this next problem?

A. $1 \div 2$
$3 \div 2$
$5 \div 2$

B. $7 \div 6$
$8 \div 6$
$9 \div 6$

C. $3 \div 3$
$5 \div 3$
$8 \div 3$

A. $5 \div 4$
$6 \div 4$
$9 \div 4$

B. $4 \div 3$
$7 \div 3$
$10 \div 3$

C. $6 \div 5$
$11 \div 5$
$16 \div 5$

A. $7 \div 5$
$12 \div 5$
$17 \div 5$

B. $9 \div 8$
$17 \div 8$
$10 \div 8$

C. $7 \div 4$
$11 \div 4$
$15 \div 4$

Category 2
Using Whole Number Divisors with Quotients Less Than 1

The number talk strings in this category are structured to help students continue with whole number division using divisors equal to or greater than the dividend. Each string consists of four problems. The structure and progression of the problems are designed to draw attention to the relationship between the dividend and the divisor, such as $2 \div 3 = \frac{2}{3}$, $2 \div 4 = \frac{2}{4}$, and $2 \div 5 = \frac{2}{5}$. This helps highlight the idea of fractions interpreted as division.

Instructions

These number talks are organized into three columns and progress in difficulty going from the first column (from A to B to C) to the second column to the third column. Feel free to work through each string in order or choose problems according to your students' needs. You may choose to pose one problem or set of problems each day, or do more than one set of problems as time allows. Introduce the first problem in each string with a story context that fosters a "fair share" approach. For example, for $2 \div 3$, consider this story context:

- *I have 2 cookies to share among 3 people. How can the cookies be shared so everyone has the same amount?*

This context requires students to continue to partition the "leftover" or remainder into a fraction.

Then collect all solutions and ask students to share their reasoning and proofs. Once the class reaches consensus, pose the next problem in the string and ask, *"How can you use what we already know to solve this next problem?"* or *"How does this new problem relate to the previous problem(s)?"* You can use the same story context for all of the problems in a string.

There are ______ cookies to share among ______ people.
How can the cookies be shared so everyone has the same amount?
How do you know?
How can you use what we already know to solve this next problem?

A. $2 \div 2$
$2 \div 3$
$2 \div 4$
$2 \div 5$

B. $3 \div 3$
$3 \div 4$
$3 \div 5$
$3 \div 6$

C. $4 \div 4$
$4 \div 5$
$4 \div 6$
$4 \div 7$

A. $5 \div 5$
$5 \div 6$
$5 \div 7$
$5 \div 8$

B. $6 \div 6$
$6 \div 7$
$6 \div 8$
$6 \div 9$

C. $7 \div 7$
$7 \div 8$
$7 \div 9$
$7 \div 10$

A. $8 \div 8$
$8 \div 9$
$8 \div 10$
$8 \div 11$

B. $9 \div 9$
$9 \div 10$
$9 \div 11$
$9 \div 12$

C. $10 \div 10$
$10 \div 11$
$10 \div 12$
$10 \div 13$

Category 3
Using a Unit Fraction as the Divisor

The number talk strings in this category are structured to help students consider the relationship between the divisor and the quotient. Each number talk string consists of three problems using the same whole number dividend. Each divisor is a unit fraction that is half of the divisor in the previous problem. This purposeful sequence offers opportunities for students to begin looking for patterns and forming generalizations about why the quotient is getting larger as the divisors in the string get smaller.

Instructions

These number talks are organized into three columns and progress in difficulty going from the first column (from A to B to C) to the second column to the third column. As you progress through each column, anticipate opportunities for conversations around equivalence and common denominators. Feel free to work through each string in order or choose problems according to your students' needs. You may choose to pose one problem or set of problems each day, or do more than one set of problems as time allows. Introduce the first problem in the string using a quotative interpretation of division (how many of the divisor are in the dividend) to support students as they begin solving the problem. For example, for the string beginning with $1 \div \frac{1}{2}$, ask, "How many halves are in 1 whole?" Collect solutions, and then ask students to share their reasoning and proofs. Once the class reaches consensus, pose the next problem in the string and ask, *"How can you use what we already know to solve this next problem?"* or *"How does this new problem relate to the previous problem(s)?"* Continue this format with each problem in the string.

How many ______ are in ______? How do you know? How can you use what we already know to solve this next problem?

A. $1 \div \frac{1}{2}$

$1 \div \frac{1}{4}$

$1 \div \frac{1}{8}$

B. $2 \div \frac{1}{2}$

$2 \div \frac{1}{4}$

$2 \div \frac{1}{8}$

C. $3 \div \frac{1}{2}$

$3 \div \frac{1}{4}$

$3 \div \frac{1}{8}$

A. $1 \div \frac{1}{5}$

$1 \div \frac{1}{10}$

$1 \div \frac{1}{20}$

B. $2 \div \frac{1}{5}$

$2 \div \frac{1}{10}$

$2 \div \frac{1}{20}$

C. $3 \div \frac{1}{5}$

$3 \div \frac{1}{10}$

$3 \div \frac{1}{20}$

A. $1 \div \frac{1}{3}$

$1 \div \frac{1}{6}$

$1 \div \frac{1}{9}$

B. $2 \div \frac{1}{3}$

$2 \div \frac{1}{6}$

$2 \div \frac{1}{9}$

C. $3 \div \frac{1}{3}$

$3 \div \frac{1}{6}$

$3 \div \frac{1}{9}$

Number Talks That Highlight the Division Strategy "Proportional Reasoning"

Once students have worked with beginning number talks, transition to number talks that further emphasize numerical relationships and the development of strategies. In this section the focus is on the division strategy, proportional reasoning.

The standard algorithm for dividing fractions is based on proportional reasoning. "Invert and multiply" or "Keep, change, flip" works because when we divide by a fraction, the dividend stays the same (keep), and then we multiply (change) by the reciprocal (flip) of the divisor. Multiplying any number by its reciprocal results in a product of 1, and when we also multiply the dividend by this same amount, we maintain a proportional relationship. Notice (as shown in Figure 9–8) that when students divide fractions using the standard algorithm it's really proportional reasoning at work. You increase the divisor and the dividend by the same amount so the proportional relationship remains the same. The amount of the increase is the reciprocal of the divisor so that the divisor will equal one. Students don't usually realize that they are changing the problem so they can divide by one.

Number Talk Tip

In this resource, each strategy is labeled to represent the thinking involved. However, in the classroom, consider naming the strategies with numbers or according to the students who invent them. The name of the strategy is not as important as the mathematical ideas the students are using.

Recording Using the Standard Algorithm for Dividing Fractions	Two Recordings Using Proportional Reasoning for Dividing Fractions
$\frac{3}{5} \div \frac{2}{3}$ $= \frac{3}{5} \times \frac{3}{2}$ $= \frac{9}{10}$	$\frac{3}{5} \div \frac{2}{3}$ $= \left(\frac{3}{5} \times \frac{3}{2}\right) \div \left(\frac{2}{3} \times \frac{3}{2}\right)$ $= \frac{9}{10} \div 1$ $= \frac{9}{10}$ *Or* $\frac{\frac{3}{5}}{\frac{2}{3}} \times \frac{\frac{3}{2}}{\frac{3}{2}} = \frac{\frac{3}{5} \times \frac{3}{2}}{1} = \frac{9}{10}$

Figure 9–8. *How Does Recording the Standard Algorithm for Dividing Fractions Compare to Recording the Proportional Reasoning Strategy?*

As students become more confident with their understanding of factors, multiples, and fractional reasoning, they may begin to investigate division from a proportional reasoning perspective. Deciding what to multiply or divide by depends on what will make the problem easier to solve. (See Figure 9–9.)

Student's Strategy and Reasoning	Recording
Conner: *Multiplying the dividend and divisor by 2 made this an easy problem because then I was just dividing 16 by 1, which is 16.*	$8 \div \frac{1}{2}$ $= (8 \times 2) \div \left(\frac{1}{2} \times 2\right)$ $= 16 \div 1$ $= 16$
Dianna: *I knew that $\frac{5}{8} \times 8$ was 5, and $\frac{3}{4} \times 8$ was 6, so when I multiplied both numbers (the dividend and the divisor) by 8 I got $6 \div 5$, which is $1\frac{1}{5}$.*	$\frac{3}{4} \div \frac{5}{8}$ $= \left(\frac{3}{4} \times 8\right) \div \left(\frac{5}{8} \times 8\right)$ $= 6 \div 5$ $= 1\frac{1}{5}$
Lawson: *When I multiply both numbers by 3 it makes the problem $12 \div 2$, which is an easier problem to solve. $12 \div 2 = 6$*	$4 \div \frac{2}{3}$ $= (4 \times 3) \div \left(\frac{2}{3} \times 3\right)$ $= 12 \div 2$ $= 6$

Figure 9–9. *Using "Proportional Reasoning" to Solve $8 \div \frac{1}{2}$, $\frac{3}{4} \div \frac{5}{8}$, and $4 \div \frac{2}{3}$*

$6 \div 3$, $3 \div 1\frac{1}{2}$, $1\frac{1}{2} \div \frac{3}{4}$: Proportional Reasoning String

Classroom Clip 9.2

Consider the following questions as you watch this number talk from a sixth-grade classroom:

1. What relationship do you notice between the problems in this number talk string?
2. How can the teacher's choice of problems help students build their mathematical understandings?
3. What can be said about Natalie's thinking based on the pattern she notices between problems?
4. What does Pablo know that helps him solve the problem?
5. What evidence of students using the mathematical practice standards do you see in this number talk?

To view this video clip, scan the QR code or access via mathsolutions.com/NTFDP9.2

These number talk strings are structured to help students notice the proportional relationships between the problems. Each string consists of four problems. The first problem starts with whole numbers to provide an accessible beginning point and then transitions to subsequent problems by halving both the dividend and divisor. The divisors and dividends in the final problems are fractions. As students begin to focus on the proportional reasoning, you may want to start with the last problem in the string to see if students use proportional reasoning to make the problem easier to solve. As you progress through each column, anticipate opportunities for conversations around equivalence and common denominators.

Number talks give students opportunities to *make sense of problems and persevere* in solving them (MP1).

Instructions

These number talks are organized into three columns and progress in difficulty going from the first column (from A to B to C, etc.) to the second column to the third column. Feel free to work through each string in order or choose problems according to your students' needs. You may choose to pose one problem or set of problems each day, or do more than one set of problems as time allows. Introduce the first problem in the string, collect solutions, then ask students to share their reasoning and proofs. Once the class reaches consensus, pose the next problem in the string and ask, *"How can you use what we just solved to help you with this next problem?"* or *"How does this new problem relate to the previous problem(s)?"* Continue this format with each problem in the string.

What is ______ ÷ ______? How do you know?
How can you use what we already know to solve this next problem?

A. $4 \div 2$

$2 \div 1$

$1 \div \frac{1}{2}$

$\frac{1}{2} \div \frac{1}{4}$

B. $8 \div 4$

$4 \div 2$

$2 \div 1$

$1 \div \frac{1}{2}$

C. $2 \div 1$

$1 \div \frac{1}{2}$

$\frac{1}{2} \div \frac{1}{4}$

$\frac{1}{4} \div \frac{1}{8}$

D. $5 \div 2$

$2\frac{1}{2} \div 1$

$1\frac{1}{4} \div \frac{1}{2}$

$\frac{5}{8} \div \frac{1}{4}$

A. $3 \div 2$

$1\frac{1}{2} \div 1$

$\frac{3}{4} \div \frac{1}{2}$

$\frac{3}{8} \div \frac{1}{4}$

B. $4 \div 3$

$2 \div 1\frac{1}{2}$

$1 \div \frac{3}{4}$

$\frac{1}{2} \div \frac{3}{8}$

C. $10 \div 4$

$5 \div 2$

$2\frac{1}{2} \div 1$

$1\frac{1}{4} \div \frac{1}{2}$

D. $5 \div 4$

$2\frac{1}{2} \div 2$

$1\frac{1}{4} \div 1$

$\frac{5}{8} \div \frac{1}{2}$

A. $9 \div 4$

$4\frac{1}{2} \div 2$

$2\frac{1}{4} \div 1$

$1\frac{1}{8} \div \frac{1}{2}$

B. $5 \div 3$

$2\frac{1}{2} \div 1\frac{1}{2}$

$1\frac{1}{4} \div \frac{3}{4}$

$\frac{5}{8} \div \frac{3}{8}$

C. $8 \div 5$

$4 \div 2\frac{1}{2}$

$2 \div 1\frac{1}{4}$

$1 \div \frac{5}{8}$

D. $6 \div 5$

$3 \div 2\frac{1}{2}$

$1\frac{1}{2} \div 1\frac{1}{4}$

$\frac{3}{4} \div \frac{5}{8}$

Number Talks That Highlight the Division Strategy "Common Denominators"

When students use this strategy, they partition the dividend and the divisor into the same number of parts. When the denominators are in common, students can focus on the relationship between the numerators. Making equivalent fractions and using the identity property of multiplication are the big ideas students build on when they use this strategy. (See Figure 9–10.)

Student's Strategy and Reasoning	Recording
Common Denominator Francis: *I thought about 8 as 16 halves, and then it was easy to know that the answer is 16 because there are 16 halves in* $\frac{16}{2}$.	$8 \div \frac{1}{2}$ $= \frac{16}{2} \div \frac{1}{2}$ $= 16$
Common Denominator DeShawn: *I thought about making common denominators so then the problem became how many* $\frac{4}{12}$ *are in* $\frac{9}{12}$. $\frac{9}{4} = 2\frac{1}{4}$ *so there are* $2\frac{1}{4}$ *thirds in* $\frac{3}{4}$.	$\frac{3}{4} \div \frac{1}{3}$ $= \frac{9}{12} \div \frac{4}{12}$ $= \frac{9}{4}$ $= 2\frac{1}{4}$

Figure 9–10. *Using "Common Denominators" to Solve* $8 \div \frac{1}{2}$ *and* $\frac{3}{4} \div \frac{1}{3}$

Learn More...

Equivalence is a critical understanding when operating with fractions. See Chapter 3, pages 69–70, for a more detailed discussion of this important idea.

Category 1
Using the Same Divisors

The number talk strings in this category are comprised of pairs of problems to begin conversation around using common denominators as a division strategy. The first problem in each pair is crafted using common denominators. The dividend in the second problem is equivalent to the dividend in the first problem, and the divisor stays the same. The denominators in the second problem of each pair are multiples of each other. The relationship between the problems provides teachers with an opportunity to ask students, "*Why are the answers the same for both problems? How are the problems related?*" As you progress through each column, anticipate opportunities for conversations around equivalence and common denominators.

Instructions

These number talks are organized into three columns and progress in difficulty going from the first column (from A to B to C, etc.) to the second column to the third column. Feel free to work through each string in order or choose problems according to your students' needs. You may choose to pose one problem or set of problems each day, or do more than one set of problems as time allows. Introduce the first problem in the string, collect solutions, and then ask students to share their reasoning and proofs. Once the class reaches consensus, pose the second problem in the string and ask, "*How can you use what we just solved to help you with this next problem?*" or "*How does this new problem relate to the previous problem? Why are the quotients the same?*"

What is ______ ÷ ______? How do you know?
How can you use what we already know to solve this next problem?
How does this new problem relate to the previous problem?
Why are the quotients the same?

A. $\frac{2}{4} \div \frac{1}{4}$

$\frac{1}{2} \div \frac{1}{4}$

B. $\frac{4}{8} \div \frac{1}{8}$

$\frac{1}{2} \div \frac{1}{8}$

C. $\frac{2}{8} \div \frac{1}{8}$

$\frac{1}{4} \div \frac{1}{8}$

D. $\frac{6}{8} \div \frac{1}{8}$

$\frac{3}{4} \div \frac{1}{8}$

E. $\frac{5}{10} \div \frac{1}{10}$

$\frac{1}{2} \div \frac{1}{10}$

F. $\frac{6}{10} \div \frac{1}{10}$

$\frac{3}{5} \div \frac{1}{10}$

A. $\frac{2}{8} \div \frac{1}{8}$

$\frac{1}{4} \div \frac{1}{8}$

B. $\frac{6}{8} \div \frac{1}{8}$

$\frac{3}{4} \div \frac{1}{8}$

C. $\frac{2}{8} \div \frac{1}{8}$

$\frac{1}{4} \div \frac{1}{8}$

D. $\frac{3}{8} \div \frac{1}{8}$

$\frac{6}{16} \div \frac{1}{8}$

E. $\frac{9}{12} \div \frac{1}{12}$

$\frac{3}{4} \div \frac{1}{12}$

F. $\frac{10}{12} \div \frac{1}{12}$

$\frac{5}{6} \div \frac{1}{12}$

A. $\frac{6}{8} \div \frac{3}{8}$

$\frac{3}{4} \div \frac{3}{8}$

B. $\frac{2}{8} \div \frac{3}{8}$

$\frac{1}{4} \div \frac{3}{8}$

C. $\frac{12}{16} \div \frac{5}{16}$

$\frac{3}{4} \div \frac{5}{16}$

D. $\frac{10}{16} \div \frac{5}{16}$

$\frac{5}{8} \div \frac{5}{16}$

E. $\frac{6}{15} \div \frac{3}{15}$

$\frac{2}{5} \div \frac{3}{15}$

F. $\frac{12}{15} \div \frac{4}{15}$

$\frac{4}{5} \div \frac{4}{15}$

Category 2
Using Equivalent Divisors

The number talk strings in this category are comprised of pairs of problems to continue the conversation around using common denominators as a division strategy. The first problem in each pair uses common denominators. The dividend and the divisor in the second problem are equivalent to the dividend and the divisor in the first problem; however, the denominators are not multiples of each other. This adds another layer of complexity. The relationship between the problems provides an opportunity for teachers to ask students, "Why are the answers the same for both problems? How are the problems related?" As you progress through each column, anticipate opportunities for conversations around equivalence and common denominators.

Instructions

These number talks are organized into three columns and progress in difficulty going from the first column (from A to B to C, etc.) to the second column to the third column. Feel free to work through each string in order or choose problems according to your students' needs. You may choose to pose one problem or set of problems each day, or do more than one set of problems as time allows. Introduce the first problem in the string, collect solutions, and then ask students to share their reasoning and proofs. Once the class reaches consensus, pose the second problem in the string and ask, *"How can you use what we just solved to help you with this next problem? How does this new problem relate to the previous problem? Why are the quotients the same?"*

What is ______ ÷ ______? How do you know?
How can you use what we already know to solve this next problem?
How does this new problem relate to the previous problem?
Why are the quotients the same?

A. $\frac{3}{6} \div \frac{2}{6}$

$\frac{1}{2} \div \frac{1}{3}$

B. $\frac{2}{6} \div \frac{3}{6}$

$\frac{1}{3} \div \frac{1}{2}$

C. $\frac{5}{10} \div \frac{2}{10}$

$\frac{1}{2} \div \frac{1}{5}$

D. $\frac{2}{10} \div \frac{5}{10}$

$\frac{1}{5} \div \frac{1}{2}$

A. $\frac{9}{12} \div \frac{4}{12}$

$\frac{3}{4} \div \frac{1}{3}$

B. $\frac{4}{12} \div \frac{9}{12}$

$\frac{1}{3} \div \frac{3}{4}$

C. $\frac{6}{15} \div \frac{5}{15}$

$\frac{2}{5} \div \frac{1}{3}$

D. $\frac{8}{20} \div \frac{5}{20}$

$\frac{2}{5} \div \frac{1}{4}$

A. $\frac{6}{10} \div \frac{5}{10}$

$\frac{3}{5} \div \frac{1}{2}$

B. $\frac{5}{10} \div \frac{6}{10}$

$\frac{1}{2} \div \frac{3}{5}$

C. $\frac{12}{20} \div \frac{5}{20}$

$\frac{3}{5} \div \frac{1}{4}$

D. $\frac{5}{20} \div \frac{8}{20}$

$\frac{1}{4} \div \frac{2}{5}$

Number Talks That Highlight the Division Strategy "Partial Quotients"

Similar to the Partial Products strategy for multiplication of whole numbers discussed in Chapter 8, this strategy focuses on decomposing the dividend into smaller, friendlier fractions to create smaller division problems. (See Figure 9–11.) This strategy works because of the distributive property.

Student's Strategy and Reasoning	Recording
Partial Quotients Valerie: *I know that* $4 \div \frac{1}{2}$ *is 8 so I broke 8 into two groups of 4 and divided each 4 by* $\frac{1}{2}$*. That gave me* $8 + 8$*, which is 16 so there are 16 halves in 8.*	$8 \div \frac{1}{2}$ $= (4 + 4) \div \frac{1}{2}$ $= \left(4 \div \frac{1}{2}\right) + \left(4 \div \frac{1}{2}\right)$ $= 8 + 8$ $= 16$
Partial Quotients Harrison: *I broke the* $\frac{3}{4}$ *into* $\frac{1}{2} + \frac{1}{4}$*. I knew that* $\frac{1}{2} \div \frac{1}{2} = 1$ *so* $\frac{1}{4} \div \frac{1}{2}$ *is* $\frac{1}{2}$*. I added* $1 + \frac{1}{2}$ *and the answer is* $1\frac{1}{2}$*. That means there are* $1\frac{1}{2}$ *halves in* $\frac{3}{4}$*.*	$\frac{3}{4} \div \frac{1}{2}$ $= \left(\frac{1}{2} + \frac{1}{4}\right) \div \frac{1}{2}$ $= \left(\frac{1}{2} \div \frac{1}{2}\right) + \left(\frac{1}{4} \div \frac{1}{2}\right)$ $= 1 + \frac{1}{2}$ $= 1\frac{1}{2}$

Figure 9–11. *Using Partial Quotients to Solve* $8 \div \frac{1}{2}$ *and* $\frac{3}{4} \div \frac{1}{2}$

When students decompose the dividend to make an easier division problem to solve, they are *looking for and making use of structure* (MP7).

The following number talk strings use a series of purposefully scaffolded problems that students can use to decompose the dividend in subsequent problems. Each string consists of four problems. The first problem offers an accessible division problem that can be used to solve any of the following problems in the string. For example, in the first string, $8 \div \frac{1}{2}$ could be solved by decomposing the 8 into fours, twos, ones, or any combination that makes 8 and then is divided by $\frac{1}{2}$.

Instructions

These number talks are organized into three columns and progress in difficulty going from the first column (from A to B to C) to the second column to the third column. Feel free to work through each string in order or choose problems according to your students' needs. You may choose to pose one problem or set of problems each day, or do more than one set of problems as time allows. Introduce the first problem in the string, collect solutions, then ask students to share their reasoning and proofs. Once the class reaches consensus, pose the next problem in the string and ask, *"How can you use what we already know to solve this next problem? How does this new problem relate to the previous problem? What relationships are you noticing between the problems?"* Continue this format with each problem in the string.

What is ______ ÷ ______? How do you know?
How can you use what we already know to solve this next problem?
What relationships are you noticing between the problems?

A. $1 \div \frac{1}{2}$

$2 \div \frac{1}{2}$

$4 \div \frac{1}{2}$

$8 \div \frac{1}{2}$

B. $1 \div \frac{1}{4}$

$2 \div \frac{1}{4}$

$4 \div \frac{1}{4}$

$8 \div \frac{1}{4}$

C. $1 \div \frac{1}{3}$

$2 \div \frac{1}{3}$

$3 \div \frac{1}{3}$

$6 \div \frac{1}{3}$

A. $\frac{1}{4} \div \frac{1}{4}$

$\frac{3}{4} \div \frac{1}{4}$

$\frac{5}{4} \div \frac{1}{4}$

$\frac{7}{4} \div \frac{1}{4}$

B. $\frac{1}{3} \div \frac{1}{3}$

$\frac{2}{3} \div \frac{1}{3}$

$\frac{4}{3} \div \frac{1}{3}$

$\frac{6}{3} \div \frac{1}{3}$

C. $\frac{4}{8} \div \frac{1}{2}$

$\frac{6}{8} \div \frac{1}{2}$

$\frac{8}{8} \div \frac{1}{2}$

$\frac{12}{8} \div \frac{1}{2}$

A. $\frac{2}{8} \div \frac{1}{4}$

$\frac{4}{8} \div \frac{1}{4}$

$\frac{6}{8} \div \frac{1}{4}$

$\frac{12}{8} \div \frac{1}{4}$

B. $\frac{1}{5} \div \frac{1}{10}$

$\frac{2}{5} \div \frac{1}{10}$

$\frac{3}{5} \div \frac{1}{10}$

$\frac{4}{5} \div \frac{1}{10}$

C. $\frac{2}{8} \div \frac{1}{16}$

$\frac{4}{8} \div \frac{1}{16}$

$\frac{6}{8} \div \frac{1}{16}$

$\frac{12}{8} \div \frac{1}{16}$

Number Talks That Highlight the Division Strategy "Multiplying Up"

Before transitioning into division with fractions, students should have a solid and flexible understanding of multiplication and division with whole numbers and the relationship between these operations. Multiplying Up is a division strategy that builds on the relationship between multiplication and division. Because of this inverse relationship, we can use one operation to "undo" or reverse the other, as indicated by the problems 4×5 and $20 \div 4$. This inverse relationship allows students to solve $20 \div 4$ as a missing factor multiplication problem, $4 \times \_\_\_\_ = 20$.

The same relationship exists when we are computing with fractions. Consider the problem $\frac{3}{2} \div \frac{1}{2}$. This idea can be represented as $\_\_\_\_ \times \frac{1}{2} = \frac{3}{2}$ and is why we can multiply up to divide. The Multiplying Up strategy provides an opportunity for students to gradually build on multiplication problems they know until they reach the dividend. (See Figure 9–12 on the next page.)

Student's Strategy and Reasoning	Recording
Multiplying Up Vickie: *I thought about "One half times what gives me 16?" I know that $\frac{1}{2} \times 20 = 10$ and $\frac{1}{2} \times 12 = 6$ so I added $20 + 12$ and that's how I knew there were 32 halves in 16.*	$16 \div \frac{1}{2}$ $\frac{1}{2} \times \square = 16$ $\frac{1}{2} \times 20 = 10$ $\frac{1}{2} \times 12 = 6$ $\frac{1}{2} \times \boxed{32} = 16$
Multiplying Up Roger: *I asked myself, "What times $\frac{1}{2}$ equals $\frac{3}{4}$?" I knew that $\frac{1}{2} \times 1 = \frac{1}{2}$ but I still needed another $\frac{1}{4}$ to get to $\frac{3}{4}$ so I multiplied $\frac{1}{2} \times \frac{1}{2}$ to get the other $\frac{1}{4}$. Then I knew that $1 + \frac{1}{2} = 1\frac{1}{2}$ so $\frac{1}{2} \times 1\frac{1}{2} = \frac{3}{4}$*	$\frac{3}{4} \div \frac{1}{2}$ $\frac{1}{2} \times \square = \frac{3}{4}$ $\frac{1}{2} \times 1 = \frac{1}{2}$ $\frac{1}{2} \times \frac{1}{2} = \frac{1}{4}$ $\frac{1}{2} \times \boxed{1\frac{1}{2}} = \frac{3}{4}$

Figure 9–12. *Using "Multiplying Up" to Solve $16 \div \frac{1}{2}$ and $\frac{3}{4} \div \frac{1}{2}$*

The following strings build from smaller multiplication problems to the final division problem to help students consider the relationship between multiplication and division. Each number talk consists of four problems. The first problem offers a beginning place to approach the problem and can be used, along with subsequent problems, to solve the final division problem in the string.

Instructions

These number talks are organized into three columns and progress in difficulty going from the first column (from A to B) to the second column to the third column. Feel free to work through each string in order or choose problems according to your students' needs. You may choose to pose one problem or set of problems each day, or do more than one set of problems as time allows. Introduce the first problem in the string, collect solutions, then ask students to share their reasoning and proofs. Once the class reaches consensus, pose the next problem in the string and ask, *"How can you use what you already know to help you solve this next problem?"* As you present the division problem, ask, *"How can our previous problems help us solve this division problem?" Continue this format for each problem in the string.*

What is ______ ÷ ______? How do you know?
How can you use what we already know to solve the next problem?
How can our previous problems help us solve this division problem?

A. $2 \times \frac{1}{2}$

$4 \times \frac{1}{2}$

$6 \times \frac{1}{2}$

$4 \div \frac{1}{2}$

B. $1 \times \frac{1}{2}$

$2 \times \frac{1}{2}$

$3 \times \frac{1}{2}$

$2 \div \frac{1}{2}$

A. $2 \times \frac{1}{4}$

$4 \times \frac{1}{4}$

$6 \times \frac{1}{4}$

$2 \div \frac{1}{4}$

B. $4 \times \frac{1}{4}$

$8 \times \frac{1}{4}$

$12 \times \frac{1}{4}$

$4 \div \frac{1}{4}$

A. $4 \times \frac{1}{2}$

$6 \times \frac{1}{2}$

$8 \times \frac{1}{2}$

$6 \div \frac{1}{2}$

B. $1 \times \frac{1}{4}$

$2 \times \frac{1}{4}$

$3 \times \frac{1}{4}$

$\frac{6}{8} \div \frac{1}{4}$

Learn More...

Anticipating student strategies for adding, subtracting, and multiplying fractions is discussed in Chapters 6, 7, and 8.

Anticipating Student Thinking

Division of fractions is a complex operation. It is often helpful to plan number talks for this operation with a partner or a team to think about how students might express their thinking and how we might record to make their ideas public for the rest of the students. Pay attention to the potential misconceptions discussed in this chapter and how you might support students by incorporating models and story contexts for the number talk problems you choose.

Looking Ahead

In this chapter, we have looked at opportunities for students to begin thinking about what happens when they divide fractions. We have also explored how a strong foundation in fractional reasoning supports students as they navigate with this operation. As you begin using number talks with your students for division of fractions, how might you use models and story problems to support students' thinking? Are there specific number talk strings that you might introduce first? In Chapter 10, we explore what it means to operate with decimals with understanding and we offer number talks to help students develop strategies for operating with decimals and fractions.

Connecting the Chapter to Your Practice

1. What are some of the common errors you see your students make when they divide with fractions?
2. Look at Figure 9–2 on page 277. What do you think your students will predict if you ask them whether the quotient will be bigger or smaller than the divisor depending on whether they are dividing by a proper fraction or a number greater than 1?
3. What have you noticed about your students' thinking when they encounter the "shifting whole" in division contexts?
4. What do you notice about the way the teacher deals with an incorrect answer in the "Inside the Classroom" excerpt on pages 279–280?
5. Examine the student's thinking and the teacher's recording in Figure 9–6 on page 284. What part of John's thinking would have been lost if the teacher had only recorded numerically?
6. How do models and story problems support students' understanding of division of fractions?
7. Examine Figure 9–8. How would you compare the standard U.S. algorithm to using Proportional Reasoning to solve a division of fractions problem?
8. Which number talk strategies are most comfortable to you? Which ones do you anticipate your students might gravitate toward?

CHAPTER 10

Number Talks for Operating with Decimals

In this chapter, we offer a place for teachers to start when planning number talks around computation with decimals. In the opening sections, we discuss student misconceptions about decimals and why the use of number talks helps students confront these misconceptions. We then explore and offer number talks that are focused on helping students build their understanding of operating with decimals. We highly recommend that students are solid and flexible in their fractional reasoning (see Chapter 4) before using the number talks in this chapter.

OVERVIEW

How Number Talks Help the Development of Computation Strategies with Decimals

Decimals is one of the most complex and difficult areas of mathematics for students (Irwin 2001; Moss and Case 1999; Okazaki and Koyama 2005; Peled and Shahbari 2009). One of the biggest reasons students struggle in this area is that they treat decimals as whole numbers and use whole number computation procedures without reasoning about the place value (Steinle and Stacey 2004). For example, when computing with decimals, students often receive instruction to "line up the decimal points" before adding or subtracting, or to ignore the decimal point and "count over the number of places" when multiplying and dividing. However, when students think about decimals as whole numbers and memorize shortcuts that ignore place value and mask the effect of multiplying or dividing by a quantity less than one, they often develop only a limited understanding of decimals.

Learn More...

For more on how procedural knowledge before conceptual understanding interferes with student understanding of rational numbers, see the Introduction, pages 7–8.

When students apply inappropriate whole number reasoning to decimals, it impacts their ability to think about the magnitude of the decimal number, which leads to two incorrect generalizations: (1) the shorter the decimal number, the larger it is, or (2) a longer decimal number is larger than a shorter decimal number. Using one-on-one interviews and written assessments with in-service and pre-service teachers, researchers found that 11 percent of the in-service teachers answered that 0.1 was larger than both 0.23 and 0.07, and 32 percent incorrectly ordered the decimals as 0.248, 0.85, 0.63, and 0.4 from the smallest to the biggest (Ubuz and Yayan 2010). This same thinking was also seen with pre-service teachers, with some indicating that 8.245 as being larger than 8.24563 and that 0.3 was larger than 0.426 (Maher and Muir 2011).

Learn More...

To read more about how students can build an understanding of comparing decimals to fractions and decimals to decimals, see Chapter 5, page 125–130.

This same whole number reasoning mindset also interferes as students operate with decimals. A study of pre-service teachers (Ryan and Williams 2007) highlights this misconception.

- 24 percent could not correctly write $912 + \frac{4}{100}$ in decimal form, with the most common error being 912.004;
- 31 percent could not give the correct answer to 300.62 divided by 100.

This is where the importance of number talks comes into play. Number talks help students focus on developing strategies to build their understanding of operating with decimals.

Specifically, there are approaches we can take during a number talk to support students in inventing and developing strategies—and thus deepen their understanding of mathematics. These approaches include:

- Making connections to strategies for computing with whole numbers
- Making connections to the arithmetic properties
- Using story problems
- Using models
- Connecting students' strategies

Each of these approaches is discussed in more detail in the sections that follow.

Making Connections to Strategies for Computing with Whole Numbers

While we do not want students to treat decimals as if they are whole numbers, we do want them to consider if the computation strategies that they have developed for operating with whole numbers will also work for decimals. The more fluent students are with whole number strategies and the better they are at composing and decomposing decimals, the more flexible they will be in their strategies for operating with decimals.

> **Number Talk Tip**
>
> For support on helping students develop strategies for whole number computation, see *Number Talks: Whole Number Computation* (Parrish 2010, 2014).

For example, during a number talk, one way a student might solve the problem *48 + 15* is to decompose the second addend into 2 + 13 and use the associative property to add the 2 to 48 to make a benchmark number of 50. Then the student adds the remaining 13 to the 50 for a sum of 63. Similarly, with the problem *0.99 + 0.15*, students will often decompose the 0.15 to 0.01 and 0.14 and add the 0.01 to 0.99 to get 1 whole. Then they add the remaining 0.14 to 1 to get a total of 1.14. (See Figure 10–1 on the next page.)

Using Benchmarks to Add Whole Numbers	Using Benchmarks to Add Decimals
$48 + 15$	$0.99 + 0.15$
$= 48 + (2 + 13)$	$= 0.99 + (0.01 + 0.14)$
$= (48 + 2) + 13$	$= (0.99 + 0.01) + 0.14$
$= 50 + 13$	$= 1.00 + 0.14$
$= 63$	$= 1.14$

Figure 10–1. *Making Connections to Strategies for Computing with Whole Numbers*

Let's continue to explore this idea with subtraction, multiplication, and division using the following three problems: *0.400 − 0.275*, *1.5 × 0.18*, and *1.25 ÷ 0.25*. Think about what strategies you could use to solve these problems. Would you use any of the strategies outlined in Figure 10–2?

CCSS

Asking students, "Will the strategies that work for adding, subtracting, multiplying, or dividing whole numbers also work with decimals?" offers an opportunity for learners to investigate mathematical structures. It also builds on these mathematical practices: *look for and make use of structure* (MP7) and *look for and express regularity in repeated reasoning* (MP8).

Testing Whole Number Strategies with Decimals	
$0.400 - 0.275$	*Adding Up* $0.400 - 0.275$ $0.275 + \_\_\_\_ = 0.400$ $0.275 + 0.025 = 0.300$ $0.300 + 0.100 = 0.400$ $0.275 + \underline{0.125} = 0.400$
	Constant Difference $0.400 - 0.275$ $= (0.400 + 0.025) - (0.275 + 0.025)$ $= 0.425 - 0.300$ $= 0.125$

Figure 10–2. *Will Strategies That Work with Whole Numbers Also Work with Decimals?*

Testing Whole Number Strategies with Decimals	
	Adjusting the Subtrahend $0.400 - 0.275$ $0.400 - (0.275 + 0.025)$ $0.400 - 0.300 = 0.100$ $0.100 + 0.025 = 0.125$
1.5×0.18	*Partial Products* 1.5×0.18 $= (1 + 0.5) \times 0.18$ $= (1 \times 0.18) + (0.5 \times 0.18)$ $= 0.18 + 0.09$ $= 0.27$
	Factoring Factors 1.5×0.18 $= 1.5 \times (2 \times 0.09)$ $= (1.5 \times 2) \times 0.09$ $= 3 \times 0.09$ $= 0.27$
	Doubling and Halving 1.5×0.18 $= (1.5 \times 2) \times \left(0.18 \times \frac{1}{2}\right)$ $= 3 \times 0.09$ $= 0.27$

Figure 10–2. *(continued)*

Testing Whole Number Strategies with Decimals	
$1.25 \div 0.25$	*Proportional Reasoning* $1.25 \div 0.25$ $= (1.25 \times 2) \div (0.25 \times 2)$ $= 2.50 \div 0.50$ $= (2.50 \times 2) \div (0.50 \times 2)$ $= 5 \div 1$ $= 5$
	Missing Factor $1.25 \div 0.25$ $0.25 \times \_\_\_\_ = 1.25$ $0.25 \times 4 = 1$ $0.25 \times 1 = 0.25$ $0.25 \times \underline{\ 5\ } = 1.25$
	Partial Quotients $1.25 \div 0.25$ $= (1 + 0.25) \div 0.25$ $= (1 \div 0.25) + (0.25 \div 0.25)$ $= 4 + 1$ $= 5$

Figure 10–2. *Will Strategies That Work with Whole Numbers Also Work with Decimals? (continued)*

Using accurate language that focuses on the numerical relationships is an important support for building understanding and it encourages students to *attend to precision* (MP6).

As students share strategies, you can support their understanding by insisting that they talk about the value of the decimal numbers. For example, rather than talking about 0.135 as "point 135," make sure students say "135 thousandths." Using accurate language that focuses on the numerical relationships is an important support for building understanding.

Making Connections to Arithmetic Properties

As students invent addition and multiplication strategies for computing with decimals, they are often using the properties of arithmetic. When teachers bring out the properties of mathematics in a number talk and connect it to the thinking students are already doing, we create opportunities to help them deepen their understanding of mathematics. We can highlight the properties during number talks by thoughtfully recording and facilitating discussions that attach students' thinking to the properties.

Consider the problem *0.26 + 0.27*. Some students will decompose the 0.26 into 0.23 and 0.03 and "give" 0.03 to the 0.27 to make a benchmark number. Figure 10–3 shows two ways to record these students' strategy. While both are correct recordings, the second recording highlights the associative property.

Recording Without Highlighting the Associative Property	Recording to Highlight the Associative Property
$\begin{array}{rcl} 0.26 & + & 0.27 \\ \underline{-.03} & & \underline{+.03} \\ 0.23 & + & 0.30 = 0.53 \end{array}$	$0.26 + 0.27$ $= (0.23 + 0.03) + 0.27$ $= 0.23 + (0.03 + 0.27)$ $= 0.23 + 0.30$ $= 0.53$

Figure 10–3. *Recording to Highlight the Associative Property*

The "Inside the Classroom" excerpt shows how a teacher might facilitate a conversation to connect the mathematical term *associative property* to student thinking as the class approaches the problem *12 × 0.25*. Because labels and symbols are social knowledge, it's fine to go ahead and tell students the names of properties, what mathematical symbols mean, and ways to record their strategies.

Learn More...

Knowing when to ask and when to tell is one of the four foundational principals of number talks. See Chapter 1, pages 28–32, for a more detailed explanation of Piaget's different kinds of knowledge.

Inside the Classroom

A Number Talk for 12 × 0.25

As this portion of the number talk begins, Matthew has explained his strategy for solving *12 × 0.25* and his teacher, Ms. Shepherd, recorded his thinking on the board:

$$\begin{aligned} &12 \times 0.25 \\ &= (3 \times 4) \times 0.25 \\ &= 3 \times (4 \times 0.25) \\ &= 3 \times 1 \\ &= 3 \end{aligned}$$

Ms. Shepherd: What did you notice about Matthew's strategy that was different from our other strategies?

Balaj: He decomposed the 12 into (4 × 3) and then multiplied the 0.25 by 4 to get one.

Amanda: Then all he had to do was multiply the 1 by the 3.

Ms. Shepherd: When we change the way the numbers are grouped in a multiplication problem, mathematicians call this the *associative property of multiplication*. Do you think it will always work? Let's do some more number talks so we can think about this idea with other problems.

Using Story Problems

One way we can help learners develop a more complete understanding of what it means to operate with decimals is to situate number talks within a story problem context. A context gives students an entry point for developing strategies and helps them make sense of the question the problem is asking and what the numbers mean in relationship to the problem.

Learn More...

Chapters 6, 7, 8, and 9 discuss specific story contexts to use with addition, subtraction, multiplication, and division of fractions.

Consider the difference between posing each of the following problems as a stand-alone problem or presenting each one framed as a story problem as seen in the following figure. (See Figure 10–4.)

Presenting a Problem in Isolation	Presenting a Problem in a Story Context
138.5 + 36.9	*After driving 138.5 miles, the Corbitt family stopped at a gas station. They still had 36.9 miles to drive before they arrived at their hotel. How many miles was their trip?*
6.2 − 3.5	*Madison's goal is to run 6.2 miles. She has already run 3.5 miles. How many more miles does she need to run to complete her goal?*
1.5 × 8	*The baby's blocks are 1.5 inches tall. If he stacks 8 of his blocks to make a tower, how many inches tall will his tower be?*
7.80 ÷ 12	*A twelve-pack of soda costs $7.80. How much does each soda cost?*

Figure 10–4. *Presenting a Problem in Isolation Versus in a Story Context*

Framing a computation problem in a story context does not mean showing students a written version of the story problem. Instead, write the computation problem as you present the story context orally. It is the context that helps students bring meaning to the numbers in the problem, visualize the action of the operation, and have a framework for evaluating the reasonableness of their answers.

Learn More...

For more on the use of story problems in building fractional reasoning, see Chapter 4, pages 73–74.

Using Models

In addition to using a story problem, teachers can incorporate models during a number talk to give students another entry point for developing strategies and finding a solution. Area and linear models can be used with decimals to (1) provide a visual context, (2) support a story problem, (3) and represent a student's strategy.

Models and story problems can offer support for students as they reason about the relationship between numbers and the action of the operation. Consider the difference between presenting the multiplication problem 0.4×0.3 in isolation versus verbally giving the following story problem and incorporating an area model partitioned into hundredths. (See Figure 10–5.)

Presenting a Problem in Isolation	Presenting a Problem with a Story Context and an Area Model
0.4×0.3	0.4 *Four-tenths of the school playground was covered in asphalt. Students wanted to reserve $\frac{3}{10}$ of the area with asphalt for playing basketball. How much of the playground would be reserved for basketball?*

Figure 10–5. *Presenting a Problem in Isolation Versus with a Story Context and an Area Model*

Using an area model with this problem can help students think about multiplication with decimals as a part of a part, confront whole number reasoning, and make sense of why the answer is in hundredths instead of tenths.

Including a model along with a story problem can further support students in understanding what a problem is asking and developing strategies to find a solution. Consider the subtraction problem *1.37 – 0.89*. When teachers use a number line to plot the minuend and subtrahend while giving the story problem verbally, they offer students an additional entry point for thinking about subtraction as the difference or distance between two amounts. (See Figure 10–6.)

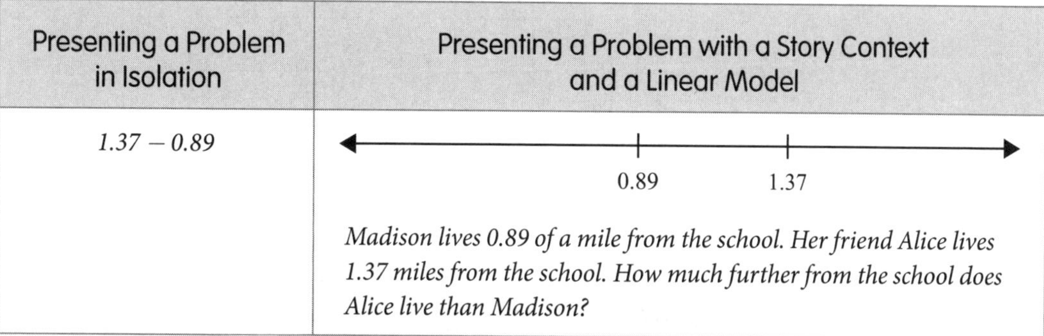

Presenting a Problem in Isolation	Presenting a Problem with a Story Context and a Linear Model
1.37 – 0.89	0.89 1.37 *Madison lives 0.89 of a mile from the school. Her friend Alice lives 1.37 miles from the school. How much further from the school does Alice live than Madison?*

Figure 10–6. *Presenting a Problem in Isolation Versus with a Story Context and a Linear Model*

During a number talk, we can record a student's mental strategy with both a model and a numerical recording. Figure 10–7 on the next page provides two examples of a teacher's recording that use area and linear models to represent a student's mental strategy for *2 ÷ 0.25*.

Student's Strategy and Reasoning	Recording Using Numerical Representation and Models
Partial Quotients Tam: *I pictured 2 squares divided into hundredths.*	*[Mr. Hardin draws 2 whole units with each one partitioned into hundredths.]* 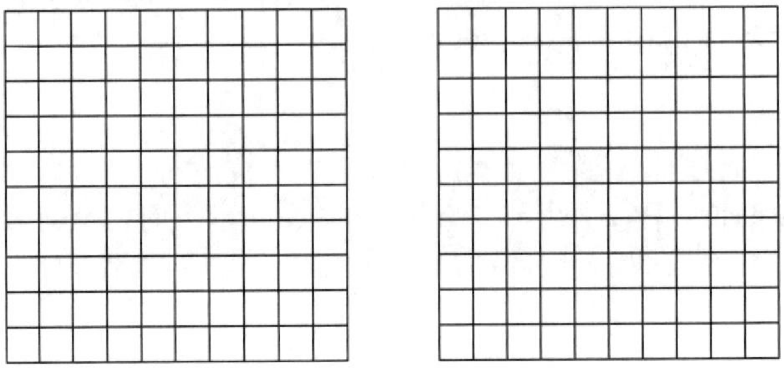
Then I thought about each whole divided into halves or 0.50. I knew there would be two 0.25 in each half. That gave me 8 groups of 0.25 to make the 2 wholes.	*[Mr. Hardin partitions each unit into two halves and circles each group of 0.25 for a total of 8 groups.]* 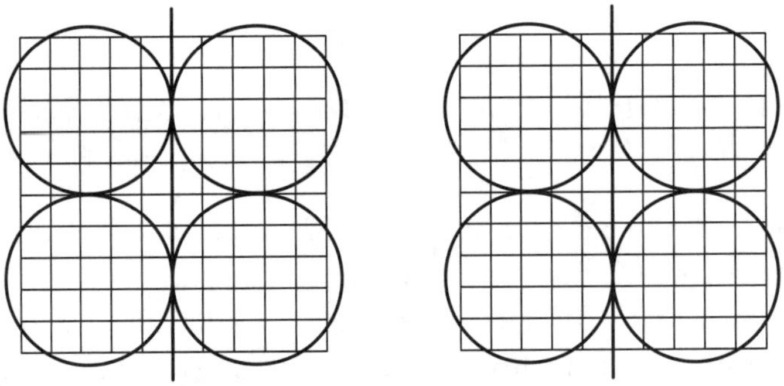
Mr. Hardin: *Does this recording match your thinking?*	*[Then he records Tam's thinking numerically.]* $2 \div 0.25$ $= (0.50 + 0.50 + 0.50 + 0.50) \div 0.25$ $= (0.50 \div 0.25) + (0.50 \div 0.25) + (0.50 \div 0.25) = (0.50 \div 0.25)$ $= 2 + 2 + 2 + 2$ $= 8$

Figure 10–7. *Using "Partial Quotients" to Solve 2 ÷ 0.25*

Student's Strategy and Reasoning	Recording Using Numerical Representation and Models
Multiplying Up	
Paulette: *I thought about a number line partitioned into fourths and each fourth was 0.25.*	*[Mrs. Tolbert draws a 0 to 2 number line partitioned into fourths.]* 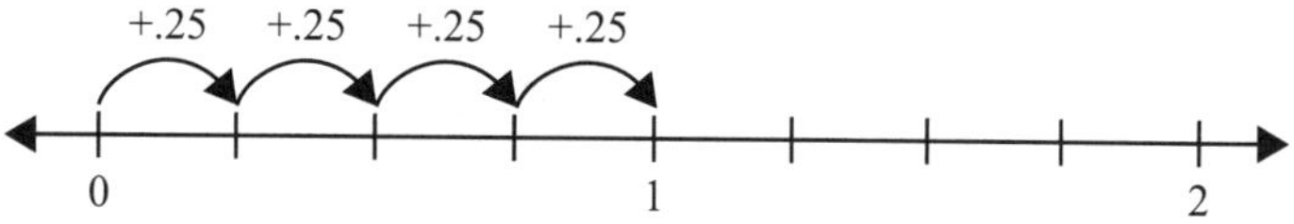 +.25 +.25 +.25 +.25 0 1 2
I know four groups of 0.25 is 1.	*[Mrs. Tolbert draws four jumps of 0.25.]*
I did the same thing again to get to 2, which gave me 4 groups of 0.25 again. That means 8 groups of 0.25 which equals 2.	*[Mrs. Tolbert draws four more jumps of 0.25 from 1 to 2.]* +.25 +.25 +.25 +.25 +.25 +.25 +.25 +.25 0 1 2 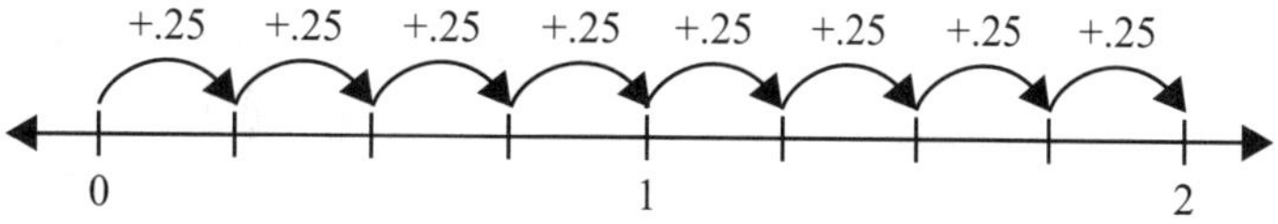 *[Mrs. Tolbert records Paulette's thinking numerically as she speaks.]*
Mrs. Tolbert: *You wondered what times 0.25 would equal 2. You knew that 4 groups of 0.25 equaled 1; and another group of 0.25 was another 1; so 8 × 0.25 equals 2.*	$2 \div 0.25$ $\_\_\_ \times 0.25 = 2$ ④$\times 0.25 = 1$ ④$\times 0.25 = 1$ $\underline{8} \times 0.25 = 2$

Figure 10–7. *(continued)*

When students analyze strategies and the mathematics behind what makes them work, they are *looking for and making use of structure* (MP7).

Connecting Students' Strategies

During number talks, teachers should look for opportunities to engage students in conversations around connections between strategies. Highlighting similarities and differences between strategies can help students focus on mathematical structures such as properties, place value, and decomposition of numbers. These discussions are especially helpful if you notice students using standard algorithms without understanding—especially as it relates to the properties and place value.

Let's think about how a number talk conversation might look around this idea using the problem *1.5* × *3.2*.

Inside the Classroom

A Number Talk for *1.5* × *3.2*

Figure 10–8 shows the standard algorithm for multiplying decimals and the Partial Products strategy students often use for solving *1.5* × *3.2*. Review these strategies, anticipate how you might engage students in comparing these two ideas, then read the dialogue excerpt that follows.

Student's Strategy and Reasoning	Recording
The Standard Algorithm Ed: *I pretended there were no decimals so it would be easier to multiply. 2 × 5 = 10 so I put down the 0 and carried the one. 3 × 5 is 15 and 15 + 1 makes 16. Then I put a 0 in the ones place on the next row. 2 × 1 is 2 and 3 × 1 is 3. Next I added 160 and 320 and got 480.*	1 3.2 × 1.5 160 + 320 4.80

Figure 10–8. *How Does the Standard Algorithm for Multiplying Fractions Compare to the Partial Products Strategy?*

Student's Strategy and Reasoning	Recording
Since there were 2 numbers behind the decimals in the problem, I moved the decimal in the answer over to the left twice and that gave me 4.80 as my final answer.	
Partial Products Catherine: *I broke 1.5 into $1 + 0.5$ because I knew that 3.2×1 was 3.2 so 3.2×0.5 was half of that or 1.6. Then I added them together. $3.2 + 1.6$ equals 4.8.*	1.5×3.2 $= (1 + 0.5) \times 3.2$ $= (1 \times 3.2) + (0.5 \times 3.2)$ $= 3.2 + 1.6$ $= 4.8$

Figure 10–8. *(continued)*

Ms. Holmes: I'd like you to turn and talk to someone about how Ed's and Catherine's strategies are the same and how they are different. *[After 45 seconds, Ms. Holmes calls the students back to a whole-group conversation.]* Would someone share what you and your partner discussed?

Juan: Stephen and I thought the two ways were different, because Ed got 160 and 320 as he solved the problem and Catherine got 1.6 and 3.2. These are different amounts.

(continued)

Number Talk Tip

As students share strategies, you can support their understanding by encouraging them to refer to decimals according to their value. For example, rather than talking about 0.5 as "zero point 5," make sure students say "five-tenths or one-half." Using accurate language that focuses on the numerical relationships is an important support for building understanding.

When students are listening to and thinking about other students' strategies during a number talk, they are *constructing viable arguments and critiquing the reasoning of others* (MP3).

Monica: Lanie and I talked about the same thing, but we also noticed that they got the same answer because 4.8 and 4.80 are equivalent. We're not sure why.

Ms. Holmes: Was anyone else confused about this? *[Several students nod their heads.]* It looks like we're unsure about the 160 and 1.6 and the 320 and 3.2. Talk to your partner about how these numbers are connected and how you think the strategies are related. *[After thirty seconds, Ms. Holmes returns them to the whole-group discussion.]* Would someone share what you and your partner discussed?

Sylvia: We noticed that both strategies broke apart the 1.5 into 1 and 0.5 and then multiplied them both by 3.2.

Reeves: We agree, and we think Ed multiplied 3.2 by 0.5 and 1 but he said he ignored the decimals and thought about the problem as 32×5 and 32×1.

Ms. Holmes: Sylvia and Reeves, are you saying that both ways used the distributive property but one kept the place value and the other didn't?

Monica: Oh, now I see! The 160 is actually 1.6 and the 320 and really 3.2. That's why Ed's final answer isn't 480.

When teachers are mindful of opportunities to make connections between ideas during a number talk, we shift the conversation from not only finding a solution but also making sense of the mathematics.

Section 1: Number Talks for Addition with Decimals

The number talks for adding decimals are organized into four sections. We first begin with number talks designed to help students reason with problems that use both a fraction and a decimal as addends, and then we transition into number talks organized around three strategies: Adding by Place Value, Adding Up by Chunks, and Making Benchmark Numbers.

Number Talks That Highlight a Place to Begin with Addition of Decimals

The following number talks consist of individual problems that use both decimals and fractions as addends. Each problem is designed to help students think about the relationship of decimals to fractions and use both representations flexibly and interchangeably. Figure 10–9 on the next page shows two ways students might use their understanding of equivalence, composing, and decomposing with tenths and eighths to solve $0.5 + \frac{5}{8}$.

Student's Strategy and Reasoning	Recording
Using Half as a Benchmark Lawrence: *I knew that 0.5 is the same as $\frac{1}{2}$ so I broke up $\frac{5}{8}$ into $\frac{4}{8}$—which is also half—and $\frac{1}{8}$. That gave me $\frac{1}{2}+\frac{1}{2}$ which is equal to 1 whole and $\frac{1}{8}$. $1+\frac{1}{8}=1\frac{1}{8}$*	$0.5+\frac{5}{8}$ $=\frac{1}{2}+\left(\frac{4}{8}+\frac{1}{8}\right)$ $=\left(\frac{1}{2}+\frac{1}{2}\right)+\frac{1}{8}$ $=1+\frac{1}{8}$ $=1\frac{1}{8}$
Using Half as a Benchmark Faye: *I was looking for another half to go with 0.5 and I knew that $\frac{1}{8}=0.125$, so I changed everything to decimals and thought about $\frac{5}{8}$ as $0.5+0.125$. Then I added 0.5 and 0.5 to get 1 and that left me with $1+0.125$, which equals 1.125.*	$0.5+\frac{5}{8}$ $=0.5+(0.5+0.125)$ $=(0.5+0.5)+0.125$ $=1+0.125$ $=1.125$

Figure 10–9. *Using "Making Benchmark Numbers" to Solve $0.5+\frac{5}{8}$*

Number Talk Tip

As students share strategies, you can support their understanding by encouraging them to refer to decimals according to their value. For example, rather than talking about 0.5 as "zero point 5," make sure students say "five-tenths or one-half." Using accurate language that focuses on the numerical relationships is an important support for building understanding.

Instructions

These individual number talk problems are organized into three columns and progress in difficulty going from problem to problem and from the first column (from A to B to C, etc.) to the second column to the third column, with an emphasis on using $\frac{1}{2}$, $\frac{1}{4}$, and $\frac{3}{4}$ as benchmarks. Feel free to work through each column in order or choose problems according to your students' needs. You may choose to pose one problem or set of problems each day. Introduce the problem, collect solutions, then ask students to share their reasoning and proofs.

What is ______ + ______? How do you know?

A. $5 + \frac{3}{4}$

B. $0.5 + \frac{5}{8}$

C. $0.5 + \frac{4}{6}$

D. $0.5 + \frac{7}{12}$

A. $0.25 + \frac{3}{4}$

B. $0.25 + \frac{3}{12}$

C. $0.25 + 1\frac{1}{12}$

D. $0.25 + \frac{7}{8}$

A. $0.75 + \frac{1}{4}$

B. $0.75 + \frac{1}{2}$

C. $0.75 + \frac{3}{4}$

D. $0.75 + 1\frac{3}{8}$

Number Talk Tip

In this resource, each strategy is named to represent the thinking involved; however, teachers often label a strategy with the name of the student who invented it. For example, if Galina offers the idea of decomposing a decimal to find and use benchmark numbers to add two decimals, the class might call this "Galina's strategy." The name of the strategy is not as important as the mathematical ideas the students are using.

Number Talks That Highlight the Addition Strategy "Adding by Place Value"

Adding by combining like place values is often one of the first strategies students invent. When using this strategy, students break the addends apart to combine like place values, and they typically work from left to right because it maintains the value of the numbers. Students often use this strategy when relationships to benchmark numbers are not efficient. The recording for *0.56 + 0.33* (see Figure 10–10) shows how a student solved the problem by using the Adding by Place Value strategy. Recording a student's thinking by writing it horizontally instead of vertically may be lengthier, but the horizontal recording highlights the associative and commutative properties.

Student's Strategy and Reasoning	Recording Vertically	Recording Horizontally to Highlight Associative and Communicative Properties
Adding by Place Value *I broke apart 0.56 into 0.50 and 0.06, and I broke apart 0.33 into 0.30 and 0.03. Then I added 0.50 + 0.30 which gave me 0.80 and 0.06 + 0.03 gave me 0.09 and 0.80 + 0.09 = 0.89.*	0.56 + 0.33 0.80 + 0.09 0.89	0.56 + 0.33 = (0.50 + 0.06) + (0.30 + 0.03) = (0.50 + 0.30) + (0.06 + 0.03) = 0.80 + 0.09 = 0.89

Figure 10–10. *Recording "Adding Up by Place Value" to Highlight the Associative and Commutative Properties*

Category 1
Adding Tenths and Hundredths

The number talk strings in this category use addends with tenths and hundredths. The addends in the first two columns have like place values, while the third column requires thinking about tenths and hundredths simultaneously.

Instructions

These number talks are organized into three columns and progress in difficulty going from the first column (from A to B to C, etc.) to the second column to the third column. Feel free to work through each string in order or choose problems according to your students' needs. You may choose to pose one problem or set of problems each day, or do more than one set of problems as time allows. Introduce the first problem in the string, collect solutions, then ask students to share their reasoning and proofs. Once the class reaches consensus, pose the next problem in the string and ask, *"How can you use what we just solved to help you with this next problem?"* or *"How does this new problem relate or connect to the previous problem(s)?"* Continue this format with each problem in the string.

What is _____ + _____? How do you know?
How can you use what we already know to solve this next problem?

A. $0.20 + 0.10$
$0.02 + 0.05$
$0.22 + 0.15$

B. $0.10 + 0.10$
$0.03 + 0.04$
$0.13 + 0.14$

C. $0.30 + 0.20$
$0.06 + 0.02$
$0.36 + 0.22$

D. $0.50 + 0.30$
$0.06 + 0.03$
$0.56 + 0.33$

E. $0.30 + 0.20$
$0.05 + 0.04$
$0.35 + 0.24$

A. $0.10 + 0.10$
$0.06 + 0.03$
$0.16 + 0.13$

B. $0.10 + 0.20$
$0.05 + 0.03$
$0.15 + 0.23$

C. $0.80 + 0.0$
$0.04 + 0.05$
$0.84 + 0.05$

D. $0.10 + 0.20$
$0.06 + 0.03$
$0.16 + 0.23$

E. $0.30 + 0.60$
$0.02 + 0.06$
$0.32 + 0.66$

A. $0.50 + 0.10$
$0.00 + 0.03$
$0.5 + 0.13$

B. $0.20 + 0.60$
$0.02 + 0.00$
$0.22 + 0.6$

C. $0.40 + 0.20$
$0.00 + 0.08$
$0.4 + 0.28$

D. $0.60 + 0.0$
$0.00 + 0.04$
$0.6 + 0.04$

E. $0.0 + 0.7$
$0.08 + 0.00$
$0.08 + 0.7$

Category 2
Adding Hundredths and Thousandths

The number talk strings in this category use addends with hundredths and thousandths. The addends in the first columns have like place values, while the second and third columns have a combination of hundredths and thousandths.

Instructions

These number talks are organized into three columns and progress in difficulty going from the first column (from A to B to C, etc.) to the second column to the third column. Feel free to work through each string in order or choose problems according to your students' needs. You may choose to pose one problem or set of problems each day, or do more than one set of problems as time allows. Introduce the first problem in the string, collect solutions, then ask students to share their reasoning and proofs. Once the class reaches consensus, pose the next problem in the string and ask, *"How can you use what we just solved to help you with this next problem?"* or *"How does this new problem relate or connect to the previous problem(s)?"* Continue this format with each problem in the string.

What is ______ + ______? How do you know?
How can you use what we already know to solve this next problem?

A. $0.200 + 0.200$
$0.060 + 0.30$
$0.007 + 0.02$
$0.267 + 0.232$

B. $0.100 + 0.200$
$0.010 + 0.070$
$0.005 + 0.002$
$0.115 + 0.272$

C. $0.200 + 0.100$
$0.010 + 0.030$
$0.006 + 0.003$
$0.216 + 0.133$

D. $0.100 + 0.200$
$0.030 + 0.010$
$0.005 + 0.003$
$0.135 + 0.213$

E. $0.300 + 0.100$
$0.010 + 0.080$
$0.005 + 0.002$
$0.315 + 0.182$

A. $0.200 + 0.100$
$0.005 + 0.030$
$0.205 + 0.13$

B. $0.500 + 0.200$
$0.080 + 0.011$
$0.58 + 0.211$

C. $0.400 + 0.300$
$0.040 + 0.025$
$0.44 + 0.325$

D. $0.700 + 0.100$
$0.040 + 0.033$
$0.74 + 0.133$

E. $0.300 + 0.200$
$0.070 + 0.002$
$0.37 + 0.202$

A. $0.200 + 0.400$
$0.039 + 0.050$
$0.239 + 0.45$

B. $0.400 + 0.300$
$0.026 + 0.030$
$0.426 + 0.33$

C. $0.100 + 0.400$
$0.021 + 0.080$
$0.121 + 0.48$

D. $0.200 + 0.300$
$0.080 + 0.019$
$0.28 + 0.319$

E. $0.200 + 0.300$
$0.028 + 0.050$
$0.228 + 0.35$

Number Talks That Highlight the Addition Strategy "Adding Up by Chunks"

This strategy is similar to the Adding by Place Value strategy except the student keeps one addend whole and decomposes the second addend to add by place value. Think about how you might use this strategy to solve the problem *0.64 + 0.33*. Figure 10–11 demonstrates two ways to record this strategy that highlight the use of the associative property.

Student's Strategy and Reasoning	Recording Highlighting the Associative Property
Decomposing 0.64 Jack: *I broke 0.64 into 0.60 and 0.04. Then I added the 0.04 to the 0.33 and got 0.37. 0.37 + 0.60 is 0.97.*	$0.64 + 0.33$ $= (0.60 + 0.04) + 0.33$ $= 0.60 + (0.04 + 0.33)$ $= 0.60 + 0.37$ $= 0.97$
Decomposing 0.33 Valita: *I split 0.33 into 0.30 and 0.03 to make an easier problem. 0.64 + 0.30 equals 0.94 + 0.03 equals 0.97.*	$0.64 + 0.33$ $= 0.64 + (0.30 + 0.03)$ $= (0.64 + 0.30) + 0.03$ $= 0.94 + 0.03$ $= 0.97$

Figure 10–11. *Recordings for "Adding Up by Chunks" That Highlight the Associative Property*

Number Talk Tip

As students share strategies, you can support their understanding by encouraging them to refer to decimals according to their value. For example, rather than talking about 0.64 as "zero point 64," make sure students say "sixty-four hundredths." Using accurate language that focuses on the numerical relationships is an important support for building understanding.

Category 1
Adding Hundredths

The number talk strings in this category are organized by pairs of problems that use hundredths. The sums for the problems in the first two columns are less than 1 and use numbers that do not require regrouping. The problems in the third column offer opportunities to regroup, and some sums are greater than 1.

Instructions

These number talks are organized into three columns and progress in difficulty going from the first column (from A to B to C, etc.) to the second column to the third column. Feel free to work through each string in order or choose problems according to your students' needs. You may choose to pose one problem or set of problems each day, or do more than one set of problems as time allows. Introduce the first problem in the string, collect solutions, then ask students to share their reasoning and proofs. Once the class reaches consensus, pose the next problem in the string and ask, *"How can you use what we just solved to help you with this next problem?"* or *"How does this new problem relate to the previous problem(s)?"*

What is ______ + ______? How do you know?
How can you use what we already know to solve this next problem?

A. $0.16 + 0.40$
$0.16 + 0.42$

B. $0.26 + 0.50$
$0.26 + 0.53$

C. $0.24 + 0.50$
$0.24 + 0.55$

D. $0.46 + 0.50$
$0.46 + 0.53$

E. $0.62 + 0.30$
$0.62 + 0.37$

A. $0.35 + 0.40$
$0.35 + 0.42$

B. $0.32 + 0.50$
$0.32 + 0.55$

C. $0.44 + 0.30$
$0.44 + 0.35$

D. $0.53 + 0.20$
$0.53 + 0.25$

E. $0.38 + 0.30$
$0.38 + 0.33$

A. $0.29 + 0.20$
$0.29 + 0.24$

B. $0.38 + 0.20$
$0.38 + 0.26$

C. $0.45 + 0.40$
$0.45 + 0.46$

D. $0.65 + 0.50$
$0.65 + 0.57$

E. $0.73 + 0.50$
$0.73 + 0.58$

Category 2
Adding Hundredths and Thousandths

The number talk strings in this category are organized by problems that use hundredths and thousandths. The first two columns use pairs of problems with addends that are a combination of hundredths and thousandths. Both addends in the third column are in the thousandths.

Instructions

These number talks are organized into three columns and progress in difficulty going from the first column (from A to B to C, etc.) to the second column to the third column. Feel free to work through each string in order or choose problems according to your students' needs. You may choose to pose one problem or set of problems each day, or do more than one set of problems as time allows. Introduce the first problem in the string, collect solutions, then ask students to share their reasoning and proofs. Once the class reaches consensus, pose the next problem in the string and ask, *"How can you use what we just solved to help you with this next problem?"* or *"How does this new problem connect to the previous problem?"* Continue this format with each problem in the string.

What is ______ + ______? How do you know?
How can you use what we already know to solve this next problem?

A. $0.156 + 0.40$
$0.156 + 0.43$

B. $0.125 + 0.60$
$0.125 + 0.68$

C. $0.247 + 0.80$
$0.247 + 0.84$

D. $0.325 + 0.70$
$0.325 + 0.74$

A. $0.237 + 0.40$
$0.237 + 0.48$

B. $0.117 + 0.30$
$0.117 + 0.32$

C. $0.315 + 0.20$
$0.315 + 0.24$

D. $0.543 + 0.50$
$0.543 + 0.55$

A. $0.345 + 0.400$
$0.345 + 0.450$
$0.345 + 0.457$

B. $0.256 + 0.300$
$0.256 + 0.340$
$0.256 + 0.342$

C. $0.134 + 0.300$
$0.134 + 0.380$
$0.134 + 0.387$

D. $0.218 + 0.400$
$0.218 + 0.450$
$0.218 + 0.456$

Number Talks That Highlight the Addition Strategy "Making Benchmark Numbers"

When numbers in a decimal addition problem are close to a half or a whole, students often decompose the addends to make benchmarks and reason through to a solution. Here are two ways students typically make benchmark numbers: (1) they decompose one addend and move part of the number to the other addend; or (2) they compensate by adding in an additional amount and then removing that amount from the sum. Figure 10–12 illustrates both of these ideas for making a benchmark number.

Student's Strategy and Reasoning	Recording
Making Benchmark Numbers Christina: *I broke 0.50 into 0.25 and 0.25. Then I added 0.75 to 0.25 to get 1, so the answer is 1.25.*	$0.75 + 0.50$ $= 0.75 + (0.25 + 0.25)$ $= (0.75 + 0.25) + 0.25$ $= 1.00 + 0.25$ $= 1.25$
Adjusting an Addend Brilynn: *I wanted to make an easier problem so I added in an extra 0.01 to 0.49 to get 0.50. Then I added 0.50 to 0.25 to get 0.75, but I needed to subtract the extra 0.01 I added in the beginning. That gave me 0.74 for my answer.*	$0.49 + 0.25$ $(0.49 + 0.01) + 0.25$ $(0.50 + 0.25) - 0.01$ $0.75 - 0.01 = 0.74$

Figure 10–12. *Using "Making a Benchmark Number" to Solve 0.75 + 0.50 and 0.49 + 0.25*

Number Talk Tip

As you work with students, listen for use of accurate language in describing solutions to this strategy. For example, some students may say they added 1 or point zero one instead of $\frac{1}{100}$. Making sure students use correct language regarding place value is critical to supporting understanding of decimals as fractional amounts.

Category 1
Adding Hundredths

The number talk strings in this category are organized by pairs of problems that use hundredths. In the second problem of each pair, one addend is one unit away from a benchmark number.

Instructions

These number talks are organized into three columns and progress in difficulty going from the first column (from A to B to C, etc.) to the second column to the third column. Feel free to work through each string in order or choose problems according to your students' needs. You may choose to pose one problem or set of problems each day, or do more than one set of problems as time allows. Introduce the first problem in the string, collect solutions, then ask students to share their reasoning and proofs. Once the class reaches consensus, pose the next problem in the string and ask, *"How can you use what we just solved to help you with this next problem?"* or *"How does this new problem relate or connect to the previous problem?"*

What is ______ + ______? How do you know?
How can you use what we already know to solve this next problem?

A. $0.20 + 0.26$
$0.19 + 0.26$

B. $0.28 + 0.40$
$0.28 + 0.39$

C. $0.40 + 0.51$
$0.39 + 0.51$

D. $0.23 + 0.50$
$0.23 + 0.49$

A. $0.16 + 0.30$
$0.16 + 0.29$

B. $0.20 + 0.12$
$0.19 + 0.12$

C. $0.30 + 0.33$
$0.29 + 0.33$

D. $0.40 + 0.16$
$0.39 + 0.16$

A. $0.60 + 0.13$
$0.59 + 0.13$

B. $0.76 + 0.20$
$0.76 + 0.19$

C. $0.46 + 0.60$
$0.46 + 0.59$

D. $0.60 + 0.73$
$0.59 + 0.73$

Category 2
Adding Mixed Decimals

Number Talk Tip

Remember that a mixed decimal number is a number that includes a whole number as well as a decimal. For instance, 2.35 and 12.7 are examples of mixed decimals.

The number talk strings in this category are organized by pairs of problems that use mixed decimals and decimals in the hundredths. One or both addends in each of the problems is close to a benchmark number.

Instructions

These number talks are organized into three columns and progress in difficulty going from the first column (from A to B to C) to the second column to the third column. Feel free to work through each string in order or choose problems according to your students' needs. You may choose to pose one problem or set of problems each day, or do more than one set of problems as time allows. Introduce the first problem in the string, collect solutions, then ask students to share their reasoning and proofs. Once the class reaches consensus, pose the next problem in the string and ask, *"How can you use what we just solved to help you with this next problem?"* or *"How does this new problem relate to the previous problem?"*

What is ______ + ______? How do you know?
How can you use what we already know to solve this next problem?

A. 1.00 + 1.38
0.99 + 1.38

B. 1.20 + 0.26
1.19 + 0.26

C. 0.36 + 1.10
0.36 + 1.09

A. 1.50 + 1.50
1.48 + 1.49

B. 1.16 + 0.30
1.16 + 0.29

C. 1.20 + 0.36
1.19 + 0.36

A. 1.40 + 1.25
1.39 + 1.27

B. 1.50 + 2.00
1.48 + 1.99

C. 2.00 + 1.00 + 0.51
1.99 + 0.99 + 0.49

Section 2: Number Talks for Subtraction with Decimals

Many of the strategies for subtraction with whole numbers also work when subtracting decimals. In this section we will explore four strategies: Adding Up, Adjusting the Subtrahend or Minuend, Constant Difference, and Partial Differences.

Number Talks That Highlight the Subtraction Strategy "Adding Up"

This strategy allows students to build on their understanding of addition and its inverse relationship to subtraction by adding up from the subtrahend (the number being subtracted) to the minuend (the number they are subtracting from). When students understand subtraction as the difference between two quantities, and when they recognize how subtraction and addition are inversely related, they can add up to find that difference. Presenting problems in a story context that suggests adding up can help bring out this strategy. (See Figure 10–13.)

Presenting a Problem in Isolation	Presenting a Problem in a Story Context
15 − 8.75	*Evan's goal is to run 15 miles in 3 days. He has run 8.75 miles. How many more miles does Evan need to run to reach his goal?* *Belinda's goal is to raise $15.00 to buy a CD. She already has $8.75. How much more money does Belinda need?*

Figure 10–13. *Presenting a Problem in Isolation Versus in a Story Context*

The story contexts in Figure 10–13 imply adding on to 8.75 to reach 15. Contexts can help students think about subtraction as the difference between two numbers.

Even with large numbers, the Adding Up strategy can be effective and efficient. The fewer the jumps, the more efficient the strategy will be.

Ask questions to help students think about how many jumps it would take to get to the nearest benchmark or friendly number. You can also represent this strategy on a number line or linear model to help students follow each other's thinking. Figure 10–14 shows how we might record a student's thinking using the Adding Up strategy both numerically and with a number line for the problem *2.31 – 0.59.*

Student's Strategy and Reasoning	Recording Using a Numerical Representation	Recording Using a Linear Model
Adding Up Betsy: *I thought about this problem as 0.59 plus what will get me to 2.31. I knew that if I added 0.01 to 0.59, I would get 0.60. Then I added 0.40 to get 1, and 1 + 1.31 gets me to 2.31. So I added up what I had to add to get from 0.59 to 2.31. My answer is 1.72.*	$2.31 - 0.59$ $0.59 + \_\_\_ = 2.31$ $0.59 + \underline{0.01} = 0.60$ $0.60 + \underline{0.40} = 1.00$ $1.00 + \underline{1.31} = 2.31$ $0.01 + 0.40 + 1.31 = 1.72$	+0.01 +0.40 +1.31 0.59 0.60 1.00 2.31

Figure 10–14. *Using "Adding Up" to Solve 2.31 – 0.59*

Category 1
Subtracting Hundredths

The number talk strings in this category are organized by pairs of problems with decimals in the hundredths. The first problem in each pair uses benchmark numbers, and the minuend in the second problem is a few units away from a benchmark number.

Instructions

These number talks are organized into three columns and progress in difficulty going from the first column (from A to B to C, etc.) to the second column to the third column. Feel free to work through each string in order or choose problems according to your students' needs. You may choose to pose one problem or set of problems each day, or do more than one set of problems as time allows. Introduce the first problem, collect solutions, then ask students to share their reasoning and proofs. Once the class reaches consensus, pose the next problem in the string and ask, *"How can you use what we just solved to help you with this next problem?"* or *"How does this new problem relate to the previous problem?"*

Number Talk Tip

As you work with students, listen for use of accurate language in describing solutions to this strategy. For example, some students may say they subtracted 2 instead of $\frac{2}{100}$. Making sure students use correct language regarding place value is critical to supporting understanding of decimals as fractional amounts.

What is ______ – ______? How do you know?
How can you use what we already know to solve the next problem?

Number Talk Tip

Consider presenting each problem in a story context along with an accompanying number line to help students consider subtraction as the difference or distance.

A. 1.00 – 0.90
1.00 – 0.89

B. 1.00 – 0.50
1.00 – 0.49

C. 1.00 – 0.40
1.00 – 0.38

D. 3.00 – 1.50
3.00 – 1.48

E. 5.00   2.50
5.00 – 2.46

A. 1.50 – 0.75
1.50 – 0.74

B. 2.50 – 1.40
2.50 – 1.37

C. 6.35 – 3.30
6.35 – 3.28

D. 5.50 – 1.20
5.50 – 1.18

E. 4.75 – 1.50
4.75 – 1.45

A. 0.200 – 0.150
0.200 – 0.147

B. 0.400 –0.275
0.400 – 0.274

C. 0.500 – 0.420
0.500 – 0.418

D. 0.750 – 0.600
0.750 – 0.599

E. 0.825 – 0.500
0.825 – 0.496

Category 2
Subtracting Multiple Place Values

The number talk strings in this category are organized by pairs of problems. The first problem in each string uses tenths, and the subtrahend in the second problem uses hundredths or thousandths. Subtracting with multiple place values encourages students to think about equivalence as they add up.

Instructions

These number talks are organized into three columns and progress in difficulty going from the first column (from A to B to C, etc.) to the second column to the third column. Feel free to work through each string in order or choose problems according to your students' needs. You may choose to pose one problem or set of problems each day, or do more than one set of problems as time allows. Introduce the first problem in the string, collect solutions, then ask students to share their reasoning and proofs. Once the class reaches consensus, pose the next problem in the string and ask, *"How can you use what we just solved to help you with this next problem?"* or *"How does this new problem relate or connect to the previous problem?"*

What is ______ – ______? How do you know?
How can you use what we already know to solve the next problem?

Column 1	Column 2	Column 3
A. 0.5 – 0.3 0.5 – 0.29	**A.** 0.5 – 0.2 0.5 – 0.198	**A.** 1.1 – 0.4 1.1 – 0.39
B. 0.8 – 0.4 0.8 – 0.38	**B.** 0.6 – 0.4 0.6 – 0.399	**B.** 2.2 – 0.5 2.2 – 0.49
C. 0.6 – 0.3 0.6 – 0.27	**C.** 0.9 – 0.5 0.9 – 0.498	**C.** 2.5 – 0.9 2.5 – 0.89
D. 0.7 – 0.4 0.7 – 0.35	**D.** 0.4 – 0.1 0.4 – 0.098	**D.** 3.3 – 0.8 3.3 – 0.79

Number Talks That Highlight the Subtraction Strategy "Adjusting the Minuend or Subtrahend"

As students become comfortable composing and decomposing decimals, a natural step is to ask them to think about how to adjust the subtrahend or minuend to make subtracting decimals easier. As they use this strategy, they have to think about (1) which number should be adjusted and why; and (2) how does their adjustment affect the final answer. Consider two subtraction problems, *2.00 – 0.59* and *0.76 – 0.59*, and think about how you would adjust the minuend or subtrahend and how this would impact the solution. After you have thought about this problem for yourself, see Figures 10–15 and 10–16 for ways that students use this strategy to solve these problems.

CCSS

Using accurate language that focuses on the numerical relationships is an important support for building understanding because it encourages students to *attend to precision* (MP6).

Student's Strategy and Reasoning	Recording
Adjusting the Minuend Grace: *Subtracting 0.59 from 1.99 makes this an easier problem, so I broke up 2.00 into 0.01 and 1.99. Then I subtracted the 0.59 from 1.99, which gave me 1.40. One hundredth plus 1.40 equals 1.41.*	$2.00 - 0.59$ $(0.01 + 1.99) - 0.59$ $0.01 + (1.99 - 0.59)$ $0.01 + 1.40 = 1.41$
Adjusting the Subtrahend Cooper: *I added 0.01 to 0.59 to get 0.60. That changed the problem to 2.00 – 0.60 which is 1.40, but when I subtracted 0.60, I was subtracting 0.01 more than the original problem asked for, so I added that to 1.40 and got 1.41 for my final answer.*	$2.00 - 0.59$ $2.00 - (0.59 + 0.01)$ $2.00 - 0.60 = 1.40$ $1.40 + 0.01 = 1.41$

Figure 10–15. *Using "Adjusting the Minuend or Subtrahend" to Solve 2.00 – 0.59*

Student's Strategy and Reasoning	Recording
Adjusting the Minuend Jevon: *I added 0.03 to 0.76 and that changed the problem to 0.79 − 0.59, which is 0.20. Since I added in an extra 0.03 to the problem, I had to take it back out so that left me with 0.17.*	$0.76 - 0.59$ $(0.76 + 0.03) - 0.59$ $0.79 - 0.59 = 0.20$ $0.20 - 0.03 = 0.17$
Adjusting the Subtrahend Eleanor: *I added 0.01 to 0.59 so the problem became 0.76 − 0.60. I knew that was 0.16 and then I had subtracted an extra 0.01, so I had to add it back. 0.16 + 0.01 = 0.17.*	$0.76 - 0.59$ $0.76 - (0.59 + 0.01)$ $0.76 - 0.60 = 0.16$ $0.16 + 0.01 = 0.17$

Figure 10–16. *Using "Adjusting the Minuend or Subtrahend" to Solve 0.76 − 0.59*

Did the problems seem easier to subtract once you adjusted the minuend or subtrahend? How did you decide whether to add or subtract the amount adjusted from your final answer? These are the same kinds of in-the-moment decisions that you will want students to share during number talks.

Category 2
Adjusting the Minuend

The number talk strings in this category are organized by pairs of problems. The minuend is adjusted from the first to the second problem; the subtrahend remains the same.

Instructions

These number talks are organized into three columns and progress in difficulty going from the first column (from A to B to C, etc.) to the second column to the third column. Feel free to work through each string in order or choose problems according to your students' needs. You may choose to pose one problem or set of problems each day, or do more than one set of problems as time allows. Introduce the first problem, collect solutions, then ask students to share their reasoning and proofs. Once the class reaches consensus, pose the next problem in the string and ask, *"How can you use what we just solved to help you with this next problem?"* or *"How does this new problem relate to the previous problem?"*

What is ______ – ______? How do you know?
How can you use what we already know to solve the next problem?

A. 0.49 – 0.18 0.50 – 0.18	**A.** 1.99 – 0.54 2.00 – 0.54	**A.** 0.999 – 0.456 1.000 – 0.456
B. 0.89 – 0.47 0.90 – 0.47	**B.** 2.49 – 1.18 2.50 – 1.18	**B.** 0.398 – 0.158 0.400 – 0.158
C. 0.69 – 0.38 0.70 – 0.38	**C.** 1.99 –1.38 2.00 – 1.38	**C.** 0.598 – 0.374 0.600 – 0.374
D. 0.79 – 0.24 0.80 – 0.24	**D.** 4.99 – 3.12 5.00 – 3.12	**D.** 0.499 – 0.265 0.500 – 0.265

Number Talks That Highlight the Subtraction Strategy "Constant Difference"

As students begin to understand subtraction as the difference between two quantities, they can investigate what occurs if both numbers are changed by the same amount. Adding or subtracting the same quantity from both the subtrahend and minuend maintains the difference between the numbers. Manipulating the numbers in this way allows students to create a friendlier problem without changing the results. How might you adjust both the minuend and subtrahend for the problem *2.15 − 1.99*? After solving this problem for yourself, see Figure 10–17 for one way a student used the Constant Difference strategy to solve this problem.

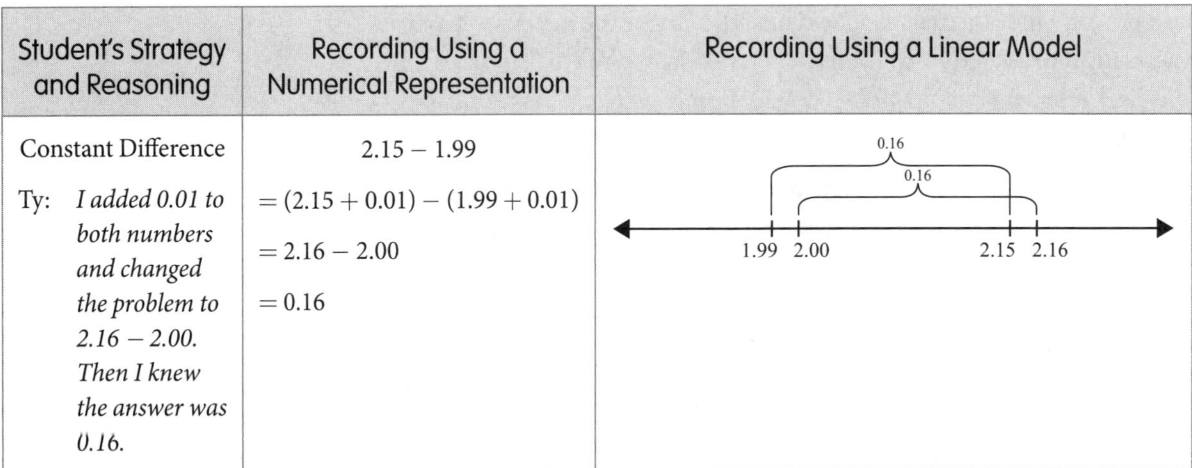

Student's Strategy and Reasoning	Recording Using a Numerical Representation	Recording Using a Linear Model
Constant Difference Ty: *I added 0.01 to both numbers and changed the problem to 2.16 − 2.00. Then I knew the answer was 0.16.*	2.15 − 1.99 = (2.15 + 0.01) − (1.99 + 0.01) = 2.16 − 2.00 = 0.16	0.16 0.16 1.99 2.00 2.15 2.16

Figure 10–17. *Using "Constant Difference" to Solve 2.15 − 1.99*

The recording using a linear model demonstrates how adding (or subtracting) the same amount from the minuend and the subtrahend "shifts" the problem up or down on the number line, but the difference remains the same.

Category 1
Subtracting Hundredths

The number talk strings in this category are designed to help students notice that when they add the same amount to the minuend and the subtrahend or subtract the same amount from the minuend or the subtrahend, the difference remains the same. The number talk strings use small numbers, and the problems progress from easier to less obvious problems to keep the focus on exploring the bigger idea of what happens when students keep a constant difference.

When students investigate and test different strategies they are using the mathematical practices: *look for and making use of structure* (MP7) and *look for and express regularity in repeated reasoning* (MP8).

Instructions

These number talks are organized into three columns and progress in magnitude going from the first column (from A to B to C) to the second column to the third column. Feel free to work through each string in order or choose problems according to your students' needs. You may choose to pose one problem or set of problems each day, or do more than one set of problems as time allows. Introduce the first problem, collect solutions, then ask students to share their reasoning and proofs. Once the class reaches consensus, pose the next problem in the string. The problems themselves are designed to be easier to solve because we want to keep the focus on the relationships between problems. Do this by asking, "*Why do you think the answers are the same even though the numbers are different? What relationships do you notice between the problems?*" Continue this format with each problem in the string.

What is _____ – _____? How do you know?
Why do you think the answers are the same even though the numbers are different?
What relationships do you notice between the problems?

A. 0.15 – 0.10
0.16 – 0.11
0.17 – 0.12
0.18 – 0.13

B. 0.20 – 0.15
0.19 – 0.14
0.18 – 0.13
0.21 – 0.16

C. 0.25 – 0.10
0.24 – 0.09
0.23 – 0.08
0.22 – 0.07

A. 0.40 – 0.20
0.39 – 0.19
0.38 – 0.18
0.37 – 0.17

B. 0.35 – 0.20
0.34 – 0.19
0.33 – 0.18
0.32 – 0.17

C. 0.40 – 0.20
0.41 – 0.21
0.42 – 0.22
0.39 – 0.19

A. 1.00 – 0.51
0.99 – 0.50
0.98 – 0.49
1.01 – 0.47

B. 0.50 – 0.25
0.49 – 0.24
0.48 – 0.23
0.51 – 0.26

C. 0.60 – 0.37
0.61 – 0.36
0.62 – 0.35
0.63 – 0.36

Category 2
Subtracting Mixed Decimals

The problems in this category are individual problems using mixed decimals and are offered as a "next step" as students begin to investigate the Constant Difference strategy.

Instructions

These number talks may be used in any order or sequence. Introduce one of the problems, collect solutions, then ask students to share their reasoning and proofs.

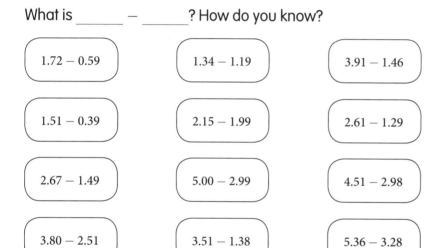

1.72 – 0.59	1.34 – 1.19	3.91 – 1.46
1.51 – 0.39	2.15 – 1.99	2.61 – 1.29
2.67 – 1.49	5.00 – 2.99	4.51 – 2.98
3.80 – 2.51	3.51 – 1.38	5.36 – 3.28

Number Talks That Highlight the Subtraction Strategy "Subtracting by Place Value"

When students subtract by place value, they decompose both the minuend and subtrahend according to place value and then subtract like place values. This strategy closely resembles the standard algorithm for subtracting decimals. One way to represent this strategy is to record each number using expanded notation, grouping place values, and then subtracting. Then the student combines the differences from each place-value subtraction. Figure 10–18 shows two ways to record this strategy.

Student's Strategy and Reasoning	Recording 1	Recording 2
Subtracting by Place Value Max: *I separated each number into its place value. 1 − 0 is 1, 0.50 − 0.30 is 0.20, and 0.06 − 0.02 is 0.04. I added it up and the answer is 1.24.*	$1.56 - 0.32$ $= (1.00 + 0.50 + 0.06) - (0.30 + 0.02)$ $= (1.00 - 0) + (0.50 - 0.30) + (0.06 - 0.02)$ $= 1 + 0.20 + 0.04$ $= 1.24$	$\begin{array}{r} 1.00 \\ -\quad 0 \\ \hline 1.00 \end{array} \quad \begin{array}{r} 0.50 \\ -0.30 \\ \hline 0.20 \end{array} \quad \begin{array}{r} 0.06 \\ -0.02 \\ \hline 0.04 \end{array}$ $1.00 + 0.20 + 0.04 = 1.24$

Figure 10–18. *Two Ways to Record "Subtracting by Place Value" to Solve 1.56 − 0.32*

When students use this strategy, it is also possible for negative values to occur. The problem *1.23 – 0.59* can help us think about this idea and how we might record a student's thinking. (See Figure 10–19.)

Student's Strategy and Reasoning	Recording 1	Recording 2
Subtracting by Place Value Bernie: *One minus 0 is 1; 0.20 – 0.50 is –0.30, and 0.03 – 0.09 = –0.06. When I combine those differences, 1 plus –0.30 is 0.70 and 0.70 plus –0.06 equals 0.64.*	1.23 –0.59 1.00 –0.30 –0.06 0.64	1.00 0.20 0.03 – 0 – 0.50 – 0.09 1.00 – 0.30 – 0.06 1.00 + (–0.30) = 0.70 0.70 + (–0.06) = 0.64

Figure 10–19. *Two Ways to Record "Subtracting by Place Value" to Solve 1.23 – 0.59*

Category 1
Using Place Values

The number talk strings in this category are organized by problems that use hundredths and thousandths. The problems are designed so that the first few problems in the string are components of the final problem.

Instructions

These number talks are organized into three columns and progress in difficulty going from the first column (from A to B to C, etc.) to the second column to the third column. Feel free to work through each string in order or choose problems according to your students' needs. You may choose to pose one problem or set of problems each day, or do more than one set of problems as time allows. Introduce the first problem, collect solutions, then ask students to share their reasoning and proofs. Once the class reaches consensus, pose the next problem in the string and ask, *"How can you use what we already know to help you with this next problem?"* or *"How does this new problem relate to the previous problem(s)?"* Continue this format with each problem in the string.

What is ______ – ______? How do you know?
How can you use what we already know to solve this problem?

A. 0.20 – 0.10
0.07 – 0.06
0.27 – 0.16

B. 0.40 – 0.20
0.07 – 0.06
0.47 – 0.26

C. 0.60 – 0.40
0.03 – 0.01
0.63 – 0.41

D. 0.40 – 0.10
0.04 – 0.03
0.44 – 0.13

A. 2.00 – 1.00
0.70 – 0.50
0.06 – 0.03
2.76 – 1.53

B. 4.00 – 2.00
0.80 – 0.50
0.03 – 0.01
4.83 – 2.51

C. 5.00 – 1.00
0.90 – 0.60
0.04 – 0.02
5.94 – 1.62

D. 6.00 – 4.00
0.50 – 0.30
0.09 – 0.05
6.59 – 4.35

A. 0.500 – 0.300
0.07 – 0.04
0.005 – 0.002
1.575 – 0.342

B. 0.9 – 0.5
0.07 – 0.05
0.006 – 0.005
2.976 – 1. 555

C. 0.7 – 0.2
0.03 – 0.01
0.004 – 0.003
2.734 – 1.213

D. 0.2 – 0.1
0.06 – 0.03
0.008 – 0.005
3.268 – 2.135

Category 2
Using Negative Numbers

The number talk strings in this category are organized by problems that use hundredths and thousandths. The problems are designed to foster discussion around what happens when you remove a larger number from a smaller number.

Instructions

These number talks are organized into three columns and progress in difficulty going from the first column (from A to B to C, etc.) to the second column to the third column. Feel free to work through each string in order or choose problems according to your students' needs. You may choose to pose one problem or set of problems each day, or do more than one set of problems as time allows. Introduce the first problem in the string, collect solutions, then ask students to share their reasoning and proofs. Once the class reaches consensus, pose the next problem and ask, *"How can you use what we already know to help you with this problem?"* or *"How does this new problem relate to the previous problem(s)?"* Continue this format with each problem in the string.

What is ______ – ______? How do you know?
How can you use what we already know to solve this problem?

A. 0.20 – 0.10
0.03 – 0.05
0.23 – 0.15

B. 0.40 – 0.10
0.05 – 0.07
0.45 – 0.17

C. 0.60 – 0.30
0.01 – 0.05
0.61 – 0.35

D. 0.30 – 0.10
0.05 – 0.08
0.35 – 0.18

A. 0.5 – 0.2
0.06 – 0.07
0.002 – 0.005
0.562 – 0.275

B. 0.7 – 0.2
0.03 – 0.05
0.006 – 0.007
0.736 – 0.257

C. 0.2 – 0.1
0.07 – 0.09
0.004 – 0.006
0.274 – 0.196

D. 0.6 – 0.3
0.01 – 0.04
0.004 – 0.008
0.614 – 0.348

A. 0.0 – 0.5
0.08 – 0.09
0.002 – 0.003
1.082 – 0.593

B. 0.40 – 0.70
0.03 – 0.08
0.0 – 0.005
1.43 – 0.785

C. 0.2 – 0.5
0.09 – 0.09
0.001 – 0.004
2.291 – 1.594

D. 0.3 – 0.5
0.01 – 0.04
0.006 – 0.008
5.316 – 2.548

Section 3: Number Talks for Multiplication with Decimals

When multiplying decimals, students often receive instructions to ignore the decimal points and multiply as if the decimals are whole numbers. Next, they are told to place a decimal point in the product by counting how many digits are behind the decimal point in the multiplicand and multiplier (the numbers being multiplied). As students implement this procedure, they often do not think about the magnitude of the numbers being multiplied or the product, and they also miss the understanding that just as in multiplication with fractions, they are taking a part of a part.

The number talks in this section offer a place for students to build on their understanding of multiplication with numbers less than one and to reason about place value and how it impacts the magnitude of the product. We first offer beginning number talks to help students think about the reasonableness of answers and patterns when multiplying by powers of 10. Next, we introduce number talks for three multiplication strategies: Partial Products, Breaking Factors into Factors, and Doubling and Halving.

Number Talks That Highlight a Place to Begin with Multiplication of Decimals

Since multiplying with decimals is based on the powers of 10, investigations that give students opportunities to consider what happens to a number when they multiply by 1, 10, 100, 1000, and 0.1, 0.01, and 0.001 are critical to help them understand this operation. The number talk strings in this section are designed to help students investigate the numerical patterns that occur when they are multiplying with decimals based on the powers of 10. The problems are purposefully chosen so the answers will be accessible to students. This will allow student conversations to focus on the relationships between the decimal point in the factors and the magnitude of the products. The number talks are organized into two categories—Ten Times Smaller and Ten Times Larger—and each category is crafted to focus on what happens when the decimal point moves to the left or right. Before you move into number talks that focus on developing specific strategies for multiplying decimals, we strongly suggest you use problems from this section.

Category 1
Ten Times Smaller

The number talk strings in this category keep one factor constant while the decimal point in the other factor moves one place to the left with each new problem. These series of problems provide opportunities to think about why the magnitude of a product becomes ten times smaller as the decimal point in a factor shifts to the left.

Instructions

These number talks are organized into three columns and progress in difficulty going from the first column (from A to B to C) to the second column to the third column. Feel free to work through each string in order or choose problems according to your students' needs. You may choose to pose one problem or set of problems each day, or do more than one set of problems as time allows. Introduce the first problem, collect solutions, then ask students to share their reasoning and proofs. Once the class reaches consensus, pose the second problem in the string. As students answer each problem, keep the problems and the answers visible to anchor the conversation on the relationship between the problems and answers in the string. Ask students, "*What do you notice about the factors and the products? Why do you think the answers are getting smaller or larger? How much smaller or larger?*"

What is ______ × ______? How do you know?
Will the answer be smaller or larger than the factors?
How much smaller or larger?
What do you notice about the factors and the products?

Number Talk Tip

Asking key questions will help students pay attention to why the product increases or decreases by powers of 10 when the decimal in the factors shifts.

A. 1×5
1×0.5
1×0.05
1×0.005

B. 5×100
5×10
5×1
5×0.1

C. 2×25
2×2.5
2×0.25
2×0.025

A. 3×50
3×5
3×0.5
3×0.05

B. 4×250
4×25
4×2.5
4×0.25

C. 4×15
4×1.5
4×0.15
4×0.015

A. 20×5
2.0×5
0.20×5
0.20×0.5

B. 50×4
5×4
0.5×4
0.5×0.4

C. 0.5×10
0.5×1.0
0.5×0.10
0.5×0.01

Category 2
Ten Times Larger

The number talk strings in this category keep one factor constant while the decimal point in the other factor moves one place to the right with each new problem. These series of problems provide opportunities to think about why the magnitude of a product becomes ten times greater as the decimal point in a factor shifts to the right.

Instructions

These number talks are organized into three columns and progress in difficulty going from the first column (from A to B to C) to the second column to the third column. Feel free to work through each string in order or choose problems according to your students' needs. You may choose to pose one problem or set of problems each day, or do more than one set of problems as time allows. Introduce the first problem, collect solutions, then ask students to share their reasoning and proofs. Once the class reaches consensus, pose the second problem in the string. As students answer each problem, keep the problems and the answers visible to anchor the conversation on the relationship between the problems and answers in the string. Ask students, "*What do you notice about the factors and the products? Why do you think the answers are getting smaller or larger? How much smaller or larger?*"

What is ______ × ______? How do you know?
Will the answer be smaller or larger than the factors?
How much smaller or larger?
What do you notice about the factors and the products?

Number Talk Tip

Asking key questions will help students pay attention to why the product increases or decreases by powers of 10 when the decimal in the factors shifts.

A. 5×0.01

5×0.1

5×1

5×10

B. 4×0.25

4×2.5

4×25

4×250

C. 2×0.025

2×0.25

2×2.5

2×25

A. 3×0.05

3×0.5

3×5

3×50

B. 25×1

25×0.1

25×0.01

25×0.001

C. 4×0.015

4×0.15

4×1.5

4×15

A. 0.5×0.02

0.5×0.20

0.5×2.0

0.5×20

B. 0.5×0.04

0.5×0.4

0.5×4

0.5×40

C. 0.5×0.010

0.5×0.10

0.5×1.0

0.5×10

Number Talks That Highlight the Multiplication Strategy "Partial Products"

An important goal for students when multiplying decimals is to think flexibly about factors. Understanding that factors can be broken into addends or smaller factors is important as students begin to develop their own strategies. The Partial Products strategy is based on the idea of decomposing one or both factors into addends and using the distributive property. While decomposing both quantities works, it is often more efficient to keep one factor intact. The standard algorithm for multiplying decimals is based on decomposing both factors into place values.

In addition to recording the Partial Products strategy numerically, we can also represent this idea using an open area model. Think about how you might record *1.5 × 2.4* numerically and with an open area model. Figure 10–20 on the next page offers four ways students might decompose 1.5 and 2.4 when using this strategy and how you might record each strategy numerically and with an area model.

Student's Strategy and Reasoning	Recording Using a Numerical Representation	Recording Using an Area Model
Decomposing 1.5 James: *I broke 1.5 into 1 and 0.5 and multiplied both parts by 2.4. One × 2.4 equals 2.4, so 0.5 × 2.4 equals half of that which is 1.2. 2.4 plus 1.2 equals 3.6.* Anna: *I thought about 1.5 as 3 halves; and I knew that half of 2.4 was 1.2 so I added 1.2 three times and that equaled 3.6.*	1.5×2.4 $= (1 + 0.5) \times 2.4$ $= (1 \times 2.4) + (0.5 \times 2.4)$ $= 2.4 + 1.2$ $= 3.6$ or 1.5×2.4 $= (0.5 + 0.5 + 0.5) \times 2.4$ $= (0.5 \times 2.4) + (0.5 \times 2.4) + (0.5 \times 2.4)$ $= 1.2 + 1.2 + 1.2$ $= 3.6$	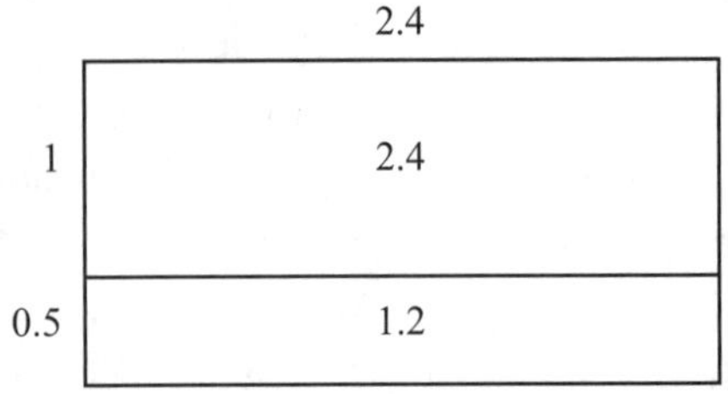 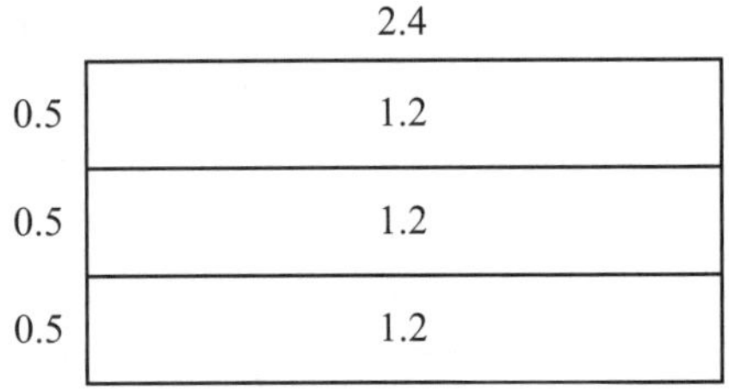 2.4 1 : 2.4 0.5 : 1.2 2.4 0.5 : 1.2 0.5 : 1.2 0.5 : 1.2
Decomposing 2.4 Lee: *I broke apart 2.4 into 2 and 0.4. I knew that 1.5 × 2 was 3, and 1.5 × 0.4 was 0.6. Three plus 0.6 equals 3.6.*	1.5×2.4 $= 1.5 \times (2 + 0.4)$ $= (1.5 \times 2) + (1.5 \times 0.4)$ $= 3 + 0.6$ $= 3.6$	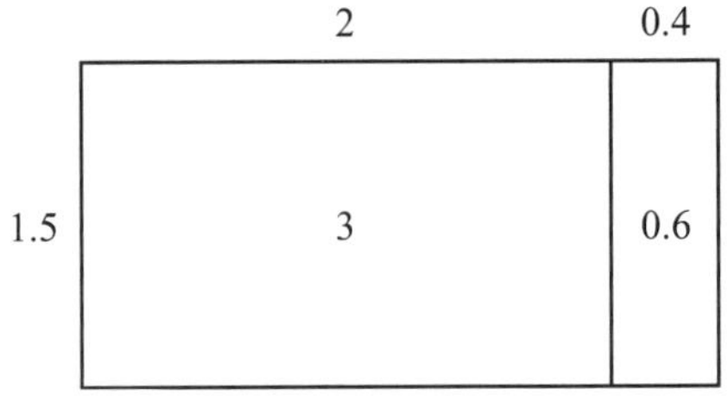 2 | 0.4 1.5 : 3 | 0.6
Decomposing 1.5 and 2.4 Ivy: *I broke up the numbers into 1 and 0.5 and 2 and 0.4 and then multiplied each part. 1 × 2 = 2 and 1 × 0.4 = 0.4. One half times 2 = 1 and 0.5 × 0.4 = 0.2. Then I added the parts and 2 + 0.4 + 1 + 0.2 = 3.6.*	1.5×2.4 $= (1 + 0.5) \times (2 + 0.4)$ $= (1 \times 2) + (1 \times 0.4) + (0.5 \times 2) + (0.5 \times 0.4)$ $= 2 + 0.4 + 1 + 0.2$ $= 3.6$	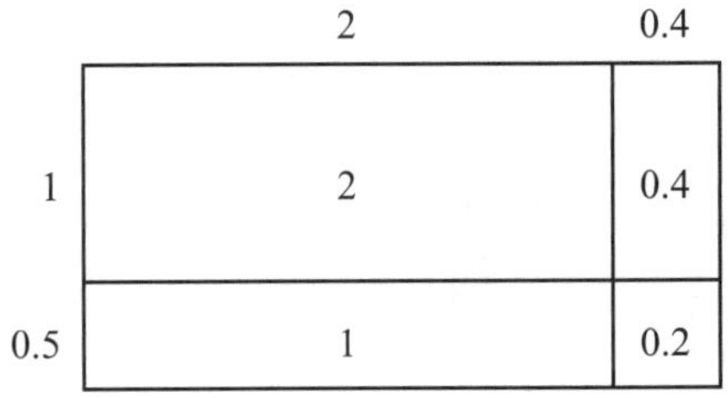 2 | 0.4 1 : 2 | 0.4 0.5 : 1 | 0.2

Figure 10–20. *Using "Partial Products" to Solve 1.5 × 2.4*

Were any of these numerical recordings or area model representations similar to how you approached this problem? As you grow more confident in facilitating number talks with your students, you will want to continue to develop the skill of accurately recording their thinking to highlight place value and the properties.

Number Talk Tip

Students can use an area model to represent their thinking, but the model itself is not a strategy. A strategy happens mentally and can be represented in various ways.

Category 1
Using Whole Numbers and Decimals

The number talk strings in this category offer a beginning place for students to think about decomposing a factor and using the distributive property. Each string begins with multiplying a whole number by a decimal to offer students an accessible starting point. The subsequent problems in the string are related to the first problem and can be used to solve the other problems in the string. For example, the first string begins with 0.2×7. The next two problems in the string are: 0.4×7 and 0.8×7. If students recognize that the first factor doubles and quadruples from the first problem to the second and third problems, they can use that information to solve the final problem in the string. Each string is designed so that students can use what they know to figure out subsequent problems.

Number Talk Tip

Make sure that area models accurately represent the numerical relationships students are considering. For example, the area representing 1×2.4 should be twice as large as the area for 0.5×2.4.

Instructions

These number talks are organized into three columns and progress in difficulty going from the first column (from A to B to C) to the second column to the third column. Feel free to work through each string in order or choose problems according to your students' needs. You may choose to pose one problem or set of problems each day, or do more than one set of problems as time allows. Introduce the first problem in the string, collect solutions, then ask students to share their reasoning and proofs. Once the class reaches consensus, pose the next problem in the string and ask, *"How can you use what we just solved to help you with this next problem?"* or *"How does this new problem relate to the previous problem(s)?"* Continue this format with each problem in the string.

What is ______ × ______? How do you know?
How can you use what we already know to solve this next problem?

A. 0.2×7

0.4×7

0.8×7

B. 0.2×8

0.4×8

0.8×8

C. 0.2×5

0.4×5

0.8×5

A. 0.2×15

0.4×15

0.6×15

0.8×15

B. 3×0.15

6×0.15

9×0.15

C. 0.3×25

0.6×25

0.9×25

A. 0.5×10

0.5×5

0.5×20

0.5×25

B. 8×0.06

8×0.10

8×0.50

8×0.56

C. 0.8×10

0.8×5

0.8×40

0.8×45

Category 2
Using Mixed Decimals

The number talk strings in this category focus on place value and using the distributive property with mixed numbers. The sequence of problems in each string is designed to encourage students to consider breaking factors into addends and then multiplying. Each number talk string is set up to encourage students to use the previous problems to solve the last problem in the string.

Instructions

These number talks are organized into three columns and progress in difficulty going from the first column (from A to B to C) to the second column to the third column. Feel free to work through each string in order or choose problems according to your students' needs. You may choose to pose one problem or set of problems each day, or do more than one set of problems as time allows. Introduce the first problem in the string, collect solutions, then ask students to share their reasoning and proofs. Once the class reaches consensus, pose the next problem in the string and ask, *"How can you use what we just solved to help you with this next problem?"* or *"How does this new problem relate to the previous problem(s)?"* Continue this format with each problem in the string.

What is ______ × ______? How do you know?
How can you use what we already know to solve this next problem?

A. 1.5×1 1.5×0.4 1.5×1.4	**A.** 1×1.6 0.2×1.6 1.2×1.6	**A.** 1×3.2 0.5×3 0.5×0.2 1.5×3.2
B. 2.5×2 2.5×0.4 2.5×2.4	**B.** 2×1.8 0.5×1.8 2.5×1.8	**B.** 2×2.5 0.5×2 0.5×0.5 2.5×2.5
C. 3×3.5 0.2×3.5 3.2×3.5	**C.** 0.4×2.5 0.8×2.5 1.2×2.5 1.6×2.5	**C.** 2×3.6 0.2×3.6 0.4×3.6 2.4×3.6

Number Talks That Highlight the Multiplication Strategy "Breaking Factors into Factors"

When students decompose factors into smaller factors, they are able to create smaller problems within larger problems. This works because of the associative property of multiplication. Consider this strategy with the problem *25 × 0.8*. (See Figure 10–21.)

Student's Strategy and Reasoning	Recording
Breaking Factors into Factors Maria: *I thought about 25 as 5 × 5 because I knew that 5 × 0.8 was 4. (I knew that because 10 × 0.8 is 8, so 5 × 0.8 is half of that.) That gave me 5 × 4 which is 20.*	25×0.8 $= (5 \times 5) \times 0.8$ $= 5 \times (5 \times 0.8)$ $= 5 \times 4$ $= 20$
Breaking Factors into Factors Pedro: *I know that 0.8 is the same as 4 × 0.2, and that 25 × 4 = 100; so the problem became 100 × 0.2—or what is 0.2 of 100—which equals 20.*	25×0.8 $= 25 \times (4 \times 0.2)$ $= (25 \times 4) \times 0.2$ $= 100 \times 0.2$ $= 20$

Figure 10–21. *Using "Breaking Factors into Factors" to Solve 25 × 0.8*

Learn More...

Chapters 6 and 8, pages 139 and 224, provide multiple examples of how to highlight the use of the associative property when recording students' addition and multiplication strategies with fractions.

Category 1
Using Tenths as a Multiplier

The number talk strings in this category consist of sets of four problems each and are structured to help students consider decomposing a factor into other factors to make a multiplication problem easier to solve. At least one factor in each problem is a whole number to provide easier access to a solution. The first three problems represent different ways to decompose the factors in the final problem in each string.

Instructions

These number talks are organized into three columns and progress in difficulty going from the first column (from A to B to C) to the second column to the third column. Feel free to work through each string in order or choose problems according to your students' needs. You may choose to pose one problem or set of problems each day, or do more than one set of problems as time allows. Introduce the first problem in the string, collect solutions, then ask students to share their reasoning and proofs. Once the class reaches consensus, pose the next problem in the string and ask, "*How can you use what we just solved to help you with this next problem*?" or "*How does this new problem relate to the previous problem(s)?*" Continue this format with each problem in the string.

What is ______ × ______? How do you know?
How can you use what we already know to solve this next problem?
How does this new problem relate to the previous problem(s)?

A. $0.2 \times 4 \times 6$

$0.4 \times 2 \times 6$

$3 \times 0.8 \times 2$

0.8×6

B. $0.3 \times 2 \times 0.3 \times 2$

$0.3 \times 3 \times 4$

$0.9 \times 2 \times 2$

0.9×4

C. $0.4 \times 4 \times 2$

$0.2 \times 8 \times 2$

$0.2 \times 2 \times 2 \times 2 \times 2$

0.4×8

A. $5 \times 0.2 \times 6$

$5 \times 0.4 \times 3$

$0.2 \times 2 \times 3 \times 5$

1.2×5

B. $4 \times 0.2 \times 5$

$5 \times 0.4 \times 2$

$2 \times 0.2 \times 5 \times 2$

0.8×5

C. $3 \times 0.2 \times 3 \times 3$

$0.6 \times 3 \times 3$

$9 \times 0.2 \times 3$

0.6×9

A. $3 \times 0.2 \times 6$

$3 \times 0.3 \times 2 \times 2$

$0.3 \times 6 \times 2$

0.6×6

B. $0.2 \times 5 \times 8$

$4 \times 5 \times 0.4$

$0.8 \times 5 \times 2$

1.6×5

C. $3 \times 0.4 \times 3$

$2 \times 9 \times 0.2$

$2 \times 3 \times 0.2 \times 3$

9×0.4

Category 2
Using Hundredths as a Multiplier

The number talk strings in this category consist of sets of four problems each and are structured to help students consider decomposing a factor into other factors to make a multiplication problem easier to solve. At least one factor in each problem is a whole number to provide a starting place to investigate this strategy. The first three problems represent different ways to decompose the factors in the final problem in each string.

Instructions

These number talks are organized into three columns and progress in difficulty going from the first column (from A to B to C) to the second column to the third column. Feel free to work through each string in order or choose problems according to your students' needs. You may choose to pose one problem or set of problems each day, or do more than one set of problems as time allows. Introduce the first problem in the string, collect solutions, then ask students to share their reasoning and proofs. Once the class reaches consensus, pose the next problem in the string and ask, *"How can you use what we just solved to help you with this next problem?"* or *"How does this new problem relate to the previous problem(s)?"* Continue this format with each problem in the string.

What is ______ $\times$ ______? How do you know?
How can you use what we already know to solve this next problem?
How does this new problem relate to the previous problem(s)?

A. $4 \times 0.25 \times 3$

$0.05 \times 12 \times 5$

$0.25 \times 2 \times 6$

0.25×12

B. $0.04 \times 8 \times 4$

$4 \times 2 \times 0.16$

$0.02 \times 4 \times 8 \times 2$

0.16×8

C. $0.04 \times 25 \times 3$

$5 \times 0.12 \times 5$

$0.02 \times 25 \times 6$

0.12×25

A. $0.05 \times 4 \times 3$

$2 \times 0.15 \times 2$

$0.03 \times 5 \times 4$

0.15×4

B. $0.08 \times 9 \times 3$

$3 \times 0.04 \times 2 \times 9$

$0.2 \times 12 \times 9$

0.24×9

C. $0.02 \times 15 \times 6$

$5 \times 0.12 \times 3$

$0.4 \times 5 \times 3 \times 3$

0.12×15

A. $5 \times 0.02 \times 12 \times 3$

$0.04 \times 16 \times 6$

$0.24 \times 5 \times 3$

0.24×15

B. $2 \times 0.35 \times 6$

$12 \times 0.05 \times 7$

$3 \times 4 \times 0.05 \times 7$

0.35×12

C. $0.6 \times 5 \times 7 \times 3$

$9 \times 5 \times 0.02 \times 7$

$7 \times 5 \times 9 \times 0.02$

0.18×35

Number Talks That Highlight the Multiplication Strategy "Doubling and Halving"

When factors in a multiplication problem are changed by multiplying one factor by any number and dividing the other factor by that same amount, the product will remain the same. This holds true whether students double and halve, triple and third, or quadruple and quarter, etc. The reason this strategy works is because of the multiplicative inverse property, which states that for every number x that is not zero, x multiplied by $\frac{1}{x}$ will equal 1. For example, $\frac{7}{1} \times \frac{1}{7} = \frac{7}{7} = 1$.

We can explore this idea of doubling and halving using the multiplicative inverse property with the problem 0.25×0.16. If we double 0.25 and halve 0.16, we change the problem to 0.5×0.08. Quartering and quadrupling will also work. (See Figure 10–22.)

Student's Strategy and Reasoning	Recording
Doubling and Halving Ruah: *I doubled 0.25 to get 0.50, and I halved 0.16 to get 0.08. I knew 0.50 × 0.08 = 0.04 because I thought about it as, "What is half of 0.08?"*	0.25×0.16 $= (2 \times 0.25) \times \left(\frac{1}{2} \times 0.16\right)$ $= 0.50 \times 0.08$ $= 0.04$
Quadrupling and Quartering Devin: *I multiplied 0.25 × 4 to get 1, so I multiplied 0.16 by $\frac{1}{4}$ and got 0.04. One times 0.04 equals 0.04.*	0.25×0.16 $= (4 \times 0.25) \times \left(\frac{1}{4} \times 0.16\right)$ $= 1 \times 0.04$ $= 0.04$

Figure 10–22. *Using "Doubling and Halving" and "Quadrupling and Quartering Strategies" to Solve 0.25 × 0.16*

If students use this strategy to multiply whole numbers, invite them to investigate this idea with decimals by asking, *"Will this strategy work with decimals?"*

When we ask students to consider whether a strategy that works with whole numbers will also work with decimals, we are asking them to *look for and make use of structure* (MP7) and *look for and express regularity in repeated reasoning* (MP8).

Using Number Talk Strings

The following number talk strings use problems that are easy to solve so the focus can be on the doubling and halving, or why the multiplicative inverse property works. Each string is made up of four sequential problems that help students investigate the relationships between problems when one factor is doubled and the other is halved.

Instructions

These number talks are organized into three columns and progress in difficulty going from the first column (from A to B to C) to the second column to the third column. Feel free to work through each string in order or choose problems according to your students' needs. You may choose to pose one problem or set of problems each day, or do more than one set of problems as time allows. Introduce the first problem in the string, collect solutions, then ask students to share their reasoning and proofs. Once the class reaches consensus, pose the next problem in the string. As students agree on the solution, ask, *"How does this problem relate to the previous problem(s)?"* When students begin to notice that each problem in the string has the same product, ask, *"Why do you think we are getting the same answer each time? How are each of the problems related? Would this idea work with other problems?"*

What is ______ × ______? How do you know?
How does this problem relate to the previous problem(s)?
Why do you think we are getting the same answer each time?

A. 8×0.5
4×1
2×2
1×4

B. 0.8×2.5
0.4×5
0.2×10
0.1×20

C. 8×0.3
4×0.6
2×1.2
1×2.4

A. 8×0.6
4×1.2
2×2.4
1×4.8

B. 0.4×8
0.8×4
1.6×2
3.2×1

C. 0.8×7.5
0.4×15
0.2×30
0.1×60

A. 2×1.6
4×0.8
8×0.4
16×0.2

B. 0.24×12.5
0.12×25
0.06×50
0.03×100

C. 3.5×0.8
7×0.4
14×0.2
28×0.1

Section 4: Number Talks for Division with Decimals

The number talks in this section offer a place for students to build an understanding of division with decimals, to reason about place value, and to compose and decompose divisors and dividends to create easier problems. We first offer number talks to investigate the Proportional Reasoning strategy followed by two additional strategies, Multiplying Up and Partial Quotients. The problems presented in each of the following sections use easier decimal numbers to provide students opportunities to think about the relationships among the dividend, divisor, and quotient and to investigate the relationship between multiplication and division. As you notice your students are becoming comfortable with the various strategies, try using numbers that are more challenging.

Number Talks That Highlight the Division Strategy "Proportional Reasoning"

The standard algorithm for dividing decimals is based on proportional reasoning. Most of us were taught to "move the decimal over" the same number of places in the dividend and in the divisor so the divisor becomes a whole number and then we divide. When we move the decimal over the same number of places, we are making the dividend and divisor proportionally larger or smaller, so the answer stays the same. As you examine the following problems, pay attention to what happens to the decimals in the dividends and the divisors.

$$100 \div 50 = 2$$
$$10.0 \div 5.0 = 2$$
$$1.00 \div 0.50 = 2$$

What did you notice about how much smaller the numbers were getting as the decimal changed places, and what did you notice about the answers? Moving the decimal one place to the left in the dividend and the divisor is the same as dividing each number by 10, and moving the decimal two places to the left divides each number by 100. This change in the magnitude of the numbers is based on the powers of 10.

Another way to consider this idea is to look at what happens to the decimal place in the answer if we multiply a number by increasing and decreasing powers of 10. In Figure 10–23, notice what happens to the magnitude of the answer—and similarly, where the decimal place goes—when we multiply and divide 85 by powers of 10. When we move the decimal to the right, it is the same as multiplying that number by 10, and moving the decimal two places to the right is the same as multiplying the number by 100. Moving the decimal to the left is the same as dividing 85 by 10, and moving the decimal two places to the left is the same as dividing 85 by 100. Figure 10–20 can help us further examine this idea.

Multiplying by 1	$85.00 \times 1 = 85$
Multiplying by 10	$85.00 \times 10 = 850$
Multiplying by 100	$85.00 \times 100 = 8{,}500$
Multiplying by 1,000	$85.00 \times 1000 = 85{,}000$
Dividing by 1	$85.00 \div 1 = 85$
Dividing by 10	$85.00 \div 10 = 8.50$
Dividing by 100	$85.00 \div 100 = 0.85$
Dividing by 1,000	$85.00 \div 1000 = 0.085$

Figure 10–23. *Multiplying and Dividing by Powers of 10*

When we think about division from a proportional reasoning perspective, the relationship of the divisor to the dividend remains proportional if we divide or multiply each number by the same amount.

The following number talks for the Proportional Reasoning strategy are organized into two categories: Using Whole Numbers and Decimals, and Using Decimals.

Category 1
Using Whole Numbers and Decimals

The number talk strings in this category are comprised of sets of three to four problems. All problems maintain a proportional relationship to the first problem by halving or thirding both the dividend and the divisor.

Instructions

These number talks are organized into three columns and progress in difficulty going from the first column (from A to B to C) to the second column to the third column. Feel free to work through each string in order or choose problems according to your students' needs. You may choose to pose one problem or set of problems each day, or do more than one set of problems as time allows. Introduce the first problem in the string, collect solutions, then ask students to share their reasoning and proofs. Once the class reaches consensus, pose the second problem in the string and ask, *"How can you use what we just solved to help you with this next problem? How does this new problem relate to the previous problem(s)? Why are the answers the same?"* Continue this format with each problem in the string.

What is ______ ÷ ______? How do you know?
How can you use what we already know to solve this next problem?
How does this new problem relate to the previous problem?
Why are the answers the same?

A. $8 \div 4$
$4 \div 2$
$2 \div 1$
$1 \div 0.5$
$0.5 \div 0.25$

B. $4 \div 1$
$2 \div 0.5$
$1 \div 0.25$
$0.5 \div 0.50$

C. $8 \div 1$
$4 \div 0.5$
$2 \div 0.25$
$1 \div 0.125$

A. $16 \div 4$
$8 \div 2$
$4 \div 1$
$2 \div 0.5$

B. $6 \div 4$
$3 \div 2$
$1.5 \div 1$
$0.75 \div 0.5$

C. $5 \div 1$
$2.5 \div 0.5$
$1.25 \div 0.25$
$0.625 \div 0.125$

A. $3 \div 0.375$
$6 \div 0.75$
$12 \div 1.5$
$24 \div 3$

B. $36 \div 5$
$18 \div 2.5$
$9 \div 1.25$
$4.5 \div 0.625$

C. $54 \div 6.75$
$18 \div 2.25$
$6 \div 0.75$
$2 \div 0.25$

Category 2
Using Decimals

The number talk strings in this category continue to focus on a proportional relationship, but they begin with a problem that can be solved through doubling both the divisor and dividend to make an easier problem.

Instructions

These number talks are organized into three columns and progress in difficulty going from the first column (from A to B to C) to the second column to the third column. Feel free to work through each string in order or choose problems according to your students' needs. You may choose to pose one problem or set of problems each day, or do more than one set of problems as time allows. Introduce the first problem in the string, collect solutions, then ask students to share their reasoning and proofs. Once the class reaches consensus, pose the second problem in the string and ask, *"How can you use what we just solved to help you with this next problem? How does this new problem relate to the previous problem(s)? Why are the answers the same?"* Continue this format with each problem in the string.

What is ______ ÷ ______? How do you know?
How can you use what we already know to solve the next problem?
How does this new problem relate to the previous problem?
Why are the answers the same?

A. $1.5 \div 0.75$

$3 \div 1.5$

$6 \div 3$

B. $0.350 \div 0.5$

$0.700 \div 1$

$1.4 \div 2$

C. $0.15 \div 0.25$

$0.30 \div 0.5$

$0.60 \div 1$

A. $0.96 \div 3.2$

$0.48 \div 1.6$

$0.24 \div 0.8$

B. $0.18 \div 0.225$

$0.36 \div 0.45$

$0.72 \div 0.9$

C. $0.35 \div 0.125$

$0.70 \div 0.250$

$1.40 \div 0.50$

A. $0.75 \div 0.25$

$1.5 \div 0.5$

$3 \div 1$

B. $0.7 \div 0.175$

$1.4 \div 0.35$

$2.8 \div 0.7$

C. $1.25 \div 0.75$

$2.5 \div 1.5$

$5 \div 3$

Number Talks That Highlight the Division Strategy "Multiplying Up"

Before transitioning into division with decimals, students should have a solid and flexible understanding of multiplication and division with whole numbers and the relationship between these operations. Multiplying Up is a division strategy that builds on the inverse relationship between multiplication and division. Because of this relationship, we can use one operation to "undo" or reverse the other, as evidenced by the problems 4×5 and $20 \div 4$. This inverse relationship allows students to solve $20 \div 4$ as a missing factor multiplication problem, $4 \times \_\_\_ = 20$.

The same relationship exists when computing with decimals. Consider the problem $4 \div 0.5$. This idea can be represented as $\_\_\_ \times 0.5 = 4$ and is why we can multiply up to divide. The Multiplying Up strategy provides an opportunity for students to gradually build on multiplication problems they know until they reach the dividend. Figure 10–24 shows two ways a student might solve $4 \div 0.5$ using the Multiplying Up strategy.

Student's Strategy and Reasoning	Recording
Multiplying Up Ralph: *I know there are 2 halves in 1, so I multiply that 4 times and I know there are 8 halves in 4.*	$4 \div 0.5$ $0.5 \times \_\_\_ = 4$ $0.5 \times \underline{\ 2\ } = 1$ $0.5 \times \underline{\ 2\ } = 1$ $0.5 \times \underline{\ 2\ } = 1$ $0.5 \times \underline{\ 2\ } = 1$
Multiplying Up Juan: *I know there are 4 halves in 2, and since there are 2 twos in 4, there are 8 halves in 4.*	$4 \div 0.5$ $0.5 \times \_\_\_ = 4$ $0.5 \times \underline{\ 4\ } = 2$ $0.5 \times \underline{\ 4\ } = 2$

Figure 10–24. *Using "Multiplying Up" to Solve $4 \div 0.5$*

The following number talk strings build from smaller multiplication problems to the final division problem to help students consider the relationship between multiplication and division. The first problem offers a beginning place to approach the problem and can be used, along with subsequent problems, to solve the final division problem in the string.

Instructions

These number talks are organized into three columns and progress in difficulty going from the first column (from A to B to C, etc.) to the second column to the third column. Feel free to work through each string in order or choose problems according to your students' needs. You may choose to pose one problem or set of problems each day, or do more than one set of problems as time allows. Introduce the first problem, collect solutions, then ask students to share their reasoning and proofs. Once the class reaches consensus, pose the second problem in the string and ask, *"How can you use what we just solved to help you with this next problem?"* As you present the division problem, ask, *"How can our previous problems help us solve this division problem?"*

What is ______ × ______? How do you know?
How can you use what we already know to solve this next problem?
How can our previous problems help us solve this division problem?
What is _____ ÷ _______?

A. 0.5×1
0.5×2
0.5×4
$4 \div 0.5$

B. 0.5×2
0.5×4
0.5×6
$6 \div 0.5$

C. 0.5×2
0.5×4
0.5×8
$8 \div 0.5$

D. 1×0.5
2×0.5
3×0.5
$2.5 \div 0.5$

A. 0.5×4
0.5×5
0.5×10
$10 \div 0.5$

B. 0.5×2
0.5×6
0.5×10
$15 \div 0.5$

C. 2×0.25
4×0.25
6×0.25
$2 \div 0.25$

D. 0.5×0.2
0.5×0.3
0.5×0.4
0.5×0.5
$0.45 \div 0.5$

A. 4×0.25
6×0.25
8×0.25
$4 \div 0.25$

B. 2×0.25
10×0.25
20×0.25
$8 \div 0.25$

C. 8×0.25
16×0.25
20×0.25
$10 \div 0.25$

D. 1×0.5
2×0.5
4×0.5
5×0.5
$4.5 \div 0.5$

Number Talks That Highlight the Division Strategy "Partial Quotients"

Similar to the Partial Quotients strategy for division of whole numbers, this strategy focuses on decomposing the dividend into smaller, friendlier numbers to create smaller division problems.

We can use the problem $4 \div 0.5$ to analyze this strategy, as recorded in Figure 10–25.

Student's Strategy and Reasoning	Recording
Partial Quotients Margaret: *I broke apart 4 into $1 + 1 + 1 + 1$. I knew there were 2 halves in each 1 and $2 + 2 + 2 + 2 = 8$.*	$4 \div 0.5$ $= (1 + 1 + 1 + 1) \div 0.5$ $= (1 \div 0.5) + (1 \div 0.5) + (1 \div 0.5) + (1 \div 0.5)$ $= 2 + 2 + 2 + 2$ $= 8$

Figure 10–25. *Using "Partial Quotients" to Solve $4 \div 0.5$*

In Figure 10–25, the dividend could have been decomposed into other addends, such as $2 + 2$ or $3 + 1$.

Learn More...

For more information on strategies for division with whole numbers, see *Number Talks: Whole Number Computation* (Parrish 2010, 2014).

The following number talk strings use a series of purposefully scaffolded problems that can be used to decompose the dividend in the last problem. The first problem offers an accessible division problem that could be used to solve any following problems in the string. For example, in the first string, $80 \div 0.5$ could be solved by decomposing the 80 into four 20s, 30 and 50, or any combination that makes 80, and then dividing each amount by 0.5.

Instructions

These number talks are organized into three columns and progress in difficulty going from the first column (from A to B to C) to the second column to the third column. Feel free to work through each string in order or choose problems according to your students' needs. You may choose to pose one problem or set of problems each day, or do more than one set of problems as time allows. Introduce the first problem in the string, collect solutions, then ask students to share their reasoning and proofs. Once the class reaches consensus, pose the second problem in the string and ask, *"How can you use what we just solved to help you with this next problem? How does this new problem relate to the previous problem?"* Continue this format with each problem in the string.

What is ______ ÷ ______? How do you know?
How can you use what we already know to solve this next problem?

Column 1	Column 2	Column 3
A. $3 \div 0.3$	**A.** $5 \div 0.5$	**A.** $12 \div 0.3$
$9 \div 0.3$	$10 \div 0.5$	$30 \div 0.3$
$12 \div 0.3$	$25 \div 0.5$	$18 \div 0.3$
$15 \div 0.3$	$50 \div 0.5$	$48 \div 0.3$
	$75 \div 0.5$	
B. $20 \div 0.4$	**B.** $40 \div 0.4$	**B.** $20 \div 0.5$
$40 \div 0.4$	$80 \div 0.4$	$50 \div 0.5$
$16 \div 0.4$	$4 \div 0.4$	$30 \div 0.5$
$56 \div 0.4$	$88 \div 0.4$	$80 \div 0.5$
C. $9 \div 0.3$	**C.** $40 \div 0.4$	**C.** $12 \div 0.6$
$30 \div 0.3$	$80 \div 0.4$	$24 \div 0.6$
$24 \div 0.3$	$16 \div 0.4$	$36 \div 0.6$
$54 \div 0.3$	$96 \div 0.4$	$72 \div 0.6$

Looking Ahead

Decimals are an essential part of the number system, and reasoning with decimals as fractions is critical to building understanding. Are there any decimal strategies you found more accessible than others? Which strategies might you anticipate your students using? While it may seem efficient to follow recipes that ignore place value when operating with decimals, this approach often circumvents attending to precision with place value and interpreting whether an answer is reasonable. A solid understanding of place value and fractional reasoning is essential as students make sense of decimals. Number talks can be an important vehicle for helping students to build that understanding with fractions, decimals, and percentages.

Connecting the Chapter to Your Practice

1. What are some of the most common errors you see students making when they operate with decimals?
2. Look at Figures 10–5 and 10–6 on pages 326 and 327. What benefits and challenges do you anticipate with presenting problems to students with story and/or models as contexts?
3. Read the "Inside the Classroom" excerpt on pages 330–332. What do you notice about the students' thinking and the teacher's questions to her students?
4. What benefits do you see in encouraging students to talk about decimals in terms of the value of the numbers?
5. In what ways do you think your recording may influence your students' thinking about operating with decimals?
6. Examine Figure 10–23 on page 388. What do you think your students already understand about multiplying and dividing by powers of 10?
7. What parts of multiplying and dividing by powers of 10 do you think they might benefit from exploring further?
8. How do you think number talks may influence your students' ability to operate with fractions, decimals, and percentages?

References

Behr, M. G., Harel, T. Post, and R. Lesh. 1992. Rational Number, Ratio, and Proportion. In D. Grouws (Ed.), *Handbook of Research on Mathematics Teaching and Learning* (pp. 296–333). New York: Macmillan.

Behr, M., I. Wachsmuth, and T. Post. 1984. Tasks to Assess Children's Perception of the Size of a Fraction. In A. Bell, B. Low, and J. Kilpatrick (Eds.), *Theory, Research and Practice in Mathematical Education* (pp. 179–81). Fifth International Congress on Mathematical Education, South Australia: Shell Centre for Mathematics Education.

Bennett, C. 1991. The Teacher as Decision Maker Program. *Journal of Teacher Education* 42: 119–31.

Boaler, J. 2016. *Mathematical Mindsets: Unleashing Students' Potential Through Creative Math, Inspiring Messages and Innovative Teaching.* San Francisco: John Wiley and Sons, Inc.

Boaler, J., and M. Staples. 2008. Creating Mathematical Futures Through an Equitable Teaching Approach: The Case of Railside School. *Teachers College Record* 110(3): 608–45.

Booth, J., and K. Newton. 2012. Fractions: Could They Really Be the Gatekeeper's Doorman? *Contemporary Educational Psychology* 37: 247–53.

Brousseau, G., N. Brousseau, and V. Warfield. 2004. Rationals and Decimals as Required in the School Curriculum. Part I: Rationals as Measurements. *Journal of Mathematical Behavior* 23: 1–20.

Brown, G., and R. J. Quinn. 2006. Algebra Students' Difficulty with Fractions: An Error Analysis. *Australian Mathematics Teacher* 62: 28–40.

Carpenter, T., M. K. Corbitt, H. Kepner, Jr., M. M. Lindquist, and R. Reyes. 1981. *Results from the Second Mathematics Assessment of the National Assessment of Educational Progress.* Reston, VA: National Council of Teachers of Mathematics.

Chapin, S., C. O'Connor, and N. Anderson. *Talk Moves: A Teacher's Guide for Using Classroom Discussions in Math.* 3d. ed. Sausalito: Math Solutions.

Cramer, K. A, T. R. Post, and R. C. del Mas. 2002. Initial Fraction Learning by Fourth- and Fifth-Grade Students: A Comparison of the Effects of Using Commercial Curricula with the Effects of Using the Rational Number Project Curriculum. *Journal for Research in Mathematics Education* 33(2): 111–44.

Dweck, C. 2006. *Mindset: The New Psychology of Success.* New York: Random House.

Fennell, F. S., and T. E. Landis. 1994. Number and Operation Sense. In C. A. Thornton and N. S. Bley (Eds.), *Windows of Opportunity: Mathematics for Students with Special Needs* (pp. 187–203). Reston, VA: National Council of Teachers of Mathematics.

Geary, D. C., M. K. Hoard, L. Nugent, and D. H. Bailey. 2012. Mathematical Cognition Deficits in Children with Learning Disabilities and Persistent Low Achievement: A Five Year Prospective Study. *Journal of Educational Psychology* 104: 206–23.

Givvin, K. B., J. W. Stigler, and B. J. Thompson. 2011. What Community College Developmental Mathematics Students Understand About Mathematics, Part II: The Interviews. *The MathAMATYC Educator* 2(3): 4–18.

Hallett, D., T. Nunes, and P. Bryant. 2010. Individual Differences in Conceptual and Procedural Knowledge When Learning Fractions. *Journal of Educational Psychology* 102(2): 395–406.

Hart, E., C. Hirsch, and S. Keller. 2007. Amplifying Student Learning in Mathematics Using Curriculum-embedded Java-based Software. In W. G. Martin and M. E. Strutchens (Eds.), *The Learning of Mathematics: 69th Yearbook of the National Council of Teachers of Mathematics.*

Hecht, S., and K. Vagi. 2010. Sources of Group and Individual Differences in Emerging Fraction Skills. *Journal of Educational Psychology* 102(4): 843–59.

Hecht, S., K. Vagi, and J. Torgesen. 2007. Fraction Skills and Proportional Reasoning. In D. Berch and M. Mazzocco (Eds.), *Why Is Math So Hard for Some Children?* (pp. 121–32). Baltimore: Paul H. Brookes.

Hiebert, J., and D. Wearne. 1993. Instructional Tasks, Classroom Discourse, and Students' Learning in Second-Grade Arithmetic. *American Educational Research Journal* 30(2): 393–425.

Irwin, K. 2001. Using Everyday Knowledge of Decimals to Enhance Understanding. *Journal for Research in Mathematics Education* 32(4): 399–420.

Isik, C., and T. KAR. 2012. The Analysis of the Problems the Pre-Service Teachers Experience in Posing Problems About Equations. *Australian Journal of Teacher Education* 37: 9.

Kamii, C., and A. Dominick. 1997. To Teach or Not to Teach Algorithms. *The Journal of Mathematical Behavior* 16(1): 51–61.

Lamon, S. J. 2006. *Teaching Fractions and Ratios for Understanding: Essential Content Knowledge and Instructional Strategies for Teachers*. New Jersey: Lawrence Erlbaum Associates, Inc.

Li, Y., and D. Smith. 2007. Prospective Middle School Teachers' Knowledge in Mathematics and Pedagogy for Teaching—The Case of Fraction Division. In J. H. Woo, Lew, H. C., Park, K. S., and Seo, D. Y. (Eds.), *Proceedings of the 31st Conference of the International Group for the Psychology of Mathematics Education* 3: 185–92. Seoul: Psychology of Mathematics Education.

Mack, N. K. 1990. Learning Fractions with Understanding: Building on Informal Knowledge. *Journal for Research in Mathematics Education* 21: 16–32.

———. 1995. Confounding Whole-Number and Fraction Concepts When Building on Informal Knowledge. *Journal for Research in Mathematics Education* 26(5): 422–441.

Maher, N., and T. Muir. 2011. I Think They Think That Zero Point Something Is Less Than Zero: Investigating Preservice Teachers' Responses to Mathematical Tasks. Proceedings of the Annual Australian Association for Research in Education Conference, 27 November–1 December 2011, Hobart, Tasmania, pp. 1–16.

Martin, W. G., M. Strutchens, and P. Elliott, eds. 2007. *The Learning of Mathematics, 69th NCTM Yearbook*. Reston, VA: National Council of Teachers of Mathematics.

Mazzocco, M. M. M., and K. T. Devlin. 2008. Parts and "Holes": Gaps in Rational Number Sense in Children with vs. Without Mathematical Learning Disabilities. *Developmental Science* 11(5): 681–91.

McNamara, J., and M. Shaughnessy. 2015. *Beyond Pizzas & Pies: 10 Essential Strategies for Supporting Fraction Sense, Grades 3–5*. 2d ed. Sausalito: Math Solutions.

Moss, J., and R. Case. 1999. Developing Children's Understanding of the Rational Numbers: A New Model and an Experimental Curriculum. *Journal for Research in Mathematics Education* 30(2): 122–47.

Mueller, M., D. Yankelewitz, and C. Maher. 2010. Sense Making as Motivation in Doing Mathematics: Results from Two Studies. *The Mathematics Educator* 20(2): 33–43.

Mullins, B., Lofgren, P., and Parker, R., et al. 2012. Challenging Courses and Curricula: A Model for All Students. *Journal of Mathematics Education Leadership* 14(2): 31–37.

National Council of Teachers of Mathematics (NTCM). 2000. *Principles and Standards for School Mathematics.* Reston, VA: National Council of Teachers of Mathematics.

———. 2014. *Principles to Actions: Ensuring Mathematical Success for All.* Reston, VA: National Council of Teachers of Mathematics.

National Governors Association Center for Best Practices, Council of Chief State School Officers. 2010. *Common Core State Standards for Mathematics.* Washington, DC: National Governors Association Center for Best Practices, Council of Chief State School Officers.

National Mathematics Advisory Panel (NMAP). 2008. *Foundations for Success: The Final Report of the National Mathematics Advisory Panel.* Washington, DC: U.S. Department of Education. www2.ed.gov/about/bdscomm/list/mathpanel/report/final-report.pdf

National Research Council (NRC). 2001. *Adding It Up: Helping Children Learn Mathematics.* J Kilpatrick, J. Swafford, and B. Findell (Eds.). Mathematics Learning Study Committee, Center for Education, Division of Behavioral and Social Sciences and Education. Washington, DC: National Academy Press.

Okazaki, M., and M. Koyama. 2005. Characteristics of 5th Graders' Logical Development Through Learning Division with Decimals. *Educational Studies in Mathematics* 60: 217–51.

Oleson, A., and M. Hora. 2014. Teaching the Way They Were Taught? Revisiting the Sources of Teaching Knowledge and the Role of Prior Experience in Shaping Faculty Teaching Practices. *Higher Education* 68(1): 29–45.

Parrish, S. 2010, 2014. *Number Talks: Whole Number Computation [Helping Children Build Mental Math and Computation Strategies].* Sausalito, CA: Math Solutions.

Peck, D., and S. Jencks. 1981. Conceptual Issues in the Teaching and Learning of Fractions. *Journal for Research in Mathematics Education* 12: 339–48.

Peled, I., and J. Shahbari. 2009. Journey to the Past: Verifying and Modifying the Conceptual Sources of Decimal Fraction Knowledge. *Canadian Journal of Science, Mathematics and Technology Education* 9(2): 4042–51.

Petit, M., R. Laird, E. Marsden, and C. Ebby. 2010. *A Focus on Fractions: Bringing Research to the Classroom.* New York: Routledge.

Piaget, J. 1971 [1967]. *Biology and Knowledge.* Chicago: University of Chicago Press.

Rizvi, N., and M. Lawson. 2007. Prospective Teachers' Knowledge: Concept of Division. *International Education Journal* 8(2): 377–92.

Ryan, J., and J. Williams. 2007. *Children's Mathematics 4–15: Learning from Errors and Misconceptions.* New York: Open University Press.

Saxe, G. B., M. Gearhart, and M. Seltzer. 1999. Relations Between Classroom Practices and Student Learning in the Domain of Fractions. *Cognition and Instruction* 17: 1–24.

Siegler, R. S., G. J. Duncan, P. E. Davis-Kean, K. Duckworth, A. Claessens, M. Engel, M. I. Susperreguy, and M. Chen. 2012. Early Predictors of High School Mathematics Achievement. *Psychological Science* 23: 691–97.

Siegler, R. S., L. K. Fazio, D. H. Bailey, and X, Zhou. 2013. Fractions: The New Frontier for Theories of Numerical Development. *Trends in Cognitive Science* 17: 13–19.

Siegler, R., C. Thompson, and M. Schneider. 2011. Integral Theory of Whole Number and Fraction Development. *Cognitive Psychology* 62: 273–96.

Stein, M., and S. Lane. 1996. Instructional Tasks and the Development of Student Capacity to Think and Reason: An Analysis of the Relationship Between Teaching and Learning in a Reform Mathematics Project. *Educational Research and Evaluation* 2(1): 50–80.

Steinle, V., and K. Stacey. 2004. Persistence of Decimal Misconceptions and Readiness to Move to Expertise. In M. J. Hoines and A. B. Fuglestad (Eds.), *Proceedings of the 28th Conference of the International Group for the Psychology of Mathematics Education* (vol. 1, pp. 225–32). Bergen-Norway: Bergen University College.

TIMSS 2011 Assessment. 2013. International Association for the Evaluation of Educational Achievement (IEA). TIMSS & PIRLS International Study Center, Lynch School of Education, Boston College.

Ubuz, B., and B. Yayan. 2010. Primary Teachers' Subject Matter Knowledge: Decimals. *International Journal of Mathematics Education in Science and Technology* 41(6): 787–804.

U.S. Department of Education, Institute of Education Sciences, National Center for Education Statistics, National Assessment of Educational Progress (NAEP). 1996. Mathematics Assessment. http://nces.ed.gov/nationsreportcard/pdf/main1996/97488.pdf

———. 2004. Mathematics Assessment. U.S. Department of Education. http://nces.ed.gov/nationsreportcard/pdf/main2005/2005464.pdf

———. 2009. Mathematics Assessment. U.S. Department of Education. http://nces.ed.gov/nationsreportcard/pdf/main2009/2010451.pdf

Van de Walle, J., Karp, K., and J. M. Bay-Williams. 2010. *Elementary and Middle School Mathematics: Teaching Developmentally*. Boston: Pearson.

Wearne, D., and V. L. Kouba. 2000. Rational Numbers. In E. A. Silver and P. A. Kenny (Eds.), *Results from the Seventh Mathematics Assessment of the National Assessment of Education Progress* (pp. 163–91). Reston, VA: National Council of Teachers of Mathematics.

Wong, M., and D. Evans. 2007. Students' Conceptual Understanding of Equivalent Fractions. Mathematics Essential Research. *Essential Practice* 2: 824–25.